Inside

Microsoft
Visual Basic,
Scripting
Edition

Scot Hillier
New Technology Solutions, Inc.

Microsoft Press

PUBLISHED BY
Microsoft Press
A Division of Microsoft Corporation
One Microsoft Way
Redmond, Washington 98052-6399

Library of Congress Cataloging-in-Publication Data
Hillier, Scot.
    Inside Microsoft Visual Basic, Scripting Edition / Scot Hillier.
        p.   cm.
    Includes index.
    ISBN 1-57231-444-3
    1. Microsoft Visual Basic   2. HTML (Document markup language)
3. World Wide Web (Information retrieval system)   I. Hillier, Scot.
II. Title.
QA76.73.B3M49   1996
005.2–dc20   96-26422
                                                              CIP

Printed and bound in the United States of America.

1 2 3 4 5 6 7 8 9   MLML   1 0 9 8 7 6

Distributed to the book trade in Canada by Macmillan of Canada, a division of Canada
Publishing Corporation.

A CIP catalogue record for this book is available from the British Library.

Microsoft Press books are available through booksellers and distributors worldwide. For further
information about international editions, contact your local Microsoft Corporation office. Or
contact Microsoft Press International directly at fax (206) 936-7329.

Acquisitions Editor: Stephen Guty
Project Editor: Xavier Callahan
Manuscript Editor: Katherine A. Krause
Technical Editor: Robert Lyon

To God for the strength, courage, and talent.

To Nancy for the faith, hope, and love.

TABLE OF CONTENTS

Foreword ix
Preface xi
Acknowledgments xiii

CHAPTER ONE

An Overview of Web Technologies   **1**
A Variation on the Internet Concept 4
Internet Development Tools 4
Opportunities for Developers 10
Assumptions Made in This Book 10
An Overview of HTML 11

CHAPTER TWO

ActiveX Scripting and VBScript   **19**
Scripting Languages 20
The VBScript Language 27
Forms and Modules 36

CHAPTER THREE

Understanding Automation and Browser Architecture   **41**
The Internet Explorer Object Model 44
Using the Internet Explorer Objects 48
The Internet Explorer Scripting Object Model 52
Using the Scripting Model in VBScript 62
Intrinsic HTML Controls 68

CHAPTER FOUR

Working with ActiveX Controls   **79**
Obtaining Class IDs for ActiveX Components 84
ActiveX Control Pad and the HTML Layout Control 90
Code Signing and Security on the Internet 92

The ActiveX Controls on the Companion CD 94
The Minesweeper and Calculator Examples 102

CHAPTER FIVE

The Microsoft Internet Information Server **121**
The Internet Services API 122
The Internet Database Connector 123
Detailed IDC Examples 138
OLEISAPI 155
A Detailed OLEISAPI Example 168
The IIS Wizards 181
CGI and IIS 190
Other IIS Services 191

CHAPTER SIX

Project #1: An Intranet Newsletter **193**
Requirements 193
Design Objective 194
Prerequisites 195
Creating the Datasource 196
Creating the HTML Page 204
Calling the Internet Database Connector 216
Sending the Newsletter 219
Running the Project 235

CHAPTER SEVEN

Project #2: An Event Registration Application **239**
Requirements 239
Design Objective 240
Prerequisites 241
Creating the Datasource 242
Creating the HTML Page 247
Creating the In-Process ActiveX Component 269
Running the Project 288

CHAPTER EIGHT

Project #3: An Online Bookstore **291**

Requirements 291
Design Objective 292
Prerequisites 293
Creating the Datasource 294
Creating the Home Page 298
Building the Search Engine 314
Creating the Selected Titles Page 315
The Book Order Query 323
Creating the Book Order Page 323
The Purchase Query 335
Creating the Confirmation Page 336
Running the Project 341

CHAPTER NINE

Project #4: An Interactive Order Form Built with ActiveX Control Pad **345**

Requirements 345
Prerequisites 346
ActiveX Control Pad Features 346
The HTML Source Editor 346
The ActiveX Control Editor 347
The Script Wizard 353
The HTML Layout and the HTML Layout Editor 358
An Interactive Order Form 369

CHAPTER TEN

Emerging Internet Technologies **389**

Windows NT 4.0 389
Normandy 390
Microsoft SQL Server 6.5 391
Microsoft dbWeb 391
Into the Future 398

APPENDIX A

An HTML PRIMER **399**
An Introduction to HTML Documents 399
The HTML Tags 403

APPENDIX B

Coding Standards **431**
HTML Standards 431
VBScript Standards 433
Comments 435
Case Sensitivity 436
The <!DOCTYPE> Tag 436

APPENDIX C

Features of Microsoft Visual Basic for Applications That Are Not Supported in Microsoft Visual Basic, Scripting Edition **437**

APPENDIX D

Interactive Web Sites **441**
Sites for Use with This Book 441
Resources for ActiveX Controls 442
Other Sites 444

APPENDIX E

Glossary **445**
Index 451

FOREWORD

Today, more people than ever before are coding, professionally or otherwise—and the open nature of the Internet is contributing daily to this phenomenon. Small-business owners, nonprofit organizations, and independent individuals are learning HTML and other Web authoring techniques in order to get their information out and create a presence on the World Wide Web. With the introduction of Microsoft Visual Basic, Scripting Edition, the legions of Visual Basic users who have been providing custom solutions to thousands of businesses around the world can now apply their current knowledge to the creation of flexible, powerful, dynamic web pages with ActiveX technologies, in the secure and robust environments of the Microsoft Internet Explorer 3.0 and the Microsoft Windows platform.

Although Visual Basic has been and will continue to be a major force in the development of mission-critical applications, it doesn't owe its success to its technical merits alone. Visual Basic's success also has much to do with the Visual Basic developer community—that group of like-minded professionals who share a passion for and a focus on building unique, powerful applications with Visual Basic and other Microsoft development tools. Developers rely on each other, learning which techniques work (or don't work) and using the experience of others who have "been there" and "done that." Because this type of feedback helps Microsoft determine future product directions, Microsoft has worked very closely with the developer community over the years to ensure that our products and support programs will continue to provide the components that allow for successful applications. Microsoft has a great commitment to the influential developer community and to the community-driven user groups, online forums, web pages, advisory councils, independent newsletters, and conferences that fuel the sharing of information and are so important to the developer community's self-sustaining character.

At the core of the worldwide developer community are individuals who, within their own fields of expertise, have taken on leadership roles. Scot Hillier of New Technology Solutions, Inc., is a prototypical leader of this community. He is truly an expert in his business—a technical guru on whom Microsoft depends for product-development feedback, and an instrumental partner, along with Dan Mezick (also of NewTech), in creating Microsoft Developer Days, the world's largest community-based developer program. Through this ongoing project for sharing the latest information with peer developers, Scot and Dan have been giving their time, knowledge, and energy back to the community.

With this book, you're getting more than the ultimate print resource for a scripting language that works with the world's greatest software development tool. You're also getting a new partner who is at the heart of the worldwide developer community and will continue to be there for years to come. If you are new to this community, I send you a warm welcome. If you're already involved, I am confident that you'll find your partnership with Scot as fruitful as Microsoft's has been.

Michael Werner
Group Manager, Microsoft Developer Community Programs,
*   Internet Platform and Tools Division*
August 1996

PREFACE

This book was written for developers who need to get started immediately on programming dynamic pages for the World Wide Web. In creating this book, my intention has been to write from the perspective of a Visual Basic programmer who is trying to make the leap from the client/server world to the intranet/Internet world.

The approach I take in the book grew out of my experience teaching thousands of people Visual Basic 3—and, now, Visual Basic 4. This experience has shown me that core information and strong examples make the best teachers. With this perspective in mind, I have focused primarily on imparting the technical principles vital to a strong foundation in web development and on providing lots of examples that show you how to accomplish your goals.

The book begins with an overview of current web technologies that can be applied to developing database solutions. It rapidly moves on to the particulars of Microsoft Visual Basic, Scripting Edition (that is, the VBScript language). If you are a Visual Basic developer, you will be interested in the key differences between VBScript and Visual Basic for Applications (VBA), and these are covered in detail. Next comes a discussion of using controls in a web page. This discussion covers not only the intrinsic controls available through HTML but also the use of ActiveX components (which we used to call OCXs). An entire chapter is devoted to using Microsoft Internet Information Server (IIS) as a back-end component, and the book's concluding chapters show examples for several complete database publishing projects.

While writing this book, I was struck by the pace of change in Internet technologies. Everyone talks about how fast things change, of course, but I was wholly amazed at the volume of technology released by Microsoft during the preparation of this book. New features were constantly being added to the Microsoft Internet Explorer—which caused a lot of scrambling on my part, to ensure that my code still worked! Nevertheless, with this book I have definitely met my goal of providing you with a sound foundation for developing dynamic web content.

The manuscript of this book was written in just ten weeks, but the process of bringing a book from conception to market is considerably longer, and so it is inevitable that by the time you read this book, changes to the current technology will have occurred that affect the book's content. To give just one example, technology allowing the use of VBScript code on the server side is just now emerging. Server-side scripting promises to allow the use of ActiveX components not only in the browser but also on the server. In fact, components on both the server and the client will be able to communicate across the Internet. This interaction, known as Distributed COM (DCOM), will revolutionize Internet development once again. I promise to include a complete treatment of emerging technologies like this one in the next edition of this book.

Looking back on the whole effort, I have to say that the compressed writing cycle of ten weeks was a plus. I certainly found the long days difficult, but I also had a tremendous amount of fun. Dan Mezick made sure that my schedule was clear so I didn't have to do anything but tackle the technology. Frankly, I think I have the best job. Where else can you get paid to play with the latest technology and not have to worry about the mundane details of the day-to-day operation?

Enjoy the book, and best of luck in your development efforts!

Scot P. Hillier
North Haven, Connecticut
August 1996

ACKNOWLEDGMENTS

Although my name appears on the cover of this book, it would be the height of arrogance for me to pretend that this work was done by me alone. One name on the cover does not tell the whole story; many other people are also responsible for the successful completion of this book, and they surely deserve significant recognition. I will thank them here, but the mere mention of their names seems inadequate. I extend my sincere appreciation and respect to each one of them.

No one can possibly pursue a dream without the loving support of a family, and I have been particularly blessed. My wife, Nancy, and my children, Matt and Ashley, have followed me all over the country while I chased after my goals. Through nine moves in just ten years of marriage, they have always been completely supportive. Thank you—I love you all.

Professionally, I could not be more fortunate. Dan Mezick, who works with me at New Technology Solutions, Inc., is one of the most honorable men I have ever met. He sacrificed opportunities for himself so that I could write this book, and it was his vision and leadership that made this effort possible. I only hope I can continue to benefit from my association with him over the years. I would also like to thank Bill Brown, who performs all the thankless jobs at NewTech.

Over the course of writing this book, I have been amazed by the professionalism and competence of the people at Microsoft Press, who have been a pleasure to work with. Several people deserve special recognition.

Steve Guty brought the project into Microsoft Press; many thanks also to Xavier Callahan, project editor and leader of the book team, who was largely responsible for the smooth production of this book.

Thanks to Katherine Krause, the manuscript editor, for making me look good, and to technical editor Robert Lyon, who had the unenviable job of testing all my code (and thanks to Mary DeJong for her keen technical eye and early feedback on the manuscript). Interior graphic design was handled by Kim Eggleston, and the cover was created by Greg Erickson and Robin Hjellen. Michael Victor, assisted by Lori Campbell, was the book's artist. E. Candace Gearhart, assisted by Susan Prettyman, was the principal compositor, with additional contributions from Linda Robinson, Paul Vautier, and Barbara Runyan.

The proofreaders were, in alphabetical order, Richard Carey, Ronald Drummond, Jocelyn Elliott, Patrick Forgette, Teri Kieffer, Roger LeBlanc, Patricia Masserman, Brenda Morris, Cheryl Penner, and Paula Thurman. Finally, many thanks to the sales and marketing teams for getting this book out there!

CHAPTER ONE

An Overview of Web Technologies

The Internet. The Internet. The Internet. Over the past several years, we have been conditioned to believe that the Internet will permeate every aspect of modern life. As software developers, we are told that Internet development is the next big wave of opportunity, and if we miss the crest, the undertow will destroy us. A significant amount of the dialogue sounds like nothing more than hype. A developer—indeed, anyone—can have a difficult time sorting fact from myth. Hype certainly abounds, but wrapped inside the hyperbole is a densely packed nugget of truth: the Internet has a significant impact on current software development.

The Internet is an international network of thousands of computers that are using the same rules to communicate. What fuels the popularity of the Internet is not just data access but also the compelling nature of the *browser* interface. Browsers are simple applications that run on computers and allow users to access the tremendous amount of information available on the Internet. Browsers are typically used to view web pages on the World Wide Web (WWW). The World Wide Web is an interlinked collection of hypertext documents (web pages) on the Internet. A typical browser offers an intuitive view of data that is easily understood even by novice users. Navigating between web pages on the WWW is a simple matter of clicking on links displayed in the browser text. Figure 1-1 shows the fundamental simplicity of the graphical user interface (GUI) for the Microsoft Internet Explorer, version 3.0, an Internet browser. The browser is displaying a sample web page on the WWW.

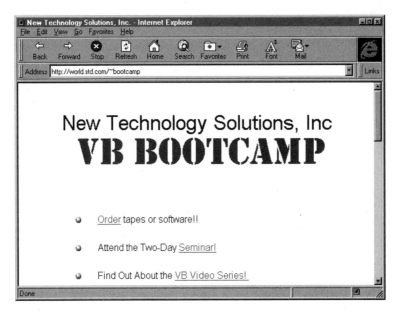

Figure 1-1.
A web page accessed via the Microsoft Internet Explorer (version 3.0 for Windows 95).

Information on the Internet is stored on *servers*. A server is a computer that provides services to connecting clients. A *web server* is a computer connected to the WWW, and it provides information for display in the browser, in the form of web pages. Each server on the web is identified by a unique Internet Protocol (IP) address. In order to connect to a particular web server, the browser must specify the IP address for the server. This address commonly takes the form of a Uniform Resource Locator (URL), which is a text string that identifies the server and the particular data to be displayed. Servers and browsers are the basic components that make up the Internet.

Computers connected to the Internet communicate by using a *protocol*. A protocol is nothing more than a set of rules used by computers to exchange information. Computers connected to the Internet communicate by the Transfer Control Protocol/Internet Protocol (TCP/IP), which allows data to be sent in small information "packets." Web servers and browsers exchange information on the WWW by using a protocol known as the Hypertext Transfer Protocol (HTTP). The data is transferred from the server in the form of text-based pages that are read by the browser. These text-based pages are written in a language known as Hypertext Markup Language (HTML). The browser recognizes and decodes HTML to present rich graphics and text through the browser interface. Figure 1-2 shows a simplified diagram of how browsers and servers function on the Internet.

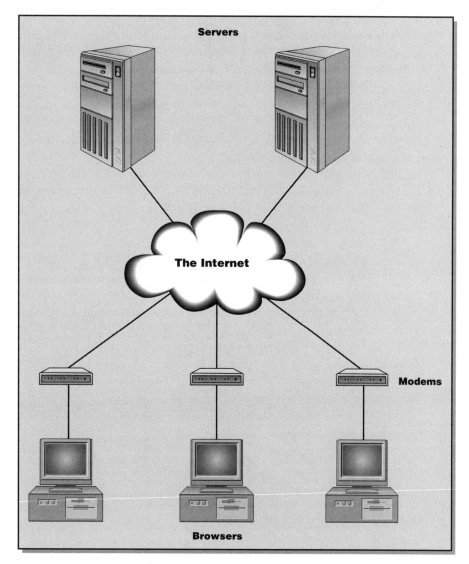

Figure 1-2.
Browsers and servers on the Internet.

A Variation on the Internet Concept

Although using the Internet can be an exciting experience, businesses are correct to question its role in the future of communications. Will the Internet become the central means of conducting business across long distances, or will it remain primarily a tool of technocrats? Internet commerce will have to overcome many barriers before it is fully viable. Bandwidth, the data transfer rate, is limited on the Internet. Most home users are connected to the WWW through an online service provider such as CompuServe, America Online, or The Microsoft Network. Access to the service provider is through a modem that operates at speeds no greater than 28.8 bits per second. These speeds cause slow browser response, which is frustrating for the user and degrades the overall experience. In addition, Internet transactions are not always secure, which makes users uneasy about conducting commerce on the web.

The good news, however, is often overlooked by businesses when they evaluate Internet technologies. Although the server/browser model was pioneered on the Internet, the same setup works on any private network that supports the same TCP/IP protocol used on the public WWW. This means that businesses can create internal networks of computers, interconnected through TCP/IP protocol, that utilize server/browser technology to provide the same intuitive interface to employees. These internal networks are known as *intranets*. Intranet solutions can overcome the traditional limitations of the WWW while maintaining the popular browser interface with which users view data. Bandwidth is generally not an issue on an intranet. Internal networks can provide secure corporate data to employees through the browsers at speeds that are more than acceptable. Employees in turn can use their interactive browser interfaces to place orders, request vacations, publish company newsletters, and so on. This technology is already in place in many companies. Everything you learn from this book is applicable to both the Internet and intranets.

KEY CONCEPT: Intranets overcome the two primary limitations of the Internet: bandwidth and security.

Internet Development Tools

For developers, the keys to capitalizing on the Internet/intranet trend are the software tools. A developer needs software tools that build on previous knowledge and that are easy to integrate with existing technology. Fortunately, that is the very description of Microsoft Visual Basic, Scripting Edition (or VBScript). VBScript is a proper subset of the Visual Basic for Applications language that has gained wide popularity in products such as Microsoft Excel. VBScript is used to transform static web pages into rich, interactive environments that are aesthetically pleasing and that provide superior content. It also integrates well with existing technology by extending the current HTML specification. Learning VBScript for Internet development is an investment in your programming skill set that will pay dividends for years.

Microsoft has created a dizzying array of Internet development tools that provide all the horsepower developers need to create interactive applications on both the client and the server side. You may initially think that you have little need to understand Microsoft's web server technologies just to use VBScript, but you'll soon discover that no developer is an island on the web. Developers who want to create outstanding applications need to have a good understanding of all the working parts of the Internet—both client and server. As an introduction, let's survey the various technologies offered by Microsoft for creating web servers, browser applications, and web content.

Developers who want to implement a web server can use technology available from Microsoft. The primary component for a web server based on Microsoft software is the operating system Windows NT version 3.51 or later. Windows NT has the ability to function as a TCP/IP network server, which is the foundation of any web site. The ability to create a TCP/IP network utilizing a Windows NT server is certainly not new, but Microsoft has added a significant new capability with the release of the Microsoft Internet Information Server (IIS). IIS installs onto a Windows NT server and provides services that allow connected users to access the World Wide Web, transfer files, and search the web. Figure 1-3 shows the fundamental architecture of IIS.

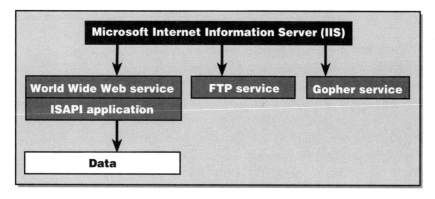

Figure 1-3.
The architecture of the Microsoft Internet Information Server.

Under the IIS umbrella you will find the WWW service, the file transfer protocol (FTP) service, and the Gopher service. These three services are the heart of IIS. Creating the simplest web site, however, requires very little knowledge of these services. Once IIS is installed on the Windows NT server, you can simply place HTML pages in the \wwwroot folder and you will have a complete vanilla web site. However, much more power is available for just a little bit of work. IIS provides two powerful dynamic-link libraries (DLLs): the Internet Database Connector (IDC) and the OLE Internet Server Application Programming Interface (OLEISAPI). These DLLs allow easy access to the strongest features of IIS, which primarily support database publishing.

When a web site needs to interact with an executable program on the server, the traditional approach has been to invoke a standard known as the Common Gateway Interface (CGI). For example, a CGI program might run each time a browser connects to it and passes a data request, such as a query, to the server. The CGI program executes and returns the results as HTML to the client browser. CGI, however, creates a new process for each request made by a browser. CGI has no memory of previous instances of itself, and this situation results in excessive overhead and slow response times. Microsoft has solved this problem in IIS by creating the Internet Server Application Programming Interface. ISAPI is an interface that allows programmers to develop DLLs that work with IIS. Since ISAPI applications are DLLs, they load into memory and initialize only once. Subsequent calls by a browser to the DLL require less overhead because the library is already resident in memory. Additionally, since the DLL has knowledge of previous calls, it can maintain state information for the entire session. This simply means that the server can now remember key information about the browser, providing flexible programmability and improved performance.

One particular ISAPI application is the Internet Database Connector (IDC). IDC is a simple mechanism for accessing any ODBC (Open Database Connectivity) datasource on the server. The technique involves three text files. The first file is the actual HTML file. For example, you could initiate a database query from the HTML file in a browser by clicking on a link to an Internet Database Connector file, which has an idc extension. The second file involved, the idc file, contains such information as the data source you want to access and the structured query language (SQL) statement you want to execute. The server then maps the idc file to the IDC, httpodbc.dll. The IDC reads the information in the idc file, connects to the ODBC datasource, retrieves the necessary data, and merges it into the HTML extension file. The third file involved, the HTML extension file, is the template for the actual HTML document that will be returned to the browser. Finally, the IDC returns the merged HTML document to the server, which returns it to the browser for display. Figure 1-4 shows the data flow as a browser queries a database and returns a result.

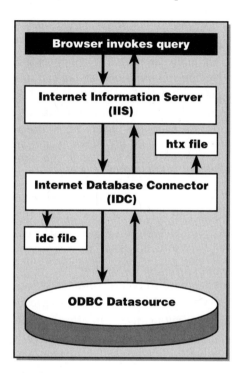

Figure 1-4.
Data flow of a database query.

A second ISAPI application is OLEISAPI. This application makes the functionality of the ISAPI interface available to any ActiveX component. ActiveX components are simply software components that support Automation. OLE servers in Visual Basic are examples of ActiveX components. You can create ActiveX components in both Visual Basic 4.0 and Visual C++. OLEISAPI allows you to access your in-process ActiveX components, which can receive a request from a client browser, execute a query or other additional functionality, and return an HTML document. Although very similar in functionality to IDC, OLEISAPI allows developers much greater flexibility because it makes the entire power of a development tool such as Visual Basic available to the programmer.

On the client side, the Internet Explorer provides an enhanced environment in which the user interacts with web information. The Internet Explorer not only recognizes the standard HTML tags but also recognizes extended HTML tags for hosting ActiveX controls. These ActiveX controls (formerly called OLE controls) are just the familiar reusable OLE custom (OCX) controls used in development tools such as Visual Basic. In some cases, the ActiveX controls have been optimized for transfer across the Internet, but they are really just OCX controls. In fact, the Internet Explorer can support any ActiveX control. Using these ActiveX controls is as simple as writing Visual Basic code. That's where VBScript enters the picture. Because VBScript is a proper subset of the Visual Basic for Applications language, the syntax for writing code and using ActiveX controls is similar to the syntax for a Visual Basic application. This is a powerful concept because Visual Basic programmers will find VBScript a natural extension of their previous programming skills.

An HTML page can contain references to ActiveX controls, much as it can contain references to other items, such as images. When an HTML page containing ActiveX controls is accessed by the Internet Explorer, the controls are downloaded to the client. The Internet Explorer registers the downloaded ActiveX components and displays the page. Once downloaded, the components are available on the client and do not have to be downloaded again.

In addition to hosting ActiveX controls, the Internet Explorer browser has its own object model. This means that it can be directly accessed through Automation, using Visual Basic. This allows Visual Basic applications to include the functionality of the Internet Explorer as a component. The Internet Explorer appears just as any other Automation component does—right in the References dialog box of the Visual Basic environment.

Automation is also used by the Internet Explorer to support a technology called ActiveX documents, an extension to OLE documents. Support for ActiveX documents enables the Internet Explorer to open an application, such as Microsoft Excel, within the browser window. To the user it appears that a stand-alone application, complete with toolbars and menus, has opened within the Internet Explorer.

The user can then interact with the application directly from the browser. The implication, of course, is that the user never has to leave the browser. Local files, network files, and the Internet can all be viewed seamlessly from inside the Internet Explorer. This capability provides a uniform look and feel for all work that occurs on the desktop, regardless of the information source. Unifying the desktop is a powerful outgrowth of Internet technology.

Don't forget Visual Basic, either. Visual Basic itself can play an important role in your overall Internet development strategy. Visual Basic executables can talk directly to the Internet Explorer through a simple ActiveX interface that behaves like an in-process DLL. Visual Basic can also utilize ActiveX controls that allow direct access to the Internet through the WinSock layer and TCP/IP protocol, completely eliminating the need for any kind of browser. Microsoft provides these ActiveX controls in a package known as the Internet Control Pack (ICP). ICP contains, for example, an ActiveX control that provides Internet browsing capability to any Visual Basic application. Grab it from the toolbox, drop it onto your form, and—presto!—instant browser.

When it comes to content, you get even more new toys. If you use Microsoft Office products, such as Microsoft Word and Microsoft PowerPoint, you will want to start off immediately by investigating the Internet Assistants for Office. These useful add-ins help you create Internet content directly from your favorite Office tool. Generating a home page for the web is as easy as writing a new Word document. It's also a great way to learn HTML because you can generate the pages and then examine them in a text editor, such as Notepad, to see all the gory details.

If you want a higher-end tool, consider Microsoft FrontPage. FrontPage is a web authoring tool for creating and maintaining HTML pages with an easy-to-use interface. The beauty of this system is that if you change the background on one HTML page, for example, FrontPage can change all the related pages as well. You also get a set of wizards to help you create the pages, as well as some automated features known as *WebBots*, which act as replacements for CGI scripts so that nonprogrammers can access advanced functionality.

Finally, if you just like to bang it all in yourself, you can always create your HTML pages in any text editor. (Notepad seems to be the favorite.) After all, HTML is just text.

Whew! What an alphabet soup! All the new tools can certainly lead to some confusion, especially when it comes to keeping the names straight. Each tool, however, is a powerful component of an overall solution, and these solutions work on both the Internet and corporate intranets. In fact, you will find that the integration among these tools is top-notch. The tools are easy to implement and have proved viable for business applications.

Opportunities for Developers

What does all of this mean to you? In essence, it means that if you're a developer you should be excited. With all the enthusiasm surrounding the Internet, developers have an opportunity to clean up. In particular, developers who use tools that employ Rapid Application Development (RAD) are in the best position. RAD is the concept of creating business solutions quickly for narrowly defined groups. RAD has gained widespread popularity through the use of tools, such as Visual Basic, with which developers can quickly generate business solutions using predefined software components. Developers skilled in RAD will certainly be in high demand on the Internet, where web page content is changed almost daily. Web development offers no room for long product cycles, beta testing, and multiple releases. Internet development is the ultimate high-tech Wild West. Make it work and get it out there now!

Because the majority of the opportunities are found in RAD development on the web, Visual Basic programmers migrating to the Internet Explorer and VBScript should do quite well in the new software marketplace. VBScript borrows from the Visual Basic for Applications language and offers the same RAD concepts through reusable software components.

Assumptions Made in This Book

Although you will gain significant knowledge of VBScript from this book, regardless of your experience level, to master the concepts and facilities of VBScript you should be a developer who is familiar with the Windows environment. In particular, you should have worked with a tool that utilizes the Visual Basic for Applications language. Visual Basic for Applications is present in many visual development tools, such as Visual Basic and Excel. This book does not attempt to teach the fundamentals of Visual Basic for Applications and assumes an understanding of properties, events, and methods.

In later chapters, knowledge of Visual Basic is essential. For example, some of the more advanced features of IIS utilize ActiveX components created with Visual Basic. Visual Basic code is provided where applicable; however, this book is not intended to teach the fundamentals of Visual Basic, either. For information on Visual Basic, see the product documentation.

This book is intended to provide developers who are already familiar with Visual Basic for Applications the fastest possible avenue to mastering VBScript and IIS. An overview of the client side is provided first, followed by an overview of the server. After the basics have been covered, complete examples are provided that utilize many of the concepts together to create valuable working applications on the Internet.

An Overview of HTML

Although HTML is getting widespread exposure, not every Visual Basic developer has mastered the language. A fundamental understanding of HTML is definitely a necessity if you want to gain the maximum benefit from this book. If you already have a firm understanding of HTML, you may want to skip this section.

HTML is nothing more than a text-based coding system used to tell a browser how to display information. The commands that make up HTML are called *tags*. Tags are indicated in HTML by angled brackets (for example, < and >). Tags form "bookends" that surround the text that they affect. Every HTML document begins with the tag <HTML> and ends with the tag </HTML>. The slash character in HTML is used to "close" a tag—that is, to indicate that its functionality no longer applies. Creating an HTML document is a simple matter of using tags to format information and provide links to other documents. Listing 1-1 shows the HTML code for the sample home page that was shown in Figure 1-1.

```
<HTML>
<HEAD>
<TITLE>New Technology Solutions, Inc.</TITLE>
<BASE HREF="http://world.std.com/~bootcamp/">
<BASEFONT FACE="ARIAL" SIZE=4>
</HEAD>

<BODY BGCOLOR="WHITE">

<CENTER>
<TABLE CELLSPACING=25>
    <TR>
        <TD COLSPAN=2>
        <IMG SRC="bootcamp.gif" ALT="VB Bootcamp"
        HEIGHT=100 WIDTH=500>
        </TD>
    </TR>
    <TR>
        <TD COLSPAN=2>
        <FONT FACE="ARIAL" SIZE=+1 COLOR=BLUE>
        <MARQUEE>Now on IE3 Steroids!!</MARQUEE>
        </FONT>
        </TD>
    </TR>
```

Listing 1-1.   *(continued)*
The HTML code for a sample home page.

11

Listing 1-1 *continued*

```
<TR>
    <TD ALIGN="RIGHT">
    <IMG SRC="knob.gif" ALT="Bullet" ALIGN="CENTER">
    </TD>
    <TD>
    <A HREF="purchase.htm">Order</A>
    tapes or software!!
    </TD>
</TR>
<TR>
    <TD ALIGN="RIGHT">
    <IMG SRC="knob.gif" ALT="Bullet" ALIGN="CENTER">
    </TD>
    <TD>
    Attend the Two-Day
    <A HREF="seminar.htm">Seminar!</A>
    </TD>
</TR>
<TR>
    <TD ALIGN="RIGHT">
    <IMG SRC="knob.gif" ALT="Bullet" ALIGN="CENTER">
    </TD>
    <TD>
    Find Out About the <A HREF="video.htm">
    VB Video Series! </A>
    </TD>
</TR>
<TR>
    <TD ALIGN="RIGHT">
    <IMG SRC="update.gif" ALT="Update" ALIGN="CENTER">
    </TD>
    <TD>
    Get info on the <A HREF="ctvbsig.htm">
    Connecticut VB Users' Group</A>
    </TD>
</TR>
<TR>
    <TD ALIGN="RIGHT">
    <IMG SRC="update.gif" ALT="Update" ALIGN="CENTER">
    </TD>
    <TD>
    WIN A COPY OF <A HREF="ctvbsig.htm">
    Visual Basic 4.0</A>
    </TD>
</TR>
```

```
    <TR>
        <TD ALIGN="RIGHT">
        <IMG SRC="new_smal.gif" ALT="New" ALIGN="CENTER">
        </TD>
        <TD>
        Get FREE <A HREF="attila.htm">Software!!</A>
        </TD>
    </TR>
    <TR>
        <TD ALIGN="RIGHT">
        <IMG SRC="new_smal.gif" ALT="New" ALIGN="CENTER">
        </TD>
        <TD>
        New Technology Solutions, Inc. is
        <A HREF="job.htm">hiring!!</A>
        </TD>
    </TR>
    <TR>
        <TD ALIGN="RIGHT">
        <IMG SRC="new_smal.gif" ALT="New" ALIGN="CENTER">
        </TD>
        <TD>
        NewTech's Special <A HREF="ie.htm">
        Internet Explorer 3.0</A> page!
        </TD>
    </TR>
    <TR>
        <TD ALIGN="RIGHT">
        <IMG SRC="new_smal.gif" ALT="New" ALIGN="CENTER">
        </TD>
        <TD>
        Special <A HREF="devday.htm">
        Developers Day</A> section
        </TD>
    </TR>
    <TR>
        <TD ALIGN="RIGHT">
        <IMG SRC="new_smal.gif" ALT="New" ALIGN="CENTER">
        </TD>
        <TD>
        VB Bootcamp Veterans get your
        <A HREF="cover.htm">Newsletter</A> here!
        </TD>
    </TR>
</TABLE>
```

(continued)

Listing 1.1 *continued*

```
<P><HR><P>
<IMG SRC="newtech.gif" ALT="NewTech" HEIGHT=103 WIDTH=300>
<P>
<FONT SIZE=-3><I>
For more information, contact us directly<P>
New Technology Solutions, Inc.<BR>
444-A Washington Avenue<BR>
North Haven, CT 06743<P>
Voice: 203-239-6874<BR>
Fax: 203-239-7997<BR>
Fax Back: 203-239-7225<P>
E-Mail: info@vb-bootcamp.com
<P>
This site is best viewed with Internet Explorer 3.0
<P>
<IMG SRC="bestwith.gif" ALT="IE3" HEIGHT=43 WIDTH=114>
</I></FONT>
</CENTER>
</BODY>
</HTML>
```

HTML documents are divided into two sections: the header and the body. The header is surrounded by the tags <HEAD> and </HEAD> and the body is surrounded by the tags <BODY> and </BODY>. All browsers display the title of the current web page in the browser's title bar. The <TITLE> tag is used to indicate the title of the page. For example, the following HTML code creates a page with no information, just a title:

```
<HTML>
<HEAD>
<TITLE>Inside Microsoft Visual Basic, Scripting Edition</TITLE>
</HEAD>
<BODY>
</BODY>
</HTML>
```

You should note that the structure of the HTML code is not important. For example, line breaks are not required. In other words, the following HTML code is equivalent to the previous example:

```
<HTML><HEAD><TITLE>Inside Microsoft Visual Basic, Scripting Edition
</TITLE></HEAD><BODY></BODY></HTML>
```

ONE: An Overview of Web Technologies

Because line breaks are not recognized, HTML provides special tags for indicating a new paragraph or a blank line. <P> causes a new paragraph and <BR> inserts a blank line. It's as simple as that to display formatted text in a browser.

Text size is controlled by heading tags. HTML recognizes six different heading tag pairs: <H1></H1> through <H6></H6>. <H1></H1> is the largest font size, and <H6></H6> is the smallest. A new tag that gives you more font control is the <FONT></FONT> tag pair. The <FONT></FONT> tag pair has several parts to it. When a tag has additional parts that help control the tag's behavior, these parts are called *attributes*. For example, the <FONT></FONT> tag pair has the attributes FACE and SIZE to modify the tag. The following code displays a resident stencil font in size 10:

```
<FONT FACE="stencil" SIZE=10>New Technology Solutions, Inc.</FONT>
```

You can make the text bold by using the <STRONG></STRONG> pair and italic by using the <EM></EM> pair. HTML also allows more exotic formatting, such as that used for lists. HTML supports three different kinds of lists: ordered, unordered, and definition. The following code creates a list of ordered (numbered) items:

```
<OL>
<LI>Visual Basic
<LI>Visual Basic for Applications
<LI>VBScript
</OL>
```

Unordered (unnumbered) lists are created with <UL></UL> tags. Unnumbered lists are bulleted lists. Definition lists use the <DL></DL> tag pair, which simply causes the items to be indented without any bullets or numbers,

How about graphics? HTML pages always have lots of cool graphics. HTML now provides support for gif and jpg graphics with the <IMG> tag. The <IMG> tag has a SRC attribute that identifies the file to be displayed:

```
<IMG SRC="newtech.gif">.
```

This displays the graphics file on the HTML page where the tag appears.

Along with graphics, links make up the primary user interface for a browser. Links are also called *jumps*. Links are indicated with the <A></A> tag pair. The attribute HREF then points to the HTML file to be displayed. For example,

```
<A HREF="contents.htm">Go to Contents</A>
```

causes a jump to the contents page when the text "Go to Contents" is clicked. A link can be either a simple filename or a fully qualified URL.

HTML is a simple language. As a result, it can be limiting. With these few tags, you obviously can't achieve the level of complex formatting provided by Word. However, HTML is growing and changing. In fact, the tag discussion here is only an overview. HTML supports many other tags and features. And Microsoft has proposed some important extensions to the HTML language to support the use of ActiveX controls in the Internet Explorer. These extensions promise to change the face of HTML pages from simple, static text and graphics to rich, interactive environments similar to the existing applications running on desktop computers.

To give an example of a simple interactive web page, and to honor our great tradition as developers, let's create a page that displays "Hello, World!" in a message dialog box when a button is clicked. We will use several of the new HTML extensions in this example. The HTML document begins with the standard structure, setting up a head and body section:

```
<HTML>
<HEAD>
<TITLE>My First VBScript Application</TITLE>
</HEAD>
<BODY>
```

This code is not particularly interesting yet. First, we will add an event subroutine that will display a message dialog box when it is called. To identify the event subroutine, we use the new <SCRIPT></SCRIPT> tags. Inside the <SCRIPT></SCRIPT> tags we simply write VBScript code:

```
<SCRIPT LANGUAGE="VBScript">
    Sub Command1_Click
        MsgBox "Hello, World!",0,"Sample"
    End Sub
</SCRIPT>
```

This is the essence of VBScript in HTML. It's a simple subset of Visual Basic for Applications written between <SCRIPT></SCRIPT> tags.

Next, we will add a form to the application, by using the <FORM></FORM> tags, and place a button on the form, by using the <INPUT> tag:

```
<FORM>
<INPUT
TYPE="BUTTON"
VALUE="Push Me"
NAME="Command1"
OnClick="Command1_Click">
</FORM>
```

Notice the OnClick attribute identifying the subroutine that gets called when the button is clicked. Now all we have to do is finish the page by adding the tags </BODY> and </HTML>. Figure 1-5 shows the finished page in the Internet Explorer after the button has been clicked.

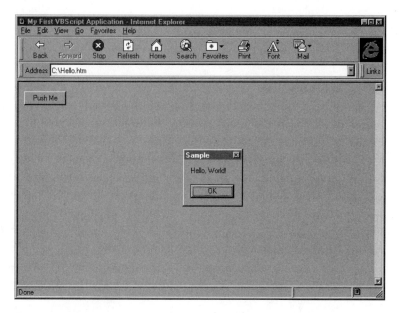

Figure 1-5.
A web page containing VBScript code, as viewed in the Internet Explorer.

Although more complex applications are certainly possible, this simple demo shows the foundation of using VBScript. We will build on this foundation throughout the book to create ever more interesting browser applications. For a detailed reference on the HTML language, see Appendix A.

CHAPTER TWO

ActiveX Scripting and VBScript

You have already seen that web browsers support a plain text syntax, known as HTML, for displaying information. HTML is a simple language and, as such, provides few mechanisms for extended interaction. Some controls, such as buttons, are supported intrinsically; however, more advanced user interface controls, such as spinners, calendars, and grids, are not implemented.

In an effort to provide a completely interactive environment, Microsoft has introduced a standard for including any scripting language within an HTML page. This standard is called *ActiveX Scripting*. ActiveX Scripting is a language-independent standard that defines the relationship between a *scripting host* and a *scripting engine*. A scripting engine is nothing more than an in-process ActiveX component, formerly called an OLE server, that conforms to the ActiveX Scripting specification. A scripting host is an application that uses the scripting engine. An example of a scripting host is the Microsoft Internet Explorer 3.0. ActiveX Scripting begins when an in-process ActiveX component representing the scripting engine is instantiated inside the process space of the Internet Explorer. After the scripting engine has been built by the Internet Explorer, it is loaded with commands for execution. The commands themselves, called the *script*, live inside the actual HTML page between the two tags <SCRIPT> and </SCRIPT>. After the script has been loaded into the engine, the Internet Explorer runs the script through the engine. This action results in the functionality defined by the commands in the code. Figure 2-1 shows the relationship between the scripting engine and the scripting host.

Figure 2-1.
ActiveX Scripting.

Microsoft Visual Basic, Scripting Edition, is implemented with the scripting engine named *vbscript.dll*. The VBScript engine and the Internet Explorer are not fundamentally joined; therefore, vbscript.dll can be used in any application that is an ActiveX scripting host. The VBScript engine understands the VBScript language, which is nothing more than a subset of the existing Visual Basic for Applications language. With the support of the Internet Explorer, VBScript can read and modify HTML form elements, perform event handling, interact with the browser, and automate any ActiveX component. We will cover the key features of the VBScript language later in this chapter.

KEY CONCEPT: VBScript is a proper subset of the Visual Basic for Applications language.

Scripting Languages

Creating interactive web content is a primary goal for many web developers and is achieved through a variety of means. Web browsers have the capability to add dynamic content through the use of video clips, sounds, and downloadable programs. Although other interactive methodologies are also capable of presenting compelling content, scripting languages offer significant advantages to the developer who is trying to create interactive web pages. For our purposes, we define a scripting language as any set of program instructions that can be embedded in an HTML page and executed by a browser.

The most significant advantage of scripting languages is their ease of use. Because these languages are contained directly in an HTML page and created in plain ASCII text, they are simple to implement and change. The developer does not have to endure the trials of the compilation and debugging process. Scripting languages are sufficient for most of the fundamental interactive functions required by a web site, such as data validation, and can easily provide interactive experiences, such as games. Currently two scripting languages are predominant: JavaScript and VBScript.

JavaScript

Perhaps the best-known scripting language prior to the introduction of VBScript was JavaScript. JavaScript is used to create interactive web applications supported by the Netscape browser. JavaScript offers many of the same advantages as VBScript. JavaScript is simple to use, lightweight, and dynamic. Developers can easily embed code functionality for interactive applications inside a web page.

The most noticeable difference between JavaScript and VBScript is the syntax. The syntax for JavaScript is similar to the syntax for the C++ programming language. Since VBScript is a subset of Visual Basic for Applications, VBScript follows the Visual Basic for Applications syntax.

Consider the "Hello, World!" VBScript example presented in Chapter 1. How much would the HTML change if we wanted to use JavaScript instead of VBScript to accomplish the same functionality? Listing 2-1 shows the complete example, but the key differences are in the scripting syntax. (Note that Listing 2-1 and all other full program listings are available on this book's companion CD, in the samples folder.) The JavaScript portion of the code looks like this:

```
<SCRIPT LANGUAGE="JavaScript">
    var rtn=false
    function push_me() {
        alert("Hello, World!")
        return true
    }
</SCRIPT>
```

Notice the syntax's similarity to C++. Curly braces are used to surround functions that return values based on success or failure. Although not overly complex, the syntax is obviously different from VBScript.

```
<HTML>
<HEAD>
<TITLE>My First JavaScript Application</TITLE>

<SCRIPT LANGUAGE="JavaScript">
    var rtn=false
    function push_me() {
        alert("Hello, World!")
        return true
    }
</SCRIPT>
```

Listing 2-1. *(continued)*

The JavaScript "Hello, World!" example.

Listing 2-1 *continued*

```
</HEAD>
<BODY>
<CENTER>

<FORM>
<INPUT TYPE = "BUTTON" VALUE = "Push Me!"
NAME = "Command1" OnClick="rtn=push_me()">
</FORM>

</CENTER>
</BODY>
</HTML>
```

The Internet Explorer 3.0 supports JavaScript directly through a scripting engine in the file jscript.dll. In fact, you can use both VBScript and JavaScript in a single web page. Listing 2-2 shows an example of utilizing JavaScript and VBScript in the same page. Figure 2-2 shows a sample output. In the Internet Explorer 3.0, both JavaScript and VBScript can read and modify HTML form elements, interact with the browser, and automate any ActiveX component.

```
<HTML>
<HEAD>
<TITLE>JavaScript and VBScript</TITLE>

<!--
This sample compares two functions that
use a text box to display a message.
Note the key differences between VBScript
and JavaScript.
-->

<SCRIPT LANGUAGE="JavaScript">
    var rtn=false
    function push_me() {

        // This function uses a literal string
        // and a property of the text box. Note
        // that JavaScript can set the values
        // for the variables when they are
        // declared with var.
```

Listing 2-2.
JavaScript and VBScript.

```
        var msg1="This is a JavaScript message: "
        var msg2=document.frmScript.txtMessage.value
        alert(msg1 + msg2)
        return true
    }
</SCRIPT>

<SCRIPT LANGUAGE="VBScript">
<!--
    Option Explicit
    Sub cmdVBS_OnClick

        ' This is a VBScript version of the
        ' JavaScript function.  VBScript must set
        ' and declare variables on separate
        ' lines.

        Dim MyForm
        Set MyForm=Document.frmScript
        Dim msg1,msg2
        msg1="This is a VBScript message: "
        msg2=MyForm.txtMessage.Value
        MsgBox msg1 & msg2
    End Sub
-->
</SCRIPT>

</HEAD>
<BODY>
<CENTER>

<FORM NAME="frmScript">
<INPUT TYPE="TEXT" NAME="txtMessage" VALUE="Test">
<P>
<INPUT TYPE="BUTTON" VALUE="JavaScript Message"
NAME="cmdJava" OnClick="rtn=push_me()">
<P>
<INPUT TYPE="BUTTON" VALUE="VBScript Message"
NAME="cmdVBS">
</FORM>

</CENTER>
</BODY>
</HTML>
```

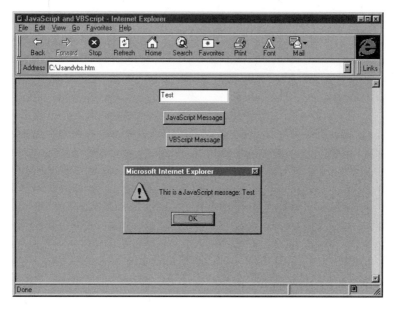

Figure 2-2.
Sample output of an HTML page that uses both JavaScript and VBScript.

VBScript

VBScript is a subset of Visual Basic for Applications. Therefore, VBScript programming has many similarities to Visual Basic for Applications programming. Many of the powerful features of Visual Basic for Applications, such as classes and API calls, were omitted to make the language portable and secure.

Although VBScript is just text and can be written with a simple text editor, a graphical design tool for VBScript is available. This visual layout tool is called *ActiveX Control Pad.* ActiveX Control Pad allows you to combine HTML code, ActiveX controls, HTML layouts, and VBScript or JavaScript. ActiveX Control Pad works in conjunction with the HTML Layout control. The HTML Layout control is a drawing board that allows you to visually add and manipulate controls. ActiveX Control Pad will be discussed in detail later in this book.

VBScript promises the same boom in ActiveX development that we have seen in OCX controls development. Because VBScript, with the support of the Internet Explorer, can automate ActiveX components, vendors can design ActiveX controls to perform particular Internet tasks. A stock ticker control is a good example of such a control. Admittedly, we already have a rich assortment of ActiveX controls in the form of OCX controls, but these controls are typically not optimized for downloading across the Internet. For example, many of these controls contain sizable design-time components that cause long delays during a download.

VBScript does not have an integrated debugging environment (IDE). This means that code debugging can be rather demanding. Typically, you run the script in a browser and troubleshoot any errors that may occur. Perhaps the most useful debugging component is a well-placed MsgBox, and until a complete IDE is available, development will remain cumbersome. The obvious need for an IDE is overwhelming, and Microsoft certainly knows that programmers want one; however, releasing VBScript "as is" allows developers to get a handle on the new concepts without waiting for a more formal product. After coding a few pages directly, you will quickly master any IDE that is delivered in the future.

Compatibility with existing browsers is another issue for VBScript. Although the Internet Explorer supports both VBScript and JavaScript, VBScript is not currently supported by the Netscape browser. In the future, we may see support from Netscape and others, but for now, interactive web sites that use VBScript are limited to platforms running the Internet Explorer.

In a bid to create standard scripting support that would broaden the appeal of VBScript while maintaining current support for other engines, such as JavaScript, Microsoft is working with the World Wide Web Consortium to develop a standard for ActiveX Scripting and the event-driven model. Such efforts will improve the viability of VBScript, but even without an absolute standard, the Internet Explorer promises to have a large market share because of tight integration with future releases of Windows. Ultimately, VBScript may take center stage in Windows development as the browser becomes the primary desktop interface. Work is ongoing at Microsoft to completely unify the desktop environment inside the browser, creating a single, comprehensive view of local files, network files, and Internet files. This new view is known as *page view*.

Implementing page view will radically alter the Windows desktop environment. First and foremost, the concept of a separate browser running on a desktop is eliminated. In fact, the browser will *be* the desktop. Imagine an environment in which the Windows Explorer is replaced by a browser interface. You will view all of the files on your local machine just as if they are web pages. Need to see a Word document? View it in a browser. Need to work on a Microsoft Excel spreadsheet? Open it in the browser.

Ultimately, the user will work with all data the same way, regardless of the location of the data. For example, local, network, and Internet files will be seamlessly integrated into the browser interface. This represents a significant advance in the user interface because users will no longer have to worry about data location and the technical knowledge necessary to connect to the data.

JavaScript Versus VBScript

JavaScript and VBScript have many similarities. In fact, anyone who has mastered VBScript will find JavaScript just as easy to learn. Since the Internet Explorer supports both languages, knowledge of the fundamentals of both is valuable. The key differences between JavaScript and VBScript are covered in the paragraphs that follow.

Syntax

As stated before, the most obvious difference is syntax. JavaScript uses curly braces to denote functions, whereas VBScript uses Function…End Function and Sub…End Sub. In fact, JavaScript supports only functions, whereas VBScript supports functions and subroutines. If you want to create a function that behaves like a subroutine in JavaScript, simply omit the return value.

Objects

Neither JavaScript nor VBScript is truly object-oriented. Without digressing into a full definition of object-oriented programming, we can safely say that neither language exhibits all of the characteristics of a truly object-oriented language. Neither language, for example, supports the concept of inheritance.

JavaScript, however, makes stronger use of objects than does VBScript. JavaScript allows for the definition of classes for the subsequent creation of objects. To define a class, you create a function that specifies the class name and the class's properties and methods. For example, the following code defines a class called *Student* that has three properties:

```
function Student (name, height, weight) {
    this.name=name
    this.height=height
    this.weight=weight
}
```

Values are assigned to properties using the *this* keyword, which always references the new object. This type of design allows JavaScript to encapsulate properties and methods inside an object. Creating an instance of the Student class is a simple matter of calling the function and using the *new* keyword:

```
mystudent=new Student("John",70,175)
```

Unfortunately, VBScript does not support object creation or user-defined classes. VBScript supports only reusable functions and subroutines. In order to use VBScript to manage the above information for multiple students, we would have to create separate variables for each student we wanted to track. We could accomplish this by using arrays, for example.

Language Scalability

A primary difference between VBScript and JavaScript is scalability. Once you learn VBScript, you are well on your way to learning Visual Basic for Applications. If you know Visual Basic or Visual Basic for Applications, you know VBScript. Although JavaScript has similarities to C++, it is a new language.

Other Scripting Languages

Because Microsoft has designed ActiveX Scripting to be an open standard, JavaScript and VBScript may soon be joined by other scripting languages. The Internet Explorer can support any scripting language that takes advantage of ActiveX Scripting. Third-party vendors may choose to design their own scripting languages.

The VBScript Language

In order to understand the VBScript language, you must first understand what's missing. VBScript is not a complete, mature development language. Many features that are a necessity in advanced languages, such as data types, are not supported in VBScript. The language is a simple collection of fundamental features taken right out of the Visual Basic for Applications language. If you have programmed with Visual Basic for Applications before, you will find VBScript familiar. Table 2-1 shows the features of the VBScript language. Appendix C shows the Visual Basic for Applications features that are not supported by VBScript. For more information, consult the VBScript documentation on this book's companion CD and at Microsoft's web site.

Table 2-1. The VBScript Language

Category	Keywords
Array handling	Array function Declaration (Dim, Static, etc.) Lbound, Ubound ReDim, Erase
Assignment	=, Let, Set
Comments	REM and '
Constants/Literals	Empty, Nothing, Null True, False User-defined literals

(continued)

Table 2-1 *continued*

Category	Keywords
Control flow	Do...Loop For...Next, For Each...Next While...Wend If...Then...Else Select...Case
Conversion	Abs Asc, Chr CBool, CByte CDate, CDbl, CInt CLng, CSng, CStr CVErr Fix, Int, Sgn Hex, Oct
Date/Time	Date function, Time function Day, Month, Weekday, Year Hour, Minute, Second Now DateSerial, DateValue TimeSerial, TimeValue
Error handling	On Error Resume Next Err Object
Input/Output	InputBox MsgBox
Math	Atn, Cos, Sin, Tan Exp, Log, Sqr Randomize, Rnd
Miscellaneous	Line continuation character (_) Line separation character (:)
Objects	Create Object
Operators	+, −, *, /, ^, Mod Integer Division (\) Negation (−) String concatenation (&) =, <>, <, >, <=, >=, Is Not, And, Or, Xor Eqv, Imp
Options	Option Explicit
Procedures	Function, Sub Exit Function, Exit Sub Call ByVal, ByRef

Category	Keywords
Strings	Asc, AscB, AscW
	Chr, ChrB, ChrW
	Instr, InStrB
	Len, LenB
	LCase, UCase
	Left, LeftB
	Mid, MidB
	Right, RightB
	Space(*number*)
	StrComp
	String(*number, character*)
	Trim, LTrim, RTrim
Variables	Procedure-level:
	Dim, Static
	Module-level:
	Private, Dim
Variants	IsArray
	IsDate, IsEmpty, IsError
	IsNull, IsNumeric, IsObject
	VarType

Key Differences Between
Visual Basic for Applications and VBScript

Because VBScript is a subset of Visual Basic for Applications, many of the familiar features of Visual Basic for Applications are supported. However, certain key differences between the two programming environments require detailed examination. The major differences are covered here in alphabetical order.

Classes

VBScript provides no support for classes as they are used in Visual Basic 4.0. You cannot use <SCRIPT></SCRIPT> tags to create anything except reusable functions and subroutines. Development in VBScript is purely procedural. However, in the Internet Explorer 3.0, VBScript can automate any ActiveX component, including OLE servers (now called ActiveX components) created in Visual Basic 4.0.

Control Arrays

VBScript does not support control arrays. (A control array is a group of duplicate controls sharing the same name.) This is unfortunate because grouping controls into arrays always simplifies coding. You can work around this limitation, however, by having controls call a centralized routine whenever their respective events are called. For example, the following HTML code shows three buttons, each of which calls the same subroutine. Note that an index is passed with the call. In the function, we can use a Select…Case statement to determine which button was pressed:

```
<SCRIPT LANGUAGE="VBScript">
    Sub WhatButton(intIndex)
        Select Case intIndex
            Case 1
                MsgBox "Button1!"
            Case 2
                MsgBox "Button2!"
            Case 3
                MsgBox "Button3!"
        End Select
    End Sub
</SCRIPT>
<INPUT TYPE="BUTTON" OnClick="WhatButton(1)">
<INPUT TYPE="BUTTON" OnClick="WhatButton(2)">
<INPUT TYPE="BUTTON" OnClick="WhatButton(3)">
```

Unfortunately, the above technique works only for controls defined with HTML. ActiveX controls downloaded into a web page do not support such events as OnClick. The events for each ActiveX control are defined as separate subroutines. Therefore, no workaround exists for control arrays in ActiveX components. We discuss events, functions, and subroutines in detail later in this chapter.

Data Access

VBScript supports data access by using data access objects, as well as by using the Internet Server API (ISAPI). Data access objects (DAOs) and remote data objects (RDOs) can be inserted into an HTML page and automated. Data access to any ODBC data source from an HTML page can be accomplished via ISAPI, provided with the Internet Information Server (IIS). IIS is discussed in detail in Chapter 5.

Debugging

VBScript does not provide any debugging features. There are no breakpoints, watches, or debug windows. Additionally, the Debug object is not supported. VBScript does not allow you to "step" through code, either; however, stepping can be simulated if you use the MsgBox function periodically in your code to report information. These MsgBox functions can then be commented out or removed from the final document.

File Operations

VBScript does not support any of the file operations found in Visual Basic for Applications, such as reading and writing to a file. Once again, this is because of the risks involved in being able to access the client machine without restriction. Clearly, allowing direct file I/O from the browser places the client machine at the mercy of any rogue executable that gets downloaded.

Forms

VBScript provides support for forms. Forms are created with the <FORM> </FORM> tags. The fundamental difference between VBScript forms and Visual Basic for Applications forms is that VBScript forms are not visible as separate "windows" in the application. Instead, forms are a way to group controls together for the purpose of referencing their properties and methods in code or submitting data to a back-end process.

Help Files

VBScript does not allow access to the Windows help file system. Unlike Visual Basic for Applications, VBScript also cannot produce context-sensitive help that displays topics for objects that currently have the focus. Help is once again limited to the text placed inside an HTML file.

Fortunately, the hypertext links available in HTML are a convenient way to provide help. For example, the language documentation for VBScript is available on this book's companion CD as an HTML file. If you run this HTML file, you will find that the hypertext links work in a way that is similar to the way any Windows-based help file system works.

Intrinsic Constants

VBScript does not support intrinsic constants, which are built-in, predefined constants. For example, to create a message box with Abort, Retry, and Ignore buttons, you would normally specify the second argument in the MsgBox statement as vbAbortRetryIgnore. However, since VBScript does not recognize intrinsic constants, you must specify the numeric values directly in code.

Menus

VBScript does not support menu structures similar to those found in Windows-based applications. Windows-style menus are typically found only in the browser itself and are used to navigate the browser. You can create menu structures, however, either by utilizing HTML directly or through an ActiveX control, but such menus do not have the same appearance or interaction as true drop-down menus.

In HTML, you can implement a menu structure using the anchor tag, <A></A>. The anchor tag denotes a link to another URL. The anchor tag has an HREF attribute that directs the browser to a new URL when the text in the anchor is clicked. The following code sets up a link to the Microsoft web site when the word *JUMP* is clicked:

```
<A HREF="http://www.microsoft.com">JUMP</A>
```

Using the anchor tag, you can set up a group of jumps that can form a simulated menu structure. HTML even supports a <MENU></MENU> tag that displays the items as a logical grouping. The following code is an example of a menu offering links to various sites:

```
<MENU>
<LI><A HREF="http://www.microsoft.com">
    Microsoft</A></LI>
<LI><A HREF="http://www.vb-bootcamp.com">
    New Technology Solutions, Inc.</A></LI>
<LI><A HREF="http://www.anysite.com">
    Any Site</A></LI>
</MENU>
```

This text appears in the browser as a grouping of links that is displayed statically on the page. The menu does not drop down and cannot be hidden. It is simply a section of text links.

ActiveX controls, however, can offer some solutions to the menu problem posed above. Utilizing an ActiveX control specifically designed to implement menus, you can create a pop-up menu that displays a series of menu choices. The pop-up menu control can be displayed on demand and is automatically hidden after a choice is made. Listing 2-3 shows a complete example using the ActiveX Popup Menu control to implement a menu. Figure 2-3, on page 35, shows a sample of the output. Note that, in order for the program in Listing 2-3 to work properly, the mnuPopUp control must reside and be registered on your computer. ActiveX controls are covered in detail in Chapter 4.

```
<HTML>
<HEAD>
<TITLE>Pop-up Menu</TITLE>

<!--
This demo uses an ActiveX
Popup Menu control to
```

Listing 2-3.
Using the ActiveX Popup Menu control to add a menu to a web page.

```
implement a pop-up menu in
a web page
-->

<SCRIPT LANGUAGE="VBScript">
    Sub cmdAdd_OnClick

        'Author: New Technology Solutions, Inc.
        'Purpose: Add a new item to the menu
        '6/2/96 Original

        Dim MyForm
        Set MyForm=Document.frmPopUp
        MyForm.mnuPopUp.AddItem MyForm.txtMenu.Value
        MsgBox "New Item Added!"
    End Sub

    Sub cmdClear_OnClick
        'Author: New Technology Solutions, Inc.
        'Purpose: Clear all menu items
        '6/2/96 Original

        Dim MyForm
        Set MyForm=Document.frmPopUp
        MyForm.mnuPopUp.Clear
        MsgBox "Menu Cleared!"
    End Sub

    Sub cmdPop_OnClick

        'Author: New Technology Solutions, Inc.
        'Purpose: Cause the menu to appear
        '6/2/96 Original

        Dim MyForm
        Set MyForm=Document.frmPopUp
        MyForm.mnuPopUp.PopUp
    End Sub

    Sub mnuPopUp_Click(intIndex)

        'Author: New Technology Solutions, Inc.
        'Purpose: Receive the click from the menu
        '6/2/96 Original
```

continued

33

Listing 2-3 *continued*

```
        Dim MyForm
        Set MyForm=Document.frmPopUp
        MsgBox "You clicked Item #" & intIndex
    End Sub
</SCRIPT>

</HEAD>
<BODY BGCOLOR="WHITE">
<CENTER>

<FORM NAME="frmPopUp">
<INPUT TYPE="TEXT" VALUE="MenuItem" NAME="txtMenu">
<P>
<INPUT TYPE="BUTTON" VALUE="AddItem" NAME="cmdAdd">
<P>
<INPUT TYPE="BUTTON" VALUE="Clear" NAME="cmdClear">
<P>
<INPUT TYPE="BUTTON" VALUE="Pop-up Menu" NAME="cmdPop">
<P>

<OBJECT
    CLASSID="clsid:7823A620-9DD9-11CF-A662-00AA00C066D2"
    ID="mnuPopUp"
    WIDTH=80
    HEIGHT=30
    >
</OBJECT>
</FORM>
</CENTER>
</BODY>
</HTML>
```

Modules

VBScript supports code modules through the <SCRIPT></SCRIPT> tag. Each script section forms an independent code module that can have its own variables, functions, and subroutines. These modules are similar to the standard BAS module found in Visual Basic.

Multiple Document Interface

There is no concept of a Multiple Document Interface (MDI) application in VBScript. MDI applications are programs that display multiple forms inside a large parent window. The child windows are confined to the boundaries of the parent window. Since VBScript does not present forms as independent objects, you cannot create MDI applications in a web browser.

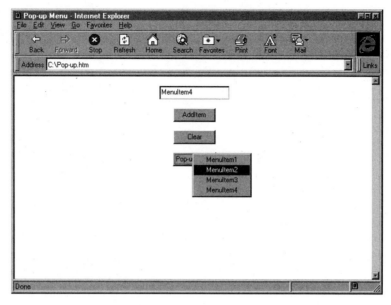

Figure 2-3.
Sample output of the ActiveX Popup Menu control.

Option Explicit

As in Visual Basic for Applications, undeclared variables in VBScript are automatically dimensioned as variants. No specific requirement exists to declare variables before you use them. However, failing to declare variables can still lead to bugs in your code. Although VBScript supports only the variant data type, Option Explicit can still be valuable because it will automatically detect any typographical errors in variable names. (The Option Explicit statement requires the explicit declaration of all variables.) Therefore, we recommend the use of Option Explicit inside every set of <SCRIPT></SCRIPT> tags. When using Option Explicit, you must remember to make it the first line of code in any script section and that the scope of Option Explicit is only inside the current <SCRIPT></SCRIPT> tags.

System Objects

Although Visual Basic for Applications supports the Screen, Printer, App, Debug, Err, and Clipboard objects, VBScript supports only the Err object. Therefore, VBScript does not allow you to access such useful objects as the mouse pointer or the clipboard. You can, however, use the Err object to provide runtime error handling for your applications.

Variables

Although Visual Basic for Applications supports a myriad of different data types, VBScript supports only the variant data type. The variant is a data type that can contain any kind of variable data (integers, strings, and objects, for example). Variables are discussed in detail later in this chapter.

The Windows API

VBScript does not allow web pages to make calls to the Windows application programming interface (API). Allowing such calls could jeopardize the security of the client. For example, viruses could easily use API calls to damage the client machine.

Forms and Modules

VBScript supports forms and modules. Forms are typically used to gather input from the user. Modules are used to group sections of code.

Forms

Forms in HTML are different from the forms found in Visual Basic and other Windows-based applications. In Visual Basic, a form is a visible container upon which controls are placed. In HTML, however, forms are principally a technique for gathering input data to pass to a back-end server. Forms are defined in HTML with the <FORM></FORM> tags. Typically, the <FORM></FORM> tags have the following syntax:

<FORM NAME="*string*" ACTION="*string*" METHOD="*string*"></FORM>

The NAME attribute is the name of the form (the name you refer to in VBScript), the ACTION attribute is the URL of the back-end process to receive the form data, and the METHOD attribute is the method of data exchange between the client and the server.

Typically, controls are placed between the form tags and are contained by the form. These controls are normally used to gather data and initiate the passing of this data to the server. Passing this data to the server is known as *submitting* a form. Submitting is accomplished through the use of a Submit control, which is one of the intrinsic controls supported by the Internet Explorer. The following code is an example of a form with a text control and a Submit control:

```
<FORM NAME="MyForm" ACTION="http://NT_SERVER/mystuff" METHOD="POST">
<INPUT TYPE="TEXT" NAME="TextField">
<INPUT TYPE="SUBMIT">
</FORM>
```

In this example, the form will send the data from the TextField text control to the mystuff executable when the Submit button is clicked. The METHOD attribute can be either POST or GET, depending upon how the information is to be handled. The POST method sends data to a back-end process, and the GET method appends the arguments to the URL and opens the URL. Regardless of the method, the form data is always passed in a plain text format as FIELD=VALUE for each input field in the form. The back-end program can then parse the text and take action based on the data.

> **KEY CONCEPT:** When a form is submitted to a back-end process, the data takes the format FIELD1=VALUE1&FIELD2=VALUE2...&FIELDn=VALUEn.

The NAME attribute of a form can be used in VBScript. The NAME attribute allows the form to behave like an object that can be accessed in code. Once the object is accessed, you can address the controls on the form in the familiar form.control.property syntax of Visual Basic for Applications. The Document object of the ActiveX Scripting model provides a way to access the form object by setting a variable equal to Document.*formname*. As an example, the following code puts text into the text control of the form:

```
<SCRIPT LANGUAGE="VBScript">
    'Notice the use of the Document object to
    'obtain a reference to the form
    Document.MyForm.Text1.Value="New Text"
</SCRIPT>
```

Once the information for a form has been entered, the data can be passed to a process running on a back-end server. When the data is passed, you can use several tools to receive data on the back end. If your server is a Windows NT platform running IIS, you can access a database directly through the Internet Database Connector (IDC) or through OLEISAPI, a dynamic-link library hosted by IIS. IDC and OLEISAPI are discussed in detail in Chapter 5, along with complete code examples.

Modules

Although there is no explicitly defined code module in VBScript, the <SCRIPT></SCRIPT> tags define a code module in the same way that the <FORM></FORM> tags define a form. Code modules are meaningful in VBScript because they allow scoping of variables and procedures at the module level. Scoping is the process that determines how long a variable or procedure exists and what parts of the application can use the variable or procedure.

Variables

There are two levels of scope for any variable in VBScript: Script and Procedure. Script-level variables are declared with the Dim keyword inside a module but outside a procedure. Script-level variables are available only to the module in which they are defined.

You can also declare Procedure-level variables. Procedure-level variables are declared inside a procedure, with the Dim keyword. Procedure-level variables are available only to the procedure in which they are defined. Here's an example that shows the declaration of each of these types of variables:

```
<SCRIPT LANGUAGE="VBScript">

    'Script-level variable
    Dim ScriptVar

    Sub MySub
        'Procedure-level variable
        Dim ProcVar
    End Sub
</SCRIPT>
```

Modules defined in a script section also support the Option Explicit statement, which was discussed earlier. When Option Explicit is used in a module, it must appear as the first line of the module.

Functions and Subroutines

Function and subroutine procedures in VBScript are scoped at only one level: Page. Any procedure that you create in VBScript can be accessed from any other portion of your application. Procedures are not qualified with the Public or Private keyword.

Event Procedures

Event procedures can be implemented in VBScript in several different ways. (An event procedure is a procedure that gets executed when an event, such as a mouse click, occurs.) Event procedures can be defined by simply coding them into VBScript directly, using attributes of the <INPUT> tag or attributes of the <SCRIPT></SCRIPT> tags.

Placing event procedures in a module is just a matter of adding a coding structure with the syntax Sub *control_eventname* to the module. This is the most common structure and the one most familiar to programmers of Visual Basic for Applications. The following code shows the definition of the OnClick event for a button named btnMine:

```
<SCRIPT LANGUAGE="VBScript">
    Sub btnMine_OnClick
        MsgBox "Event Text"
    End Sub
</SCRIPT>
<FORM>
<INPUTNAME="btnMine" TYPE="BUTTON" VALUE="Click Here">
</FORM>
```

The <SCRIPT></SCRIPT> tags also have attributes, however, that allow a module to explicitly support only one event. The following code shows the code designed to support only the OnClick event for btnMine:

```
<SCRIPT LANGUAGE="VBScript" FOR="btnMine" EVENT="OnClick">
    MsgBox "Event Test"
</SCRIPT>
<FORM>
<INPUT>NAME="btnMine" TYPE="BUTTON" VALUE="Click Here">
</FORM>
```

Finally, you can attach code to controls by using the appropriate attribute of the control itself. The following code shows how VBScript code can be attached to a button OnClick event:

```
<SCRIPT LANGUAGE="VBScript">
</SCRIPT>
<FORM>
<INPUT TYPE="BUTTON" OnClick="MsgBox 'Event Test'"
    VALUE="Click Here">
</FORM>
```

Immediate Execution

Although VBScript is generally organized into functions and subroutines, such procedures are not required. VBScript code can actually be executed inline if code is placed directly in between the <SCRIPT></SCRIPT> tags. The following code declares a variable and initializes its value automatically when the page is loaded:

```
<SCRIPT LANGUAGE="VBScript">
    Dim MyVar
    MyVar=100
</SCRIPT>
```

Notice that the code is not contained between Function…End Function or Sub…End Sub keywords. When code is created this way, it is executed when the page loads, and never again. This coding technique is known as *immediate execution.* Immediate execution is useful for initializing data or for dynamically changing a web page when it is loaded.

> **KEY CONCEPT:** Code that is not contained in a function or subroutine is executed when the page is loaded. This is called *immediate execution.*

C H A P T E R   T H R E E

Understanding Automation and Browser Architecture

Automation allows applications to communicate, exchange data, and control one another. Specifically, Automation allows a client application to create and control an object, using the exposed object's interface. Automation is powerful because programmers can use this technology to access the functionality of any application that supports Automation. For example, if you were writing a mortgage calculation application, you could write the calculation engine yourself, but Automation gives you another option. Using Automation, you can access the calculation engine of Microsoft Excel and get Excel to do the calculations for you. In this way, developers can use the functionality of existing applications without recreating the same functionality in their own applications.

Software objects play an important role in Automation. For the purposes of this discussion, objects are nothing more than self-contained functional software components. Like objects in Microsoft Visual Basic, these components contain properties and methods. In fact, objects that are accessible through Automation behave just like the tools in the Visual Basic toolbox—if you know the properties and methods, you can easily use the component. The Microsoft Visual Basic for Applications language supports Automation by means of several keywords. In order to access an object, you use the CreateObject function. For example, the following code creates an instance of an Excel spreadsheet from Visual Basic:

```
Dim objWorksheet as Object
Set objWorksheet = CreateObject("Excel.Sheet")
```

In general, the syntax for the CreateObject function is

CreateObject("*ServerName.Class*")

where *ServerName* is the name of the application supplying the object and *Class* is the type of object you want to create. Once the object is created, the program can use any of the exposed properties and methods defined for the object. For example, Listing 3-1 shows how a Visual Basic program can access the spell checking method of an Excel worksheet object through Automation. Figure 3-1 shows a sample of the output from the program in Listing 3-1. Note that Listing 3-1 and all other full program listings are available on this book's companion CD in the samples folder.

```
'This demo uses the spell checking capabilities
'of Microsoft Excel.
'This is accomplished by accessing the CheckSpelling
'method of Excel using Automation.


Private Sub Command1_Click()
    Dim objWorksheet As Object
    Set objWorksheet = CreateObject("Excel.Sheet")
    objWorksheet.Cells(1, 1).Value = Text1.Text
    objWorksheet.CheckSpelling
    Text1.Text = objWorksheet.Cells(1, 1).Value
    Set objWorksheet = Nothing
End Sub
```

Listing 3-1.
Using Excel's spell checker through Automation.

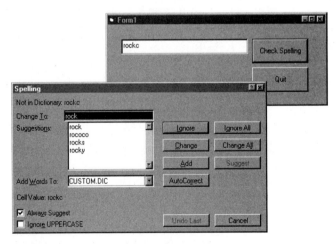

Figure 3-1.
Using Excel's spell checker.

When using Automation to develop new applications, programmers are often frustrated by the lack of documentation describing the functionality of various software objects that can be used in an application. When object documentation is provided, manufacturers typically supply it in the form of an *object model.* An object model is a hierarchical representation of the objects contained in an application and their interrelationships.

Figure 3-2 shows a partial Excel object model. Excel actually contains dozens of objects, but the partial model clearly shows the relationships among some of the objects. For example, Excel is presented in a workbook/worksheet paradigm, which is represented by the Workbook and Worksheet objects. The relationship between a workbook and a worksheet is indicated by the placement of the objects in the hierarchy.

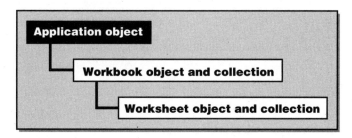

Figure 3-2.
A partial Excel object model.

KEY CONCEPT: Object models are used to describe various objects in an application, as well as their relationships.

Another good source of object information is the *object browser.* The object browser is an application that presents objects, properties, and methods in a dialog box. Visual Basic has a built-in object browser that can be used to view object information. Figure 3-3 shows the Visual Basic 4.0 Object Browser displaying the Microsoft Internet Explorer version 3.0 object, along with the corresponding methods and properties. These properties and methods are discussed in detail later in this chapter. Like Excel objects, Internet Explorer objects can be used directly from Visual Basic. If you need more information on any object model, contact the manufacturer of the application. Manufacturers should be able to provide a complete Automation object model.

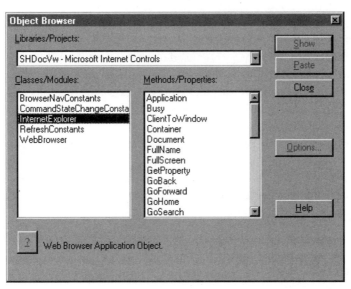

Figure 3-3.
The Visual Basic 4.0 Object Browser.

The Internet Explorer Object Model

The Internet Explorer version 3.0 object model is flat—that is, it has only one level. In this respect it is unlike many other object models. The single-level architecture of the Internet Explorer model makes it significantly easier to master than many other applications. Figure 3-4 shows the complete Internet Explorer object model, and Tables 3-1 and 3-2 describe the object's properties and methods.

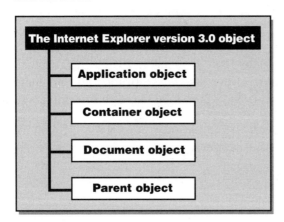

Figure 3-4.
The Internet Explorer object model.

Table 3-1. **Properties of the Microsoft Internet Explorer, Version 3.0**

Property	Type	Description	Usage
Application	Object	Returns a reference to the Internet Explorer object.	Set MyObject = *browser.*Application
Busy	Boolean	Returns a Boolean value indicating whether the Internet Explorer is busy downloading data or performing some other activity. True indicates busy; False indicates not busy.	If *browser.*Busy Then...EndIf
Container	Object	Returns a reference to the container/parent of the Internet Explorer, if any exists.	Set MyObject = *browser.*Container
Document	Object	Returns a reference to the active document, if any exists.	Set MyDocument = *browser.*Document
FullName	String	Returns the full pathname to the Internet Explorer executable. (Example: C:\ PROGRAM FILES\Plus!\ MICROSOFT INTERNET\ IEXPLORE.EXE)	MsgBox *browser.*FullName
FullScreen	Boolean	Returns or sets the Internet Explorer window mode. True indicates that the window is maximized and that the status bar, toolbar, menu bar, and title bar are hidden.	If *browser.*FullName Then...EndIf *browser.*FullScreen = True
Height, Width	Long	Returns or sets the dimensions in pixels of the Internet Explorer window.	MsgBox *browser.*Height *browser.*Height = 400
HWND	Long	Returns the window handle of the current Internet Explorer window.	MsgBox *browser.*HWND
Left, Top	Long	Returns or sets the position in pixels of the Internet Explorer window relative to the screen/container.	MsgBox *browser.*Left *browser.*Left = 100
LocationName	String	Returns the name of the file currently being viewed. (Example: Microsoft Corporation)	MsgBox *browser.*LocationName

(continued)

Table 3-1. *continued*

Property	Type	Description	Usage
LocationURL	String	Returns the full URL for the file currently being viewed. (Example: http://www.microsoft.com/)	MsgBox *browser*.LocationURL
MenuBar	Boolean	Returns or sets the display of the menu bar. True indicates that the menu bar is visible; False indicates that it is hidden.	If *browser*.MenuBar Then…EndIf *browser*.MenuBar = True
Name	String	Returns the name of the Internet Explorer application. (Example: Microsoft Internet Explorer)	MsgBox *browser*.Name
Parent	Object	Returns a reference to the container/parent of the Internet Explorer.	Set MyObject = *browser*.Parent
Path	String	Returns the full pathname to the Internet Explorer application. (Example: C:\PROGRAM FILES\PLUS!\MICROSOFT INTERNET\)	MsgBox *browser*.Path
StatusBar	Boolean	Returns or sets the display of the status bar. True indicates that the status bar is visible; False indicates that it is hidden.	*If browser*.StatusBar Then…EndIf *browser*.StatusBar = True
StatusText	String	Returns or sets the text for the status bar.	MyString = *browser*.StatusText *browser*.StatusText = MyString
ToolBar	Long	Returns or sets which toolbar is shown. For example, 0 indicates no toolbar; 1 indicates the default toolbar.	MsgBox *browser*.toolbar *browser*.toolbar = 1
TopLevelContainer	Boolean	Returns a Boolean value indicating whether the current object is the top-level container. True indicates that the object is the top-level container; False indicates that it is not.	If *browser*.TopLevelContainer Then…EndIf

Property	Type	Description	Usage
Type	String	Returns the type of document in the Internet Explorer.	MyType = *browser*.Type
Visible	Boolean	Returns or sets the display of the Internet Explorer. True indicates that the Internet Explorer is visible; False indicates that it is hidden.	If *browser*.Visible Then...EndIf *browser*.Visible = True

**Table 3-2. Methods of the
Microsoft Internet Explorer, Version 3.0**

Method	Description	Usage
ClientToWindow(*pcx, pcy*)	Converts client sizes into window sizes. *pcx* and *pcy* are defined as long.	
GetProperty (*szProperty*)	Returns the value for the specified property. *szProperty* is defined as a string.	
GoBack, GoForward	Used to navigate the Internet Explorer, based on values in the history list.	*browser*.GoBack
GoHome, GoSearch	Used to navigate the Internet Explorer.	*browser*.GoHome
Navigate (*URL* [, *Flags*] [, *TargetFrameName*] [, *PostData*] [, *Headers*])	Jumps to the specified URL. *Flags* is one of the following constants or values: navOpenInNewWindow=1 navNoHistory=2 navNoReadFromCache=4 navNoWriteToCache=8 *TargetFrameName* is a string that specifies the name of the frame in which results will be displayed. *PostData* is the data to send with the HTTP post transaction. *Headers* is a value that specifies the HTTP headers to send.	*browser*.Navigate ("http://www .vb-bootcamp.com")
PutProperty(*szProperty, vtValue*)	Sets the property to the specified value. *szProperty* is defined as a string and *vtValue* is defined as a variant.	
Quit	Exits the Internet Explorer application and closes the open document.	*browser*.Quit

(continued)

Table 3-2. *continued*

Method	Description	Usage
Refresh	Refreshes the current document.	*browser*.Refresh
Refresh2 [*Level*]	Refreshes the current document. *Level* is one of the following constants or values: REFRESH_NORMAL=0 REFRESH_IFEXPIRED=1 REFRESH_CONTINUE=2 REFRESH_COMPLETELY=3	*browser*.Refresh2(0) *browser*. Refresh2(REFRESH_ NORMAL)
Stop	Stops loading the current document.	*browser*.Stop

Using the Internet Explorer Objects

Since the Internet Explorer supports Automation, you can access its functionality from Visual Basic. You can make the objects in the Internet Explorer available to Visual Basic 4.0 through the References dialog box. The References dialog box lists all the objects available to Visual Basic. You access the dialog box by selecting Tools/References from the menu bar. Figure 3-5 shows the References dialog box with a reference set to the Internet Explorer object library. The proper reference is described in the dialog box as "Microsoft Internet Controls."

Once a reference is set in Visual Basic, you can exploit the objects in code. For example, to get an instance of the Internet Explorer browser that can be accessed from Visual Basic, you could use the following code:

```
Dim MyBrowser As SHDocVw.InternetExplorer
Set MyBrowser = New SHDocVw.InternetExplorer
```

The first line of this code is a variable declaration, and the second line creates an instance of the Internet Explorer. The syntax SHDocVw.InternetExplorer refers to the name of the server, SHDocVw, and the type of object that you want to create, Internet Explorer. SHDocVw itself is actually a server that contains more than just the Internet Explorer objects. This server defines constants and events as well. You can use all of these from Visual Basic to make any Visual Basic application Internet-enabled.

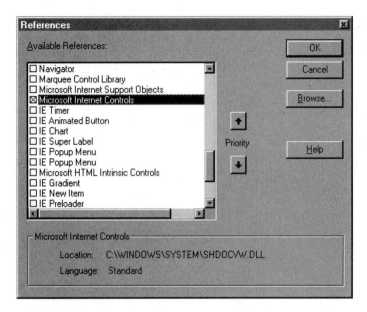

Figure 3-5.
The References dialog box in Visual Basic.

Once you have an instance of the Internet Explorer, you can manipulate it through properties and methods. For example, if you want the browser to appear and navigate to the New Technology Solutions, Inc., web site, you could use the following code:

```
MyBrowser.Visible = True
MyBrowser.Navigate "http://www.vb-bootcamp.com"
```

You can use this type of coding to add browsing capabilities to Visual Basic projects or to create utilities for the browser. Listing 3-2 shows a complete project in Visual Basic that implements a Favorites list for the Internet Explorer browser. The project uses a small Microsoft Access database to keep track of your favorite URLs. These URLs are placed in a list box, from which users can pick a specified URL and cause the browser to navigate to it. Figure 3-6, on page 51, shows an example of the Favorites list box.

```
'This demo implements a Favorites list for the Internet
'Explorer 3.0. The list of favorite URLs is stored
'in a Microsoft Access database.
'This demo automatically launches the Internet Explorer.
'The user can jump to a favorite URL by selecting it from
'the list and clicking on the Navigate button or just
'double-clicking on the URL.


Option Explicit
Public MyBrowser As SHDocVw.InternetExplorer

Private Sub Form_Load()
    'Get an instance of Internet Explorer 3.0
    Set MyBrowser = New SHDocVw.InternetExplorer
    MyBrowser.Visible = True
    'Fill list box with favorites
    Call FillList
End Sub

Private Sub cmdNavigate_Click()
    If lstFavorites.ListIndex = -1 Then Exit Sub
    'Use the Navigate method to display the
    'selected URL
    MyBrowser.Navigate lstFavorites.List(lstFavorites.ListIndex)
End Sub

Private Sub lstFavorites_DblClick()
    cmdNavigate.Value = True
End Sub

Private Sub FillList()

    'Author: New Technology Solutions, Inc.
    'Purpose: Fill list box from Favorites database
    '6/2/96 Original

    Dim dbFavorites As DAO.Database
    Dim rsFavorites As DAO.Recordset
    'Get favorites from database
    Set dbFavorites = DBEngine.Workspaces(0) _
```

Listing 3-2.
The Favorites list.

```
        .OpenDatabase(App.Path & "\favorite.mdb")
        Set rsFavorites = dbFavorites.OpenRecordset _
        ("SELECT * FROM Favorites", dbOpenSnapshot)
        If rsFavorites.BOF And rsFavorites.EOF Then Exit Sub
        lstFavorites.Clear
        rsFavorites.MoveFirst
        'Fill list box
        Do While Not rsFavorites.EOF
            lstFavorites.AddItem rsFavorites!URL
            rsFavorites.MoveNext
        Loop
        rsFavorites.Close
        dbFavorites.Close
        Set rsFavorites = Nothing
        Set dbFavorites = Nothing
    End Sub


    Private Sub cmdExit_Click()
        Unload Me
    End Sub
```

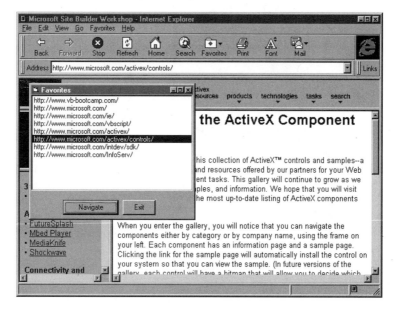

Figure 3-6.
The Favorites list box.

The Internet Explorer Scripting Object Model

Just as you can access the Internet Explorer object model from Visual Basic, you can access the scripting object model from Microsoft Visual Basic, Scripting Edition. The scripting object model, which provides access to the browser, is a collection of objects that can be accessed by any scripting engine. VBScript accesses the scripting object model when it is executing code in an HTML page. Developers can also exploit the scripting object model in VBScript code. The scripting object model supports a variety of properties and methods for use directly in VBScript. Figure 3-7 shows the complete scripting model, which is discussed in detail in the sections that follow.

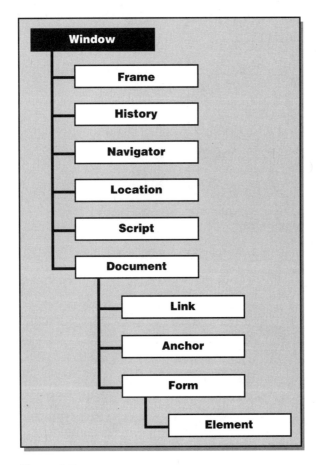

Figure 3-7.
The Internet Explorer scripting object model.

The Window Object

The Window object is the object that represents the Internet Explorer. The properties, methods, and events defined in Tables 3-3, 3-4, and 3-5 can be called directly in VBScript without qualification—meaning that the Window object does not need to be specified. The following code shows an example using the Confirm method:

```
<SCRIPT LANGUAGE="VBScript">
    MyVar = Confirm ("Are you sure?")
</SCRIPT>
```

Table 3-3.   Window Object Properties

Property	Type	Description	Usage
Name	String	Returns the name of the current window.	MsgBox Name
Parent	Object	Returns a reference to the Parent object.	Set MyObject=Parent
Self	Object	Returns a reference to the Window object itself.	Set MyObject=Self
Top	Object	Returns a reference to the topmost Window object.	Set MyObject=Top
Location	Object	Returns a reference to the Location object.	Set MyObject= Location
DefaultStatus	String	Returns or sets the text in the lower left corner of the status bar. (At this writing, this property does not set the specified string to be the default status message. Therefore, it is the same as calling Status.)	DefaultStatus="Ready"
Status	String	Returns or sets the text in the lower left corner of the status bar.	Status="Busy"
Frames	Object	Returns a reference to the Frames array.	Set MyObject= Frames(1)
History	Object	Returns a reference to the History object of the current window.	Set MyObject=History
Navigator	Object	Returns a reference to the Navigator object of the current window.	Set MyObject= Navigator
Document	Object	Returns a reference to the Document object of the current window.	Set MyObject= Document

Table 3-4. Window Object Methods

Method	Return Type	Description	Usage
Alert	None	Displays an OK message box.	Alert "Stop that!"
Confirm	Boolean	Displays an OK/Cancel message box and returns a Boolean value. True if user clicked on OK; False if not.	MyVar=Confirm ("Are you sure?")
Prompt	String	Displays an OK/Cancel input box that returns the text in the input box. The message and the initial text in the input box can be specified.	MyVar=Prompt ("Enter your name", "name")
Open	Object	Opens a new window.	open("*url*", "*windowName*", "*windowFeatures*", *width, height*)
Close	None	Closes the window.	Close
SetTimeout	Long	Executes the code contained in the string after *msec* milliseconds have elapsed.	MyID=SetTimeout ("*string*", *msec*)
ClearTimeout	None	Clears the timer specified.	ClearTimeout(MyID)
Navigate	None	Jumps to a specified URL.	Navigate "http://www.vb-bootcamp.com"

Table 3-5. Window Object Events

Event	Arguments	Description	Usage
OnLoad	None	Fires when page is loaded	<BODY OnLoad="MySub">
OnUnload	None	Fires when page is unloaded	<BODY OnUnload="MySub">

The Document Object

The Document object represents the current HTML page in the browser. The Document object also represents any object on the HTML page, such as a link, a form, a button, or an ActiveX object. The properties and methods for the Document object must be fully qualified when used. The Document object supports many properties and methods that modify the HTML page. These properties and methods, such as LinkColor and Write, must be used inline when the HTML page is loading. These properties and methods cannot be called after the HTML page is loaded because the Internet Explorer parses the HTML only during page load. VBScript code can be executed inline as the load occurs. The following code shows an example where text is being written to an HTML page and the background color is being set to white:

```
<SCRIPT LANGUAGE="VBScript">
    Document.Write "<H2>Inline HTML modification</H2>"
    Document.BGColor="#FFFFFF"
</SCRIPT>
```

Executing inline code to modify an HTML page while it loads is known as *immediate execution*. Immediate execution is a valuable technique because it allows you to create web pages that are different each time they are loaded. As a simple example, the following code displays the date of the last update for the web page:

```
Document.Write "<P><CENTER>"
Document.Write "Page last updated"
Document.Write Document.LastModified
Document.Write "</CENTER><P>"
```

This technique can be expanded to display new pictures or text on the basis of the current date, or even randomly.

Tables 3-6 and 3-7 describe the properties and methods of the Document object.

Table 3-6. Document Object Properties

Property	Type	Description	Usage
LinkColor	String	Returns or sets the link color. Accepts a string input representing the hexadecimal color value or a specific color command.	Document.LinkColor= "#FF0000" Document.LinkColor= "Red"
ALinkColor	String	Returns or sets the anchor color. Accepts a string input representing the hexadecimal color value or a specific color command.	Document.ALinkColor= "#FF0000" Document.ALinkColor= "Red"
VLinkColor	String	Returns or sets the visited link color. Accepts a string input representing the hexadecimal color value or a specific color command.	Document.VLinkColor= "#FF0000" Document.VLinkColor= "Red"

(continued)

55

Table 3-6 *continued*

Property	Type	Description	Usage
BGColor	String	Returns or sets the background color. Accepts a string input representing the hexadecimal color value or a specific color command.	Document.BGColor= "#FF0000" Document.BGColor= "Red"
FGColor	String	Returns or sets the foreground color. Accepts a string input representing the hexadecimal color value or a specific color command.	Document.FGColor= "#FF0000" Document.FGColor= "Red"
Anchors	Object	Returns an Anchors array.	Set MyObject= Document.Anchors(1)
Links	Object	Returns a Links array.	Set MyObject= Document.Links(1)
Forms	Object	Returns a Forms array.	Set MyObject= Document.Forms(1)
Location	String	Returns a string representing the complete URL for the current document.	MyVar= Document.Location
LastModified	String	Returns a string representing the date when the current page was last modified.	MyVar= Document .LastModified
Title	String	Returns the read-only title of the current HTML page.	MyVar= Document.Title
Cookie	String	Returns or sets the cookie for the current document.	MyVar= Document.Cookie
Referrer	String	Returns the URL of the referring document.	MyVar= Document.Referrer

Table 3-7. Document Object Methods

Method	Return Type	Description	Usage
Write	None	Writes the given string into the current document.	Document.Write "Hello"
WriteLn	None	Writes the given string into the current document with the addition of a newline character at the end. (This works only if the scripting section is surrounded by <PRE></PRE> tags.)	Document.WriteLn "Hello"

Method	Return Type	Description	Usage
Open	None	Opens the document stream for output.	Document.Open
Close	None	Updates the screen to display all the strings written after the last Open method call.	Document.Close
Clear	None	Closes the document output stream and writes the data to the screen.	Document.Clear

The Form Object

The Form object represents a form created by the <FORM></FORM> tags. The Form object can be accessed as a property of the Document object. Using forms in VBScript is similar to using forms in Visual Basic for Applications. Any controls contained within the <FORM></FORM> tags are accessed with the *Form.Control.Property* syntax. Additionally, the Internet Explorer provides complete support for all of the events for a control contained in a form. Tables 3-8, 3-9, and 3-10 show the properties, method, and event for the Form object.

Table 3-8. Form Object Properties

Property	Type	Description	Usage
Action	String	Returns or sets the ACTION attribute.	MyForm.Action= "http://www.vb-bootcamp"
Encoding	String	Returns or sets the ENCODING attribute.	MyForm.Encoding="text/html"
Method	String	Returns or sets the METHOD attribute.	MyForm.Method="POST"
Target	String	Returns or sets the TARGET attribute.	MyForm.Target= "NewWindow"
Elements	Object	Returns an Elements array.	Set MyObject=MyForm.Elements(1)
Hidden		Not yet implemented.	

Table 3-9. Form Object Method

Method	Return Type	Description	Usage
Submit	None	Submits form contents.	MyForm.Submit

Table 3-10. Form Object Event

Event	Arguments	Description	Usage
OnSubmit	None	Fires when form contents are submitted.	MyForm.OnSubmit= "*VBScript code*"

The Location Object

The Location object represents the current URL. The Location object can be accessed directly in VBScript. Table 3-11 describes the Location object properties. The following code shows an example of the Href property being used to navigate to a specified URL:

```
<SCRIPT LANGUAGE="VBScript">
    Location.Href = "http://www.vb-bootcamp.com"
</SCRIPT>
```

Table 3-11. Location Object Properties

Property	Type	Description	Usage
Href	String	Returns or sets the complete URL for the current location. (Example: http://www.microsoft.com)	MyVar=Location.Href
Protocol	String	Returns or sets the protocol portion of the URL for the current location. (Example: http:, ftp:)	MyVar= Location.Protocol
Host	String	Returns or sets the Host:Port for the current location. (For example, for http://www.microsoft.com, www.microsoft.com:80 is returned. For file: protocols, "" is returned.)	MyVar=Location.Host

Property	Type	Description	Usage
HostName	String	Returns or sets the host portion of the URL for the current location. (For example, for http://www .microsoft.com, www.microsoft.com is returned. For file: protocols, "" is returned.)	MyVar= Location.HostName
Port	String	Returns or sets the port for communicating with the current location. (For example, for http://www.microsoft .com, 80 is returned. For file: protocols, "" is returned.)	MyVar=Location.Port
PathName	String	Returns or sets the pathname portion of the URL for the current location. (For example, for http://www .microsoft.com/intdev, intdev is returned.)	MyVar= Location.PathName
Search	String	Returns or sets the search portion of the URL beginning with a ?, representing a query. (For example, for http://www.microsoft.com/ intdev?user, ?user is returned. For http://www.microsoft.com/intdev, NULL is returned.)	MyVar= Location.Search
Hash	String	Returns or sets the hash portion of the URL beginning with a #. (For example, for http://www.microsoft. com/intdev#user, #user is returned.)	MyVar=Location.Hash

The Link Object

The Link object references a read-only property array that represents every link in the current HTML page. Links are defined as anchor tags with the HREF attribute set. The following code, which continues on the next page, shows how the links on a page can be referenced:

```
<SCRIPT LANGUAGE="VBScript">
    Sub Button1_OnClick
        MsgBox Document.Links(1).href
    End Sub
</SCRIPT>
<A HREF="http://www.microsoft.com">Microsoft</A><BR>
```

```
<A HREF="http://www.vb-bootcamp.com">VB-Bootcamp</A>
<FORM>
<INPUT TYPE="BUTTON" NAME="BUTTON1">
</FORM>
```

Tables 3-12 and 3-13 describe the properties and events of the Link object.

Table 3-12.   Link Object Properties

Property	Type	Description	Usage
Href	String	Returns the complete URL for the current link (http://www.microsoft.com).	MyVar=Links(2).Href
Protocol	String	Returns the protocol portion of the URL for the current link (http:, ftp:).	MyVar= Links(2).Protocol
Host	String	Returns the Host:Port for the current link. (For http://www.microsoft.com, www.microsoft.com:80 is returned.)	MyVar=Links(2).Host
HostName	String	Returns the host portion of the URL for the current link. (For example, http://www.microsoft.com, www.microsoft.com is returned.)	MyVar= Links(2).HostName
Port	Integer	Returns the port for communicating with the current link. (For example, for http://www.microsoft.com, 80 is returned.)	MyVar=Links(2).Port
PathName	String	Returns the pathname portion of the complete URL for the current link. (For example, for http://www.microsoft.com/intdev, intdev is returned.)	MyVar= Links(2).PathName
Search	String	Returns the search portion of the URL beginning with a ?, representing a query. (For example, for http://www.microsoft.com/intdev?user, ?user is returned.)	MyVar= Links(2).Search
Hash	String	Returns the hash portion of the URL string beginning with a #. (For example, for http://www.microsoft.com/intdev#user, #user is returned.)	MyVar=Links(2).Hash
Target	String	Returns the target of the link, if specified.	MyVar=Links(2).Target

Table 3-13.   Link Object Events

Event	Arguments	Description	Usage
MouseMove	*Shift, Button, X, Y*	Fires whenever the mouse moves over the link. Also passes the following arguments: *Shift* indicates the status of the Shift key. *Button* indicates which button was pushed, if any. *X* indicates the horizontal position of the pointer in pixels. *Y* indicates the vertical position of the pointer in pixels.	Sub Link1_MouseMove (*Shift, Button, X, Y*) ... End Sub
OnMouseOver	None	Fires whenever the mouse moves over the link.	Sub Link2_OnMouseOver ... End Sub
OnClick	None	Fires whenever the link is clicked.	Sub Link3_OnClick ... End Sub

The Anchor Object

The Anchor object references a read-only property array representing all anchors in the HTML document. An anchor is defined as any item between <A></A> tags. Table 3-14 describes the Anchor object property.

Table 3-14.   Anchor Object Property

Property	Type	Description	Usage
Name	String	Returns or sets the name of the anchor.	Document. Anchors(2)= Name.

The Elements Array

The Elements array represents all of the controls in the current HTML page. These controls can be intrinsic controls or controls inserted with the <OBJECT> </OBJECT> tags. The intrinsic HTML controls are discussed later in this chapter. ActiveX controls, which are inserted with the <OBJECT></OBJECT> tags, are discussed in Chapter 4.

Other Objects

At the time of this writing, the remaining objects were not fully documented. The History object is used for navigating through the current history. It is expected to have the following property and methods:

Property

Length	Returns the length of the history list

Methods

Back, Forward, Go	Navigate a specified number of steps in the history list

The Navigator object provides information to script writers about the browser application. The Navigator object is expected to have the following properties:

Properties

AppCodeName	Returns the code name of the application
AppName	Returns the name of the application
AppVersion	Returns the version of the application
UserAgent	Returns the user agent for the current application

Using the Scripting Model in VBScript

To review, the scripting model gives you access to the browser, the current document, and any forms on your page. You can use these objects to facilitate development and maintain a fresh web site. Here we present three examples that utilize the Internet Explorer scripting object model from VBScript.

A Window Object Example

This example uses the Window object to navigate to a new URL with VBScript. The example also updates the status text to reflect the move to the new URL. Listing 3-3 shows the complete code, but note specifically that the Window object properties and methods can be called with or without explicit reference to the object. For example, the following lines of code are equivalent:

```
Window.Navigate "http://www.vb-bootcamp.com"
Navigate "http://www.vb-bootcamp.com"
```

```
<HTML>
<HEAD>
<TITLE>Window object</TITLE>

<!--
This demo uses the Window object
to navigate to a new URL
-->

<SCRIPT LANGUAGE="VBScript">
<!--
    'These comment marks hide code from
    'browsers that do not support the
    'SCRIPT tag
    'Sub cmdNavigate_OnClick
        Dim MyForm
        Set MyForm=Document.frmForm
        Window.Status="Opening " & MyForm.txtURL.Value & "..."
        Window.Navigate MyForm.txtURL.Value
    End Sub
-->
</SCRIPT>

</HEAD>
<BODY>
<CENTER>

<FORM NAME="frmForm">
<INPUT TYPE="TEXT" NAME="txtURL"
VALUE="http://www.vb-bootcamp.com">
<INPUT TYPE="BUTTON" VALUE="Navigate" NAME="cmdNavigate">
</FORM>

</CENTER>
</BODY>
</HTML>
```

Listing 3-3.
The Window object in VBScript.

Figure 3-8 shows a sample of the output.

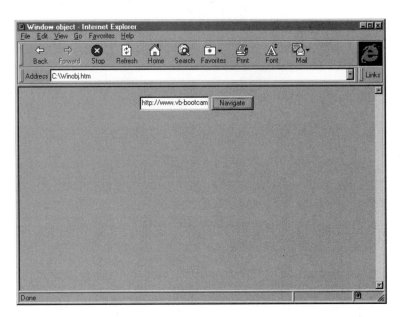

Figure 3-8.
Sample output using the Window object.

The Window object represents the Internet Explorer itself and gives you control over the browser. The Window object is used from VBScript and is similar to the browser object we instantiated from Visual Basic earlier in this chapter. The Window object, however, offers less flexibility than the browser object accessed from Visual Basic. The Window object is limited primarily for security reasons. The VBScript code must be contained inside the browser and must allow no access to the client machine.

A Document Object Example

The Document object allows access to the currently loaded web page. The properties of the Document object can be accessed through VBScript to affect the appearance of the web page. The example shown in Listing 3-4 changes the heading based on the current month. Figure 3-9 shows a sample of the output.

```
<HTML>
<HEAD>
<TITLE>Immediate Execution</TITLE>
<!--
This demo uses the Write method of the
Document object to create dynamic HTML code.
The web page will display a different
heading, based on the current month.
-->

<SCRIPT LANGUAGE="VBScript">
<!--
    Hide code from old browsers
    Dim strSpecial
    If Month(Now)=1 Then strSpecial="Steaks"
    If Month(Now)=2 Then strSpecial="Chicken"
    If Month(Now)=3 Then strSpecial="Hot Dogs"
    If Month(Now)=4 Then strSpecial="Hamburgers"
    If Month(Now)=5 Then strSpecial="Porterhouse"
    If Month(Now)=6 Then strSpecial="Filet Mignon"
    If Month(Now)=7 Then strSpecial="NY Strip"
    If Month(Now)=8 Then strSpecial="Lamb"
    If Month(Now)=9 Then strSpecial="Veal"
    If Month(Now)=10 Then strSpecial="Pork Chops"
    If Month(Now)=11 Then strSpecial="Ham"
    If Month(Now)=12 Then strSpecial="Turkey"
    Document.Write "<CENTER><H2>" & strSpecial & _
    "</H2></CENTER>"
-->
</SCRIPT>

</HEAD>
<BODY BGCOLOR=#FFFFFF>
<H2><CENTER>Check out our special this month!<CENTER></H2>
<P>
<P>
</BODY>
</HTML>
```

Listing 3-4.
The Document object in VBScript.

Figure 3-9.
Sample output using the Document object.

Although this example shows other uses, the most common use of the Document object is to reference forms contained inside the document. These forms are always referenced by the syntax Document.*formname*. With this reference, you can access any control on any form.

A Form Object Example

The Form object offers properties and methods for any form on the current page. The Form object also contains an Element object that can reference any control on the form either by array or by name. Elements are intrinsic HTML controls and are discussed in more detail later in this chapter. As an example, Listing 3-5 shows code that accesses all of the controls on a form and changes their values. Figure 3-10 on page 68 shows a sample of the output.

```
<HTML>
<HEAD>
<TITLE>Forms and Elements</TITLE>

<!--
This demo loops through
all of the controls and
changes their value to
"Changed!"
-->

<SCRIPT LANGUAGE="VBScript">
<!--
    Sub cmdChange_OnClick
        For i=0 To Document.frmForm.Elements.Count-1
            Document.frmForm.Elements(i).Value="Changed!"
        Next
    End Sub
-->
</SCRIPT>

</HEAD>
<BODY>
<CENTER>

<FORM NAME="frmForm">
<INPUT TYPE="TEXT"><P>
<INPUT TYPE="TEXT"><P>
<INPUT TYPE="TEXT"><P>
<INPUT TYPE="TEXT"><P>
<INPUT TYPE="TEXT"><P>
<INPUT TYPE="BUTTON" NAME="cmdChange"
VALUE="Push and Watch the Controls!"><P>
</FORM>

</CENTER>
</HTML>
```

Listing 3-5.
Form and Element objects in VBScript.

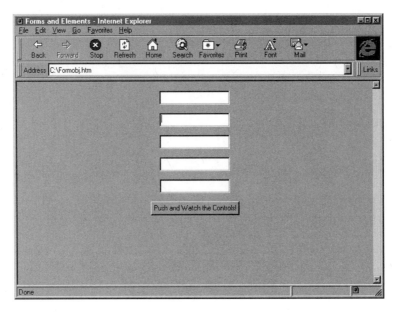

Figure 3-10.
Sample output using Form and Element objects.

Intrinsic HTML Controls

The Internet Explorer supports a set of controls that are built into the browser itself. These controls, called *intrinsic HTML controls,* do not have to be downloaded across the Internet to be used on the client machine. Intrinsic controls are not defined with the <OBJECT></OBJECT> tags, as ActiveX controls are. Instead, they are defined either with the <INPUT> tag or such special tags as the <SELECT></SELECT> tags or <TEXTAREA></TEXTAREA> tags. The intrinsic controls are used with these tags because these tags support the original HTML specification for controls on a web page. Prior to the introduction of ActiveX controls and downloadable objects, HTML supported several controls through these special HTML tags. For example, inserting a button into a web page is done with the <INPUT> tag, as shown here:

```
<INPUT TYPE="BUTTON" NAME="Command1">
```

The intrinsic controls are often used in conjunction with an HTML form. Forms are created with the <FORM></FORM> tags. Controls are subsequently defined inside the form. The following code defines two text fields and a button inside a form:

```
<FORM NAME="frmOne">
<INPUT TYPE="TEXT" NAME="Text1">
<INPUT TYPE="TEXT" NAME="Text2"><BR>
<INPUT TYPE="BUTTON" NAME="Command1">
</FORM>
```

When controls are defined inside a form, the Internet Explorer automatically supports their events in VBScript code. In the above case, the button supports an OnClick event that the Internet Explorer will fire, executing code in a VBScript event-handling subroutine, shown here:

```
<SCRIPT LANGUAGE="VBScript">
    Sub Command1_OnClick
        MsgBox "Event Routine Fired!"
    End Sub
</SCRIPT>
```

Notice that the name of the event-handling subroutine is OnClick. This initially looks strange to developers who are familiar with Visual Basic for Applications syntax. In Visual Basic, for example, the event-handling subroutine for a pressed button is called Click. Why the difference? Isn't VBScript a proper subset of Visual Basic for Applications? The answer rests in the fact that intrinsic HTML controls existed before VBScript, so the Internet Explorer supports them for backward compatibility. The OnClick event is defined in the HTML standard, not in Visual Basic for Applications. Click events are supported for ActiveX components that are downloaded with the <OBJECT> </OBJECT> tags. Table 3-15 lists the properties, events, and methods for the intrinsic HTML controls.

Table 3-15. Intrinsic HTML Controls

Intrinsic HTML Control	Properties	Events	Methods
Button	Form, Enabled Name Value	OnClick OnFocus	Click Focus
CheckBox	Form, Enabled Name Value Checked DefaultChecked	OnClick OnFocus	Click Focus
Hidden	Name Value		

(continued)

69

Table 3-15 *continued*

Intrinsic HTML Control	Properties	Events	Methods
Password	Form, Enabled Name Value DefaultValue	OnFocus OnBlur	Focus Blur Select
Radio	Form, Enabled Name Value Checked	OnClick OnFocus	Click Focus
Reset	Form, Enabled Name Value	OnClick OnFocus	Click Focus
Select	Name Length Options SelectedIndex	OnFocus OnBlur OnChange	Focus Blur
Submit	Form, Enabled Name Value	OnClick OnFocus	Click Focus
Text TextArea	Form, Enabled Name Value DefaultValue	OnFocus OnBlur OnChange OnSelect	Focus Blur Select

KEY CONCEPT: Intrinsic HTML controls exist to support the original use of controls in HTML. Intrinsic HTML controls are part of the Internet Explorer architecture.

Although the intrinsic HTML controls support ActiveX concepts such as properties, events, and methods, they are typically defined with standard HTML syntax. Therefore, the rest of this chapter provides an explanation of each control for the Visual Basic for Applications developer not intimately familiar with HTML syntax.

The Intrinsic Button Control

The intrinsic Button control is simply used to supply a general-purpose button control on a form. The button is implemented with the <INPUT> tag.

Attributes

NAME	A string representing the name of the Button control
VALUE	A string representing the text that appears on the button

Events

OnClick	Fires whenever the control is clicked
OnFocus	Fires when the control receives the focus

Syntax

<INPUT TYPE="BUTTON" [NAME="*string*"] [VALUE="*string*"]
[OnClick="*subroutine*"] [OnFocus="*subroutine*"]>

Example

```
<FORM>
<INPUT TYPE="BUTTON" NAME="btnOne" VALUE="Push Me!">
</FORM>
```

The Intrinsic CheckBox Control

The intrinsic CheckBox control implements a simple check box by using the
<INPUT> tag. When a form containing CheckBox controls is submitted to the
server, only the information from the selected check boxes is submitted.

Attributes

NAME	A string representing the name of the CheckBox control
VALUE	A string representing the value of the control when submitted (by default, this value is ON)
CHECKED	An option that causes the check box to be checked by default

Events

OnClick	Fires whenever the control is checked
OnFocus	Fires when the control receives the focus

Syntax

<INPUT TYPE="CHECKBOX" [NAME="*string*"] [VALUE="*string*"]
[CHECKED] [OnClick="*subroutine*"] [OnFocus="*subroutine*"]>

Example

```
<FORM>
<INPUT TYPE="CHECKBOX" NAME="chkOne" VALUE="Checked" CHECKED>
</FORM>
```

The Intrinsic Hidden Control

The intrinsic Hidden control is used to provide data that is invisible to the user in the form. Hidden controls are useful when you want to pass data from a form to another process and send along key information that is supplied by the web page and not the user.

Attributes

NAME   A string representing the name of the Hidden control

VALUE   A string representing the default value of the control

Syntax

<INPUT TYPE="HIDDEN" [NAME="*string*"] [VALUE="*string*"]>

Example

```
<FORM>
<INPUT TYPE="HIDDEN" NAME="txtOne" VALUE="SECRET_CODE">
</FORM>
```

The Intrinsic Password Control

The intrinsic Password control is similar to a Text control, but when the user enters data into a Password control, only asterisks appear. This control is useful for preventing others from seeing the data on the screen, but be aware that the ASCII text is sent directly over the network without encryption.

Attributes

NAME	A string representing the name of the Password control
VALUE	A string representing the default value of the control
SIZE	An integer representing the length of the control in characters
MAXLENGTH	An integer representing the maximum number of characters allowed in the control

Events

OnFocus	Fires when the control receives the focus
OnBlur	Fires when the control loses the focus

Syntax

<INPUT TYPE="PASSWORD" [NAME="*string*"] [VALUE="*string*"] [SIZE="*integer*"] [MAXLENGTH="*integer*"] [OnFocus="*subroutine*"] [OnBlur="*subroutine*"] >

Example

```
<FORM>
<INPUT TYPE="PASSWORD" NAME="txtOne" VALUE="changeme" SIZE="10"
MAXLENGTH="8">
</FORM>
```

The Intrinsic Radio Control

The intrinsic Radio control allows a user to select one choice from a number of options. Radio controls are also called *option buttons*. Radio controls can be grouped by using the same NAME attribute.

Attributes

NAME	A string representing the name of the Radio control
VALUE	A string representing the value of the control when submitted (each radio button should have a unique value)
CHECKED	An option that causes the Radio control to be selected by default

Events

OnClick	Fires when the control is clicked
OnFocus	Fires when the control receives the focus

Syntax

<INPUT TYPE="RADIO" [NAME="*string*"] [VALUE="*string*"]
[CHECKED][OnClick="*subroutine*"][OnFocus="*subroutine*"]>

Example

```
<FORM>
<INPUT TYPE="RADIO" NAME="OPTIONS" VALUE="One" CHECKED>One
<INPUT TYPE="RADIO" NAME="OPTIONS" VALUE="Two">Two
<INPUT TYPE="RADIO" NAME="OPTIONS" VALUE="Three">Three
</FORM>
```

The Intrinsic Reset Control

The intrinsic Reset control clears all the text fields in the current form. The Reset control appears in the browser as a button and by default has the caption "Reset."

Attributes

NAME	A string representing the name of the Reset control
VALUE	A string representing the text that appears in the Reset button caption

Events

OnClick	Fires whenever the control is clicked
OnFocus	Fires when the control receives the focus

Syntax

<INPUT TYPE="RESET" [NAME="*string*"] [VALUE="*string*"]
[OnClick="*subroutine*"][OnFocus="*subroutine*"]>

Example

```
<FORM>
<INPUT TYPE="TEXT">
<INPUT TYPE="RESET" VALUE="Reset Me">
</FORM>
```

The Intrinsic Select Control

The intrinsic Select control is used to create a list of selections. It is similar to the ComboBox control in Visual Basic. The Select control is implemented in HTML with the <SELECT></SELECT> tags. The <OPTION> tag is used to identify each element in the list.

Attributes

NAME	A string representing the name of the Select control
SIZE	An integer representing the number of items in the list that are visible at one time
MULTIPLE	An option that allows multiple items in a list to be selected
SELECTED	An option that causes the element in the list to be selected by default

Events

OnFocus	Fires when the control receives the focus
OnBlur	Fires when the control loses the focus
OnChange	Fires when the control is changed

Syntax

<SELECT NAME="*string*" [SIZE="*integer*"] [MULTIPLE]
[OnFocus="*subroutine*"] [OnBlur="*subroutine*"] [OnChange="*subroutine*"]
<OPTION [SELECTED] VALUE="*string*">*Item* </SELECT>

Example

```
<FORM>
<SELECT NAME="FirstLanguage" MULTIPLE>
<OPTION VALUE="1">Visual Basic
<OPTION SELECTED VALUE="2">VBScript
<OPTION VALUE="3">C++
</SELECT>
</FORM>
```

The Intrinsic Submit Control

The intrinsic Submit control is a button used to pass all the elements in a form to a back-end process. When a form is submitted, the data entered into the input controls is sent as ASCII text to the process identified in the ACTION attribute of the form. Every form with more than one field *must* have a Submit control. Typically, you have one, and only one, Submit control, but it is possible to have more than one.

Attributes

NAME	A string representing the name of the Submit control
VALUE	A string representing the text that appears in the Submit button caption

Events

OnClick	Fires whenever the control is clicked
OnFocus	Fires when the control receives the focus

Syntax

<INPUT TYPE="SUBMIT" [NAME="*string*"] [VALUE="*string*"]
[OnClick="*subroutine*"] [OnFocus="*subroutine*"]>

Example

```
<FORM METHOD="POST" ACTION="http://www.vb-bootcamp.com/test">
<INPUT TYPE="TEXT">
<INPUT TYPE="SUBMIT" VALUE="Submit Form">
</FORM>
```

The Intrinsic Text Control

The intrinsic Text control is used as an input device to receive text. It is quite similar to the TextBox control in Visual Basic. The intrinsic Text control is implemented with the <INPUT> tag.

Attributes

NAME	A string representing the name of the Text control
VALUE	A string representing the default value of the control
SIZE	An integer representing the length of the control in characters
MAXLENGTH	An integer representing the maximum number of characters allowed in the control

Events

OnFocus	Fires when the control receives the focus
OnBlur	Fires when the control loses the focus
OnSelect	Fires when the contents of the control are selected
OnChange	Fires when the control is changed

Syntax

<INPUT TYPE="TEXT" [NAME="*string*"] [VALUE="*string*"]
[SIZE="*integer*"] [MAXLENGTH="*integer*"] [OnFocus="*subroutine*"]
[OnBlur="*subroutine*"] [OnSelect="*subroutine*"] [OnChange="*subroutine*"]>

Example

```
<FORM>
<INPUT TYPE="TEXT" NAME="Text1" VALUE="Default Text" SIZE="50" MAXLENGTH="30">
</FORM>
```

The Intrinsic TextArea Control

The intrinsic TextArea control is similar to the Text control but allows multiline user input. Text areas are created with the <TEXTAREA></TEXTAREA> tags.

Attributes

NAME	A string representing the name of the TextArea control
ROWS	An integer representing the height of the control in lines
COLS	An integer representing the width of the control in characters

Events

OnFocus	Fires when the control receives the focus
OnBlur	Fires when the control loses the focus
OnSelect	Fires when the contents of the control are selected
OnChange	Fires when the control is changed

Syntax

<TEXTAREA [NAME="*string*"] [ROWS="*integer*"] [COLS="*integer*"]
[Onfocus="*subroutine*"] [OnBlur="*subroutine*"]
[OnSelect="*subroutine*"] [OnChange="*subroutine*"]></TEXTAREA>

Example

```
<FORM>
<TEXTAREA NAME="txtWords" ROWS="20" COLS="20">
</TEXTAREA>
</FORM>
```

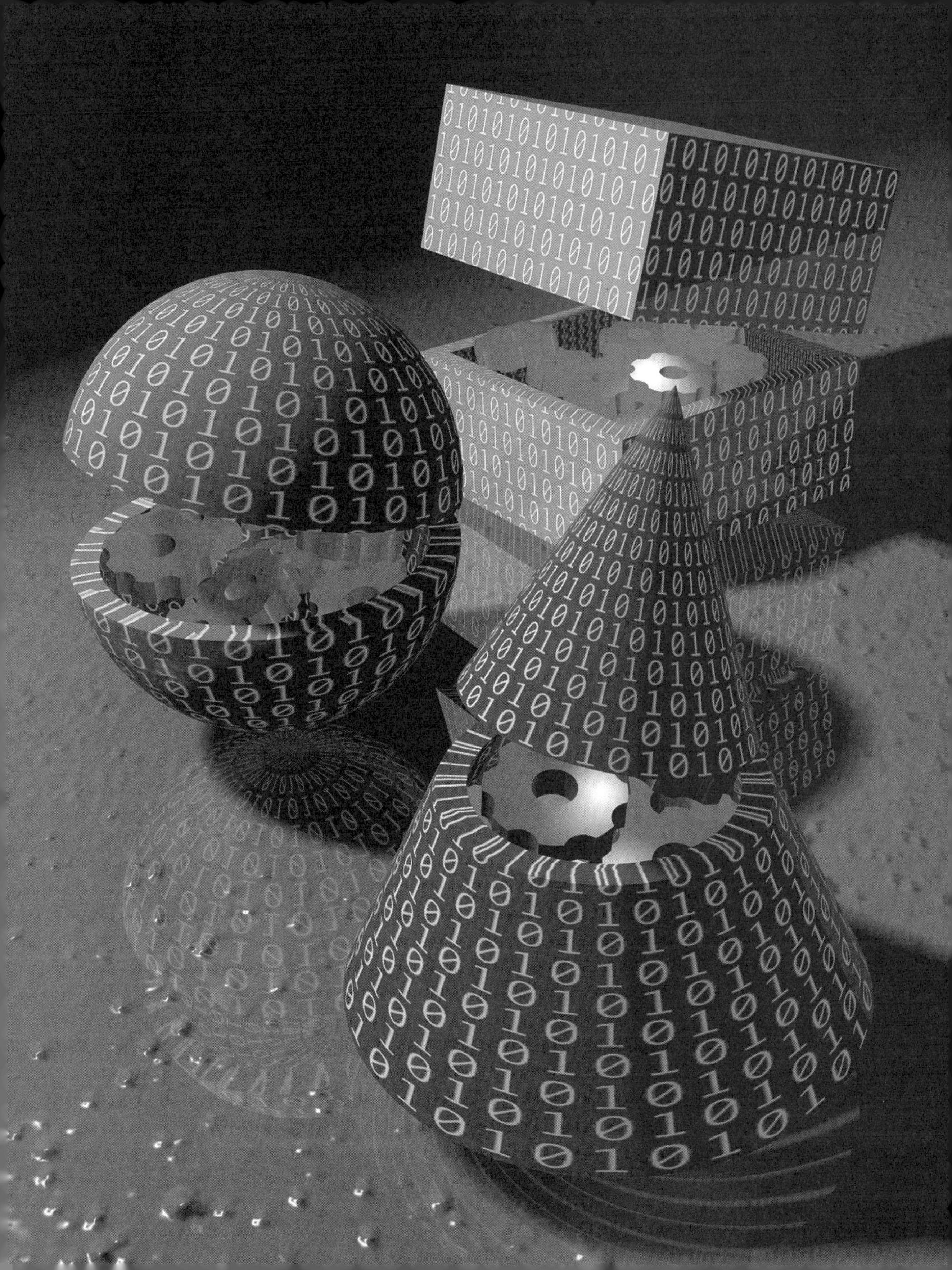

Working with ActiveX Controls

Although the Microsoft Internet Explorer 3.0 supports a reasonable assortment of standard controls, the intrinsic control set is certainly limited. If you try to use the intrinsic controls to add special functionality to a web page, you'll find that the controls come up short. Fortunately, in addition to intrinsic controls, the Internet Explorer supports ActiveX controls through the new HTML <OBJECT></OBJECT> tags. At the time of this writing, the <OBJECT></OBJECT> tags have the attributes listed here. The information that follows comes from a working draft by the World Wide Web Consortium. Since this information is regularly updated, it is advisable to review the current information at the website, http://www.w3.org/pub/WWW/.

ALIGN specifies where to place the object. The ALIGN tag recognizes the LEFT, CENTER, RIGHT, TEXTTOP, MIDDLE, TEXTMIDDLE, BASELINE, and TEXTBOTTOM arguments.

BORDER specifies the width of the border that is displayed around the visible area of the object when the object is part of a hypertext link.

CLASSID specifies a URL used to locate the object, or it specifies a class identifier for the object. For ActiveX controls, CLASSID is used to specify the class identifier. The class identifier is a unique alphanumeric code assigned to each ActiveX control and is stored in the system Registry of the client computer.

CODEBASE specifies a URL used to locate the object.

CODETYPE specifies the Internet Media Type of the code specified by the CLASSID attribute. Since this information can be accessed before the code is retrieved, it is possible to skip over unsupported media types.

DATA specifies a URL that references the object's data (for example, a gif file for an image object).

DECLARE is used to indicate that the object is not to be instantiated, only declared.

HEIGHT specifies the height of a box enclosing the visible area of the object. Use HEIGHT instead of accessing the Height property.

HSPACE specifies the space to the left and right of the visible area of the object.

ID specifies the name of the object as it is referenced in code. The ID attribute is just like the Name property of an OCX control.

NAME provides a way to determine whether an object within a form block should be involved in the Submit process. If the object has its NAME attribute specified, its VALUE property will be included in any Submit action for a form.

SHAPES indicates that the object element contains shape-defined links on the visible area of the object.

STANDBY specifies a text string that can be displayed in the browser while the object and data are being loaded.

TYPE specifies the Internet Media Type of the data specified by the DATA attribute. Since this information can be accessed before the data is retrieved, it is possible to skip over unsupported media types.

USEMAP specifies a URL for a client-side image map in a format proposed by Spyglass, Inc.

VSPACE specifies the space to the top and bottom of the visible area of the object.

WIDTH specifies the width of a box enclosing the visible area of the object. Use WIDTH instead of accessing the Width property.

For the </OBJECT> attributes that specify a positioning or size value, the unit of measurement can be either screen pixels or a percentage of the current displayable region. Additional units, such as points and inches, can be used if you include a suffix after the value. See the World Wide Web Consortium web site for more information.

Although the <OBJECT></OBJECT> tags have an exhausting array of attributes, only two of the attributes are generally required: CLASSID and ID. These attributes tell the browser which ActiveX control to load and how the control is referenced in code.

While you are loading the ActiveX control, you can set its properties with the <PARAM> tag. The <PARAM> tag has the following attributes:

NAME specifies the property name.

VALUE specifies the value for the named property.

VALUETYPE specifies REF, OBJECT, or DATA.

> **REF** indicates that the value is a URL.
>
> **OBJECT** indicates that the value is a URL of an OBJECT element in the same document.
>
> **DATA** indicates that the value is to be passed directly to the object as a string.

KEY CONCEPT: ActiveX controls are the same as the reusable OCX controls found in Visual Basic but are optimized so that they can be downloaded more quickly across the Internet.

When an object has been inserted into an HTML page, you can access its properties, events, and methods by using a format that is the same as that of Microsoft Visual Basic for Applications. Listing 4-1 shows an example of an ActiveX control in HTML, and Figure 4-1 shows a sample of the output. This example uses the Visual Basic Gauge control and an intrinsic Button control that increments the gauge. Notice the connection between the OnClick event of the button and the event procedure written in Microsoft Visual Basic, Scripting Edition. Initially, events such as OnClick will be confusing to Visual Basic developers because the same event in Visual Basic for Applications is called *Click*. The difference is due to the fact that OnClick is part of the HTML language, not the Visual Basic for Applications language. HTML has always supported some intrinsic controls, and these are supported by the Internet Explorer for backward compatibility. You can get absolute adherence to Visual Basic for Applications standards simply by downloading a Button object instead of using an intrinsic Button control. Once you learn the intrinsic controls, however, you will find them fairly simple to use. Listing 4-1 and all other full program listings are available on this book's companion CD, in the samples folder.

Also, note that if you want to run the Gauge control example, the Gauge control must be registered on your computer.

```
<HTML>
<HEAD>
<TITLE>Gauge Control</TITLE>

<!--
This demo shows how to use an ActiveX control.
It uses the Gauge control from Visual Basic 4.0
and increments it with a standard HTML button.
-->

<SCRIPT LANGUAGE="VBScript">
<!--
    'Notice that VBScript does not
    'support data types.  All variables
    'are variants.

    Dim intValue

    'This routine is called when the
    'button is clicked.  Note that
    'an intrinsic button is being used.
    'This means that only the Gauge control
    'is downloaded. The button is always
    'available.

    Sub cmdChange_Click
        'Increment variable
        intValue=intValue + 1
        'Check bounds
        If intValue>9 then
            intValue=0
        End If
        'Set gauge property
        Gauge1.Value=intValue
    End Sub
```

Listing 4-1.
An ActiveX Gauge control in VBScript.

```
-->
</SCRIPT>

</HEAD>
<BODY>
<CENTER>


<!--
This is the key to the example.  The OBJECT
tag is a new tag used to download ActiveX
components.  Once the ActiveX component is available,
you can set its properties by using the PARAM tag.
-->

<OBJECT
    CLASSID="clsid:7A080CC5-26E2-101B-AEBD-04021C009402"
    ID="Gauge1"
    HEIGHT=100
    WIDTH=100
    >
    <PARAM NAME="Style" VALUE=3>
    <PARAM NAME="NeedleWidth" VALUE=5>
    <PARAM NAME="Min" VALUE=0>
    <PARAM NAME="Max" VALUE=10>
    <PARAM NAME="Value" VALUE=0>
</OBJECT>

<P>


<!--
Set up an intrinsic HTML button
-->
<INPUT TYPE="BUTTON" NAME="cmdChange" VALUE="Change Gauge"
OnClick="cmdChange_Click">

</CENTER>
</BODY>
</HTML>
```

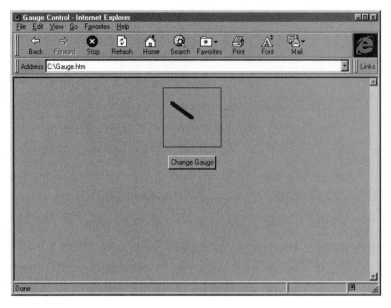

Figure 4-1.
An example of a Gauge control used in HTML code.

Obtaining Class IDs for ActiveX Components

Acquiring the CLASSID attribute for an ActiveX component can be cumbersome. The CLASSID attribute is the class identifier for an object and is used within the <OBJECT></OBJECT> tags. The class ID is stored in the system Registry. Because many programmers find the Registry mysterious, an explanation is provided here.

The System Registry

Every Windows operating system needs to keep track of information about users, hardware, and software. In Windows 3.x, this function was performed by special files called *initialization* (INI) *files*. INI files are text files that are divided into *sections* and *keywords*. Sections are delineated by square brackets, and keywords are used to set values inside each section. For example, if you wanted a program to remember the name of the last person who used it, you might establish a section called *Users* and a keyword called *Last* to track the information. The INI file entry for this information would look like this:

```
[Users]
Last=John Smith
```

Once the program had been properly set up, the name of the last user and any user-specified options could be stored in the INI file. With the information saved in the INI file, the program could read the INI file on startup and restore the options specified by the last user.

INI files can be used for all sorts of similar information storage. They are convenient and quick storage devices, and because they can be edited with any text editor, such as Notepad, they are extremely easy to use.

The problem with INI files is that they are inefficient. Using a text file to store a few pieces of data is fine, but mayhem can result if you need to store a large amount of data, especially if that data must be cross-referenced with other data. Text files just don't work when the situation calls for a true database.

Recognizing the inherent problems with INI files, Microsoft has developed the Windows 95 Registry. The Registry is a unified database for storing system and application configuration information in a hierarchical format. The Registry can be compared to INI files. For example, the bracketed sections in INI files are similar to Registry keys, and the keyword entries are similar to Registry values. The Registry contains information ranging from the name of the last user to the ActiveX components available on your computer.

The Registry has a special role to play in Automation. Software components, such as servers and ActiveX controls, have entries in the Registry that describe them. In particular, every component stores its class ID in the Registry. The class ID is a unique sequence of characters that is used by the Windows operating system to identify a component. In this way, the operating system can track and maintain ActiveX components.

Class IDs are particularly important in VBScript. As mentioned earlier, VBScript uses the CLASSID attribute in the new <OBJECT></OBJECT> tags to identify the ActiveX component that is to be loaded into memory. When the browser encounters the <OBJECT></OBJECT> tags, it checks the client's Registry for the component with the specified class ID. If the component does not exist on the client machine, the browser can request a download from the server on the basis of a location specified by the web page creator. The ActiveX control will then be downloaded, and appropriate entries will be made in the Registry to identify the component the next time it is required. Because a component's class ID is unique, no confusion exists about which component is needed by the web page.

The Registry is simply a database, so you can actually look at its contents. Windows 95 provides a utility called the Registry Editor (REGEDIT.EXE) for viewing and editing the Registry. REGEDIT opens the Registry and allows you to browse the keys and values. You can even search for a key. Figure 4-2 shows the Registry Editor window, which is composed of two panes. The left pane displays the keys, and the right pane displays the value entries of the selected key.

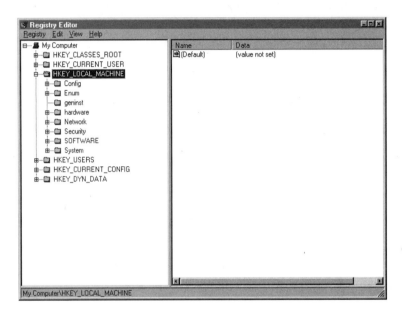

Figure 4-2.
The Registry as displayed by REGEDIT.

> CAUTION: If you examine your Registry by using the utility REGEDIT.EXE, do not make any changes to the information you find. Changing the information in the Registry can cause serious problems in your operating system.

By browsing the Registry, you can find class IDs for ActiveX components and use these sequences of characters in your web pages. Class IDs can be found under HKEY_LOCAL_MACHINE\SOFTWARE\Classes\. In this area, search for the name of the control you are interested in. For example, if you wanted to use the Gauge control and it is registered on your computer, you could search for the word *gauge*. In this case, you would find an entry for the Gauge control that has the key {7A080CC5-26E2-101B-AEBD-04021C009402}, which is the class ID. Figure 4-3 shows the class ID for the Gauge control in the system Registry.

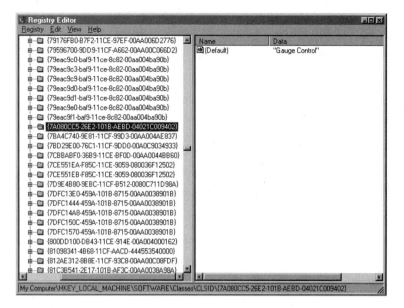

Figure 4-3.
The class ID for the Gauge control in the system Registry.

This sequence of characters can be used directly in the <OBJECT> </OBJECT> tags. An example is shown here:

```
<OBJECT>
    CLASSID="clsid:7A080CC5-26E2-101B-AEBD-04021C009402"
    ID="/Gauge1/"
</OBJECT>
```

NOTE: Be sure to remove the curly braces from the Registry's class ID before you insert it into the <OBJECT></OBJECT> tags.

The ActiveX Control Lister

The ActiveX Control Lister is a tool you can use to insert controls into a web page. The Control Lister was developed by Microsoft to retrieve class ID information from the Registry. A list box displays the available controls. All you do is double-click on the desired control. The Control Lister generates the necessary code, including the <OBJECT></OBJECT> tags, for inserting the control. This code is copied to the clipboard, and from there it can be pasted into your HTML code. You can also right-click on the desired control and select Options. This will display a dialog box that allows you to see the code and adjust additional settings. Figure 4-4 shows the ActiveX Control Lister and the Options dialog box.

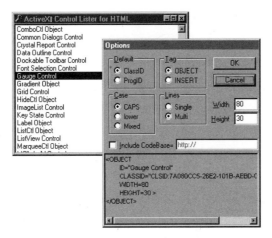

Figure 4-4.
The ActiveX Control Lister and the Options dialog box.

ActiveX Control Pad

Microsoft has introduced a simple design environment called ActiveX Control Pad. ActiveX Control Pad is another utility that can be used to insert controls into an HTML page and is available on this book's companion CD. When you launch ActiveX Control Pad, it shows a text editor with the beginning code for an HTML page. When you select Insert ActiveX Control from the Edit menu, a dialog box that shows the available ActiveX controls is displayed. Figure 4-5 shows the Insert ActiveX Control dialog box with the Gauge control selected.

After you select a control and click the OK button, the ActiveX Control Editor window and the Properties window are displayed. You can size the control in the ActiveX Control Editor window and set the properties in the Properties window. After the appropriate settings have been made in the ActiveX Control Editor window and the Properties window, these windows can be closed. At this point, the appropriate code for the control, including the <OBJECT></OBJECT> and <PARAM> tags, is inserted into the HTML code. Figure 4-6 shows a sample of the code inserted for the Gauge control in the HTML Source Editor window.

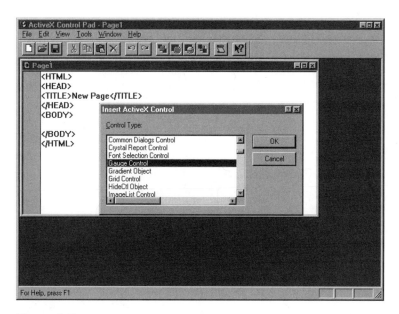

Figure 4-5.
The Insert ActiveX Control dialog box.

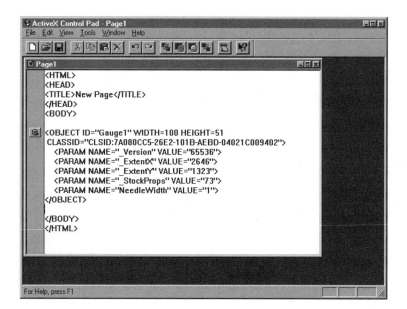

Figure 4-6.
A sample of the HTML code after the Gauge control has been inserted.

ActiveX Control Pad and the HTML Layout Control

The techniques already discussed are useful in obtaining class IDs for ActiveX controls and in inserting the controls into web pages, but you'll find that using the <OBJECT></OBJECT> tags to place ActiveX controls has definite limitations. A big problem for a developer creating an interactive web page is the placement of controls on the page. For example, developers of Visual Basic applications are accustomed to placing controls precisely on forms, but this can be difficult in HTML. Control placement in HTML is merely a suggestion to the browser, and the browser is generally free to reformat the page as necessary. Therefore, developers cannot guarantee the final placement of any ActiveX control by simply using the <OBJECT></OBJECT> tags.

In an attempt to allow developers to specify exact placement of ActiveX controls in a web page, Microsoft has created the HTML Layout control, to be used with ActiveX Control Pad. ActiveX Control Pad and the HTML Layout control are discussed in detail in Chapter 9, but an example of what the HTML Layout control can do is provided here.

In this example, a Hangman game was created with the HTML Layout control. The Hangman game requires the exact placement of image controls to provide the graphics. Figure 4-7 depicts the Hangman layout as shown in the HTML Layout control, and Figure 4-8 shows the Hangman game in the Internet Explorer.

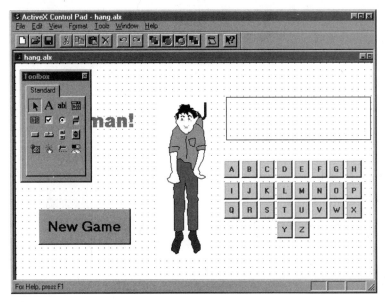

Figure 4-7.
The Hangman layout in the HTML Layout control.

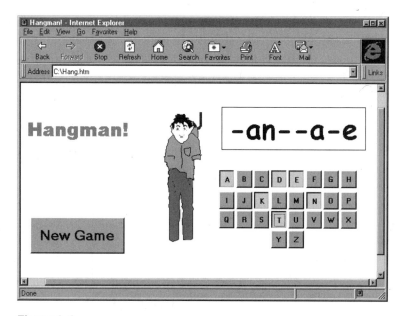

Figure 4-8.
The Hangman game in the Internet Explorer.

Listing 4-2 shows the contents of the Hangman HTML file. If you are interested in the alx layout file for Hangman, you can find it on the companion CD, in the samples folder.

```
<HTML>
<HEAD>
<TITLE>Hangman!</TITLE>
</HEAD>

<BODY BGCOLOR="WHITE">
<CENTER>
<FORM NAME="frmHangman">

<OBJECT CLASSID="CLSID:812AE312-8B8E-11CF-93C8-00AA00C08FDF"
ID="hang" STYLE="LEFT:0;TOP:0">
<PARAM NAME="ALXPATH" REF VALUE="file:hang.alx">
</OBJECT>

</FORM>
</BODY>
</HTML>
```

Listing 4-2.
The Hangman HTML file.

Code Signing and Security on the Internet

As you can see, many web pages today have controls and applications that must be downloaded and run locally on the user's computer. This brings up the question of whether to trust the code that you download. After all, ActiveX controls are executable components, so it would be possible to design a control that reformats the hard drive! The Internet Explorer now displays a dialog box, similar to the one shown in Figure 4-9, indicating to the user that code is about to be downloaded. The dialog box does give the user the option of not downloading the code, but it is basically up to the user to decide whether the code is safe.

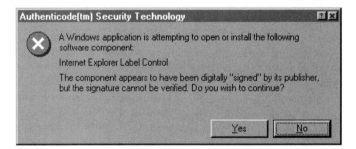

Figure 4-9.
Sample of a security dialog box when code is about to be downloaded.

In an effort to address this issue head-on, Microsoft is pioneering a concept called *code signing*. Code signing is a process by which software manufacturers can digitally "sign" their code. The browser can then match the signature on the code with the manufacturer's known signature to ensure that the code has not been tampered with. To begin this process, the software manufacturer works with a third party, called a *certificate authority*, to obtain a digital certificate. Once the software manufacturer has finished testing the code, the digital certificate is used to sign the code. Signing the code involves embedding a *signature block* in the code. The signature block is a structure that contains information about the code, the digital certificate, and the software manufacturer's credentials.

When a browser is preparing to download code that has been signed, a method is required to verify it. Verification involves extracting the information from the signature block, validating the certificate, and determining whether the code has been modified. If the code is determined to be secure, it will be downloaded. Otherwise, a warning is displayed to the user, indicating the potential problem, and the user can decide whether it is safe to download the code.

Figure 4-10 shows a sample of what a user might see when downloading software over the Internet, using the Internet Explorer. It is a mock certificate that displays the credentials of software that is to be downloaded.

Figure 4-10.
A mock code-signature certificate.

In addition to code signing, the Internet Explorer also incorporates cryptographic technology. Cryptography is the encoding and decoding of data for secure transmission and storage. The Internet Explorer has access to cryptographic functions through the Microsoft Cryptographic Application Programming Interface (CryptoAPI). The CryptoAPI, along with code signing, is expected to provide an environment in which third-party tools flourish and are widely distributed on the Internet.

The ActiveX Controls on the Companion CD

Many new ActiveX controls are beginning to appear on the market. Several of these new controls are on the companion CD that comes with this book. In this section, we discuss a few of these ActiveX controls, to give you some ideas about how to use the controls in your web pages.

The Label Control

The Label control is just like the Label control in Visual Basic except that it can be rotated. The Label control supports an Angle property that is set in degrees. This is useful for labeling a web page. Many of the examples in this book use the Label control to place a vertical label on a page. Listing 4-3 shows the code that places a vertical label on a web page, and Figure 4-11 shows a sample of the output.

```
<HTML>
<HEAD>
<TITLE>Label Control</TITLE>
</HEAD>
<BODY>
<CENTER>

<OBJECT
    CLASSID="clsid:99B42120-6EC7-11CF-A6C7-00AA00A47DD2"
    ID="Label1"
    HEIGHT=350
    WIDTH=50
    >
    <PARAM NAME="Angle" VALUE="90">
    <PARAM NAME="FontSize" VALUE="30">
    <PARAM NAME="ForeColor" VALUE="#000000">
    <PARAM NAME="Caption" VALUE="Super!!">
</OBJECT>

</CENTER>
</BODY>
</HTML>
```

Listing 4-3.
The Label control used in HTML code.

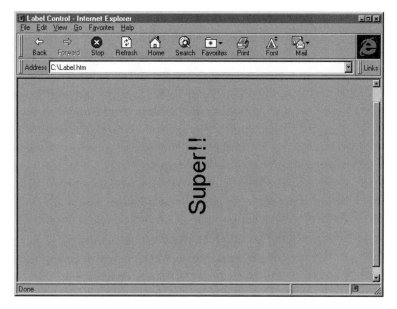

Figure 4-11.
Sample output of the Label control.

The Timer Control

Another useful control is the Timer control. The timer works just the way the Visual Basic timer does. It supports an Interval property that takes as an argument the number of milliseconds between Time events. Listing 4-4 shows an example of a timer used to display a MsgBox after 5 seconds have elapsed. Figure 4-12 shows a sample of the output.

```
<HTML>
<HEAD>
<TITLE>Timer Control</TITLE>

<SCRIPT LANGUAGE="VBScript">
<!--
    Sub timer1_timer
        timer1.enabled=False
```

Listing 4-4.   *(continued)*
The Timer control used in HTML code.

Listing 4-4 *continued*

```
        MsgBox "It has been 5 seconds!"
    End Sub
-->
</SCRIPT>

<OBJECT
    CLASSID="clsid:59CCB4A0-727D-11CF-AC36-00AA00A47DD2"
    ID=timer1
    >
    <PARAM NAME="Interval" VALUE="5000">
    <PARAM NAME="Enabled" VALUE="True">
</OBJECT>

</HEAD>
<BODY>
</BODY>
</HTML>
```

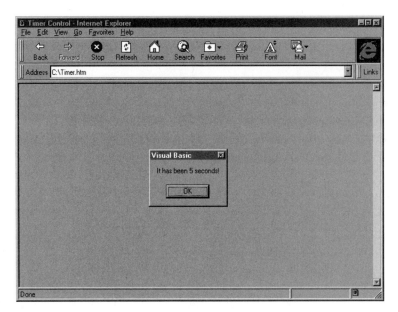

Figure 4-12.
Sample output of the Timer control.

The timer is useful for adding a dynamic look and feel to your web page. Use it to change label captions or play music.

The New Item Control

The New Item control is a simple control that displays a "New!" banner, or any specified image, until a specified date. This is good for drawing attention to new areas and items on a web site. The beauty of the control is that you do not have to manually update the site later—the banner simply stops displaying after a specified date. Listing 4-5 shows the code for displaying an image until January 31, 1997. Figure 4-13 shows a sample of the output.

```
<HTML>
<HEAD>
<TITLE>New Item Control</TITLE>
</HEAD>
<BODY>
The COOL image will be displayed until January 31, 1997

<OBJECT
    CLASSID="clsid:642B65C0-7374-11CF-A3A9-00A0C9034920"
    ID="NewItem Object"
    WIDTH=80
    HEIGHT=30
    >
    <PARAM NAME="date" VALUE="1/31/1997">
    <PARAM NAME="image" VALUE="cool.bmp">
</OBJECT>

</BODY>
</HTML>
```

Listing 4-5.
The New Item control used in HTML code.

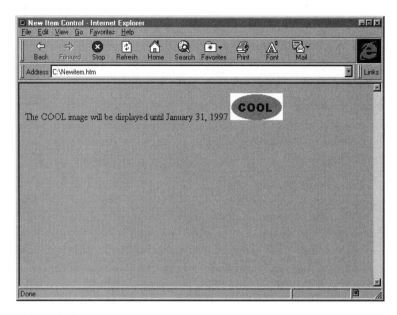

Figure 4-13.
Sample output of the New Item control.

The Stock Ticker Control

The Stock Ticker control is an example of a vertical application control. (A *vertical application* is an application that is specific to one industry.) Although not useful for general purposes, the stock ticker represents a new generation of ActiveX controls that are targeted at specific niche groups on the web. Listing 4-6 shows the code used to implement a stock ticker in a web page. (Notice that the information displayed by the stock ticker is from a file on Microsoft's web site.) Figure 4-14 shows a sample of the output.

```
<HTML>
<HEAD>
<TITLE>Stock Ticker Control</TITLE>
</HEAD>
<BODY>

<OBJECT
    CLASSID="clsid:0CA4A620-8E3D-11CF-A3A9-00A0C9034920"
    ID="Ticker"
```

Listing 4-6.
The Stock Ticker control used in HTML code.

```
     WIDTH=300
     HEIGHT=50
     >
     <PARAM NAME="DataObjectName"
     VALUE="http://www.microsoft.com/workshop/activex/gallery/ms/
ticker/other/iexrt.xrt">
     <PARAM NAME="DataObjectActive" VALUE="1">
     <PARAM NAME="ScrollWidth" VALUE="5">
     <PARAM NAME="ForeColor" VALUE="#FF0000">
     <PARAM NAME="BackColor" VALUE="#0000FF">
     <PARAM NAME="ReloadInterval" VALUE="5000">
</OBJECT>

</BODY>
</HTML>
```

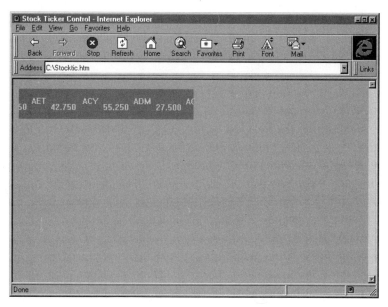

Figure 4-14.
Sample output of the Stock Ticker control.

The Marquee Control

The Marquee control is a special control that allows you to easily animate any web page. The Marquee control takes another HTML document as input and scrolls it inside the current document. This adds a "grand marquee" look to the page. Listing 4-7 shows two HTML documents. The first HTML document shows the implementation of the Marquee control and the reference to the HTML page to be scrolled. The second HTML document shows the actual code for the page to be scrolled. Figure 4-15 shows a sample of the output.

```
<HTML>
<HEAD>
<TITLE>Marquee Control</TITLE>
</HEAD>
<BODY>
<CENTER>

<OBJECT
    CLASSID="clsid:1A4DA620-6217-11CF-BE62-0080C72EDD2D"
    ID="objMarquee"
    ALIGN="CENTER"
    WIDTH=200 HEIGHT=250
    >
    <PARAM NAME="ScrollStyleX" VALUE="Circular">
    <PARAM NAME="ScrollStyleY" VALUE="Circular">
    <PARAM NAME="szURL" VALUE="scrollpg.htm">
    <PARAM NAME="ScrollDelay" VALUE=60>
    <PARAM NAME="LoopsX" VALUE=-1>
    <PARAM NAME="LoopsY" VALUE=-1>
    <PARAM NAME="ScrollPixelsX" VALUE=0>
    <PARAM NAME="ScrollPixelsY" VALUE=-3>
    <PARAM NAME="DrawImmediately" VALUE=0>
    <PARAM NAME="Whitespace" VALUE=0>
    <PARAM NAME="PageFlippingOn" VALUE=0>
    <PARAM NAME="Zoom" VALUE=100>
    <PARAM NAME="WidthOfPage" VALUE=200>
</OBJECT>

</CENTER>
</BODY>
</HTML>
```

Listing 4-7.
The Marquee control used to scroll another HTML document within the current document.

```
<!--
Code for the scrolling page
-->

<HTML>
<HEAD>
<TITLE>Page to Scroll</TITLE>
</HEAD>
<BODY BGCOLOR="#ffffff">
<CENTER>
<H2>Scrolling Text</H2>
<BR><BR>
Scrolling Image
<BR>
<IMG SRC="book.bmp">
<BR>
</CENTER>
</BODY>
</HTML>
```

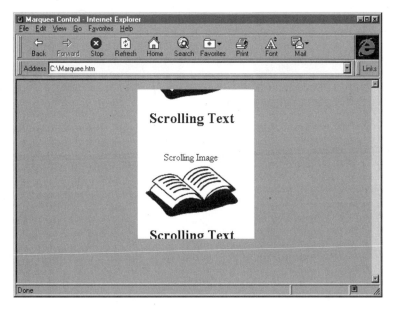

Figure 4-15.
Sample output of the Marquee control.

The Minesweeper and Calculator Examples

The following two programming examples, Minesweeper and Calculator, utilize ActiveX controls and VBScript. These examples show how ActiveX controls, along with some VBScript code, can be used to create interesting interactive web pages. The complete code for these examples can be found at the end of this chapter and on the companion CD that comes with this book.

The Minesweeper example is a simple Internet version of the popular Microsoft Minesweeper game that shipped with Windows 3.1. Players are presented with a 5-by-5 grid of cells. Cells are "swept" when they are clicked. If the cell doesn't contain a mine, it is cleared along with all the adjacent cells that do not contain mines. Uncovering a mine ends the game. When the player believes that all the mines have been identified, he or she clicks on the Done Sweeping button to see whether he or she has won. Figure 4-16 shows a sample of the minesweeper interface. Listing 4-8, starting on page 104, shows the code for the Internet version of the Minesweeper game. Since some of the code for the Minesweeper example is repetitive, only the basic code structure is included in Listing 4-8. The full program listing is available on the companion CD, in the samples folder.

Figure 4-16.
The Minesweeper interface.

The Minesweeper grid of cells is an HTML table defined by the <TABLE></TABLE> tags. A label control is placed inside each cell with the <OBJECT></OBJECT> tags. Note that this control is not the same as the Label control found in Visual Basic 4.0 and does not support control arrays, which are discussed in more detail later in this section. Therefore, all of the code was created with discrete instances of the Label control. The following code shows the definition of the Label control:

```
<OBJECT
CLASSID="clsid:99B42120-6EC7-11CF-A6C7-00AA00A47DD2"
ID="lblCell5" HEIGHT=20 WIDTH=20>
<PARAM NAME="Caption" VALUE="X">
</OBJECT>
```

The controls are all built into a form called frmSweeper, using the <FORM></FORM> tags. The intrinsic Button controls are added to the form with the <INPUT> tag, as shown here:

```
<INPUT TYPE="BUTTON" ID="cmdShow" VALUE="Show All Mines" WIDTH=30>
<INPUT TYPE="BUTTON" ID="cmdNew" VALUE="New Game" WIDTH=30>
<INPUT TYPE="BUTTON" ID="cmdDone" VALUE="Done Sweeping" WIDTH=30>
```

These controls will automatically call the associated OnClick event subroutine as coded in VBScript.

As shown in the Minesweeper example, many controls in the Internet Explorer do not support control arrays. A control array is a group of the same controls, all of which have the same name. The controls are differentiated by the values of their Index property. Every control in the array can call the same event-handling routine and pass its Index value as an argument. Control arrays are great timesavers because when you use them you don't have to write an event-handling routine for each control.

The second example presented in this section is a simple four-function calculator. It uses the OnClick event of intrinsic Button controls to simulate control arrays. In the OnClick event, a separate routine is called, and an index is passed. Listing 4-9, starting on page 113, shows the complete project, but the following code shows the workaround for the control array:

```
<INPUT TYPE="BUTTON" NAME="btnOne" VALUE="1"
OnClick="Call NumPad(1)">
```

Note that the OnClick event can be used to execute code directly. This strategy is in contrast to that used in the Minesweeper example, in which the Click events were called because the controls were part of a form. Using the

OnClick event, as we did for the calculator, results in HTML code that is considerably shorter than the code for the Minesweeper game. Figure 4-17 shows a sample of the calculator interface.

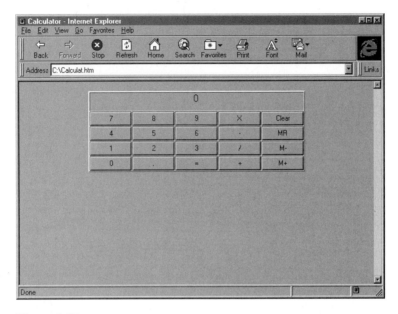

Figure 4-17.
The four-function calculator interface.

The remaining portion of this chapter contains the program listings for the Minesweeper and Calculator examples.

```
<HTML>
<HEAD>
<TITLE>Minesweeper</TITLE>

<!--
This sample creates a Minesweeper game that uses
25 label controls in a table structure.  Players
clear cells by clicking on them. If a cell doesn't
contain a mine, it's cleared along with all
adjacent cells that don't contain mines.  If a cell
contains a mine and the player tries to clear it,
the game is over.
-->
```

Listing 4-8.
The Minesweeper example.

```
<SCRIPT LANGUAGE="VBScript">
<!--
    Sub lblCell1_Click
        Call Sweep(1,Document.frmSweeper.lblCell1)
    End Sub

    Sub lblCell2_Click
        Call Sweep(2,Document.frmSweeper.lblCell2)
    End Sub

    Sub lblCell3_Click
        Call Sweep(3,Document.frmSweeper.lblCell3)
    End Sub

    Sub lblCell4_Click
        Call Sweep(4,Document.frmSweeper.lblCell4)
    End Sub

    Sub lblCell5_Click
        Call Sweep(5,Document.frmSweeper.lblCell5)
    End Sub

                        .
                        .
                        .

    Sub lblCell25_Click
        Call Sweep(25,Document.frmSweeper.lblCell25)
    End Sub

    Sub Sweep(intIndex,lblCell)

    'Author: New Technology Solutions, Inc.
    'Purpose: This code handles the Click
    'events for all the labels.  When a
    'label is clicked, we check to see if it
    'contains a mine.
    '5/1/96 Original

        Dim i
        Dim MyForm
        Set MyForm=Document.frmSweeper

        If Playing=0 Then Exit Sub
        If Mine(intIndex)=0 Then
            lblCell.Caption=""
            Call ClearOthers(intIndex)
```

(continued)

Listing 4-8 *continued*

```
        Else
            lblCell.Caption="*"
            Call YouLose()
        End If
End Sub

'Author: New Technology Solutions, Inc.
'Purpose: The variables are dimensioned
'here. They are dimensioned inline so that
'they are available to all code in the page.
'They are declared when the page loads.
'5/9/96 Original

Dim Playing
Dim Mine(25)

Sub SetCellCaption(ByVal intMine,ByVal strCaption)

'Author: New Technology Solutions, Inc.
'Purpose: Set the caption of a label in the grid
'5/1/96 Original

    Dim MyForm
    Set MyForm=Document.frmSweeper

    Select Case intMine
    Case 1
        MyForm.lblCell1.Caption=strCaption
    Case 2
        MyForm.lblCell2.Caption=strCaption
    Case 3
        MyForm.lblCell3.Caption=strCaption
    Case 4
        MyForm.lblCell4.Caption=strCaption
    Case 5
        MyForm.lblCell5.Caption=strCaption
                    .
                    .
                    .
    Case 25
        MyForm.lblCell125.Caption=strCaption
    End Select
End Sub
```

```
    Function GetCellCaption(ByVal intMine)

    'Author: New Technology Solutions, Inc.
    'Purpose: Return the current label caption
    '5/1/96 Original

        Dim MyForm
        Set MyForm=Document.frmSweeper

        If intMine=1 Then _
            GetCellCaption=MyForm.lblCell1.Caption
        If intMine=2 Then _
            GetCellCaption=MyForm.lblCell2.Caption
        If intMine=3 Then _
            GetCellCaption=MyForm.lblCell3.Caption
        If intMine=4 Then _
            GetCellCaption=MyForm.lblCell4.Caption
        If intMine=5 Then _
            GetCellCaption=MyForm.lblCell5.Caption
                            .
                            .
                            .

        If intMine=25 Then _
            GetCellCaption=MyForm.lblCell25.Caption
    End Function
-->
</SCRIPT>

<SCRIPT LANGUAGE="VBScript">
<!--
    Sub ResetGame()

    'Author: New Technology Solutions, Inc.
    'Purpose: Reset the variables and the game board
    '5/1/96 Original

        Dim i
        Dim n

        For i=1 to 25
            Mine(i)=0
            Call SetCellCaption(i,"X")
        Next
        Randomize Timer
```

(continued)

Listing 4-8 *continued*

```
      For i=1 to 5
            n=Int(25*Rnd)+1
            Mine(n)=1
      Next
      Playing=1
End Sub

Sub ClearOthers(ByVal intMine)

'Author: New Technology Solutions, Inc.
'Purpose: This routine clears adjacent
'cells that do not have a mine in them
'5/1/96 Original

      Dim MyForm
      Set MyForm=Document.frmSweeper

      Select Case intMine
      Case 1
            If Mine(2)=0 Then MyForm.lblCell2.Caption=""
            If Mine(6)=0 Then MyForm.lblCell6.Caption=""
            If Mine(7)=0 Then MyForm.lblCell7.Caption=""
      Case 2
            If Mine(1)=0 Then MyForm.lblCell1.Caption=""
            If Mine(3)=0 Then MyForm.lblCell3.Caption=""
            If Mine(6)=0 Then MyForm.lblCell6.Caption=""
            If Mine(7)=0 Then MyForm.lblCell7.Caption=""
            If Mine(8)=0 Then MyForm.lblCell8.Caption=""
      Case 3
            If Mine(2)=0 Then MyForm.lblCell2.Caption=""
            If Mine(4)=0 Then MyForm.lblCell4.Caption=""
            If Mine(7)=0 Then MyForm.lblCell7.Caption=""
            If Mine(8)=0 Then MyForm.lblCell8.Caption=""
            If Mine(9)=0 Then MyForm.lblCell9.Caption=""
      Case 4
            If Mine(3)=0 Then MyForm.lblCell3.Caption=""
            If Mine(5)=0 Then MyForm.lblCell5.Caption=""
            If Mine(8)=0 Then MyForm.lblCell8.Caption=""
            If Mine(9)=0 Then MyForm.lblCell9.Caption=""
            If Mine(10)=0 Then MyForm.lblCell10.Caption=""
      Case 5
            If Mine(4)=0 Then MyForm.lblCell4.Caption=""
```

```
                    If Mine(9)=0 Then MyForm.lblCell9.Caption=""
                    If Mine(10)=0 Then MyForm.lblCell10.Caption=""
                                    .
                                    .
                                    .
            Case 25
                    If Mine(24)=0 Then MyForm.lblCell24.Caption=""
                    If Mine(19)=0 Then MyForm.lblCell19.Caption=""
                    If Mine(20)=0 Then MyForm.lblCell20.Caption=""
        End Select
End Sub

Sub YouLose()

'Author: New Technology Solutions, Inc.
'Purpose: Display losing message
'5/1/96 Original

    MsgBox "Oh, no! You Lose!",32,"Minesweeper"
    Playing=0
End Sub

Sub YouWin()

'Author: New Technology Solutions, Inc.
'Purpose: Display winning message
'5/1/96 Original

    MsgBox "Congratulations! You Win!",64,"Minesweeper"
    Playing=0
End Sub


Sub cmdNew_OnClick()

'Author: New Technology Solutions, Inc.
'Purpose: Initialize game
'5/1/96 Original

    Call ResetGame()
    MsgBox "Ready to Play!",64,"Minesweeper"

End Sub
```

(continued)

Listing 4-8 *continued*

```
Sub cmdDone_OnClick()

'Author: New Technology Solutions, Inc.
'Purpose: This routine is called when the
'player thinks he or she has found all the mines
'5/1/96 Original

    Dim blnWinLose
    Dim i

    blnWinLose=1
    For i=1 to 25
        If Mine(i)=0 And GetCellCaption(i)="X" Then
            blnWinLose=0
        End if
    Next
    If blnWinLose=1 Then
        Call YouWin()
    Else
        Call YouLose()
    End If
End Sub

Sub cmdShow_OnClick()

    'Author: New Technology Solutions, Inc.
    'Purpose: This routine shows all the
    'mine locations for the current game
    '5/1/96 Original

    Dim i

    For i=1 to 25
        If Mine(i)=1 Then
            Call SetCellCaption(i,"*")
        Else
            Call SetCellCaption(i,"")
        End If
    Next
    Playing=0
End sub
-->
</SCRIPT>
```

```
</HEAD>
<BODY BGCOLOR="White">
<CENTER>
<H2>Minesweeper!</H2><BR>


<!--
This HTML code builds the form that
contains the label controls and
the buttons
-->


<FORM NAME="frmSweeper">
<FONT FACE="Arial" Size="12">
    <TABLE BORDER CELLPADDING="5" WIDTH=100>
        <TR ALIGN="MIDDLE" VALIGN="BASELINE">
            <TD ALIGN="CENTER" NOWRAP WIDTH=20>
            <OBJECT
            CLASSID=
            "clsid:99B42120-6EC7-11CF-A6C7-00AA00A47DD2"
            ID="lblCell1" HEIGHT=20 WIDTH=20>
            <PARAM NAME="Caption" VALUE="X">
            </OBJECT>
            </TD>

            <TD ALIGN="CENTER" NOWRAP WIDTH=20>
            <OBJECT
            CLASSID=
            "clsid:99B42120-6EC7-11CF-A6C7-00AA00A47DD2"
            ID="lblCell2" HEIGHT=20 WIDTH=20>
            <PARAM NAME="Caption" VALUE="X">
            </OBJECT>
            </TD>

            <TD ALIGN="CENTER" NOWRAP WIDTH=20>
            <OBJECT
            CLASSID=
            "clsid:99B42120-6EC7-11CF-A6C7-00AA00A47DD2"
            ID="lblCell3" HEIGHT=20 WIDTH=20>
            <PARAM NAME="Caption" VALUE="X">
            </OBJECT>
            </TD>

            <TD ALIGN="CENTER" NOWRAP WIDTH=20>
            <OBJECT
            CLASSID=
```

(continued)

Listing 4-8 *continued*

```
                "clsid:99B42120-6EC7-11CF-A6C7-00AA00A47DD2"
                ID="lblCell4" HEIGHT=20 WIDTH=20>
                <PARAM NAME="Caption" VALUE="X">
                </OBJECT>
                </TD>

                <TD ALIGN="CENTER" NOWRAP WIDTH=20>
                <OBJECT
                CLASSID=
                "clsid:99B42120-6EC7-11CF-A6C7-00AA00A47DD2"
                ID="lblCell5" HEIGHT=20 WIDTH=20>
                <PARAM NAME="Caption" VALUE="X">
                </OBJECT>
                </TD>
            </TR>

                        .
                        .
                        .

                <TD ALIGN="CENTER" NOWRAP WIDTH=20>
                <OBJECT
                CLASSID=
                "clsid:99B42120-6EC7-11CF-A6C7-00AA00A47DD2"
                ID="lblCell125" HEIGHT=20 WIDTH=20>
                <PARAM NAME="Caption" VALUE="X">
                </OBJECT>
                </TD>
            </TR>
            <CAPTION ALIGN="BOTTOM">Click on a cell</CAPTION>
        </TABLE>

<INPUT TYPE="BUTTON" ID="cmdShow" VALUE="Show All Mines"
WIDTH=30>
<INPUT TYPE="BUTTON" ID="cmdNew" VALUE="New Game" WIDTH=30>
<INPUT TYPE="Button" ID="cmdDone" VALUE="Done Sweeping"
WIDTH=30>
<BR>

</FONT>
</FORM>
</CENTER>

<SCRIPT LANGUAGE="VBScript">
<!--
```

```
     'This code is called inline after
     'the rest of the page is set up.
     'It initializes the game.

     Call ResetGame()
-->
</SCRIPT>

</BODY>
</HTML>
```

```
<HTML>
<HEAD>
<TITLE>Calculator</TITLE>

<!--
This demo implements a simple four-function
calculator
-->

<SCRIPT LANGUAGE="VBScript">
<!--
     'Author: New Technology Solutions, Inc.
     'Purpose:
     'These are variables used throughout
     'the calculator.  They are declared
     'inline as the page loads and are
     'available to the entire application.
     '5/1/96 Original

     'Variable for user storage
     Dim dblMemory
     'Flag indicating whether decimal button
     'has been clicked
     Dim blnDecimal
     'Display cache
     Dim dblDisplay
     'Temporary storage for chain calculations
     Dim dblStorage
     'Number of keystrokes entered
     Dim intKeyStrokes
     'Any pending mathematical operations
     Dim intPending
```

Listing 4-9.

(continued)

The four-function calculator example.

113

Listing 4-9   *continued*

```
    'Initialize variables
    dblMemory = 0
    blnDecimal = 0
    intKeyStrokes = 0
    dblDisplay = 0
    dblStorage = 0
    intPending = 0
-->
</SCRIPT>

<SCRIPT LANGUAGE="VBScript">
<!--
    Sub NumPad(intIndex)

        'Author: New Technology Solutions, Inc.
        'Purpose:
        'Receive all button clicks for
        'numbers on the calculator.
        'The buttons do not support control
        'arrays, but note how the OnClick
        'attribute is used as a workaround to
        'call the same routine for each button.
        '5/1/96 Original

        intKeyStrokes = intKeyStrokes + 1
        If blnDecimal=0 Then
            dblDisplay = dblDisplay * 10 + intIndex
        Else
            dblDisplay = dblDisplay + _
            intIndex/(10 ^ intKeyStrokes)
        End If
        Call UpdateDisplay(dblDisplay)
    End Sub
-->
</SCRIPT>

<SCRIPT LANGUAGE="VBScript">
<!--
    Sub btnClear_OnClick

        'Author: New Technology Solutions, Inc.
        'Purpose: Clear the calculator display
        '5/1/96 Original
```

```
            intKeyStrokes = 0
            dblDisplay = 0
            blnDecimal = 0
            dblStorage = 0
            dblMemory = 0
            Call UpdateDisplay(0)
      End Sub

      Sub btnDecimal_OnClick

            'Author: New Technology Solutions, Inc.
            'Purpose: Handle the Decimal button
            '5/1/96 Original

            intKeyStrokes = 0
            blnDecimal = 1
      End Sub
-->
</SCRIPT>

<SCRIPT LANGUAGE="VBScript">
<!--
      Sub OperationPad(intIndex)

            'Author: New Technology Solutions, Inc.
            'Purpose: Handle addition, subtraction,
            'multiplication, and division
            '5/1/96 Original

            Call DoPending()
            'Reset all flags
            intKeyStrokes = 0
            blnDecimal = 0
            intPending = intIndex
            dblDisplay = 0
            'Update calculator display
            Call UpdateDisplay(dblStorage)
      End Sub

      Sub btnEquals_OnClick

            'Author: New Technology Solutions, Inc.
            'Purpose: Handle Equals key
            '5/1/96 Original
```

(continued)

Listing 4-9 *continued*

```
        intKeyStrokes = 0
        blnDecimal = 0
        Call DoPending()
        dblDisplay = 0
        Call UpdateDisplay(dblStorage)
        dblStorage = 0
    End Sub

    Sub DoPending()

        'Author: New Technology Solutions, Inc.
        'Purpose:
        'Handle any pending actions
        'during chain calculations
        '5/1/96 Original

        'No pending operations
        If intPending = 0 Then
            dblStorage = dblDisplay
        End If
        'Chain addition
        If intPending = 1 Then
            dblStorage = dblStorage + dblDisplay
        End If
        'Chain subtraction
        If intPending = 2 Then
            dblStorage = dblStorage - dblDisplay
        End if
        'Chain multiplication
        If intPending = 3 Then
            dblStorage = dblStorage * dblDisplay
        End if
        'Chain division
        If intPending = 4 Then
            If dblStorage = 0 Then
                intPending = 0
                Exit Sub
            End If
            dblStorage = dblStorage / dblDisplay
        End If
        intPending = 0
    End Sub
```

```
     Sub UpdateDisplay(dblValue)

          'Author: New Technology Solutions, Inc.
          'Purpose: Refresh the display
          '5/1/96 Original

          Dim MyForm
          Set MyForm = Document.frmCalculator
          MyForm.lblDisplay.Caption = dblValue
     End Sub
-->
</SCRIPT>

<SCRIPT LANGUAGE="VBScript">
<!--
     'Author: New Technology Solutions, Inc.
     'Purpose:
     'All of these routines handle the
     'user-defined storage variable
     '5/1/96 Original

     Sub btnMemRecall_OnClick
          dblDisplay = dblMemory
          Call UpdateDisplay(dblDisplay)
     End Sub

     Sub btnMemMinus_OnClick
          dblMemory = dblMemory - dblDisplay
     End Sub

     Sub btnMemPlus_OnClick
          dblMemory = dblMemory + dblDisplay
     End Sub
-->
</SCRIPT>

</HEAD>
<BODY>
<CENTER>

<FORM NAME="frmCalculator">

<!--
     This HTML builds the actual calculator form
-->
```

(continued)

Listing 4-9 *continued*

```
<TABLE BORDER=2 CELLSPACING=0 CELLPADDING=0 WIDTH=250>
    <TR>
        <TH COLSPAN=5>
        <!--
        This is the label for displaying the results
        -->
        <OBJECT
        CLASSID=
        "clsid:99B42120-6EC7-11CF-A6C7-00AA00A47DD2"
        ID="lblDisplay" WIDTH=250 HEIGHT=30>
        <PARAM NAME="Caption" VALUE="0">
        <PARAM NAME="Alignment" VALUE="1">
        <PARAM NAME="ForeColor" VALUE="#000000">
        </OBJECT>
        </TH>
    </TR>
    <TR>
        <TD>
        <INPUT TYPE="BUTTON" NAME="btnSeven"
        VALUE="7" OnClick="Call NumPad(7)">
        </TD>
        <TD WIDTH=50>
        <INPUT TYPE="BUTTON" NAME="btnEight"
        VALUE="8" OnClick="Call NumPad(8)">
        </TD>
        <TD WIDTH=50>
        <INPUT TYPE="BUTTON" NAME="btnNine"
        VALUE="9" OnClick="Call NumPad(9)">
        </TD>
        <TD WIDTH=50>
        <INPUT TYPE="BUTTON" NAME="btnMultiply"
        VALUE="X" OnClick="Call OperationPad(3)">
        </TD>
        <TD WIDTH=50>
        <INPUT TYPE="BUTTON" NAME="btnClear"
        VALUE="Clear">
        </TD>
    </TR>
    <TR>
        <TD>
        <INPUT TYPE="BUTTON" NAME="btnFour"
        VALUE="4" OnClick="Call NumPad(4)">
        </TD>
```

```
            <TD WIDTH=50>
            <INPUT TYPE="BUTTON" NAME="btnFive"
            VALUE="5" OnClick="Call NumPad(5)">
            </TD>
            <TD WIDTH=50>
            <INPUT TYPE="BUTTON" NAME="btnSix"
            VALUE="6" OnClick="Call NumPad(6)">
            </TD>
            <TD WIDTH=50>
            <INPUT TYPE="BUTTON" NAME="btnMinus"
            VALUE="-" OnClick="Call OperationPad(2)">
            </TD>
            <TD WIDTH=50>
            <INPUT TYPE="BUTTON" NAME="btnMemRecall"
            VALUE="MR">
            </TD>
    </TR>
    <TR>
            <TD>
            <INPUT TYPE="BUTTON" NAME="btnOne"
            VALUE="1" OnClick="Call NumPad(1)">
            </TD>
            <TD WIDTH=50>
            <INPUT TYPE="BUTTON" NAME="btnTwo"
            VALUE="2" OnClick="Call NumPad(2)">
            </TD>
            <TD WIDTH=50>
            <INPUT TYPE="BUTTON" NAME="btnThree"
            VALUE="3" OnClick="Call NumPad(3)">
            </TD>
            <TD WIDTH=50>
            <INPUT TYPE="BUTTON" NAME="btnDivide"
            VALUE="/" OnClick="Call OperationPad(4)">
            </TD>
            <TD WIDTH=50>
            <INPUT TYPE="BUTTON" NAME="btnMemMinus"
            VALUE="M-">
            </TD>
    </TR>
    <TR>
            <TD>
            <INPUT TYPE="BUTTON" NAME="btnZero"
            VALUE="0" OnClick="Call NumPad(0)">
            </TD>
            <TD WIDTH=50>
```

(continued)

Listing 4-9 *continued*

```
            <INPUT TYPE="BUTTON" NAME="btnDecimal"
            VALUE=".">
            </TD>
            <TD WIDTH=50>
            <INPUT TYPE="BUTTON" NAME="btnEquals"
            VALUE="=">
            </TD>
            <TD WIDTH=50>
            <INPUT TYPE="BUTTON" NAME="btnPlus"
            VALUE="+" OnClick="Call OperationPad(1)">
            </TD>
            <TD WIDTH=50>
            <INPUT TYPE="BUTTON" NAME="btnMemPlus"
            VALUE="M+">
            </TD>
        </TR>
    </TABLE>
</FORM>

</CENTER>
</BODY>
</HTML>
```

CHAPTER FIVE

The Microsoft Internet Information Server

Although Microsoft Visual Basic, Scripting Edition, itself offers some compelling functionality for creating interactive web sites, no book about Internet technology would be complete without a discussion of back-end processing. Until recently, web masters had few options. Some companies, operating under the constraints of limited resources, opted to use an Internet service provider (ISP). An ISP rents out space on a large server, such as a UNIX platform, to many customers who can then set up simple web sites. The server provides the customers with a connection to the World Wide Web and maps the proper URLs to folders on the server. Back-end processing is typically provided by a limited set of Common Gateway Interface (CGI) scripts that are called from the customer's HTML code. For example, a CGI script might be provided to allow a web browser to send email directly to an ISP customer. Although ISPs provide simple, basic access to the Internet, they obviously cannot provide unique solutions to particular business problems.

To achieve greater flexibility, a company with more resources will often choose to purchase its own server for creating a web presence. Connecting the server to the Internet also requires an access line with sufficient bandwidth, such as ISDN or T-1. ISDN (Integrated Services Digital Network) is a connection that allows data to be transferred at a speed of 64 to 128 kilobytes per second, while a T-1 connection allows approximately 1.5 megabytes per second. Although providing a dedicated in-house server is certainly more expensive than using an ISP, back-end processing with an in-house server can be customized to meet particular business needs such as database access. Until recently, the choice for an in-house server might have been a UNIX system that used CGI scripts for back-end processing. However, with the release of the Microsoft Internet Information Server (IIS), developers can easily set up a web site using a Windows NT server.

IIS is designed to run as a set of services on a Windows NT server. Windows NT supports the TCP/IP protocol and is therefore an ideal platform for creating a web server. In fact, IIS can easily be used not only to create a presence on the WWW but also as a corporate intranet, or wide area network (WAN), running the TCP/IP protocol. When installed, IIS provides services for the Hypertext Transfer Protocol (HTTP), the file transfer protocol (FTP), and the Gopher protocol. HTTP is the service primarily used to create interactive web pages and is the focus of this chapter. IIS makes it simple to create powerful back-end processes that allow database access and more.

The Internet Services API

Back-end processes are typically triggered by input from a browser. CGI scripts represent the bulk of back-end processing present on the web today. An HTML form is used to invoke a CGI script. HTML recognizes a special intrinsic control called a *Submit button*. Submit buttons package all of the form's input variables and pass them to the back-end process. The following code passes three form input variables—Name, Address, and Phone—to a CGI script called email.pl:

```
<FORM ACTION="http://www.myweb.com/email.pl" METHOD="POST">
<INPUT TYPE="Text" NAME="Name">
<INPUT TYPE="Text" NAME="Address">
<INPUT TYPE="Text" NAME="Phone">
<INPUT TYPE="Submit" VALUE="Send Mail">
</FORM>
```

The ACTION attribute of the form specifies the process that will receive the data. The METHOD attribute is set to POST, which means that data is sent from the form to the process. The data is delineated by the NAME attribute of each of the text input fields. When the user clicks on the Submit button, the text entered into each text field is sent to the email.pl process as a single string in the form *Field=Value*. The back-end process parses the data and takes action. In this simple example, email would be sent to the ISP customer designated by the Name, Address, and Phone values.

CGI scripts are useful, and most can be used by IIS; however, IIS also implements some other powerful back-end processing. CGI spawns a new process for each transaction. Thus, CGI scripts cannot remember the status of a transaction because each new call represents a new transaction. Remembering information throughout several transactions is the key to rendering smooth interactive behavior on a web page. For this reason, we will not focus on CGI as a solution. Instead, we will devote this chapter to the new, more powerful Internet Server API (ISAPI).

ISAPI is an interface that allows programmers to develop DLLs that work with IIS. A DLL is superior to a CGI script because DLLs can remain resident in memory throughout a series of transactions. The ability to remain resident means that ISAPI can operate faster than CGI and can remember the state of a transaction. These are significant advantages over the classic CGI script and make IIS a formidable competitor in the web server market. ISAPI is utilized in two components that ship with IIS: the Internet Database Connector (IDC) and OLEISAPI.

KEY CONCEPT: ISAPI is an interface that allows programmers to develop DLLs that work with IIS.

The Internet Database Connector

The Internet Database Connector (IDC) is a specific implementation of ISAPI. IDC is designed to allow communication between a front-end HTML page and a back-end ODBC (Open Database Connectivity) datasource. IDC uses the HTTP protocol to accept input and responds to requests by returning a complete HTML web page for display. Figure 5-1 (page 124) shows the flowpath of the action when a browser uses IDC to query a database for information.

Consider an example in which you use IDC to make a database query from an HTML page to IIS. IIS communicates the request to a DLL called httpodbc.dll, which is the Internet Database Connector. IDC, embodied in httpodbc.dll, invokes the appropriate ODBC driver to access the database. The ODBC driver executes a structured query language (SQL) statement that can either update the database or retrieve records from the database. When retrieving records, httpodbc.dll formats the resulting record set and returns it to the browser as an HTML page ready for display.

IDC requires three different ASCII text files for implementation. These three files control the flow and content of database information handled by IDC. The files required to utilize IDC are the HTML (htm) file, the Internet Database Connector (idc) file, and the HTML extension (htx) file.

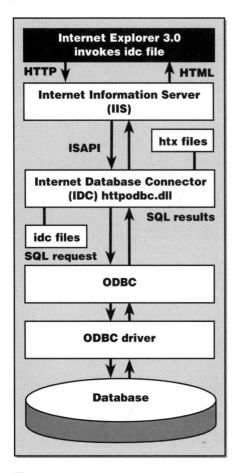

Figure 5-1.
The Internet Database Connector (IDC) flowpath.

IDC can be called from an HTML web page with a form. The following code shows an example of IDC being called from a form. This is a slight variation on the previous CGI example:

```
<FORM ACTION="/scripts/myfile.idc" METHOD="POST">
<INPUT TYPE="Text" NAME="Name">
<INPUT TYPE="Text" NAME="Address">
<INPUT TYPE="Text" NAME="Phone">
<INPUT TYPE="Submit" VALUE="Send Mail">
</FORM>
```

In this example, the ACTION attribute of a form is used to call a special file called the idc file. The idc file contains information used by IDC to query an ODBC datasource. The following is an example of an idc file:

```
Datasource:MyODBCSource
Template:MyHTX.htx
SQLStatement:
+SELECT * FROM MyTable
```

The idc file is a simple text file containing information such as the name of the ODBC datasource to query, the HTML extension file used to return the results, and the SQL statement to be executed. IDC reads this information and executes the query through the appropriate ODBC driver.

The results of any query are returned by IDC as an HTML web page. The format of the web page is determined by the HTML extension file. The htx file is nothing more than a template describing how the results are to be displayed. The browser receives the resulting web page and displays the results. The following shows the structure of the htx file:

```
<HTML>
<HEAD>
<TITLE>A Sample htx File</TITLE>
</HEAD>
<BODY>
<%begindetail%>

<!--
The HTML in this area is repeated for each row
returned in a result set. You can format the
data with tables, for example.
-->

<%enddetail%>
</BODY>
</HTML>
```

KEY CONCEPT: The Internet Database Connector requires three files:

❏ htm, which contains the HTML that calls IDC

❏ idc, which contains the name of the ODBC datasource, the name of the htx file, and the SQL query command

❏ htx, which contains a template for the returned HTML page

Setting Up an ODBC Source

During the IIS setup, you can choose to install the SQL Server ODBC driver. No other drivers are provided with IIS. If you want to work with other databases, such as Microsoft Access and Microsoft FoxPro, you must install the appropriate ODBC drivers. Typically, ODBC drivers are included with database software, but additional ODBC drivers are available on the companion CD and also from Microsoft.

Once the drivers have been installed, the next step is to configure an ODBC datasource. Configuring ODBC datasources is done with the ODBC Administrator, which is typically located in the ODBC program group or in the Control Panel of the Main program group. Figure 5-2 shows the ODBC Data Sources dialog box, which is displayed after you double-click on the ODBC Administrator icon.

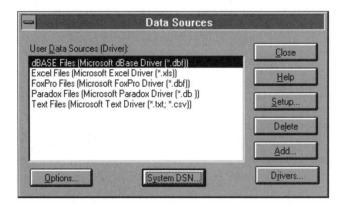

Figure 5-2.
The ODBC Data Sources dialog box.

IIS works only with system datasources. You set up a system datasource by clicking on the System DSN button in the ODBC Data Sources dialog box. After you click on the System DSN button, the System Data Sources dialog box appears. Figure 5-3 shows the System Data Sources dialog box.

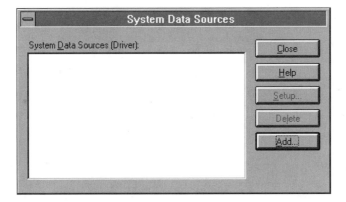

Figure 5-3.
The System Data Sources dialog box.

In the System Data Sources dialog box, click on the Add button to view a list of all ODBC drivers available. Figure 5-4 shows the Add Data Source dialog box.

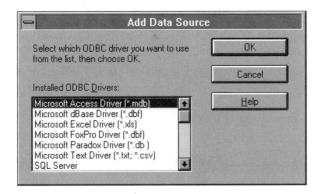

Figure 5-4.
The Add Data Source dialog box.

When you select an ODBC driver and click on the OK button, an ODBC setup dialog box is displayed. Each ODBC setup dialog box is different; its contents depend upon which driver you select. Figure 5-5 shows the ODBC setup dialog box for the Microsoft Access ODBC driver.

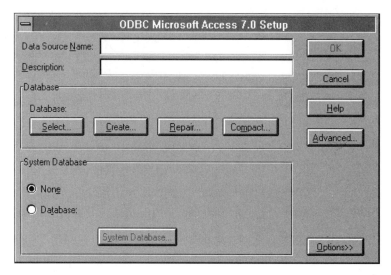

Figure 5-5.
The Access ODBC driver setup dialog box.

The ODBC driver setup dialog box allows you to locate the database you want to associate with the system datasource and to specify a name for the datasource. The datasource name is the same name used in idc files to address the database. You can select a database by clicking on the Select button and locating the database from the Select Database dialog box. Figure 5-6 shows the Select Database dialog box.

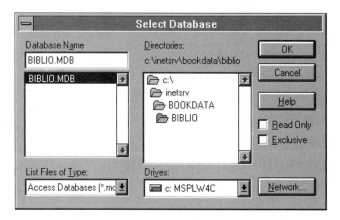

Figure 5-6.
The Select Database dialog box.

After all the dialog boxes are closed, the system datasource is set up and ready for use.

KEY CONCEPT: IDC works only with *system* datasources.

Using IDC

As an example, let's use IDC to retrieve records from an Access database. We will use a database called biblio.mdb, which ships with Microsoft Visual Basic. The biblio database is simply a database of publishers and book titles. Since the Access ODBC driver is not installed with the IIS installation, you will have to install it separately. Access ODBC drivers are available on this book's companion CD and also from Microsoft.

This example creates a web page that presents the names of several publishing companies in a list box. The user can select a company and view all of the books published by that company that are listed in the database. The results are listed in tabular format on a resulting web page. Figure 5-7 and Figure 5-8 (page 130) show the two web pages in action.

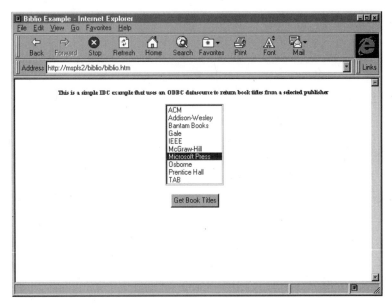

Figure 5-7.
The web page that lists the company names from the biblio database.

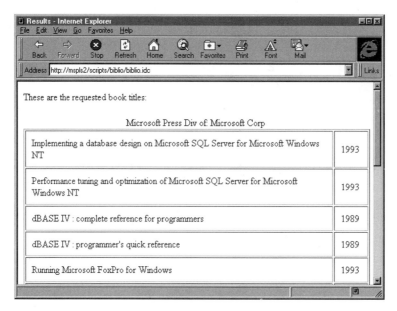

Figure 5-8.
The web page that displays the books of the selected company.

Listing 5-1 shows the HTML file that invokes IDC. Note the ACTION attribute that calls the biblio.idc file. Listing 5-1 and all other full program listings are available on this book's companion CD, in the samples folder.

```
<HTML>
<HEAD>
<TITLE>Biblio Example</TITLE>
</HEAD>
<BODY BGCOLOR="#FFFFFF">

<CENTER><H6>
This is a simple IDC example that uses
an ODBC datasource to return book titles
from a selected publisher
</H6>
<P>

<FORM NAME="frmQuery" METHOD="POST"
ACTION="/scripts/biblio/biblio.idc">
```

Listing 5-1.
The biblio HTML file that invokes IDC.

```
<!--
An intrinsic combo box is used
to hold the selections.  The
NAME attribute is referenced in
the SQL statement defined in the
biblio.idc file.
-->

<SELECT NAME="lstName" SIZE="10">
    <OPTION>ACM
    <OPTION>Addison-Wesley
    <OPTION>Bantam Books
    <OPTION>Gale
    <OPTION>IEEE
    <OPTION>McGraw-Hill
    <OPTION SELECTED>Microsoft Press
    <OPTION>Osborne
    <OPTION>Prentice Hall
    <OPTION>TAB
</SELECT>
<P>

<!--
Clicking on the Submit button sends
all of the form input variables to
the biblio.idc file for processing.
In this case, there is only one
variable, lstName.
-->

<INPUT TYPE="SUBMIT" VALUE="Get Book Titles">
</FORM>
</CENTER>
</BODY>
</HTML>
```

IDC exists in the file httpodbc.dll but is never called directly. Instead, the idc file is called through the ACTION attribute of a form. When IIS is installed, entries are made in the system Registry to associate idc files with the httpodbc.dll file. The system Registry is nothing more than a centralized database on your Windows NT server that stores important application information. In this case, it remembers that when idc files are called, httpodbc.dll should start and read the contents of the idc file. Listing 5-2 (page 132) shows the contents of biblio.idc.

```
Datasource:biblio
Template:c:\inetsrv\scripts\biblio\biblio.htx
SQLStatement:
+SELECT [Company Name],Title,[Year Published]
+FROM Publishers,Titles
+WHERE (Publishers.Name='%lstName%') AND
+(Publishers.PubID=Titles.PubID)
```

Listing 5-2.
The biblio.idc file.

IDC uses the information in biblio.idc to execute a SQL query on the biblio system datasource. (The biblio system datasource name is just an alias for the biblio.mdb database.) Note that the form input variable %lstName% appears in the idc file. Form input variables can be used in idc files to make SQL statements more flexible. In this case, you can return a subset of the book titles contained in the database. The form input variable corresponds exactly to the NAME attribute used in the form in the original HTML file. Several other fields are permitted in idc files. Table 5-1 lists all of the required fields in an idc file.

Table 5-2 lists the optional fields in an idc field. The optional fields are used in the idc file in the following way:

field_name:value

Here is an example of a statement in the idc file that refreshes a cached output page after 60 seconds:

Expires:60

Table 5-3 (page 134) lists the ODBC options available in an idc file. These options allow the user to debug and manipulate the ODBC driver. For more information on these ODBC options, consult the ODBC driver documentation. The ODBC options are used in the idc file in the following way:

ODBCOptions: *option_name1=value1*[, *option_name2=value2*] [...]

Here is an example of a statement in the idc file that aborts any SQL statement that takes over 10 seconds and also enables the tracing of ODBC function calls:

ODBCOptions: SQL_QUERY_TIME=10, SQL_OPT_TRACE=1

For more information, consult the IIS help files available on this book's companion CD.

Table 5-1. Required Fields in an idc File

Field	Description
Datasource	The name of the ODBC system datasource as it appears in the ODBC setup dialog box.
Template	The name of the HTML extension (htx) file that contains the structure for the returned records.
SQLStatement	The SQL statement to be executed. The statement can use form input variables (which are enclosed in % signs). The statement can be several lines long. The + sign is used as a line continuation character.

Table 5-2. Optional Fields in an idc File

Field	Description
ContentType	Any valid MIME (Multipurpose Internet Mail Extensions) type indicating what will be returned to the client. Generally, this is text/html.
DefaultParameters	The parameter values to use if a parameter is not specified by the client. The format is as follows: *param1=value1*[, *param2=value2*][...].
Expires	The number of seconds to wait before the database is requeried and the cached output page refreshed. Output pages are cached only when the Expires field is used.
MaxFieldSize	The maximum size allocated by IDC for each field. If the data exceeds the field size, it is truncated. The default is 8192 bytes.
MaxRecords	The maximum number of records that IDC will return for one query. This has no default value but can return up to 4 billion records.
Password	The password the user must enter to access the database. If password is null, this field does not need to be specified.
RequiredParameters	A list of the parameters that must be passed by the client. If any are missing, IDC will return an error. The required parameters are separated by commas (for example, RequiredParameters: FirstName, LastName).
UserName	A valid user name to access the database. When SQL Server databases are accessed anonymously, IIS uses the user name and password from the anonymous user. By default, the anonymous user is IUSR_*computername*.

Table 5-3. ODBC Options Available in an idc File.

Option	Description
SQL_ACCESS_MODE	0 Read/write
	1 Read-only
SQL_LOGIN_TIMEOUT	The number of seconds to wait for a logon request to complete before terminating the connection.
SQL_MAX_LENGTH	The maximum amount of data that the driver will return from a character or binary column.
SQL_MAX_ROWS	The maximum number of rows that can be returned by a SELECT statement. The default is 0, which causes all rows to be returned.
SQL_NOSCAN	A value that specifies whether the driver should scan SQL strings for escape clauses, which are enclosed by curly braces.
	0 Scan for escape clauses
	1 Do not scan for escape clauses
SQL_OPT_TRACE	0 Trace off
	1 Write ODBC function calls to trace file
SQL_OPT_TRACEFILE	The name of the trace file to use if tracing is enabled. The default is \sql.log
SQL_PACKET_SIZE	The size, in bytes, of the network packet that will be used to exchange information between IIS and the DBMS (database management system).
SQL_QUERY_TIMEOUT	The number of seconds to wait before aborting a SQL query. The default is 0, which indicates no time-out.
SQL_TRANSLATE_DLL	The name of a DLL that contains the functions SQL DriverToDataSource and SQL DataSourceToDriver, loaded by the driver. It can be used for character set translation.
SQL_TRANSLATE_OPTION	An integer value used to control the translation DLL.
SQL_TXN_ISOLATION	An integer that sets the transaction isolation level.
	1 Read uncommitted
	2 Read committed
	4 Repeatable read
	8 Serializable
	16 Versioning
integer	A value that allows driver-specific options to be set (for example, 4322=1, 234=String).

Once the results of the query are obtained, IDC formats them according to the structure provided by the HTML extension file. The htx file is called out in the idc file and contains the template for returned rows. Listing 5-3 shows the complete htx file for this example. The htx file also uses special tags. In particular, the <%begindetail%> and <%enddetail%> tags are used to delineate the structure for returning rows as HTML code.

```
<HTML>
<HEAD>
<TITLE>Results</TITLE>
</HEAD>
<BODY BGCOLOR="#FFFFFF">

These are the requested book titles:

<P>
<CENTER>
<TABLE BORDER CELLPADDING=10>
<CAPTION ALIGN="Top"><%Company Name%></CAPTION>

<!--
The %begindetail% and %enddetail% variables
define the HTML code that is repeated for
each row in the result set.
In this case, the HTML code builds a table for
the results.
-->

<%begindetail%>
    <TR>
        <!--
        In code, you can use
        any field from the
        SQL statement as a variable
        simply by enclosing it in %
        signs
        -->

        <TD COLSPAN=4>

            <!--
            The if...else...endif
            blocks can be used to
```

Listing 5-3. *(continued)*
The biblio.htx file.

Listing 5-3 *continued*

```
                    do special things when a
                    particular item is found
                    -->

                    <%if Title EQ
                        "Inside Microsoft Visual Basic, Scripting Edition"%>
                        <FONT COLOR="#FF0000">
                        <%TITLE%>
                        </FONT>
                    <%else%>
                        <%Title%>
                    <%endif%>
                </TD>
                <TD>
                <%Year Published%>
                </TD>
            </TR>
<%enddetail%>

</TABLE>
</CENTER>
</BODY>
</HTML>
```

Because a query returns an indeterminate number of rows, you cannot specify an exact structure in an HTML extension file. Instead, you use the special tags <%begindetail%> and <%enddetail%> to create a loop through which IDC travels when building the returned web page. For each row in the result, IDC builds a template identical to the HTML specified between the detail tags. Note that within the detail tags you can access any field returned by the results for display.

HTML extension files also support program flow. For example, biblio.htx uses the special tags <%if%>, <%else%>, and <%endif%> to take special action if one of the returned book titles is *Inside Microsoft Visual Basic, Scripting Edition.* If the book is part of the result set, the book title will be colored red when it is displayed. You can use this type of code to take action when any desired record is returned. Table 5-4 lists the tags and variables available in HTML extension files. There are also several HTTP variables that are available in HTML extension files. HTTP variables can provide information about the server environment and the client connected to the server. Table 5-5 lists the HTTP variables available in HTML extension files. For more information, consult the IIS help files available on this book's companion CD.

Table 5-4. Tags and Variables Available in HTML Extension Files

Tag or Variable	Description
<%begindetail%> <%enddetail%>	These tags are used to specify a section of the HTML extension file in which data from the database will be merged.
<%*field_name*%>	This tag is used to mark where the data for the specified field will be placed.
<%if%> <%else%> <%endif%>	These tags are used for conditional control in the HTML extension file. Here is the syntax: <%if *condition*%> *HTML code* [<%else%> *HTML code*] <%endif%> Here is the format of condition: *value1 operator value2* Here are the available operators: EQ Equals LT Less than GT Greater than CONTAINS Contains the string
CurrentRecord	This returns the number of times the <%begindetail%> section has been processed. The first time through the section, the value is zero.
MaxRecords	This returns the maximum number of records as specified in the idc file. It can be used only with the tag <%if%>.
Form input variables	Any form input variable used in the idc file can be accessed by the htx file using the syntax <%idc.*variable*%>.

Table 5-5. HTTP Variables Available in HTML Extension Files

HTTP Variable	Description
ALL_HTTP	All HTTP headers that were not parsed into variables
AUTH_TYPE	The type of authentication used by IIS
CONTENT_LENGTH	The number of bytes the script can expect to receive from the client
CONTENT_TYPE	The content type of information supplied in the body of a POST request
GATEWAY_INTERFACE	The version of the CGI used by the server

(continued)

Table 5-5 *continued*

HTTP Variable	Description
HTTP_ACCEPT	A special-case HTTP header.
PATH_INFO	Additional path information from the client. This consists of the part of the URL that comes after the script name but before the query string, if one exists.
PATH_TRANSLATED	The PATH_INFO, but with any virtual path expanded into a directory specification.
QUERY_STRING	The string following the question mark in the URL that called the script.
REMOTE_ADDR	The client's IP address.
REMOTE_HOST	The client's host name.
REMOTE_USER	The user name of the client.
REQUEST_METHOD	POST or GET.
SCRIPT_NAME	The name of the currently executing script.
SERVER_NAME	The server's host name or IP address.
SERVER_PORT	The TCP/IP port that received the request.
SERVER_PROTOCOL	The name and version of the protocol related to the request (typically HTTP/1.0).
SERVER_SOFTWARE	The name and version of the server running IIS.

Detailed IDC Examples

The following examples show in detail how the Internet Database Connector can be used to interface with a database from a web page. The code and the Access databases for each example are available on the companion CD included with this book. However, if you wanted to target other ODBC sources, such as SQL Server, you would use the same techniques.

The User Group Event Registration Example

The first example uses IDC to display a list of upcoming events for a Visual Basic user group. When the events are displayed, the user is invited to register for any event. After registering, the user is given a confirmation screen showing his or her name and the event for which he or she is registered.

On the initial web page, the user simply sees a button. Clicking on the button displays the events that are contained in the database. As the database is updated, the events page is automatically updated. Figure 5-9 shows the initial web page, and Listing 5-4 shows the code for implementing the web page.

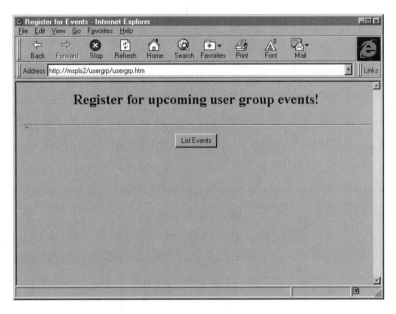

Figure 5-9.
The initial web page for the user group registration example.

```
<HTML>
<HEAD>
<TITLE>Register for Events</TITLE>
</HEAD>

<BODY>
<CENTER><H2>Register for upcoming user group events!</H2></CENTER>
<P>
<HR>
<CENTER>
```

Listing 5-4.   *(continued)*
usergrp.htm.

Listing 5-4 *continued*

```
<!--
This form is used to run the
SQL query that returns all
the events in the database
-->

<FORM NAME="frmEvents" METHOD="POST"
ACTION="/scripts/usergrp/events.idc">
<INPUT TYPE="SUBMIT" VALUE="List Events">
</FORM>

</CENTER>
</BODY>
</HTML>
```

The button invokes the idc file, shown in Listing 5-5, which runs a SQL statement returning all of the events. The results are formatted according to the htx file shown in Listing 5-6.

```
Datasource:usergrp
Template:c:\inetsrv\scripts\usergrp\events.htx
SQLStatement:SELECT * FROM Events
```

Listing 5-5.
events.idc.

```
<HTML>
<HEAD>
<TITLE>Upcoming Events</TITLE>
</HEAD>
<BODY BGCOLOR="#FFFFFF">
<CENTER>

<H2>Here are the upcoming events!!</H2>
<P>

<!--
The events in the database are returned
in a table format so that they can all
be easily browsed
```

Listing 5-6.
events.htx.

```
-->

<TABLE BORDER>
    <TR>
        <TH>Event ID</TH>
        <TH>Event Name</TH>
        <TH>Date</TH>
        <TH COLSPAN=3>Description</TH>
    </TR>
<%begindetail%>
    <TR>
        <TH><%EventID%></TH>
        <TH><%EventName%></TH>
        <TD><%EventDate%></TD>
        <TD COLSPAN=3><%EventDescription%></TD>
    </TR>
<%enddetail%>
</TABLE>

<!--
Now that the user has the results,
let the user register, using another form.
This method of cascading forms in htx
files to call idc files can be used
again and again.
-->

<HR>
<P>
<H2>Register Online!</H2>

<FORM NAME="frmRegister" METHOD="POST"
ACTION="/scripts/usergrp/register.idc">
Name
<INPUT TYPE="Text" NAME="txtName"><P>
Email Address
<INPUT TYPE="Text" NAME="txtEmail"><P>
Event ID
<INPUT TYPE="Text" NAME="txtEvent"><P>
<INPUT TYPE="SUBMIT" VALUE="Register">
<INPUT TYPE="RESET">
</FORM>

</CENTER>
</BODY>
</HTML>
```

After the events have been listed in a table, the user can immediately use another form to register for any event. Note how we use cascading forms in the htx file to call the idc file again and again. This is a good strategy for working through a database transaction with a user. Figure 5-10 shows a sample of the events and registration page.

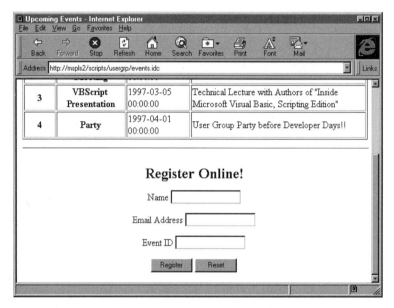

Figure 5-10.
The events and registration page for the user group registration example.

Listings 5-7 and 5-8 show the details of the event registration process. A simple SQL INSERT statement is used to store the user's information in the database.

```
Datasource:usergrp
Template:c:\inetsrv\scripts\usergrp\register.htx
SQLStatement:
+INSERT INTO Attendees
+(AttendeeName,AttendeeEmail,EventID)
+VALUES ('%txtName%','%txtEmail%','%txtEvent%')
```

Listing 5-7.
register.idc.

```
<HTML>
<HEAD>
<TITLE>Members Attending</TITLE>
</HEAD>
<BODY BGCOLOR="#FFFFFF">
<CENTER>

<!--
A confirmation screen
-->

<H2>
<%idc.txtName%> is registered for Event #<%idc.txtEvent%>
</H2>

</CENTER>
</BODY>
</HTML>
```

Listing 5-8.
register.htx.

The Product Showcase Example

The product showcase example displays photographs of three different products that are available from a company. The photos are links that can invoke the Internet Database Connector when clicked. You access IDC directly through the <A></A> anchor tags by using the HREF attribute. When you access IDC through an anchor, you can pass the data for the SQL query directly, using a ? to separate the call from the data. The following code passes the value Software through the form input variable Product to an idc file called buy.idc:

```
<A HREF="http://NT_SERVER/scripts/buy.idc?Product=Software">
</A>
```

Using anchor tags to invoke IDC allows you to create a "point-and-click" interface, which is easier to use than the standard text-boxes-and-buttons interface.

Figure 5-11 (page 144) shows a sample of the initial web page for the product showcase example. Listing 5-9 contains the HTML code to display the products and set up the links that can invoke IDC.

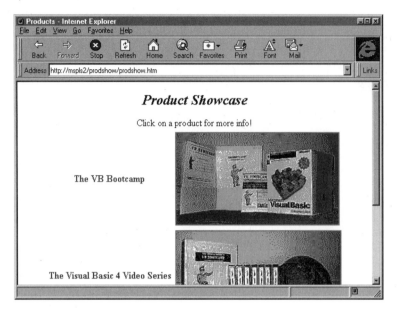

Figure 5-11.
The initial web page for the product showcase example.

```
<HTML>
<HEAD>
<TITLE>Products</TITLE>
</HEAD>

<!--
This example shows photos of products
and allows the user to order them
-->

<BODY BGCOLOR="#FFFFFF">
<CENTER>
<H2><EM>Product Showcase</EM></H2>

<!--
Note that the HREF attribute of the anchor tag
is used to invoke IDC.  You pass a parameter
to IDC by using the ? operator.
-->
```

Listing 5-9.
prodshow.htm.

```
<TABLE>
    <CAPTION>Click on a product for more info!</CAPTION>
    <TR>
        <TH>
        <FONT COLOR="#008000">The VB Bootcamp</FONT>
        </TH>
        <TD>
        <A HREF=
        "/scripts/prodshow/order.idc?txtCode=Training">
        <IMG SRC="product1.jpg" ALT="Training">
        </A>
        </TD>
    </TR>
    <TR>
        <TH>
        <FONT COLOR="#008000">The Visual Basic 4 Video Series</FONT>
        </TH>
        <TD>
        <A HREF=
        "/scripts/prodshow/order.idc?txtCode=Videos">
        <IMG SRC="product2.jpg" ALT="Videos">
        </A>
        </TD>
    </TR>
    <TR>
        <TH>
        <FONT COLOR="#008000">Attila/VB</FONT>
        </TH>
        <TD>
        <A HREF=
        "/scripts/prodshow/order.idc?txtCode=Attila">
        <IMG SRC="product3.jpg" ALT="Attila/VB">
        </A>
        </TD>
    </TR>
</TABLE>

</CENTER>
</BODY>
</HTML>
```

After the user has selected a product, an order form is presented. When the user has completed the order form, IDC is invoked again to save the information, allowing the company to fill the order at a later date. Figure 5-12 shows a sample of the order form. Listing 5-10 shows the idc file used to return the product information, and Listing 5-11 shows the htx file used to display the order form.

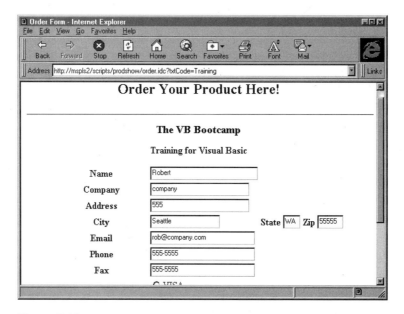

Figure 5-12.
A sample order form for the product showcase example.

```
Datasource:prodshow
Template:c:\inetsrv\scripts\prodshow\order.htx
SQLStatement:
+SELECT * FROM Products WHERE Code='%txtCode%'
```

Listing 5-10.
order.idc.

```
<HTML>
<HEAD>
<TITLE>Order Form</TITLE>
</HEAD>
```

Listing 5-11.
order.htx.

```
<BODY BGCOLOR="#FFFFFF">
<CENTER>

<H2>Order Your Product Here!</H2>

<P>
<HR>
<P>

<!--
Note that the field names from
the SQL statement can be used directly
in the HTML page generated by the htx
file
-->

<H3><%Product Name%></H3>
<P>
<H4><%ProductDescription%></H4>
<P>

<SCRIPT LANGUAGE="VBScript">
<!--
    'This routine is used to return
    'to the Product Showcase page
    'when the user clicks on the Exit
    'button.  Notice the use of the
    'Navigate method, which can be
    'called directly in VBScript.

    Sub btnExit_OnClick
        Navigate "/prodshow/prodshow.htm"
    End Sub
-->
</SCRIPT>

<!--
This HTML generates the order
form for actually purchasing the
product
-->

<FORM NAME="frmOrder" METHOD="POST"
ACTION="/scripts/prodshow/purchase.idc">
```

(continued)

147

Listing 5-11 *continued*

```
<TABLE>
    <TR>
        <TH>Name</TH>
        <TD><INPUT TYPE="Text" SIZE=33
            NAME="txtName"></TD>
    </TR>
    <TR>
        <TH>Company</TH>
        <TD><INPUT TYPE="Text" SIZE=30
            NAME="txtCompany"></TD>
    </TR>
    <TR>
        <TH>Address</TH>
        <TD><INPUT TYPE="Text" SIZE=30
            NAME="txtAddress"></TD>
    </TR>
    <TR>
        <TH>City</TH>
        <TD><INPUT TYPE="Text" SIZE=20
            NAME="txtCity"></TD>
        <TH>State</TH>
        <TD><INPUT TYPE="Text" SIZE=2
            NAME="txtState"></TD>
        <TH>Zip</TH>
        <TD><INPUT TYPE="Text" SIZE=5
            NAME="txtZip"></TD>
    </TR>
    <TR>
        <TH>Email</TH>
        <TD><INPUT TYPE="Text" SIZE=32
            NAME="txtEmail"></TD>
    </TR>
    <TR>
        <TH>Phone</TH>
        <TD><INPUT TYPE="Text" SIZE=32
            NAME="txtPhone"></TD>
    </TR>
    <TR>
        <TH>Fax</TH>
        <TD><INPUT TYPE="Text" SIZE=32
            NAME="txtFax"></TD>
    </TR>
    <TR>
        <TH>Credit Card Information</TH>
        <TD ROWSPAN=6>
```

```
                <INPUT TYPE="RADIO" NAME="optCard"
                    VALUE="VISA">VISA<BR>
                <INPUT TYPE="RADIO" NAME="optCard"
                    VALUE="MC">MasterCard<BR>
                <INPUT TYPE="RADIO" NAME="optCard"
                    VALUE="AMEX">American Express<BR>
                <P>
                Expiration Date
                <INPUT TYPE="Text" SIZE=10 NAME="txtExpDate">
            </TR>
</TABLE>

<!--
We use a hidden field here to hold
the name of the product the user will
purchase. The value of the hidden field
depends on the product that was clicked
on the Showcase page. Note how you can
access form input variables that were
referenced in the idc file by using
the idc prefix.
-->

<%if idc.txtCode EQ "Training"%>
    <INPUT TYPE="HIDDEN" NAME="txtProduct"
        VALUE="VB Bootcamp">
<%endif%>

<%if idc.txtCode EQ "Videos"%>
    <INPUT TYPE="HIDDEN" NAME="txtProduct"
        VALUE="VB4 Video Series">
<%endif%>

<%if idc.txtCode EQ "Attila"%>
    <INPUT TYPE="HIDDEN" NAME="txtProduct"
        VALUE="Attila/VB">
<%endif%>

<P>
<INPUT TYPE="SUBMIT" VALUE="Purchase">
<INPUT TYPE="RESET">
<INPUT TYPE="BUTTON" NAME="btnExit" VALUE="Exit">
</FORM>

</CENTER>
</BODY>
</HTML>
```

After the Purchase button has been clicked and the information is stored in the database, we display a confirmation screen for the user that allows him or her to return to the Product Showcase screen. Figure 5-13 shows a sample of the confirmation screen. Listing 5-12 shows the idc file invoked to write the purchase information to the database, and Listing 5-13 shows the htx file that presents the confirmation screen.

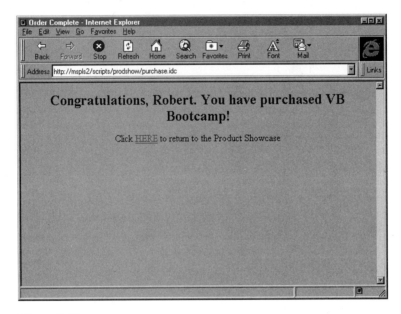

Figure 5-13.
A sample confirmation screen for the product showcase example.

```
Datasource:prodshow
Template:c:\inetsrv\scripts\prodshow\purchase.htx
SQLStatement:
+INSERT INTO orders
+(Name,Company,Address,City,State,Zip
+,Email,Phone,Fax,CreditCard,ExpDate,Product)
+VALUES
+('%txtName%','%txtCompany%','%txtAddress%',
+'%txtCity%','%txtState%','%txtZip%','%txtEmail%'
+,'%txtPhone%','%txtFax%','%optCard%','%txtExpDate%'
+,'%txtProduct%')
```

Listing 5-12.
purchase.idc.

```
<HTML>
<HEAD>
<TITLE>Order Complete</TITLE>
</HEAD>
<BODY>
<CENTER>

<!--
This is a simple confirmation screen
-->

<H2>Congratulations, <%idc.txtName%>. You
have purchased <%idc.txtProduct%>!</H2>
<P>

Click <A HREF="/prodshow/prodshow.htm">HERE</A> to return
to the Product Showcase

</CENTER>
</BODY>
</HTML>
```

Listing 5-13.
purchase.htx.

The Members-Only Page Example

The last example in this section creates a members-only page that requires an account name and a password for entry. A database is checked for records matching the account name and password combination. If the combination exists, access is allowed. Otherwise, a message box is displayed and the user is returned to the login page. This example takes advantage of the fact that the <%begindetail%> <%enddetail%> section is not executed if no records are returned from a query. The example also uses an inline VBScript variable as a flag to check and see whether records were returned. Figure 5-14 (page 152) shows a sample of the initial members-only web page. Figure 5-15 (page 152) shows a sample web page that is displayed if the proper account name and password are entered. Beginning on page 153, Listings 5-14 through 5-16 show the code.

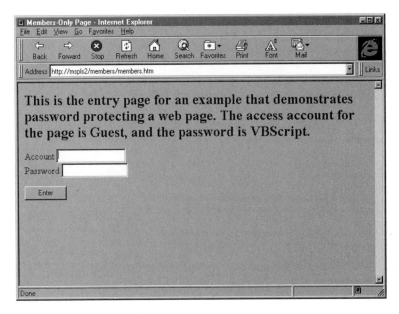

Figure 5-14.
The entry web page for the members-only example.

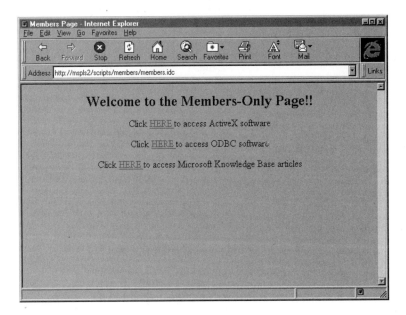

Figure 5-15.
A sample web page that is displayed when the proper account name and password are entered.

```
<HTML>
<HEAD>
<TITLE>Members-Only Page</TITLE>
</HEAD>
</BODY>
</CENTER>

<H2>This is the entry page for an
example that demonstrates password
protecting a web page. The access
account for the page is Guest, and
the password is VBScript.</H2>

<FORM NAME="frmMember" METHOD="POST"
ACTION="/scripts/members/members.idc">
Account
<INPUT TYPE="TEXT" SIZE=20 NAME="txtAccount"><BR>
Password
<INPUT TYPE="PASSWORD" SIZE=19 NAME="txtPassword"><P>
<INPUT TYPE="SUBMIT" VALUE="Enter"><P>
</FORM>

</CENTER>
</BODY>
</HTML>
```

Listing 5-14.
members.htm.

```
Datasource:members
Template:c:\inetsrv\scripts\members\members.htx
SQLStatement:
+SELECT * FROM Passwords WHERE Account='%txtAccount%'
+AND Password='%txtPassword%'
```

Listing 5-15.
members.idc.

```
<HTML>
<HEAD>
<TITLE>Members Page</TITLE>
</HEAD>
```

Listing 5-16.
members.htx.

(continued)

153

Listing 5-16 *continued*

```
<BODY>

<!--
This file is used to generate
the Members-Only page if the
account and password are
correct
-->

<SCRIPT LANGUAGE="VBScript">
<!--
    'A variable is declared inline
    'to be used as a flag to determine
    'whether access is denied

    Dim blnAccess
    blnAccess=False
-->
</SCRIPT>

<!--
Only one record is expected
for this.  If no records are
returned, the %begindetail%
section is skipped.
-->

<%begindetail%>
    <%if CurrentRecord EQ 0%>

        <!--
        Note how we use the FTP protocol
        here to allow downloading of files
        -->

        <CENTER>
        <H2>Welcome to the Members-Only Page!!</H2>
        Click <A HREF=
        "ftp://ftp.microsoft.com/msdownload/activex/">
        HERE </A> to access ActiveX software<P>
        Click <A HREF=
        "ftp://ftp.microsoft.com/developr/odbc/public/">
        HERE </A> to access ODBC software<P>
```

```
    Click <A HREF=
    "ftp://ftp.microsoft.com/kbhelp/">
    HERE </A> to access Microsoft Knowledge Base articles<P>
    </CENTER>

    <SCRIPT LANGUAGE="VBScript">
    <!--
        'Set the flag to
        'True if a record
        'was returned

        blnAccess=True
    -->
    </SCRIPT>

<%endif%>
<%enddetail%>

<SCRIPT LANGUAGE="VBScript">
<!--
    'The flag is checked inline
    'and action is taken if access
    'is denied.  A message is displayed,
    'and the user is sent to the
    'original page.

    If blnAccess=False Then
        MsgBox "Access Denied",16,"Members-Only"
        Navigate "/members/members.htm"
    End If
-->
</SCRIPT>

</BODY>
</HTML>
```

OLEISAPI

OLEISAPI is designed to allow web page users to access the functionality of software components on IIS. OLEISAPI is implemented in a DLL called oleisapi.dll. Although IDC is useful for accessing ODBC datasources, its functionality is strictly limited to databases. You will often want to create additional interactive functionality for web pages that goes beyond simple data access.

OLEISAPI provides the means for employing the additional functionality. The oleisapi.dll file is a DLL that allows users to access in-process ActiveX components (formerly called OLE servers) on IIS from a web page.

ActiveX components are software components that can expose their properties and methods to client applications that are using Automation. ActiveX components come in two different varieties: out-of-process components and in-process components. An out-of-process ActiveX component is a stand-alone application that runs in its own memory space. The application might have a user interface, or it might run without a GUI. For example, using Automation, a Visual Basic application can access Microsoft Project's calendar functionality. In this case, Project is the ActiveX component and Visual Basic is the client application. An in-process component runs in the same memory space as the client application. It remains resident in the memory of the client throughout the session.

Because in-process ActiveX components can be created directly in the 32-bit versions of Visual Basic and C++, OLEISAPI provides the web developer with an incredibly powerful mechanism for accessing the complete functionality of these development tools. Not only can OLEISAPI be used to access data, it can also be used to provide complex mathematical functionality or improved algorithms that are not possible with HTML alone.

Setting Up OLEISAPI

The first step in implementing OLEISAPI in your HTML page is to obtain the DLL called oleisapi.dll. The OLEISAPI DLL does not ship with IIS but is typically available for downloading from Microsoft's web site. When you download the DLL, it is a collection of C++ files. In order to use OLEISAPI, you will have to compile the files into a DLL using C++. If you do not have C++, you can obtain a compiled version of oleisapi.dll from the New Technology Solutions, Inc., web site at http://www.vb-bootcamp.com or from the companion CD included with this book.

After you obtain a copy of oleisapi.dll, you typically place it in the scripts folder of the Internet Information Server. The scripts folder is a special folder in which executable files are placed. In IIS, when a folder is designated as *executable*, files are not read from the folder, as is normal for HTML. Instead, applications in the folder are executed when they are called. The Execute property can be set in the Directory Properties dialog box, which is available from within the IIS service manager. Figure 5-16 shows the Directory Properties dialog box for the scripts folder with the Execute check box selected. By default, the Execute property is set for the scripts folder.

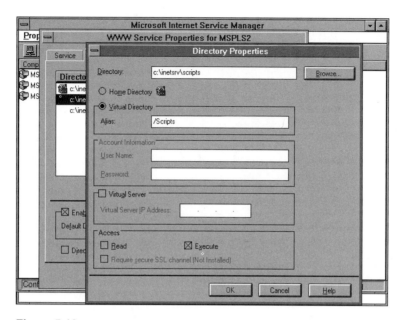

Figure 5-16.
The IIS Directory Properties dialog box.

KEY CONCEPT: The oleisapi.dll file *must* be located in an execute-enabled directory of IIS.

Once you have oleisapi.dll in the scripts folder, you can create an in-process ActiveX component to use with it. In-process ActiveX components can easily be created in the 32-bit version of Visual Basic 4.0.

Building an ActiveX Component in Visual Basic 4.0 for Use with OLEISAPI

Although this book is not designed to teach Visual Basic programming skills, using Visual Basic with the Internet Information Server is a powerful approach that deserves detailed treatment. Because many readers might not be familiar with ActiveX component construction, this section will discuss the concepts involved in building a simple in-process ActiveX component for use with OLEISAPI. Some fundamental knowledge of the Visual Basic Integrated Debugging Environment (VBIDE) is assumed.

When you are creating an in-process ActiveX component in Visual Basic, several requirements must be met. First, an ActiveX component requires at least one *public, creatable* class module. Public, creatable class modules are implemented using the properties of the Visual Basic class module. The Public property should be set to True, and the Instancing property should be set to Creatable Multi-Use. See your Visual Basic documentation for further explanation of the Public and Creatable properties.

For an ActiveX component to be usable with OLEISAPI, it must have a Public method that accepts two arguments. The arguments are both string data types: one is the request string sent by the client, and one is the return string sent by the ActiveX component back to the client. This is the fundamental operation of OLEISAPI. OLEISAPI passes arguments to the ActiveX component, which creates an HTML string for display in the client.

KEY CONCEPT: The method used by OLEISAPI must meet the following requirements:

❑ It can have any name, but it *must* be public.

❑ It *must* accept two arguments.

❑ Both accepted arguments *must* be string data types.

❑ Both accepted arguments *must* be passed by reference.

The request string is structured as a concatenation of the form input variables and their values. Specifically, the string is passed as *Field=Value*. In the ActiveX component, you must use Visual Basic code to parse the string to find the fields and values passed.

Once you have decoded the request string, you can use any algorithm you need to create an HTML page as the return string. The return string is formatted as standard HTML.

After you have completed all the necessary Visual Basic coding, you will need to create an ActiveX component. In Visual Basic 4.0, you do this by selecting Make OLE DLL File from the File menu. This action will create a DLL file. For further information, consult your documentation.

After you build your in-process ActiveX component, it must be registered on the Windows NT server. Registering your component places important information about the DLL in the Windows NT system Registry. If the DLL is created with Visual Basic on the Windows NT server, the component is automatically registered. Otherwise, to register your component you will need a copy of the registration utility regsvr32.exe. The registration utility will write the information about your component to the system Registry. The registration utility can typically be found in the clisvr folder of any Visual Basic 4.0 32-bit installation. The registration utility can be executed from MS-DOS or from the Windows Run command using the following syntax:

drive:\path regsvr32 *drive:\path\myserver*.dll

KEY CONCEPT: For an in-process ActiveX component to be usable with oleisapi.dll, it *must*

❑ Have at least one public, creatable class module

❑ Have at least one public method that accepts two string arguments

❑ Be properly registered in the system Registry

Finally, to call OLEISAPI from your web page, you will need a form with the ACTION attribute set to call oleisapi.dll. The argument for the ACTION attribute must invoke OLEISAPI and provide the name of the ActiveX component, the public class module, and the method to call. Here is how this is typically formatted in HTML:

```
<FORM
ACTION="[oleisapi path]/oleisapi.dll/[DLL name].[class name].[method]"
METHOD="[POST or GET]">
<INPUT ...
</FORM>
```

Assuming you have put oleisapi.dll in the scripts folder of your IIS installation and have properly registered the ActiveX component, the HTML that follows shows an example of how OLEISAPI is invoked and a component named *parser* is called. Parser has a public class module named *echo* and a public method named *process,* which will receive a request and return a string.

```
<FORM
ACTION="/scripts/oleisapi.dll/parser.echo.process"
METHOD="POST">
<INPUT TYPE="Text" NAME="Name">
<INPUT TYPE="Text" NAME="Address">
<INPUT TYPE="Text" NAME="Phone">
</FORM>
```

Assuming that the values for the Name, Address, and Phone fields are Scot, Washington Ave, and 2035551212, the following string would be passed to the component named *parser.*

```
Name=Scot&Address=Washington+Ave&Phone=2035551212
```

This string can then be parsed and a return string generated. If you wanted to simply return the parsed values in a table, the return string might look like the following:

```
"Content-Type: text/html" & vbCrLf & vbCrLf _
& </TABLE><TR><TD>" & Field1 & "</TD><TD>" & Value1 _
```

```
& </TD></TR><TR><TD>" & Field2 & "</TD><TD>" & Value2 _
& </TD></TR><TR><TD>" & Field3 & "</TD><TD>" & Value3 _
& </TD></TR></TABLE>"
```

The next several pages describe the code for creating a simple in-process
ActiveX component to exercise oleisapi.dll. You will need the 32-bit version of
Visual Basic 4.0 to write the ActiveX component, or you can use the completed
component, named *parser*, located on the companion CD.

A Simple OLEISAPI Parsing Example

Let's consider the code for an example that creates a simple OLEISAPI DLL
that performs parsing. The DLL receives arguments from the web page and
parses them. The parsed arguments are echoed back to the client and displayed. Although relatively simple, these techniques are the cornerstones for
each project you create.

Figure 5-17 shows a sample of the initial web page, and Figure 5-18 shows
a sample of output.

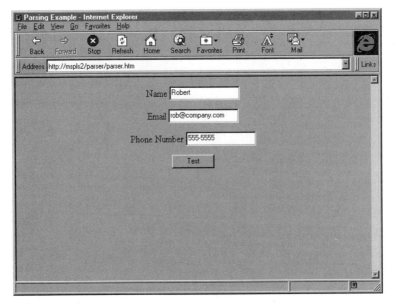

Figure 5-17.
The initial web page for the parsing example.

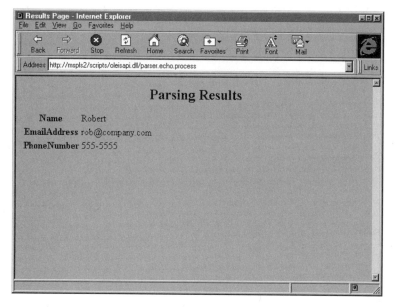

Figure 5-18.
The output displayed for the parsing example.

The following Visual Basic code is implemented in the echo class module. This code accepts the request string from OLEISAPI, calls the parsing subroutine, and then passes the results of the parsing subroutine to a function that creates the HTML.

```
Public Sub Process(strRequest As String, strReturn As String)

On Error GoTo ProcessErr:

    ReDim arrArgVal(0) As String

    'Parse the incoming string
    Call sParseRequest(strRequest, arrArgVal())

    'Return the HTML page to the browser
    strReturn = fCreateHTML(arrArgVal())

ProcessExit:
    Exit Sub

ProcessErr:
    strReturn = fCreateHTMLError(Err.Number, Err.Description)
    Resume ProcessExit

End Sub
```

The following pages show the echo class module code necessary to parse the request string into fields and values. This code can be used in any ActiveX component for parsing HTML fields and is an integral part of other examples in this book:

```
Private Sub sParseRequest(strRequest, arrArgVal() As String)

On Error GoTo ParseRequestErr

    'Incoming string is in the format
    'Argument1=Value1&Argument2=Value2

    Dim intIndex As Integer
    Dim intPosition As Integer
    Dim intStart As Integer
    Dim strParse As String
    Dim strTemp As String

    intIndex = 0
    intStart = 1
    Do While InStr(intStart, strRequest, "=", 1) > 0
        intIndex = intIndex + 1
        ReDim Preserve arrArgVal(intIndex + 1)

        'Search for = and get argument name
        intPosition = InStr(intStart, strRequest, "=", 1)
        arrArgVal(intIndex) = Mid$(strRequest, intStart, _
            intPosition - intStart)
        intIndex = intIndex + 1
        intStart = intPosition + 1
        intPosition = InStr(intStart, strRequest, "&", 1)

        'Search for & and get value
        If intPosition > 0 Then
            arrArgVal(intIndex) = Mid$(strRequest, intStart, _
                intPosition - intStart)
            intStart = intPosition + 1
        Else
            arrArgVal(intIndex) = Right$(strRequest, _
                Len(strRequest) - intStart + 1)
            intStart = Len(strRequest)
        End If
    Loop
    For intIndex = 1 To UBound(arrArgVal)

        'This loop cleans up each entry.
        'Plus signs are used as spaces, and
```

```
                'ASCII characters are in hex notation,
                'preceded by a % sign.

                strTemp = ""
                intPosition = 1
                Do
                    Select Case Mid$(arrArgVal(intIndex), intPosition, 1)
                        Case "+"
                            strTemp = strTemp & " "
                            intPosition = intPosition + 1
                        Case "%"
                            strTemp = strTemp & Chr$(Val("&H" & _
                                Mid$(arrArgVal(intIndex), _
                                intPosition + 1, 2)))
                            intPosition = intPosition + 3
                        Case Else
                            strTemp = strTemp & Mid$(arrArgVal(intIndex), _
                                intPosition, 1)
                            intPosition = intPosition + 1
                    End Select
                Loop While intPosition <= Len(arrArgVal(intIndex))
                arrArgVal(intIndex) = strTemp
            Next

ParseRequestExit:
        Exit Sub

ParseRequestErr:
        ReDim arrArgValue(4)
        arrArgValue(1) = "Error"
        arrArgValue(2) = Err.Description
        arrArgValue(3) = "Number"
        arrArgValue(4) = Format$(Err.Number)
        Resume ParseRequestExit

End Sub
```

The following echo class module code is used to return an error page to the browser if the ActiveX component fails:

```
Private Function fCreateHTMLError(lngNumber As Long, strDescription
As String) As String

Dim strHTML As String

strHTML = "Content-type: text/html" & vbCrLf & vbCrLf
strHTML = strHTML & _
    "<HTML><HEAD><TITLE>Error Report</TITLE></HEAD><BODY>"
strHTML = "<H2><CENTER>OLEISAPI ERROR!</CENTER></H2><P>"
```

```
strHTML = strHTML & "<TABLE><TR><TH>NUMBER</TH><TD>" & _
    Format$(lngNumber) & "</TD></TR>"
strHTML = strHTML & "<TR><TH>DESCRIPTION</TH><TD>" & _
    strDescription & "</TD></TR>"
strHTML = strHTML & "</TABLE></BODY></HTML>"
fCreateHTMLError = strHTML
End Function
```

Listing 5-17 and Listing 5-18 show the full program listings for the parsing example. Listing 5-17 shows the HTML code, and Listing 5-18 shows the Visual Basic code for the echo class module, which is available in the samples folder of the companion CD.

```
<HTML>
<HEAD>
<TITLE>Parsing Example</TITLE>
</HEAD>
<BODY>
<CENTER>

<FORM METHOD="POST"
ACTION="/scripts/oleisapi.dll/parser.echo.process">
Name
<INPUT TYPE="Text" NAME="Name"><P>
Email
<INPUT TYPE="Text" NAME="EmailAddress"><P>
Phone Number
<INPUT TYPE="Text" NAME="PhoneNumber"><P>
<INPUT TYPE="SUBMIT" VALUE="Test">
</FORM>

</CENTER>
</BODY>
</HTML>
```

Listing 5-17.
HTML code for the parsing example.

```
Option Explicit

Public Sub Process(strRequest As String, strReturn As String)

'Author: New Technology Solutions, Inc.
'Purpose: Receive a call from OLEISAPI
```

Listing 5-18.
The echo class Visual Basic code for the parsing example.

```
'5/1/96 Original

On Error GoTo ProcessErr

    ReDim arrArgVal(0) As String

    'Parse the incoming string
    Call sParseRequest(strRequest, arrArgVal())

    'Return the HTML page to the browser
    strReturn = fCreateHTML(arrArgVal())

ProcessExit:
    Exit Sub

ProcessErr:
    strReturn = fCreateHTMLError(Err.Number, Err.Description)
    Resume ProcessExit

End Sub

Private Sub sParseRequest(strRequest, arrArgVal() As String)

'Author: New Technology Solutions, Inc.
'Purpose: Parse request string into entries in array
'5/1/96 Original

On Error GoTo ParseRequestErr

    'Incoming string is in the format
    'Argument1=Value1&Argument2=Value2

    Dim intIndex As Integer
    Dim intPosition As Integer
    Dim intStart As Integer
    Dim strParse As String
    Dim strTemp As String

    intIndex = 0
    intStart = 1
    Do While InStr(intStart, strRequest, "=", 1) > 0
        intIndex = intIndex + 1
        ReDim Preserve arrArgVal(intIndex + 1)

        'Search for = and get argument name
        intPosition = InStr(intStart, strRequest, "=", 1)
```

(continued)

Listing 5-18 *continued*

```
        arrArgVal(intIndex) = Mid$(strRequest, intStart, _
            intPosition - intStart)
        intIndex = intIndex + 1
        intStart = intPosition + 1
        intPosition = InStr(intStart, strRequest, "&", 1)

        'Search for & and get value
        If intPosition > 0 Then
            arrArgVal(intIndex) = Mid$(strRequest, intStart, _
                intPosition - intStart)
            intStart = intPosition + 1
        Else
            arrArgVal(intIndex) = Right$(strRequest, _
                Len(strRequest) - intStart + 1)
            intStart = Len(strRequest)
        End If
Loop
For intIndex = 1 To UBound(arrArgVal)

    'This loop cleans up each entry.
    'Plus signs are used as spaces, and
    'ASCII characters are in hex notation,
    'preceded by a % sign.

    strTemp = ""
    intPosition = 1
    Do
        Select Case Mid$(arrArgVal(intIndex), intPosition, 1)
            Case "+"
                strTemp = strTemp & " "
                intPosition = intPosition + 1
            Case "%"
                strTemp = strTemp & Chr$(Val("&H" & _
                    Mid$(arrArgVal(intIndex), _
                    intPosition + 1, 2)))
                intPosition = intPosition + 3
            Case Else
                strTemp = strTemp & Mid$(arrArgVal(intIndex), _
                    intPosition, 1)
                intPosition = intPosition + 1
        End Select
    Loop While intPosition <= Len(arrArgVal(intIndex))
    arrArgVal(intIndex) = strTemp
Next
```

```
ParseRequestExit:
    Exit Sub

ParseRequestErr:
    ReDim arrArgValue(4)
    arrArgValue(1) = "Error"
    arrArgValue(2) = Err.Description
    arrArgValue(3) = "Number"
    arrArgValue(4) = Format$(Err.Number)
    Resume ParseRequestExit

End Sub

Private Function fCreateHTMLError(lngNumber As Long, _
    strDescription As String) As String

'Author: New Technology Solutions, Inc.
'Purpose: Create an HTML page describing an error
'5/1/96 Original

    Dim strHTML As String

    strHTML = strHTML = "Content-Type: text/html" & vbCrLf & vbCrLf
    strHTML = strHTML & _
        "<HTML><HEAD><TITLE>Error Report</TITLE></HEAD><BODY>"
    strHTML = "<H2><CENTER>OLEISAPI ERROR!</CENTER></H2><P>"
    strHTML = strHTML & "<TABLE><TR><TH>NUMBER</TH><TD>" & _
        Format$(lngNumber) & "</TD></TR>"
    strHTML = strHTML & "<TR><TH>DESCRIPTION</TH><TD>" & _
        strDescription & "</TD></TR>"
    strHTML = strHTML & "</TABLE></BODY></HTML>"
    fCreateHTMLError = strHTML
End Function

Private Function fCreateHTML(arrArgVal() As String) As String

'Author: New Technology Solutions, Inc.
'Purpose: Generate a sample return HTML page
'5/1/96 Original

On Error GoTo CreateHTMLErr
    Dim i As Integer
    Dim strHTML As String
```

(continued)

Listing 5-18 *continued*

```
        strHTML = "Content-Type: text/html" & vbCrLf & vbCrLf
        strHTML = strHTML & _
            "<HTML><HEAD><TITLE>Results Page</TITLE></HEAD><BODY>"
        strHTML = strHTML & _
            "<H2><CENTER>Parsing Results</CENTER></H2><P><TABLE>"
        For i = 1 To UBound(arrArgVal) Step 2
            strHTML = strHTML & "<TR><TH>" & arrArgVal(i) & _
            "</TH><TD>" & arrArgVal(i + 1) & "</TD></TR>"
        Next
        strHTML = strHTML & "</TABLE></BODY></HTML>"
        fCreateHTML = strHTML

CreateHTMLExit:
    Exit Function

CreateHTMLErr:
    fCreateHTML = fCreateHTMLError(Err.Number, Err.Description)
    Resume CreateHTMLExit

End Function
```

A Detailed OLEISAPI Example

The following is a more detailed example that utilizes OLEISAPI. The example uses an in-process ActiveX component created in Visual Basic. Knowledge of Visual Basic is assumed in this example.

The OLEISAPI Minesweeper Game

Chapter 4 presented an Internet version of the Microsoft Minesweeper game that ran completely on the client. Built with ActiveX controls and VBScript, the application downloaded all of the necessary components to the client for execution. The advantage of such client-side processing is execution speed; with all of the components on the client, very little support is needed from the server across the Internet.

The example presented here shows how the Minesweeper game can be implemented on the server. An in-process component created in Visual Basic handles all of the game logic under IIS. The client is sent updated web pages to reveal the current state of the game. The current state is stored in the server's system Registry. Access to the system Registry is through the Visual Basic functions GetSetting and SaveSetting. The state of the game is tracked with two arrays in the DLL. One array, arrMines, is used to track the location of mines on the playing field, and another array, arrExposed, is used to track whether or not the cell has been "swept" by the user. The following code is used to read and write the status to the system Registry:

```
Private Sub sWriteGameData(strPlayerName As String)

'Author: New Technology Solutions, Inc.
'Purpose: Save the state of the game to a text file
'5/9/96 Original

    Dim i As Integer
    For i = 1 To 25
        If arrMines(i) = True Then
            SaveSetting "Minesweeper", strPlayerName, "Mines" _
            & Format$(i), "True"
        Else
            SaveSetting "Minesweeper", strPlayerName, "Mines" _
            & Format$(i), "False"
        End If
        If arrExposed(i) = True Then
            SaveSetting "Minesweeper", strPlayerName, "Exposed" _
            & Format$(i), "True"
        Else
            SaveSetting "Minesweeper", strPlayerName, "Exposed" _
            & Format$(i), "False"
        End If
    Next

End Sub

Private Sub sGetGameData(strPlayerName As String)

'Author: New Technology Solutions, Inc.
'Purpose: Get the state of the game from the text file
'5/9/96 Original

    Dim i As Integer
    Dim strTemp As String

    For i = 1 To 25
        strTemp = GetSetting("Minesweeper", strPlayerName, "Mines" _
        & Format$(i))
        If strTemp = "True" Then
            arrMines(i) = True
        Else
```

(continued)

continued

```
            arrMines(i) = False
        End If
        strTemp = GetSetting("Minesweeper", strPlayerName, _
        "Exposed" & Format$(i))
        If strTemp = "True" Then
            arrExposed(i) = True
        Else
            arrExposed(i) = False
        End If
    Next
End Sub
```

The key to interacting with the user is invoking oleisapi.dll each time a cell is selected. The in-process DLL then builds a dynamic web page to update the game board. Figure 5-19 shows an example of the web page returned by the DLL.

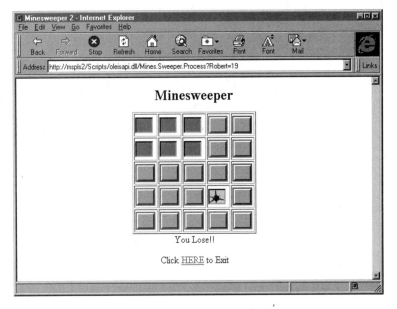

Figure 5-19.
The Minesweeper interface.

The game starts from a simple web page that invokes oleisapi.dll through a simple form. The form passes the name of the user as an argument. The name is used by the DLL on the server to track the state of all the current games. Using the names of the players allows the server to track many games at once.

Listing 5-19 shows the initial web page HTML code, and Listing 5-20 shows the sweeper class Visual Basic code contained in the in-process ActiveX component.

```
<HTML>
<HEAD>
<TITLE>Minesweeper 2</TITLE>
</HEAD>
<BODY BACKGROUND="backgrnd.gif" BGCOLOR="#FFFFFF">
<CENTER>

<H2>Welcome to Minesweeper!</H2>
<P>
<MARQUEE><H4>Enter your name to start</H4></MARQUEE>

<FORM METHOD="POST"
ACTION="/scripts/oleisapi.dll/mines.sweeper.resetgame">
<INPUT TYPE="TEXT" SIZE=30 NAME="Name"><P>
<INPUT TYPE="SUBMIT" VALUE="Start Game">
</FORM>

</CENTER>
</BODY>
</HTML>
```

Listing 5-19.
mines.htm.

```
Option Explicit

Private arrMines(1 To 25) As Boolean
Private arrExposed(1 To 25) As Boolean
Private strPlayerName As String

Public Sub ResetGame(strRequest As String, strReturn As String)

'Author: New Technology Solutions, Inc.
'Purpose: Initialize game
'5/9/96 Original

On Error GoTo ResetGameErr
    Dim i As Integer
    Dim n As Integer
    ReDim arrArgVal(0) As String
    Randomize Timer
```

Listing 5-20.
sweeper.cls.

(continued)

Listing 5-20 *continued*

```
    'Parse data to get player's name
    Call sParseRequest(strRequest, arrArgVal())
    strPlayerName = arrArgVal(2)

    'Reset arrays
    For i = 1 To 25
        arrMines(i) = False
        arrExposed(i) = False
    Next

    'Set four arrMines
    For i = 1 To 4
            n = Int(Rnd * 25) + 1
            arrMines(n) = True
    Next

    'Write data to Registry
    sWriteGameData strPlayerName

    'Generate the initial HTML page
    strReturn = fCreateHTMLPage(strPlayerName)

ResetGameExit:
    Exit Sub

ResetGameErr:
    strReturn = fCreateHTMLError(Err.Number, Err.Description, _
    "ResetGame")
    Resume ResetGameExit

End Sub

Public Sub Process(strRequest As String, strReturn As String)

'Author: New Technology Solutions, Inc.
'Purpose: Handle calls from client
'5/9/96 Original

On Error GoTo ProcessErr
    Dim intIndex As Integer

    'Parse the incoming string.
    'The format is expected to be
    'PlayerName=n, where n is the cell
    'number selected.
```

```
ReDim arrArgVal(0) As String
Call sParseRequest(strRequest, arrArgVal())
strPlayerName = arrArgVal(1)

'Get the game data for this player
sGetGameData strPlayerName

'Expose the selected cell
intIndex = Val(arrArgVal(2))
arrExposed(intIndex) = True

'Expose surrounding cells
If arrMines(intIndex) = False Then

    Select Case intIndex
        Case 1
            If arrMines(2) = False Then arrExposed(2) = True
            If arrMines(6) = False Then arrExposed(6) = True
            If arrMines(7) = False Then arrExposed(7) = True
        Case 5
            If arrMines(4) = False Then arrExposed(4) = True
            If arrMines(9) = False Then arrExposed(9) = True
            If arrMines(10) = False Then arrExposed(10) = True
        Case 21
            If arrMines(16) = False Then arrExposed(16) = True
            If arrMines(17) = False Then arrExposed(17) = True
            If arrMines(22) = False Then arrExposed(22) = True
        Case 25
            If arrMines(19) = False Then arrExposed(19) = True
            If arrMines(20) = False Then arrExposed(20) = True
            If arrMines(24) = False Then arrExposed(24) = True
        Case 6, 11, 16
            If arrMines(intIndex + 1) = False Then _
            arrExposed(intIndex + 1) = True
            If arrMines(intIndex + 5) = False Then _
            arrExposed(intIndex + 5) = True
            If arrMines(intIndex - 5) = False Then _
            arrExposed(intIndex - 5) = True
            If arrMines(intIndex - 4) = False Then _
            arrExposed(intIndex - 4) = True
            If arrMines(intIndex + 6) = False Then _
            arrExposed(intIndex + 6) = True
        Case 10, 15, 20
            If arrMines(intIndex - 1) = False Then _
            arrExposed(intIndex - 1) = True
```

(continued)

Listing 5-20 *continued*

```
              If arrMines(intIndex + 5) = False Then _
              arrExposed(intIndex + 5) = True
              If arrMines(intIndex - 5) = False Then _
              arrExposed(intIndex - 5) = True
              If arrMines(intIndex + 4) = False Then _
              arrExposed(intIndex + 4) = True
              If arrMines(intIndex - 6) = False Then _
              arrExposed(intIndex - 6) = True
          Case 2, 3, 4
              If arrMines(intIndex + 1) = False Then _
              arrExposed(intIndex + 1) = True
              If arrMines(intIndex - 1) = False Then _
              arrExposed(intIndex - 1) = True
              If arrMines(intIndex + 4) = False Then _
              arrExposed(intIndex + 4) = True
              If arrMines(intIndex + 5) = False Then _
              arrExposed(intIndex + 5) = True
              If arrMines(intIndex + 6) = False Then _
              arrExposed(intIndex + 6) = True
          Case 22, 23, 24
              If arrMines(intIndex + 1) = False Then _
              arrExposed(intIndex + 1) = True
              If arrMines(intIndex - 1) = False Then _
              arrExposed(intIndex - 1) = True
              If arrMines(intIndex - 4) = False Then _
              arrExposed(intIndex - 4) = True
              If arrMines(intIndex - 5) = False Then _
              arrExposed(intIndex - 5) = True
              If arrMines(intIndex - 6) = False Then _
              arrExposed(intIndex - 6) = True
          Case 7, 8, 9, 12, 13, 14, 17, 18, 19
              If arrMines(intIndex + 1) = False Then _
              arrExposed(intIndex + 1) = True
              If arrMines(intIndex - 1) = False Then _
              arrExposed(intIndex - 1) = True
              If arrMines(intIndex + 5) = False Then _
              arrExposed(intIndex + 5) = True
              If arrMines(intIndex - 5) = False Then _
              arrExposed(intIndex - 5) = True
              If arrMines(intIndex + 6) = False Then _
              arrExposed(intIndex + 6) = True
              If arrMines(intIndex - 6) = False Then _
              arrExposed(intIndex - 6) = True
              If arrMines(intIndex + 4) = False Then _
              arrExposed(intIndex + 4) = True
```

```
                    If arrMines(intIndex - 4) = False Then _
                arrExposed(intIndex - 4) = True
        End Select

    End If

    'Write data to Registry
    sWriteGameData strPlayerName

    'Process selected cell
    strReturn = fCreateHTMLPage(strPlayerName)

ProcessExit:
    Exit Sub

ProcessErr:
    strReturn = fCreateHTMLError(Err.Number, Err.Description, _
    "Process")
    Resume ProcessExit

End Sub

Private Sub sParseRequest(strRequest As String, arrArgVal() As String)

'Author: New Technology Solutions, Inc.
'Purpose: Parse request string into entries in array
'5/1/96: Original

On Error GoTo ParseRequestErr

    'Incoming string is in the format
    'Argument1=Value1&Argument2=Value2

    Dim intIndex As Integer
    Dim intPosition As Integer
    Dim intStart As Integer
    Dim strParse As String
    Dim strTemp As String
    Dim intTest As Integer
    intIndex = 0
    intStart = 1

    Do While InStr(intStart, strRequest, "=", 1) > 0
        intIndex = intIndex + 1
        ReDim Preserve arrArgVal(intIndex + 1)
```

(continued)

Listing 5-20 *continued*

```
        'Search for = and get argument name
        intPosition = InStr(intStart, strRequest, "=", 1)
        arrArgVal(intIndex) = Trim$(Mid$(strRequest, intStart, _
        intPosition - intStart))
        intIndex = intIndex + 1
        intStart = intPosition + 1
        intPosition = InStr(intStart, strRequest, "&", 1)

        'Search for & and get value
        If intPosition > 0 Then
            arrArgVal(intIndex) = Trim$(Mid$(strRequest, intStart, _
            intPosition - intStart))
            intStart = intPosition + 1
        Else
            arrArgVal(intIndex) = Trim$(Right$(strRequest, _
            Len(strRequest) - intStart + 1))
            intStart = Len(strRequest)
        End If
    Loop

    For intIndex = 1 To UBound(arrArgVal)

        'This loop cleans up each entry.
        'Plus signs are used as spaces, and
        'ASCII characters are in hex notation,
        'preceded by a % sign.

        strTemp = ""
        intPosition = 1
        Do
            Select Case Mid$(arrArgVal(intIndex), intPosition, 1)
                Case "+"
                    strTemp = strTemp & " "
                    intPosition = intPosition + 1
                Case "%"
                    strTemp = strTemp & Chr$(Val("&H" & _
                    Mid$(arrArgVal(intIndex), intPosition + 1, 2)))
                    intPosition = intPosition + 3
                Case Else

                    'Get rid of any ASCII characters not supported
                    'by Windows
                    intTest = Asc(Mid$(arrArgVal(intIndex), _
                    intPosition, 1))
```

```
                    If Not (intTest < 32 Or (intTest > 126 And _
                    intTest < 145) _
                    Or (intTest > 146 And intTest < 160)) Then
                        strTemp = strTemp & _
                        Mid$(arrArgVal(intIndex), intPosition, 1)
                    End If
                    intPosition = intPosition + 1
            End Select
        Loop While intPosition <= Len(arrArgVal(intIndex))
        arrArgVal(intIndex) = strTemp
    Next

ParseRequestExit:
    Exit Sub

ParseRequestErr:
    ReDim arrArgValue(4)
    arrArgValue(1) = "Error"
    arrArgValue(2) = Err.Description
    arrArgValue(3) = "Number"
    arrArgValue(4) = Format$(Err.Number)
    Resume ParseRequestExit

End Sub

Private Function fCreateHTMLPage(strPlayerName As String) As String

'Author: New Technology Solutions, Inc.
'Purpose: Create the HTML page to send back to the client
'5/9/96 Original

On Error GoTo CreateHTMLPageErr
    Dim i As Integer, j As Integer
    Dim strHTML As String
    Dim blnLoser As Boolean
    Dim blnWinner As Boolean

    blnLoser = False
    blnWinner = True
    strHTML = "Content-Type: text/html" & vbCrLf & vbCrLf
    strHTML = strHTML & "<HTML><HEAD>"
    strHTML = strHTML & "<TITLE>Minesweeper 2</TITLE>"
    strHTML = strHTML & "<HEAD><BODY BGCOLOR=#FFFFFF BACKGROUND=" _
    & Chr$(34) & "http://mspls2/mines/blueback.gif" & Chr$(34) & ">"
```

(continued)

Listing 5-20 *continued*

```
strHTML = strHTML & "<CENTER><H2>Minesweeper</H2>"
strHTML = strHTML & "<P><TABLE BORDER>"
For i = 1 To 21 Step 5
    strHTML = strHTML & "<TR>"
    For j = 0 To 4

        'If any good spaces are still covered, player is
        'not yet a winner!
        If arrMines(i + j) = False And arrExposed(i + j) = _
        False Then
            blnWinner = False
        End If
        If arrExposed(i + j) And arrMines(i + j) Then
            strHTML = strHTML & "<TD>"
            strHTML = strHTML & "<IMG SRC=" & Chr$(34) _
            & "http://mspls2/mines/mine.gif" _
            & Chr$(34) & "ALT=" & Chr$(34) _
            & "cell" & Chr$(34) & "></TD>"

            'If a mine is exposed, player loses!!
            blnLoser = True
        ElseIf arrExposed(i + j) Then
            strHTML = strHTML & "<TD>"
            strHTML = strHTML & "<IMG SRC=" & Chr$(34) _
            & "http://mspls2/mines/empty.gif" _
            & Chr$(34) & "ALT=" & Chr$(34) _
            & "cell" & Chr$(34) & "></TD>"
        Else
            strHTML = strHTML & "<TD>"
            strHTML = strHTML & "<A HREF=" & Chr$(34) _
            & "/Scripts/oleisapi.dll/Mines.Sweeper.Process?" & _
            strPlayerName & "=" & Format$(i + j) & Chr$(34) & ">"
            strHTML = strHTML & "<IMG SRC=" & Chr$(34) _
            & "http://mspls2/mines/covered.gif" _
            & Chr$(34) & "ALT=" & Chr$(34) _
            & "cell" & Chr$(34) & "></A></TD>"
        End If
    Next
    strHTML = strHTML & "</TR>"
Next
If blnLoser Then

    'Generate loser message
    strHTML = strHTML & "<CAPTION ALIGN=" & Chr$(34) _
    & "BOTTOM" & Chr$(34) & ">You Lose!!</CAPTION>"
```

```
        strHTML = strHTML & "</TABLE><P>"
        strHTML = strHTML & "Click <A HREF=" & _
        Chr$(34) & "http://mspls2/mines/mines.htm" _
        & Chr$(34) & ">HERE</A> to Exit</CENTER></BODY></HTML>"

        'Clear Registry contents
        DeleteSetting "Minesweeper", strPlayerName
    ElseIf blnWinner Then

        'Generate winner message
        strHTML = strHTML & "<CAPTION ALIGN=" & Chr$(34) _
        & "BOTTOM" & Chr$(34) & ">You Win!!</CAPTION>"
        strHTML = strHTML & "</TABLE><P>"
        strHTML = strHTML & "Click <A HREF=" & _
        Chr$(34) & "http://mspls2/mines/mines.htm" _
        & Chr$(34) & ">HERE</A> to Exit</CENTER></BODY></HTML>"

        'Clear Registry contents
        DeleteSetting "Minesweeper", strPlayerName
    Else

        'Keep playing
        strHTML = strHTML & "<CAPTION ALIGN=" & Chr$(34) _
        & "BOTTOM" & Chr$(34) & ">Click on a cell</CAPTION>"
        strHTML = strHTML & "</TABLE></CENTER></BODY></HTML>"
    End If

CreateHTMLPageExit:
    fCreateHTMLPage = strHTML
    Exit Function

CreateHTMLPageErr:
    fCreateHTMLPage = fCreateHTMLError(Err.Number, Err.Description, _
    "fCreateHTMLPage")
    Resume CreateHTMLPageExit
End Function


Private Function fCreateHTMLError(lngNumber As Long, _
strDescription As String, strProcedure As String) As String

'Author: New Technology Solutions, Inc.
'Purpose: Create an HTML page describing an error
'5/1/96 Original

    On Error GoTo 0
    Dim strHTML As String
```

(continued)

Listing 5-20 *continued*

```
    strHTML = "Content-Type: text/html" & vbCrLf & vbCrLf
    strHTML = strHTML & _
    "<HTML><HEAD><TITLE>Error Report</TITLE></HEAD><BODY>"
    strHTML = strHTML & _
    "<H2><CENTER>OLEISAPI ERROR!</CENTER></H2><P>"
    strHTML = strHTML & _
    "<H5><CENTER>Reported from Server Mines.Sweeper</CENTER></H5><P>"
    strHTML = strHTML & _
    "<TABLE><TR><TH>NUMBER</TH><TD>" & Format$(lngNumber) & _
    "</TD></TR>"
    strHTML = strHTML & _
    "<TR><TH>DESCRIPTION</TH><TD>" & strDescription & "</TD></TR>"
    strHTML = strHTML & _
    "<TR><TH>PROCEDURE</TH><TD>" & strProcedure & "</TD></TR>"
    strHTML = strHTML & _
    "</TABLE></BODY></HTML>"
    fCreateHTMLError = strHTML
End Function

Private Sub sWriteGameData(strPlayerName As String)

'Author: New Technology Solutions, Inc.
'Purpose: Save the state of the game to a text file
'5/9/96 Original

    Dim i As Integer
    For i = 1 To 25
        If arrMines(i) = True Then
            SaveSetting "Minesweeper", strPlayerName, "Mines" _
            & Format$(i), "True"
        Else
            SaveSetting "Minesweeper", strPlayerName, "Mines" _
            & Format$(i), "False"
        End If
        If arrExposed(i) = True Then
            SaveSetting "Minesweeper", strPlayerName, "Exposed" _
            & Format$(i), "True"
        Else
            SaveSetting "Minesweeper", strPlayerName, "Exposed" _
            & Format$(i), "False"
        End If
```

```
     Next
End Sub

Private Sub sGetGameData(strPlayerName As String)

'Author: New Technology Solutions, Inc.
'Purpose: Get the state of the game from the text file
'5/9/96 Original

    Dim i As Integer
    Dim strTemp As String

    For i = 1 To 25
        strTemp = GetSetting("Minesweeper", strPlayerName, "Mines" _
        & Format$(i))
        If strTemp = "True" Then
            arrMines(i) = True
        Else
            arrMines(i) = False
        End If
        strTemp = GetSetting("Minesweeper", strPlayerName, _
        "Exposed" & Format$(i))
        If strTemp = "True" Then
            arrExposed(i) = True
        Else
            arrExposed(i) = False
        End If
    Next
End Sub
```

The IIS Wizards

The companion CD contains two wizards that we designed to make it easier to develop applications with the Internet Information Server. The first wizard is an Internet Database Connector Wizard, and the second is an OLEISAPI Wizard. The wizards can be found on the companion CD under the filenames idcwiz.exe and isapiwiz.exe. Both wizards were built in Visual Basic 4.0.

The IDC Wizard generates an idc, an htm, and an htx file for a given datasource. You provide simple information about the datasource, and the wizard generates the files automatically. The wizard generates a simple HTML template for calling IDC and a simple htx file for returning results from IDC.

Figures 5-20, 5-21, and 5-22 show sample dialog boxes of the IDC Wizard.

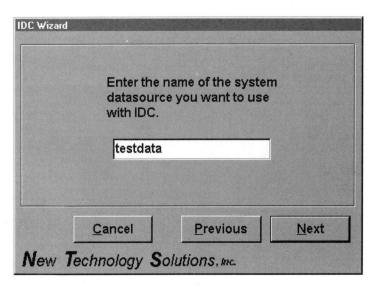

Figure 5-20.
The datasource name dialog box of the IDC Wizard.

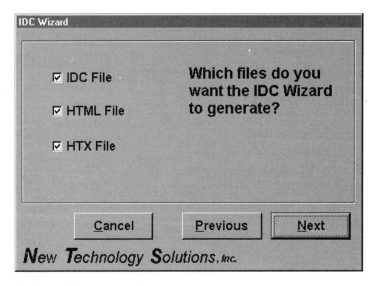

Figure 5-21.
The file selection dialog box of the IDC Wizard.

Figure 5-22.
The file set name dialog box of the IDC Wizard.

Here is the code generated by the IDC Wizard. In this example, the three files are test.htm, test.idc, and test.htx. The following is test.htm:

```
<HTML>
<HEAD>
<TITLE>HTML page</TITLE>
</HEAD>

<BODY>
<CENTER>
<FORM METHOD="POST"
<ACTION="/Scripts/test.idc">
<INPUT>
<INPUT TYPE="SUBMIT" VALUE="Submit">
</FORM>

</CENTER>
</BODY>
</HTML>
```

Here is test.idc:

```
Datasource:testdata
Template:test.htx
SQLStatement:Enter your SQL statement here!!!
```

Here is test.htx:

```
<HTML>
<HEAD>
<TITLE>Return Page</TITLE>
</HEAD>

<BODY>
<%begindetail%>
<!--
Structure your return htx file here!!
-->
<%enddetail%>

</CENTER>
</BODY>
</HTML>
```

The OLEISAPI Wizard generates a complete in-process ActiveX component project for Visual Basic. The wizard generates all of the necessary files and code to receive a request string, parse the string, and return an HTML page. In order to use the output from the OLEISAPI Wizard, you must have the 32-bit version of Visual Basic 4.0. After the wizard has generated the project, simply open the project in Visual Basic, customize it as desired, and compile it as an in-process ActiveX component. If the component is not compiled on the server, you will have to register it after you copy it to the server.

Figures 5-23, 5-24, and 5-25 (page 186) show sample dialog boxes from the OLEISAPI Wizard.

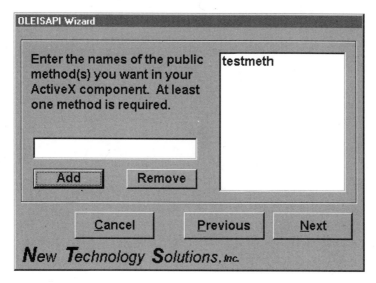

Figure 5-23.
The method names dialog box of the OLEISAPI Wizard.

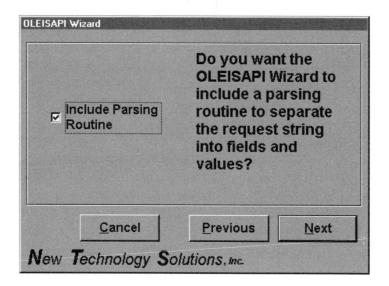

Figure 5-24.
The parsing selection dialog box of the OLEISAPI Wizard.

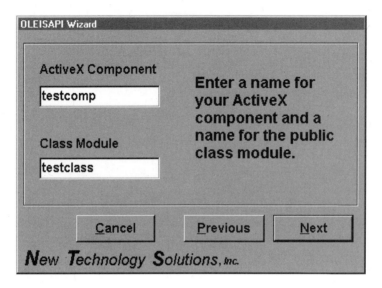

Figure 5-25.
The component name dialog box of the OLEISAPI Wizard.

Here is the Visual Basic code generated by the OLEISAPI Wizard:

```
Option Explicit

Public Sub testmeth(strRequest As String, strReturn As String)

'Author: New Technology Solutions, Inc.
'Purpose: Receive a call from OLEISAPI
'5/1/96 Original

On Error GoTo testmethErr

    ReDim arrArgVal(0) As String

    'Parse the incoming string
    Call sParseRequest(strRequest, arrArgVal())

    'Return the HTML page to the browser
    strReturn = fCreateHTML(arrArgVal())

testmethExit:
    Exit Sub

testmethErr:
    strReturn = fCreateHTMLError(Err.Number, Err.Description)
    Resume testmethExit

End Sub
```

```
Private Sub sParseRequest(strRequest As String, arrArgVal() _
As String)

'Author: New Technology Solutions, Inc.
'Purpose: Parse request string into entries in array
'5/1/96 Original

On Error GoTo ParseRequestErr

    'Incoming string is in the format
    'Argument1=Value1&Argument2=Value2

    Dim intIndex As Integer
    Dim intPosition As Integer
    Dim intStart As Integer
    Dim strParse As String
    Dim strTemp As String
    Dim intTest As Integer

    intIndex = 0
    intStart = 1

    Do While InStr(intStart, strRequest, "=", 1) > 0

        intIndex = intIndex + 1
        ReDim Preserve arrArgVal(intIndex + 1)

        'Search for = and get argument name
        intPosition = InStr(intStart, strRequest, "=", 1)
        arrArgVal(intIndex) = Trim$(Mid$(strRequest, intStart, _
        intPosition - intStart))

        intIndex = intIndex + 1
        intStart = intPosition + 1
        intPosition = InStr(intStart, strRequest, "&", 1)

        'Search for & and get Value
        If intPosition > 0 Then
            arrArgVal(intIndex) = Trim$(Mid$(strRequest, _
            intStart, intPosition - intStart))
            intStart = intPosition + 1
        Else
            arrArgVal(intIndex) = Trim$(Right$(strRequest, _
            Len(strRequest) - intStart + 1))
```

(continued)

continued

```
            intStart = Len(strRequest)
        End If

Loop

For intIndex = 1 To UBound(arrArgVal)

'This loop cleans up each entry.
'Plus signs are used as spaces, and
'ASCII characters are in hex notation,
'preceded by a % sign.

    strTemp = ""

intPosition = 1
Do

    Select Case Mid$(arrArgVal(intIndex), intPosition, 1)
        Case "+"
            strTemp = strTemp & ""
            intPosition = intPosition + 1
        Case "%"
            strTemp = strTemp & Chr$(Val("&H" & _
            Mid$(arrArgVal(intIndex), intPosition + 1, 2)))
            intPosition = intPosition + 3
        Case Else

            'Get rid of any ASCII characters not supported
            'by Windows
            intTest = Asc(Mid$(arrArgVal(intIndex), _
            intPosition, 1))

            If Not (intTest < 32 Or (intTest > 126 And _
            intTest < 145) _
            Or (intTest > 146 And intTest < 160)) Then
                strTemp = strTemp & Mid$(arrArgVal(intIndex), _
                intPosition, 1)
            End If

            intPosition = intPosition + 1

    End Select

Loop While intPosition <= Len(arrArgVal(intIndex))
```

```
        arrArgVal(intIndex) = strTemp

Next

ParseRequestExit:
    Exit Sub

ParseRequestErr:
    ReDim arrArgValue(4)
    arrArgValue(1) = "Error"
    arrArgValue(2) = Err.Description
    arrArgValue(3) = "Number"
    arrArgValue(4) = Format$(Err.Number)
    Resume ParseRequestExit

End Sub

Private Function fCreateHTMLError(lngNumber As Long, _
strDescription As String) As String

'Author: New Technology Solutions, Inc.
'Purpose: Create an HTML page describing an error
'5/1/96 Original

    Dim strHTML As String

    strHTML = strHTML = "Content-Type: text/html" & _
    vbCrLf & vbCrLf
    strHTML = strHTML & _
    "<HTML><HEAD><TITLE>Error Report</TITLE></HEAD><BODY>"
    strHTML = strHTML & _
    "<H2><CENTER>OLEISAPI ERROR!</CENTER></H2><P>"
    strHTML = strHTML & _
    "<TABLE><TR><TH>NUMBER</TH><TD>" & Format$(lngNumber) & _
    "</TD></TR>"
    strHTML = strHTML & _
    "<TR><TH>DESCRIPTION</TH><TD>" & strDescription & "</TD></TR>"
    strHTML = strHTML & "</TABLE></BODY></HTML>"

    fCreateHTMLError = strHTML

End Function

Private Function fCreateHTML(arrArgVal() As String) As String

'Author: New Technology Solutions, Inc.
```

(continued)

continued

```
'Purpose: Generate a sample return HTML page
'5/1/96 Original

On Error GoTo CreateHTMLErr

    Dim strHTML As String

    strHTML = "Content-Type: text/html" & vbCrLf & vbCrLf
    '***************************************************************
    'Enter additional HTML code here and format it however you want!!
    'Just append it to strHTML to build the return page.
    '***************************************************************

    fCreateHTML = strHTML

CreateHTMLExit:
    Exit Function

CreateHTMLErr:
    fCreateHTML = fCreateHTMLError(Err.Number, Err.Description)
    Resume CreateHTMLExit

End Function
```

CGI and IIS

Not only can IIS use IDC and OLEISAPI, it also provides support for the Common Gateway Interface (CGI) and Windows CGI standards. CGI and Windows CGI are older standards that are used to communicate with back-end processes. CGI is a platform-independent standard that was designed to allow a browser to communicate with a server. Windows CGI is a standard in which passed data is written to an initialization (INI) file so that any Windows application can retrieve the data. Before OLEISAPI was introduced, this technique was often used to pass data to Visual Basic programs, which can read INI files.

In Windows, CGI is generally implemented as a batch file. The batch file is invoked from the HTML code on the client in a manner similar to that used to invoke the Internet Database Connector. For example, to call a batch file from HTML, we might use the following code:

```
<A HREF="/scripts/cgi-test.bat?test+parameters">
Click here to test CGI
</A>
```

This HTML calls the batch file and includes the argument test+parameters. IIS maps the batch file to cmd.exe, which executes it. IIS maps both bat and cmd files to cmd.exe, so you can prepare scripts with either extension. In fact, you can specify additional mappings by editing the system Registry entries made by IIS at installation. The system Registry keys for mappings are contained in HKEY_LOCAL_MACHINE\SYSTEM\CurrentControlSet\Services\W3SVC\Parameters\ScriptMap.

> CAUTION: Do *not* edit the system Registry keys unless you are experienced with the Registry. Improperly edited Registry keys can cause serious malfunctions on the server.

Overall, IDC and OLEISAPI have some advantages over the CGI technology. ISAPI-based solutions run faster and can remain resident in memory. New web installations using IIS and Windows NT have little reason to implement CGI solutions.

Other IIS Services

In addition to the WWW service, IIS also provides FTP and Gopher services. Though not an integral part of VBScript, these services certainly play a key role in creating interactive web sites.

The File Transfer Protocol

The file transfer protocol (FTP) is used to move files between computers on a TCP/IP network. The protocol is platform-independent, which allows files to be transferred between computers on different platforms. Although the WWW service has replaced much of the FTP functionality (for example, browsers do not need FTP to download files from a web site), FTP is commonly used to transfer files from a client computer to a server. The FTP service in IIS is extremely easy to use. You simply copy the files you want to make available for downloading into the ftproot folder of your IIS installation and reference the URL from a web page. When the user clicks on an anchor tag that references FTP, the download begins. The files transferred via FTP can be in any format.

Gopher

Gopher, which also allows files to be transferred over the Internet, is similar to FTP. Gopher, however, is an improved file transfer mechanism. Gopher implements features such as links to other computers and identification of the MIME type for files. In IIS, the Gopher folder is gophroot. When you place files in the Gopher folder, browsers can easily access and download them.

Project #1:
An Intranet Newsletter

The project presented in this chapter creates an intranet newsletter for a hypothetical company's internal use. The project allows employees to "subscribe" to the newsletter through the Microsoft Internet Explorer 3.0 browser. The newsletter is distributed periodically through the interoffice email system, which can be Microsoft Exchange or Microsoft Mail. The subscriptions are registered in an ODBC datasource with the Internet Database Connector (IDC) that is associated with the Microsoft Internet Information Server (IIS). The newsletter is distributed to the circulation list by means of a separate Visual Basic application.

The discussion of this project assumes that you are familiar with Microsoft Visual Basic 4.0 and the use of custom controls. You should also be familiar with Microsoft Windows NT Server and Microsoft Windows 95. In this chapter we also assume that you are building the solution directly on a Windows NT server. However, it is possible to construct the necessary files on a computer using Windows 95 and then transfer them to a Windows NT server for final configuration and testing. No matter which method you use, it is a good idea to have Visual Basic installed on the server so that changes can be made on the server.

Requirements

Construction of the intranet newsletter project requires the following components:

- Windows NT Server version 3.51 or 4.0 with IIS installed and access to email

- Windows 95, with the Microsoft Internet Explorer 3.0 installed

- Visual Basic 4.0, Enterprise Edition

- Microsoft Access 7.0 ODBC drivers (available on the companion CD)
- Microsoft PowerPoint Animation Player (available on the companion CD)
- Microsoft Access (optional)
- Microsoft PowerPoint for Windows 95 (optional)
- Microsoft PowerPoint Animation Publisher (available on the companion CD)
- Microsoft Label control (available on the companion CD)

Design Objective

The design objective for this project is to create an intranet newsletter for a hypothetical company. The system will provide a form for subscribing, a way to validate the entered data, and a method to store the entered data in a server-side database. Users will subscribe online with an HTML form that uses form input variables to store the data. The form input variables will contain the subscriber's name, department, and email address. Figure 6-1 shows the subscription form.

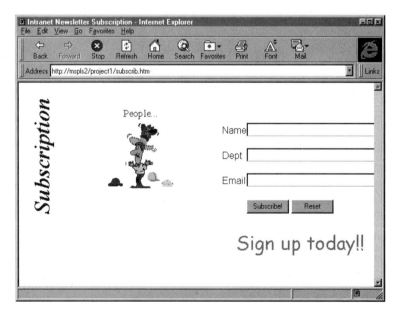

Figure 6-1.
The subscription form.

The data for each subscription will be stored in an ODBC datasource. This ODBC datasource will subsequently be used as a mailing list for a Visual Basic application called Publish, which distributes the newsletter via email. Employees whose names are in the database will receive the newsletter in their email inboxes whenever the Publish application is used. Figure 6-2 shows a sample of the Publish application interface.

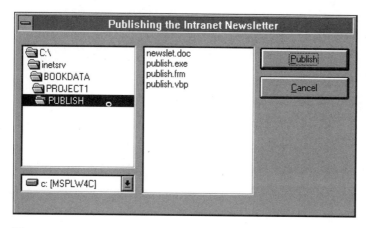

Figure 6-2.
The Publish application interface.

Prerequisites

Prior to starting the project, you will need to create a folder structure to hold your work. If you have done any of the other projects in this book, some of this structure might already be in place. From the Windows NT server's File Manager, create the following folders (note that for a standard installation of IIS, you should already have a folder named inetsrv and two subfolders named wwwroot and scripts):

drive:\inetsrv\bookdata	For files related to this book
drive:\inetsrv\bookdata\project1	For the subscription database and the Publish application
drive:\inetsrv\scripts\project1	For the idc and htx files
drive:\inetsrv\wwwroot\project1	For the HTML and associated files

Figure 6-3, on page 196, shows an example of the folder structure.

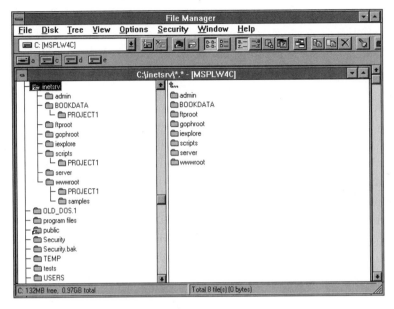

Figure 6-3.
An example of the Project #1 folder structure.

Creating the Datasource

Before you build the application, you must create a database in which to store the information for the subscribers. In this section you will install ODBC drivers for Microsoft Access, build an Access database, and create an ODBC datasource for use with the project. You need to understand ODBC datasources if you want to develop Internet applications. A thorough understanding of the subject will allow you to access any ODBC back-end data storage element. For example, if you choose to use a Microsoft SQL Server database instead of a Microsoft Access database, ODBC will be able to work with it equally well. Although Access databases are fine for demonstration purposes, they are not useful for handling high-traffic web sites with many transactions. However, the techniques you will employ to interact with an Access database are the same ones you would use for any ODBC datasource, including a SQL Server datasource.

Installing the Access ODBC Drivers

Before you can create an ODBC datasource, the ODBC drivers must be properly installed on your Windows NT server. If the drivers have already been installed, you can skip this section. You can determine whether or not the drivers have been installed by opening the ODBC Administrator, which can be found in the Control Panel in the Main program group or in an ODBC group.

When you start the ODBC Administrator, you will see the Data Sources dialog box. The Data Sources dialog box lists all the user datasources that are registered on your machine. You can set up two different kinds of datasources in the ODBC Administrator: user datasources and system datasources. User datasources are defined for the use of individual users, and system datasources are intended for use by other processes. IIS uses only system datasources. Figure 6-4 shows a sample of the Data Sources dialog box.

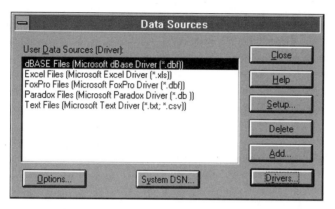

Figure 6-4.
The Data Sources dialog box.

In the Data Sources dialog box, click on the Drivers button to see a list of all the ODBC drivers on your server. If the Access drivers have been installed, you will see an appropriate entry. Figure 6-5, on page 198, shows a sample of the Drivers dialog box as it appears when the Access drivers and others have been installed. If the Access drivers haven't been installed on your server, close the Drivers dialog box and the Data Sources dialog box. You will return to the ODBC Administrator after you have installed the drivers.

To install the Access drivers, you will need either the companion CD included with this book or a copy of Microsoft Access. To install the drivers from the companion CD, run the ODBC setup and follow the directions. To install the ODBC drivers from Microsoft Access, run the setup program from the product CD. When you run the setup program, you will see a dialog box asking you if you want to perform a complete setup or a custom setup. Select Custom from the dialog box. When you perform a custom setup of Microsoft Access, you will be presented with a list of components that you can install.

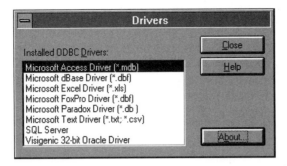

Figure 6-5.
The Drivers dialog box showing installed ODBC drivers.

From the setup dialog box, choose to install only the Data Access component. Choosing the Data Access component will install the appropriate ODBC drivers on your machine. Follow the rest of the instructions for the setup routine, and then return to the ODBC Administrator and verify that the Access drivers are now present in the Drivers dialog box.

Creating the Access Database

The next step in creating the datasource is to actually construct a database in Microsoft Access. You can build the database either by using Microsoft Access directly or by using the Data Manager included with Visual Basic. For this project, you will create the database by using the Data Manager. If you prefer to create the database in Access, you may do so and then turn to the exercise in the "Defining the Datasource" section on page 201. In any case, you will create a database with the structure shown in Table 6-1.

Table 6-1. The People Table

Field Name	Data Type
Name	Text
Department	Text
Email	Text

Step 1

Start Visual Basic 4.0. Open the Data Manager by selecting Add-Ins/Data Manager from the Visual Basic menu bar. The Data Manager will start, and you will see a form with File and Help menus.

Step 2

Create a new database by selecting File/New Database from the Data Manager menu bar. After the New Database dialog box appears, navigate to the folder \bookdata\project1, type in the file name subscrib.mdb, and then click on the OK (or Save) button. Figure 6-6 shows the resulting Data Manager window that is displayed.

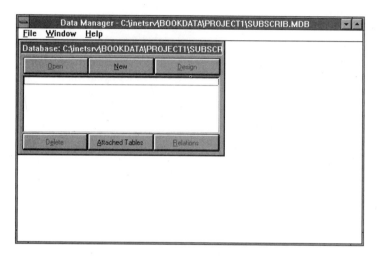

Figure 6-6.
The subscribers database created with the Data Manager.

Step 3

Add a new table to the database by clicking on the New button. The Add Table dialog box should appear. Name the new table People.

Step 4

Add the fields from Table 6-1 to the database one at a time by filling in the Field Name text box with the appropriate name. For each field, select Text from the Data Type combo box and set the field size to 250. Click on the right arrow button to add each field. The fields will appear in the list box in the center of the dialog box. Figure 6-7, on page 200, shows the completed People table in the Add Table dialog box.

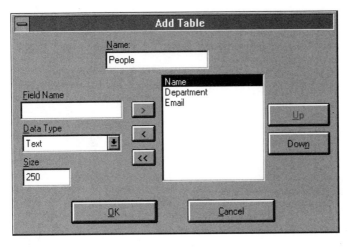

Figure 6-7.
The Add Table dialog box showing the completed People table.

Step 5

Click on the OK button in the Add Table dialog box. The People table should appear in the Data Manager. Figure 6-8 shows the subscribers database with the People table added. Minimize the Data Manager so that you can access the database directly anytime during the exercise. When you are working with ODBC drivers, direct access via the Data Manager can be helpful for trouble-shooting.

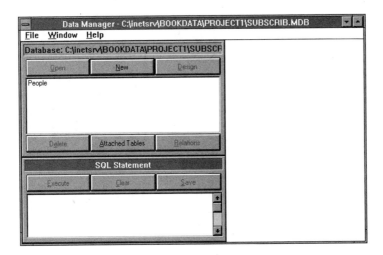

Figure 6-8.
The subscribers database with the People table added.

Defining the Datasource

At this point in the exercise, you should have built the database by using either the Data Manager or Microsoft Access. Regardless of which method you used, your database should have the structure shown in Table 6-1. If your database is ready, you can go on to create the ODBC datasource used in the exercise. Make sure that the database is complete and that the appropriate ODBC drivers have been installed.

Step 1

From the Control Panel or an ODBC group, start the ODBC Administrator. When the ODBC Administrator starts, you will see the Data Sources dialog box. Figure 6-9 shows the Data Sources dialog box.

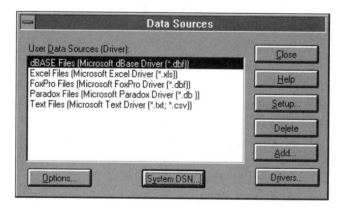

Figure 6-9.
The Data Sources dialog box.

Step 2

Install the new datasource by clicking on the System DSN button in the Data Sources dialog box. The System Data Sources dialog box should appear. Figure 6-10, on page 202, shows the System Data Sources dialog box.

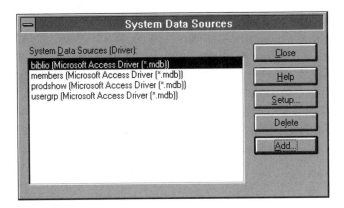

Figure 6-10.
The System Data Sources dialog box.

In the System Data Sources dialog box, click on the Add button. The Add Data Source dialog box will then appear. Figure 6-11 shows the Add Data Source dialog box.

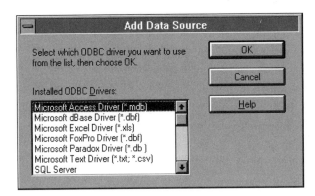

Figure 6-11.
The Add Data Source dialog box.

Step 3
In the Add Data Source dialog box, select the Microsoft Access ODBC driver and click on the OK button. The ODBC Microsoft Access Setup dialog box should appear. This dialog box is used to set up the datasource.

Step 4
Give your datasource a name by typing the word *subscribers* into the Data Source Name text box. This is the name you will use to identify the database whenever

you utilize an ODBC driver. This name can be anything you want and is not directly related to the name of the database you created previously.

Step 5

Enter a brief description for your datasource in the Description text box. This can be any text you want and has no effect on the application.

Step 6

To establish the database you created previously as your datasource, click the Select button. A dialog box appears that lets you select the file for this datasource. Navigate to the \bookdata\project1 folder, and select the sub-scrib.mdb database you created previously. Figure 6-12 shows a sample of the ODBC Microsoft Access Setup dialog box with the information for the subscribers datasource filled in. When you have finished, click on the OK button. Your new datasource should now be visible in the System Data Source dialog box.

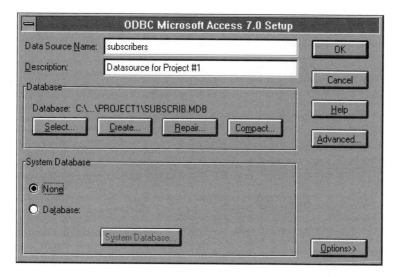

Figure 6-12.
The ODBC Microsoft Access Setup dialog box.

Step 7

Click on the Close buttons in the System Data Sources dialog box and in the Data Sources dialog box to exit the ODBC Administrator. Your datasource is now ready to be accessed from the web.

Creating the HTML Page

The HTML page for this project will allow users to subscribe to the intranet newsletter by using the Internet Explorer. The page is a simple form that takes the name, department, and email address of the subscriber and stores them in a database. The database transaction will use IDC. This HTML page utilizes two ActiveX controls—the Label control and the Microsoft PowerPoint Animation Player control—to improve the interaction between the user and the browser. The page you will create was shown earlier, in Figure 6-1. The complete HTML code, along with comments, is shown in Listing 6-1, starting on page 213. The following text describes how to create the HTML code.

The Head Section

The head section of the HTML file contains the title and base reference for the page. The head section will eventually contain the script section, in which you will perform some simple client-side data validation. The script section is covered in detail after the discussion of the body section. For now, you will simply add some basic HTML code to this section.

Because HTML code is only ASCII text, you can construct a page by using Notepad. Any text editor will work, including Microsoft Word, but all files must be saved as ASCII text and typically have the extension htm.

While you are creating this file, you should be aware of one special consideration: some text editors, such as the one included with Windows NT 3.51, support the Unicode format. Unicode, a text format that uses 2 bytes per character, was designed to provide support for languages with more than 256 characters. When you are using a text editor that supports Unicode, be sure to save the text in ASCII format, not in Unicode format. ASCII format uses only 1 byte per character and is the format that browsers will expect.

Open a new document in a text editor such as Notepad to start creating your web page at the head section. The head section always contains the title and the base reference for the page. Add the following code to your project to create a title and base reference:

```
<HTML>
<HEAD>
<TITLE>Intranet Newsletter Subscription</TITLE>
<BASE HREF="/project1/">
</HEAD>
```

The base reference points to the root folder for this page. Obviously, if you change the folder for this page, you will have to change the base reference. We have specified a relative address here, but it may be necessary to specify a full HTTP address—for example, <BASE HREF="http://*myserver*/project1/ ">, where *myserver* is the name of your server. You can obtain the name of your Windows NT server by clicking on the Network icon in the Control Panel.

The Body Section

In the body section, you will create the form used to gather data from the user. You will also use an ActiveX control called the *PowerPoint Animation Player*. The PowerPoint Animation Player is an ActiveX control that runs Microsoft PowerPoint presentations. With this control, you can add some dramatic animation to your web page without having to write any additional code. You simply create a PowerPoint slide show, save it, and pass it as a property to the PowerPoint Animation Player. Since PowerPoint presentations can be fairly large files, a PowerPoint for Windows 95 extension, called the Microsoft PowerPoint Animation Publisher, can be used to compress the presentation. The PowerPoint Animation Publisher is available from Microsoft and on the companion CD.

Step 1

Most of the body section is used to create a form for collecting data and including controls. You will build the form with HTML tables. HTML tables allow sophisticated formatting of the content of a web page. You can space text, images, and controls with precision and create web pages that would otherwise not be possible. Begin the form by adding the following code to your HTML page:

```
<BODY BGCOLOR="WHITE">
<CENTER>

<FORM NAME="frmSubscribe" METHOD="POST"
ACTION="/scripts/project1/subscrib.idc">
<TABLE BORDER=0 CELLPADDING=0 CELLSPACING=0>
```

This code opens the form and directs the submitted data to the idc file subscrib.idc. The POST method is used to direct the data to the back-end process. In this case, the data is received by the Internet Database Connector file httpodbc.dll, which runs the query specified by the idc file. You will build the idc file later in this project.

Step 2

Now that the table is open, you can fill in each cell. The <TR></TR> tags define table rows, and the <TD></TD> tags define table cells. You can place text, images, or controls in cells. Add the code at the top of page 206 to place an ActiveX label in the first row of the table in your HTML page.

```
<TR>
    <TD ROWSPAN=5>

    <OBJECT
    CLASSID="clsid:99B42120-6EC7-11CF-A6C7-00AA00A47DD2"
    ID="lblSubscribe"
    WIDTH=60
    HEIGHT=200
    >
    <PARAM NAME="Angle" VALUE="90">
    <PARAM NAME="ForeColor" VALUE="0">
    <PARAM NAME="FontName" VALUE="Times New Roman">
    <PARAM NAME="FontSize" VALUE="28">
    <PARAM NAME="FontBold" VALUE="True">
    <PARAM NAME="FontItalic" VALUE="True">
    <PARAM NAME="Caption" VALUE="Subscription">
    <PARAM NAME="Visible" VALUE="True">
    </OBJECT>
    </TD>
```

You can use the Angle property to rotate a label control through 360 degrees. In this example, you set the property to 90 degrees by using the <PARAM> tag when the label is loaded. The label acts as a vertical banner for the web page; this is a common use for such a label.

Step 3

Now you will add the code to display a PowerPoint animation in the web page. Add the following code to the first row of your HTML table to use the PowerPoint Animation Player in your web page:

```
    <TD ROWSPAN=5>
    <OBJECT
    CLASSID="clsid:EFBD14F0-6BFB-11CF-9177-00805F8813FF"
    WIDTH=284
    HEIGHT=213
    >
    <PARAM NAME="File" VALUE="ppanim.ppz">
    <EMBED
    WIDTH=284 HEIGHT=213 SRC="ppanim.ppz"
    >
    </EMBED>
    <NOEMBED>
    This page contains a Microsoft PowerPoint
    animation that your browser was unable to view.
    </NOEMBED>
    </OBJECT>
    </TD>
</TR>
```

In this HTML code, the <EMBED></EMBED> tags are used to insert the PowerPoint presentation in the page if the browser does not understand the <OBJECT></OBJECT> tags. The <NOEMBED></NOEMBED> tags are used to display a message if the browser can't embed the presentation.

To view the PowerPoint animation, the user must have the PowerPoint Animation Player installed. The PowerPoint Animation Player is simply an ActiveX control. If a user tries to view this page and doesn't have the player installed on the computer, the presentation will not play. Therefore, either each user will have to install the PowerPoint Animation Player or you will have to add PowerPoint animation support to the web server. Step 4 describes both how to install the PowerPoint Animation Player and how to add PowerPoint animation support to the web server.

In the HTML code on page 206, the actual PowerPoint animation that will be displayed with the PowerPoint Animation Player is stored in the file ppanim.ppz, which is a compressed PowerPoint presentation file. The PowerPoint Animation Player can display a standard PowerPoint presentation, but compressed versions are much faster to download. You create compressed animations by using an extension to PowerPoint for Windows 95 called the Microsoft PowerPoint Animation Publisher. Step 4 describes how to install the PowerPoint Animation Publisher.

Step 4

In this step, you will install the PowerPoint Animation Player and the PowerPoint Animation Publisher. The PowerPoint Animation Player should be installed on the computer that will be using the Internet Explorer to view the web page. To install just the PowerPoint Animation Player, use the setup program called axplayer.exe, which is available on the companion CD and on Microsoft's PowerPoint web site. Copy this self-extracting file to your computer, and run it by double-clicking on its icon.

If you want to install both the PowerPoint Animation Player and the PowerPoint Animation Publisher, use the setup program called axpub.exe. This file is available on the companion CD and on Microsoft's PowerPoint web site. When you run axpub.exe, it will install the PowerPoint Animation Player and PowerPoint Animation Publisher.

You can add PowerPoint Animation support to your web server. If you are using IIS, first install the PowerPoint Animation Player on your server and then add the following Registry entries on your server:

```
[HKEY_LOCAL_MACHINE\SYSTEM\CurrentControlSet\Services
\InetInfo\Parameters\MimeMap]
"application/ms-powerpoint,ppt,,5"=""
"application/ms-powerpoint,ppz,,5"=""
```

"application/ms-powerpoint,pps,,5"=""
"application/ms-powerpoint,pot,,5"=""

For more information, consult the PowerPoint Animation user's guide on the Microsoft PowerPoint web site and consult the MIME mapping section of your server documentation.

Step 5

This step describes how to create compressed PowerPoint animations with the PowerPoint Animation Publisher extension in PowerPoint for Windows 95. If you just want to use the ppanim.ppz file, or if you do not have PowerPoint for Windows 95, you can copy the ppanim.ppz file from the project1 folder on the companion CD and place it in the \wwroot\project1 folder you created at the beginning of this project.

Launch PowerPoint for Windows 95, and open the file called ppanim.ppt on the companion CD. Feel free to modify the presentation or simply create your own. Select the File menu and notice the new entry: Export as PowerPoint Animation. Figure 6-13 shows a sample of the Export as PowerPoint Animation dialog box. This option takes any PowerPoint presentation and creates a com-

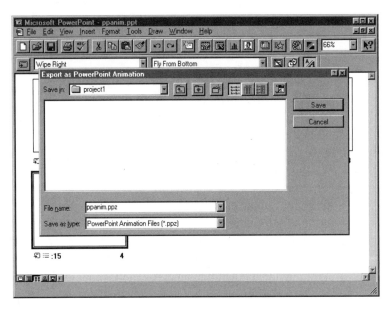

Figure 6-13.
The export as PowerPoint Animation dialog box.

pressed animation file with a ppz extension. When you are finished creating the PowerPoint presentation, simply select the command Export as PowerPoint Animation from the File menu. Save the file with the name ppanim.ppz in the \wwwroot\project1 folder you created at the beginning of this project.

The Export as PowerPoint Animation command will create two files: one compressed animation file, called ppanim.ppz; and one sample HTML file, called ppanim.htm. You can see the results of your work immediately by viewing the sample ppanim.htm file in the Internet Explorer. Figure 6-14 shows a sample of the ppanim.htm file as viewed in the Internet Explorer.

Figure 6-14.
The sample HTML file created with the PowerPoint Animation Publisher extension to PowerPoint for Windows 95.

Step 6

The subscriber data is collected with simple intrinsic controls. In this step, you specify three text boxes to contain the name, department, and email address. All these controls are implemented with the <INPUT> tag. You need to maintain control of the layout, so these controls are used in an HTML table. Add the code at the top of page 210 to place the text boxes on the web page.

```
<TR>
    <TD>
    </TD>
    <TD>
    <FONT FACE="ARIAL" SIZE=3>
    Name
    </FONT>
    </TD>
    <TD>
    <INPUT TYPE="TEXT" SIZE=40 NAME="txtName">
    </TD>
</TR>
<TR>
    <TD>
    </TD>
    <TD>
    <FONT FACE="ARIAL" SIZE=3>
    Dept
    </FONT>
    </TD>
    <TD>
    <INPUT TYPE="TEXT" SIZE=40 NAME="txtDept">
    </TD>
</TR>
<TR>
    <TD>
    </TD>
    <TD>
    <FONT FACE="ARIAL" SIZE=3>
    Email
    </FONT>
    </TD>
    <TD>
    <INPUT TYPE="TEXT" SIZE=40 NAME="txtEmail">
    </TD>
</TR>
```

In the script section, you will use the OnBlur events for each of these controls to perform validation on the data entered. For now, however, just insert the controls.

Step 7

Once your program has collected the data from the user, it must submit the information to the back-end process. In HTML, the ACTION attribute of a form is used to specify the file that will receive the data. In Step 1 of this section, you added code to post the data to subscrib.idc. This file is associated with the httpodbc.dll file.

The user initiates the transfer of data from the form to the back end by clicking on an intrinsic control called a Submit control. When clicked, the Submit control packages all the data in the form input variables and sends it to the process identified by the ACTION attribute of the form. The data is sent as a single string which has the following format:

field1=value1&field2=value2…&fieldn=valuen

The back-end process can then parse this string and take action. Add the following code to add the Submit and Reset controls to the HTML page:

```
<TR>
    <TD>
    </TD>
    <TD>
    </TD>
    <TD>
    <INPUT TYPE="SUBMIT" VALUE="Subscribe!" NAME="cmdSubscribe">
    <INPUT TYPE="RESET">
    </TD>
</TR>
</TABLE>

</FORM>
```

Take note of the other control you inserted, the Reset control. When clicked, this control simply clears all text boxes in the input form. The user can take advantage of this button to start over if he or she makes any mistakes. After the data boxes are filled in, the user clicks on the Subscribe! button. IDC receives the data and adds it to the database. You will construct the idc file later in this exercise.

Step 8

You finish the web page by adding some simple text to the bottom. The last few lines of code present a message prompting the user to subscribe right away and then close the form. Add the following code to finish the body section:

```
<P ALIGN="RIGHT">
<FONT FACE="Comic Sans MS" SIZE=6 COLOR="BLUE">
Sign up today!!
</FONT>
</P>

</CENTER>
</BODY>
</HTML>
```

The Script Section

In this section, you will add some Microsoft Visual Basic, Scripting Edition, code to your web page to perform data validation. The data validation consists of simply checking to see whether information has been entered into the text boxes. The code will not perform more sophisticated validation, such as verifying the user's email address. More advanced validation can be performed with OLEISAPI back-end processes. Although this project does not use OLEISAPI, Project 2 in this book uses it extensively.

Each of the validation routines for this section uses the OnBlur event to determine whether data has been entered into a text field. OnBlur is the intrinsic HTML equivalent of the Visual Basic LostFocus event. In this way, you check to see whether the field has data in it when the user exits the field. Add the following VBScript code to your HTML file after the <BASE HREF="/ project1/"> tag, to create the validation routines (remember, VBScript standards require the script section to be in the head section, for consistency):

```
<SCRIPT LANGUAGE="VBScript">
<!--
    Sub txtName_OnBlur
        Dim MyForm
        Set MyForm=Document.frmSubscribe
        If MyForm.txtName.Value="" Then
            Msgbox "Please enter your name.",16,"Newsletter"
            Exit Sub
        End If
    End Sub

    Sub txtDept_OnBlur
        Dim MyForm
        Set MyForm=Document.frmSubscribe
        If MyForm.txtDept.Value="" Then
            Msgbox "Please enter your department.",16,"Newsletter"
            Exit Sub
        End If
    End Sub

    Sub txtEmail_OnBlur
        Dim MyForm
        Set MyForm=Document.frmSubscribe
        If MyForm.txtEmail.Value="" Then
            Msgbox "Please enter your email address.",16,"Newsletter"
            Exit Sub
        End If
    End Sub
-->
</SCRIPT>
```

In the preceding code, notice the beginning comment tag <!-- and the closing comment tag -->. Their purpose is to hide script code from browsers that do not understand it.

The web page is now complete. Save your web page as subscrib.htm in the folder \wwwroot\project1, which you created at the beginning of this project. Listing 6-1 shows the entire code for subscrib.htm, along with comments, and Figure 6-15, on page 217, shows its output.

```
<HTML>
<HEAD>
<TITLE>Intranet Newsletter Subscription</TITLE>
<BASE HREF="/project1/">

<!--
This demo allows a user to subscribe to a
company newsletter published through the
intranet
-->

<SCRIPT LANGUAGE="VBScript">
<!--
    Sub txtName_OnBlur
        Dim MyForm
        Set MyForm=Document.frmSubscribe
        If MyForm.txtName.Value="" Then
            Msgbox "Please enter your name.",16,"Newsletter"
            Exit Sub
        End If
    End Sub

    Sub txtDept_OnBlur
        Dim MyForm
        Set MyForm=Document.frmSubscribe
        If MyForm.txtDept.Value="" Then
            Msgbox "Please enter your department.",16,"Newsletter"
            Exit Sub
        End If
    End Sub

    Sub txtEmail_OnBlur
        Dim MyForm
        Set MyForm=Document.frmSubscribe
        If MyForm.txtEmail.Value="" Then
            Msgbox "Please enter your email address.", _
                16,"Newsletter"
            Exit Sub
```

Listing 6-1.
The complete code for subscrib.htm.

(continued)

213

Listing 6-1 *continued*

```
        End If
    End Sub
-->
</SCRIPT>

</HEAD>
<BODY BGCOLOR="WHITE">
<CENTER>

<FORM NAME="frmSubscribe" METHOD="POST"
ACTION="/scripts/project1/subscrib.idc">
<TABLE BORDER=0 CELLPADDING=0 CELLSPACING=0>
    <TR>
        <TD ROWSPAN=5>

        <!--
        This is a Label control, rotated 90 degrees.
        It is used to place a label on the web page.
        -->

        <OBJECT
         CLASSID="clsid:99B42120-6EC7-11CF-A6C7-00AA00A47DD2"
        ID="lblSubscribe"
        WIDTH=60
        HEIGHT=200
        >
        <PARAM NAME="Angle" VALUE="90">
        <PARAM NAME="ForeColor" VALUE="0">
        <PARAM NAME="FontName" VALUE="Times New Roman">
        <PARAM NAME="FontSize" VALUE="28">
        <PARAM NAME="FontBold" VALUE="True">
        <PARAM NAME="FontItalic" VALUE="True">
        <PARAM NAME="Caption" VALUE="Subscription">
        <PARAM NAME="Visible" VALUE="True">
        </OBJECT>
        </TD>
        <TD ROWSPAN=5>

        <!--
        This is a Microsoft PowerPoint Animation Player
        control. It is used to display PowerPoint
        presentation files. It can also display a
        compressed PowerPoint presentation file, which
        typically has a ppz extension.
        The ppz file can be created with the Microsoft
        Powerpoint Animation Publisher, a PowerPoint for
```

```
        Windows 95 extension.
        -->

        <OBJECT
        CLASSID="clsid:EFBD14F0-6BFB-11CF-9177-00805F8813FF"
        WIDTH=284
        HEIGHT=213
        >
        <PARAM NAME="File" VALUE="ppanim.ppz">
        <EMBED
        WIDTH=284 HEIGHT=213 SRC="ppanim.ppz"
        >
        </EMBED>
        <NOEMBED>
        This page contains a Microsoft PowerPoint
        animation that your browser was unable to view.
        </NOEMBED>
        </OBJECT>
        </TD>
</TR>
<TR>
    <TD>
    </TD>
    <TD>
    <FONT FACE="ARIAL" SIZE=3>
    Name
    </FONT>
    </TD>
    <TD>
    <INPUT TYPE="TEXT" SIZE=40 NAME="txtName">
    </TD>
</TR>
<TR>
    <TD>
    </TD>
    <TD>
    <FONT FACE="ARIAL" SIZE=3>
    Dept
    </FONT>
    </TD>
    <TD>
    <INPUT TYPE="TEXT" SIZE=40 NAME="txtDept">
    </TD>
</TR>
<TR>
    <TD>
    </TD>
```

(continued)

Listing 6-1 *continued*

```
        <TD>
        <FONT FACE="ARIAL" SIZE=3>
        Email
        </FONT>
        </TD>
        <TD>
        <INPUT TYPE="TEXT" SIZE=40 NAME="txtEmail">
        </TD>
    </TR>
    <TR>
        <TD>
        </TD>
        <TD>
        </TD>
        <TD>
        <INPUT TYPE="SUBMIT" VALUE="Subscribe!" NAME="cmdSubscribe">
        <INPUT TYPE="RESET">
        </TD>
    </TR>
</TABLE>
</FORM>

<P ALIGN="RIGHT">
<FONT FACE="Comic Sans MS" SIZE=6 COLOR="BLUE">
Sign up today!!
</FONT>
</P>

</CENTER>
</BODY>
</HTML>
```

Up to this point, you have created a database, set up the ODBC drivers, and created the HTML page. Now you need to create the necessary files so that subscriber information on the web page can be added to the database when the Subscribe! button is clicked. This will be accomplished with the Internet Database Connector (IDC).

Calling the Internet Database Connector

IDC is invoked from a web page by the ACTION attribute of a form. In this section, you will create the idc file called by the form in subscrib.htm, and you will add a confirmation screen informing the user that he or she is properly registered.

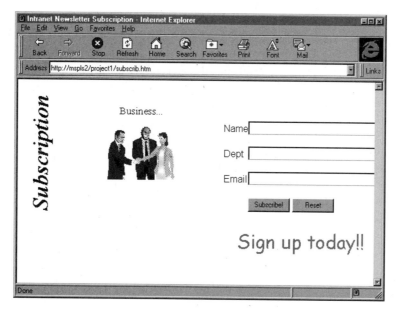

Figure 6-15.
Sample output for subscrib.htm.

The idc File

The idc file identifies the datasource, the return page template, and the SQL statement for IDC to use when the data is submitted. Begin this file by opening a new document in a text editor such as Notepad. The file you create will be called subscrib.idc.

Step 1

The Datasource field is used to identify an ODBC datasource for IDC to use. This datasource is the same one you set up earlier in this project. Identify the datasource for this transaction by adding the following code to the idc file:

```
Datasource:subscribers
```

Step 2

The Template field is used to identify an HTML extension (htx) file that acts as a template for the return page. This field should contain the complete path to the file. Add the following code to identify the HTML extension file to be used with this transaction:

```
Template:c:\inetsrv\scripts\project1\subscrib.htx
```

Step 3

The SQLStatement field is used to identify the SQL statement you want IDC to run when the idc file is called. This field can reference the form input variables used in the form. You reference these variables by using the NAME attribute as specified in the HTML page. Treat the variables as you would any SQL variables. For example, if you enclose the variables in single quotes, the variables will be read as strings. Add the following code to the idc file to insert the new data into the database:

```
SQLStatement:
+INSERT INTO People (Name,Department,Email)
+VALUES ('%txtName%','%txtDept%','%txtEmail%')
```

The plus signs in the statement are line continuation characters and are required at the start of each new line. When you have finished this file, save it with the name subscrib.idc in the folder \scripts\project1, which you created at the beginning of the project.

The htx File

After the database has been updated, you will return a confirmation screen to the user, saying that the registration is complete. The HTML extension (htx) file is the return page template. This template is similar to any other HTML page except that you can access special variables within the page. The htx file should be formatted into head, script, and body sections.

Step 1

The head section of the htx file is just like any other HTML head section. You can specify a title and a base reference, and you can include a script section. Begin this file by opening a new document in a text editor such as Notepad. Add the following code to create the head section of the return web page:

```
<HTML>
<HEAD>
<TITLE>Account Information</TITLE>
</HEAD>
```

Step 2

The rest of the page is a simple confirmation screen thanking the user for subscribing. This page uses a form input variable from the idc file to include the user's name in the page. You access the form input variables by prefixing them with the letters *idc*. Add the following code to complete the htx file:

```
<BODY BGCOLOR="WHITE" BACKGROUND="/project1/backgnd.gif">
<CENTER>
```

```
<FONT FACE="TIMES NEW ROMAN" SIZE=6>
Thanks for subscribing, <%idc.txtName%>!<P>
</FONT>
</CENTER>
</BODY>
</HTML>
```

Save this file as subscrib.htx in the folder \scripts\project1, which you created at the beginning of this project. From the companion CD, copy the file backgnd.gif, located in the project1 folder, and place it in the folder \wwwroot\project1. The file backgnd.gif is used to display a background on the confirmation screen. Figure 6-16 shows a sample of the web page returned after a user subscribes.

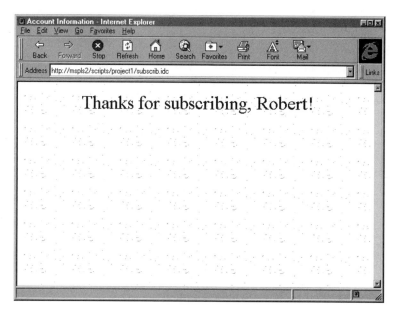

Figure 6-16.
The confirmation screen.

Sending the Newsletter

Once the data has been collected in the database, you can publish a newsletter. The newsletter is distributed by a Visual Basic application that can connect to both the datasource and the intranet mail server. This part of the project uses only Visual Basic.

The Visual Basic files used for this portion of the project, along with an executable called publish.exe, are available on the companion CD, in the project1 folder. Listing 6-2, starting on page 231, shows the complete code. The following steps show you how to create the Visual Basic application called Publish.

Creating the Interface

The graphical user interface (GUI) for your project will consist of a Visual Basic form with controls that allow the user to select the file to be sent to the subscribers. Two buttons are also included. One allows the user to publish the newsletter, and the other lets the user exit the application. There are also two invisible Mail API (MAPI) controls that are used to access email and send the newsletter to the subscribers.

Step 1

Start a new project in Visual Basic 4.0. Form1 will be the primary user interface for the application. Change the form properties for Form1 as follows:

BorderStyle	3 - Fixed Dialog
Caption	Publishing the Intranet Newsletter
Height	3735
MaxButton	False
MinButton	False
Name	frmPublish
Width	6600

Step 2

The user will employ a set of file controls to select the files to publish. These controls allow him or her to select the drive, folder, and file for publishing. Place a DriveListBox control on the form, and change the properties as follows:

Left	90
Name	drvPublish
Top	2700
Width	2175

Step 3

The DirListBox control works with the DriveListBox control to specify the complete path to the file. Place a DirListBox control on the form, and change the properties as follows:

Height	2280
Left	90
Name	dirPublish
Top	270
Width	2175

Step 4

The FileListBox control allows the user to select the file to be published. Place a FileListBox control on the form, and set the properties as follows:

Height	2790
Left	2430
Name	filPublish
Top	270
Width	2130

Step 5

In this step you add a button to the form to allow the user to exit the application. Place a CommandButton control on the form, and set the properties as follows:

Cancel	True
Caption	&Cancel
Height	420
Left	4680
Name	cmdCancel
Top	810
Width	1725

Step 6

A second button is used to initiate the publishing process. Place another CommandButton control on the form, and set its properties as follows:

Caption	&Publish
Default	True
Height	420
Left	4680
Name	cmdPublish
Top	270
Width	1725

Step 7

The mail system is accessed through the MAPI controls that ship with Visual Basic. Add the MAPI controls to your project by selecting Tools/Custom Controls from the Visual Basic menu bar. In the Custom Controls dialog box, select Microsoft MAPI Controls and then click on the OK button. The MAPI controls should then be added to your toolbox. When the controls are visible in the toolbox, place a MAPISession control and a MAPIMessages control on your form. Your form should now look like the one in Figure 6-17.

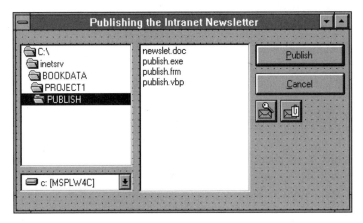

Figure 6-17.
The Publish application interface.

You have now completed the interface for the Publish application. Save this form as publish.frm and this project as publish.vbp. The next section describes the code for implementing the Publish application.

Coding the Application

The Publish application must connect to both the ODBC datasource you built earlier and the email system that will be used to send the newsletter. In this section you will use Remote Data Objects (RDOs) to connect to the ODBC datasource. These objects allow you to connect to a database, execute queries, and modify the information. RDOs are a feature of Visual Basic, Enterprise Edition, and are not available in the Professional or Standard Editions of Visual Basic. If you have the Professional Edition of Visual Basic, it is possible to interface with a database by using Data Access Objects (DAOs), but that type of implementation is not discussed here. The email system will be accessed through the MAPI controls that you have already placed on the form.

Step 1

Before you can use Remote Data Objects to access the ODBC source, you must set a reference to the RDO component. You set a reference to any component by using the References dialog box that is accessed through the Visual Basic Tools/References command. Open the References dialog box, and set a reference to the component named Microsoft Remote Data Object 1.0.

The RDO component is designed specifically to communicate with ODBC datasources. It is made up of a set of objects that can interface directly with ODBC drivers. Table 6-2 lists the Remote Data Objects. Figure 6-18, on page 224, shows the Remote Data Object model.

Table 6-2. **The Remote Data Objects**

Object	Description
rdoEngine	An object that represents the ODBC datasource itself.
rdoEnvironment	An object that represents a set of connections to various datasources for a particular user name. This object also provides for batch transactions between datasources.
rdoError	An object that contains information about errors that might occur while a datasource is being accessed.
rdoConnection	An object that represents an open connection to a specific database on a datasource.
rdoTable	An object that represents a table inside a datasource.
rdoPreparedStatement	An object that represents a predefined query.
rdoResultset	An object that represents the results of a query on the datasource.
rdoColumn	An object that represents a column of data in a table or result set.
rdoParameter	An object that represents a parameter associated with a predefined query.

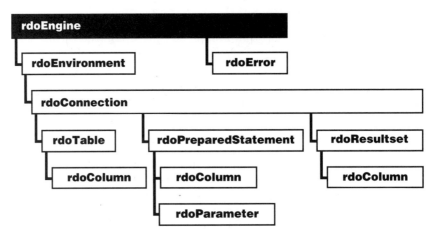

Figure 6-18.
The Remote Data Object model.

Step 2

Open the code window associated with frmPublish by selecting the form in the Project window and clicking on the View Code button. In the code window, define two variables for accessing the ODBC datasource by adding the following code:

```
Option Explicit

Private dbSubscribers As RDO.rdoConnection
Private rsSubscribers As RDO.rdoResultset
```

Note how these variables are defined. Each of the variables represents an object in the RDO component; you will use one to access the datasource and the other to return a set of records. The variables can have any name you want, but the data types are defined by the RDO component. The definitions use the syntax *Component_Name.Object*. The name of the component for Remote Data Objects is RDO, and the object names are those that were defined in Table 6-2. These variables will give you the necessary functionality to open the datasource and retrieve records.

Step 3

Begin building your project in the Form_Load event procedure of the form. In this procedure, you will open the datasource and connect to the mail server. You will also handle routine functions, such as changing the mouse pointer and handling errors. Add the following code to the Form_Load procedure:

```
Private Sub Form_Load()
On Error GoTo LoadErr

    Dim intPrevPointer As Integer
    intPrevPointer = Screen.MousePointer
    Screen.MousePointer = 11
```

This code sets up an error-handling structure for the function and changes the mouse to an hourglass while the form loads. Both error handling and mouse handling are critical to making the application robust. The error-handling structure simply identifies a line label that directs execution to an error-handling routine in the event of an error. You will build the actual error-handling routine later. The mouse-handling code saves the current value of the mouse pointer to an intermediate variable and changes the mouse pointer to an hourglass. Later in the code, you will restore the mouse pointer to its previous value.

Step 4

Connecting to the datasource is a function of the RDO component. You will use the rdoConnection object to establish a connection to the datasource, and you will use the rdoResultset object to retrieve records from the source. Add the following code to the Form_Load procedure to establish a connection and run a query:

```
Set dbSubscribers = rdoEngine.rdoEnvironments(0). _
OpenConnection("subscribers")
Set rsSubscribers = dbSubscribers.OpenResultset _
("SELECT * FROM People", rdOpenDynamic)
```

The OpenConnection method of the rdoEnvironment object is used to create a connection to the datasource. The argument for the OpenConnection method is the name of the datasource you want to open. If your datasource requires other information, such as a user ID and password, that can be specified here as well.

The OpenResultset method of the rdoConnection object is used to perform a query on the datasource. The arguments for the method allow you to specify a query, as well as the type of result set to return. In the preceding code, you are returning all the entries in the datasource and making the result set "dynamic," which means that you will be able to navigate the result set completely, without restriction.

Step 5

You connect to the mail server with the MAPI controls. There are two differ-ent MAPI controls: MAPISession and MAPIMessages. The MAPISession con-trol connects to the server, and the MAPIMessages control sends or receives messages. The MAPISession control has four commonly used properties and two commonly used methods. Table 6-3 lists the properties, and Table 6-4 lists the methods that you will use in this project.

Table 6-3. MAPISession Properties Used in This Project

Property	Description
UserName	The name of the user account that will connect to the mail server
Password	The password for the given user account
SessionID	A property that returns a nonzero value identifying the connection if the connection is successful
DownloadMail	A Boolean property that determines whether mail is downloaded for the given account when a connection is made

Table 6-4. MAPISession Methods Used in This Project

Method	Description
SignOn	Connects to the mail server with the given user name and password
SignOff	Disconnects from the mail server

To connect to the mail server under the administrator account, add the following code to the Form_Load procedure:

```
MAPISession1.DownloadMail = False
MAPISession1.UserName = "POSTMASTER"
MAPISession1.Password = "your password"
MAPISession1.SignOn
```

Note that you would need to enter the appropriate user name and pass-word for your mail server.

Step 6

Once the connection is established, the mail is sent via the MAPIMessages control. The MAPIMessages control allows you to construct a message, add attachments, and send the message to a recipient. The commonly used MAPIMessages properties and methods are shown in Table 6-5 and Table 6-6, respectively.

Table 6-5. MAPIMessages Properties Used in This Project

Property	Description
SessionID	A number that identifies the current session. This number comes from the MAPISession control when the connection is made.
MsgSubject	The text for the subject line of the message.
MsgNoteText	The body of the message.
RecipDisplayName	The name of the recipient as it is displayed in email. This is not the user account. For example, a user account called *JOHNS* might correspond to a RecipDisplayName of *John Smith*. User accounts can be accessed through the RecipAddress property.
RecipAddress	The address of the recipient—for example, *JOHNS*.
AttachmentPathName	The fully qualified path and filename of an attachment to the message.

Table 6-6. MAPIMessages Methods Used in This Project

Method	Description
Compose	Resets the message buffer and allows a new message to be created
Send	Sends the message and all attachments to the recipient

Add the following code to the Form_Load procedure to enable the MAPIMessages control.

```
MAPIMessages1.SessionID = MAPISession1.SessionID
```

Step 7

To complete the Form_Load event procedure, you must restore the mouse pointer and provide the error-handling routine. The mouse pointer is restored just before you exit the procedure, and the error-handling call is separated from the rest of the procedure. Add the following code to complete the Form_Load procedure:

```
LoadExit:
    Screen.MousePointer = intPrevPointer
    Exit Sub

LoadErr:
    ErrorHandler Err.Number, Err.Description, "Form_Load"
    Resume LoadExit
End Sub
```

Step 8

The Publish application allows the user to select a file to include as an attachment. This attachment is the newsletter itself. In this way, the user can create a newsletter in any application that the mail system supports and simply select it, using the file controls that you placed on the form.

The file controls used in this project are independent controls; however, you can make them work together by adding some simple code. The following code causes the drive box, folder box, and file box to coordinate their behavior so that they display the correct folders and files for any drive and folder combination:

```
Private Sub dirPublish_Change()
    filPublish.Path = dirPublish.Path
End Sub

Private Sub drvPublish_Change()
    dirPublish.Path = drvPublish.Drive
End Sub
```

Step 9

Publishing the newsletter is a matter of reading all the recipients' names from the database, composing a message, and mailing the newsletter. You will implement these steps in the Publish routine. You will also build error handling and mouse handling into the Publish routine. The publishing occurs when the user clicks on the Publish button. To begin the Publish routine, add the following code to the cmdPublish_Click procedure:

```
Private Sub cmdPublish_Click()
On Error GoTo PublishErr
    Dim intPrevPointer As Integer
    intPrevPointer = Screen.MousePointer
    Screen.MousePointer = 11
```

Step 10

Before the user can send any messages, the Publish application must make sure that a file has been selected and that there are names of subscribers in the database. If a file has not been properly selected, or if there are no subscribers in the database, an error will result. Add the following code to check whether a file has been selected and whether the database has subscribers:

```
If filPublish.filename = "" Then
    MsgBox "Please pick a file to mail.", 16, "Publisher"
    GoTo PublishExit
End If

If rsSubscribers.BOF And rsSubscribers.EOF Then
    MsgBox "No subscribers are in the database.", 16, "Publish"
    GoTo PublishExit
End If
```

Step 11

The newsletter is published by means of a loop in which the user creates a series of messages to send. The names are retrieved from the database one by one. The Compose method is used to start the message, and then the MsgSubject and MsgNoteText are assigned. The RecipDisplayName and the RecipAddress properties are set to the Name and Email fields in the subscribers database. Note that the transport protocol, SMTP, was added to the RecipAddress property in the code below. (SMTP stands for Simple Mail Transfer Protocol.) This might not be required; it depends on your mailing system. Finally, the user attaches the newsletter, using the AttachmentPathName property, and mails it with the Send method. Add the following code to allow the user to send the newsletter to all recipients in the subscribers datasource:

```
rsSubscribers.MoveFirst
Do While Not rsSubscribers.EOF
    MAPIMessages1.Compose

    MAPIMessages1.MsgSubject = "Company Newsletter"
```

(continued)

229

continued

```
    MAPIMessages1.MsgNoteText _
        = "The Monthly Company Newsletter is attached!"

    MAPIMessages1.RecipDisplayName = rsSubscribers!Name

    MAPIMessages1.RecipAddress = "SMTP:" & _
        rsSubscribers!email

    MAPIMessages1.AttachmentPathName = filPublish.Path & _
        "\" & filPublish.filename

    MAPIMessages1.Send

    rsSubscribers.MoveNext
Loop

MsgBox "Newsletter Published!", 0, "Publisher"
```

Step 12

You complete the Publish routine by adding error handling and mouse handling, just as for other routines. Add the following code to complete the cmdPublish_Click procedure:

```
PublishExit:
    Screen.MousePointer = intPrevPointer
    Exit Sub

PublishErr:
    ErrorHandler Err.Number, Err.Description, "Publish"
    Resume PublishExit

EndSub
```

Step 13

The ErrorHandler routine takes care of error handling. This routine simply displays a message box that describes any errors that occur. Add the following code to construct the error-handling procedure:

```
Private Sub ErrorHandler(lngNumber As Long, _
    strDescription As String, strProcedure As String)

    On Error GoTo 0
    MsgBox "System Error!" & Chr$(10) & "Error #" & _
    Format$(lngNumber) & Chr$(10) & strDescription & _
    Chr$(10) & "In Procedure " & strProcedure, 16, "Publisher"
End Sub
```

Step 14

Your project also supplies a Cancel button that can be used to exit the project
without publishing the newsletter. This button simply unloads the form and
terminates the project. Add the following code to the cmdCancel_Click procedure to allow the user to exit the project without publishing the newsletter:

```
Private Sub cmdCancel_Click()
    Unload Me
End Sub
```

Step 15

The user can exit the application in two different ways: either by selecting the
Cancel button or by clicking on the control box to close the form. In both cases,
the Form_Unload event will trigger. In the Form_Unload procedure, you will
close the database connection and the mail server connection. Add the following code to the Form_Unload procedure to complete the code for the Publish
application:

```
Private Sub Form_Unload (Cancel As Integer)
    MAPISession1.SignOff
    rsSubscribers.Close
    dbSubscribers.Close
    Set rsSubscribers = Nothing
    Set dbSubscribers = Nothing
    End
End Sub
```

   Listing 6-2 shows the complete Visual Basic code, along with comments
for the Publish application.

```
Option Explicit

Private dbSubscribers As RDO.rdoConnection
Private rsSubscribers As RDO.rdoResultset

Private Sub Form_Load()

'Author: New Technology Solutions, Inc.
'Purpose: Connect to datasource and mail server
'6/10/96 Original

On Error GoTo LoadErr
```

Listing 6-2.   *(continued)*
The Visual Basic code for the Publish application.

Listing 6-2 *continued*

```
    'Change pointer to hourglass
    Dim intPrevPointer As Integer
    intPrevPointer = Screen.MousePointer
    Screen.MousePointer = 11

    'Connect to datasource
    Set dbSubscribers = rdoEngine.rdoEnvironments(0). _
    OpenConnection("subscribers")
    Set rsSubscribers = dbSubscribers. _
    OpenResultset("SELECT * FROM People", rdOpenDynamic)

    'Connect to mail server
    MAPISession1.DownloadMail = False
    MAPISession1.UserName = "POSTMASTER"
    MAPISession1.Password = "your password"
    MAPISession1.SignOn

    MAPIMessages1.SessionID = MAPISession1.SessionID

LoadExit:
    Screen.MousePointer = intPrevPointer
    Exit Sub

LoadErr:
    ErrorHandler Err.Number, Err.Description, "Form_Load"
    Resume LoadExit
End Sub

Private Sub dirPublish_Change()
    filPublish.Path = dirPublish.Path
End Sub

Private Sub drvPublish_Change()
    dirPublish.Path = drvPublish.Drive
End Sub

Private Sub cmdPublish_Click()

'Author: New Technology Solutions, Inc.
'Purpose: Publish the newsletter
'6/10/96 Original

On Error GoTo PublishErr

    'Change pointer to hourglass
    Dim intPrevPointer As Integer
```

```
intPrevPointer = Screen.MousePointer
Screen.MousePointer = 11

'Make sure a file has been selected
If filPublish.filename = "" Then
    MsgBox "Please pick a file to mail.", 16, "Publisher"
    GoTo PublishExit
End If

'Make sure there is someone to send it to
If rsSubscribers.BOF And rsSubscribers.EOF Then
    MsgBox "No subscribers are in the database.", 16, "Publish"
    GoTo PublishExit
End If

rsSubscribers.MoveFirst
Do While Not rsSubscribers.EOF

    'Build the message to send
    MAPIMessages1.Compose

    MAPIMessages1.MsgSubject = "Company Newsletter"
    MAPIMessages1.MsgNoteText _
    = "The Monthly Company Newsletter is attached!"

    'Specify the name as it will appear in the email
    MAPIMessages1.RecipDisplayName = rsSubscribers!Name

    'Specify the transport protocol and the
    'email address.  This may vary, depending on
    'your mailing system.
    MAPIMessages1.RecipAddress = "SMTP:" & _
        rsSubscribers!email

    'Attach the newsletter
    MAPIMessages1.AttachmentPathName = filPublish.Path & _
        "\" & filPublish.filename

    'Send the message
    MAPIMessages1.Send

    'Move to next recipient
    rsSubscribers.MoveNext
Loop
```

(continued)

Listing 6-2 *continued*

```
    MsgBox "Newsletter Published!", 0, "Publisher"

PublishExit:
    Screen.MousePointer = intPrevPointer
    Exit Sub

PublishErr:
    ErrorHandler Err.Number, Err.Description, "Publish"
    Resume PublishExit

End Sub

Private Sub ErrorHandler(lngNumber As Long, _
    strDescription As String, strProcedure As String)

'Author: New Technology Solutions, Inc.
'Purpose: Handle runtime errors
'6/10/96 Original

    On Error GoTo 0
    MsgBox "System Error!" & Chr$(10) & "Error #" & _
    Format$(lngNumber) & Chr$(10) & strDescription & _
    Chr$(10) & "In Procedure " & strProcedure, 16, "Publisher"
End Sub

Private Sub cmdCancel_Click()
    Unload Me
End Sub

Private Sub Form_Unload(Cancel As Integer)

    'Disconnect from mail server
    MAPISession1.SignOff

    'Close datasource
    rsSubscribers.Close
    dbSubscribers.Close

    'Destroy objects
    Set rsSubscribers = Nothing
    Set dbSubscribers = Nothing

    'End application
    End
End Sub
```

Now that the code for the Publish application is finished, you can make an executable file. First save the Publish project, and then select Make EXE File from the File menu. Name the file publish.exe, and click the OK button. You can test the application by entering some data in the subscribers database with the Visual Basic Data Manager and running the application. Combined with the HTML page you created previously, this project is a simple but complete intranet publishing system.

Running the Project

To run the project, first make sure that you have saved subscrib.htm, backgnd.gif, and ppanim.ppz in the folder \wwwroot\project1, subscrib.htx and subscrib.idc in the \scripts\project1 folder, and subscrib.mdb in the folder \bookdata\project1. (Refer to Figure 6-3 for the folder structure.)

Once all of the files are placed in the proper folders, you can test the HTML subscription form by opening subscrib.htm in the Internet Explorer. Test the data validation routine for the subscription form by leaving the Department field blank. A message box should appear, prompting you to enter some data. Figure 6-19 shows a sample of the subscription form with the message box displayed.

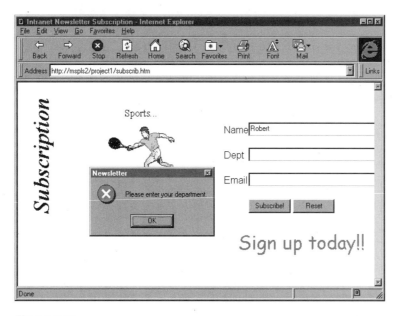

Figure 6-19.
The subscription form demonstrating simple data validation.

After testing the validation procedure, fill in the form completely and submit it to the Internet Database Connector by clicking on the button on the form. If your code is correct, you will see a confirmation screen.

After you have tested the data entry routine, you can publish the newsletter, using the Visual Basic Publish application you created. Run the Publish application, and use the file controls to select a file for the newsletter. The newsletter can be any file that your mail system supports. Then simply click the Publish button. The Publish application mails the newsletter as an attachment to each subscriber in the database.

Figure 6-20 shows the Publish application as it appears after a newsletter has been published.

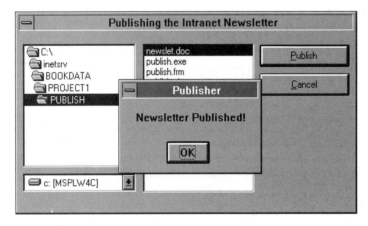

Figure 6-20.
The Publish application.

Figure 6-21 shows a sample of the email the subscribers will receive from the Publish application, as viewed in Microsoft Exchange. It shows the message that is received, along with an attached newsletter that was created in Microsoft Word.

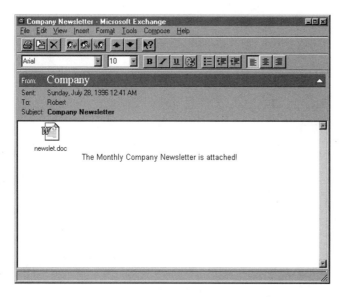

Figure 6-21.

The newsletter subscribers will receive from the Publish application as shown in Microsoft Exchange.

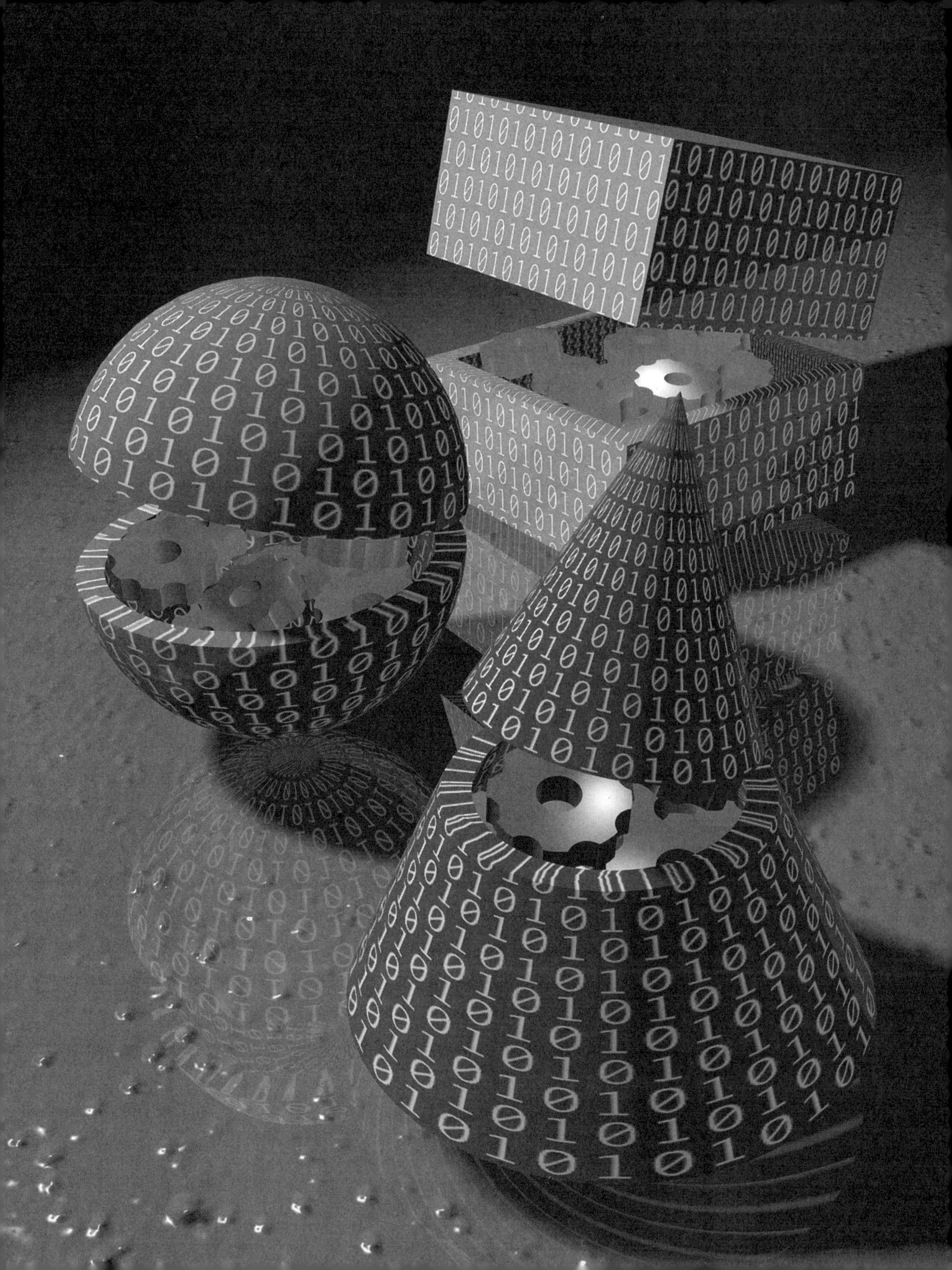

Project #2: An Event Registration Application

The project presented in this chapter creates an online registration program for a hypothetical event. The project uses a back-end database to store information about the registrants. The program accesses the database on the Microsoft Internet Information Server (IIS) by using OLEISAPI technology. OLEISAPI calls an in-process ActiveX component, formerly called an OLE server, that you will create by using Microsoft Visual Basic 4.0. Front-end validation is performed with Microsoft Visual Basic, Scripting Edition.

The discussion of this project assumes that you are familiar with Visual Basic 4.0. Detailed knowledge of ActiveX components is not required but is helpful. Because this project is intended to be a complete online solution, you will need to be familiar with Microsoft Windows NT Server, Microsoft Windows NT networks in general, and Microsoft Windows 95. We also assume that you are building the solution directly on a Windows NT server. However, it is possible to construct the necessary files on a computer with Windows 95 and then transfer them to a Windows NT server for final configuration and testing. No matter which method you use, it is a good idea to have Visual Basic installed on the server so that changes can be made on the server.

Requirements

Construction of the event registration project requires the following components:

- Windows NT Server version 3.51 or 4.0 with IIS installed
- Windows 95 with the Microsoft Internet Explorer 3.0 installed
- Visual Basic 4.0, Enterprise Edition

- Microsoft Access 7.0 Open Database Connectivity (ODBC) drivers (available on the companion CD)

- Microsoft Access (optional)

- Microsoft Label and Timer controls (available on the companion CD)

- oleisapi.dll (available on the companion CD)

Design Objective

The design objective for this project is to create an online event registration system. The system will provide a form for registering, a way to validate the entered data, and data storage in a server-side database. Users will register online with an HTML form that uses form input variables to store the data. The form input variables will contain all of the vital information for each registrant, including such items as name, company, and credit card number. The form will also contain and display the total cost incurred by each registrant. Figure 7-1 shows the event registration form.

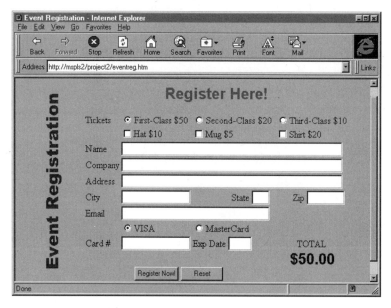

Figure 7-1.
The event registration form.

Because it is faster to use client-side calculations than to send data back to the server for calculation, all intermediate calculations will be performed on the client. The client will also perform all data validation. The performance of intermediate tasks (such as data validation and the calculation of running totals) on the client allows for faster response to the user's input and offers the user a more pleasant experience with the application.

When the transaction is complete, data will be transferred in a batch to the server for processing. The back end stores information about the user and the cost for the event. Although this example simply stores the entered data, you could add more functionality to process the data in different ways. After the processing has been completed, the program returns an acknowledgment message to the user.

Prerequisites

Prior to starting the project, you will need to create a folder structure to hold your work. If you have done any of the other projects in this book, some of this structure might already be in place. From the Windows NT server's File Manager, create the following folders (note that for a standard installation of IIS, you should already have a folder named inetsrv and two subfolders named wwwroot and scripts):

drive\inetsrv\bookdata\project2	For the events registration database and Visual Basic files
drive\inetsrv\scripts\project2	For the DLL created with Visual Basic
drive\inetsrv\wwwroot\project2	For the HTML file and background graphic

Figure 7-2 (page 242) shows an example of the folder structure.

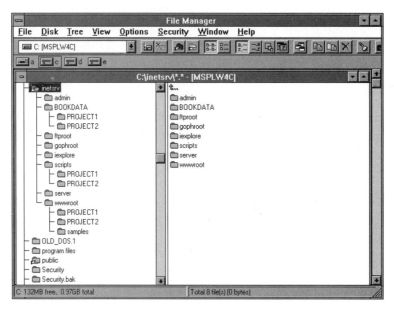

Figure 7-2.
An example of the Project #2 folder structure.

Creating the Datasource

To complete this project, you must create an ODBC datasource to store the information for each registrant. Before you can create the datasource, you must have the ODBC drivers for Microsoft Access properly installed. If you need to install ODBC drivers, see the newsletter project in Chapter 6, which explains in detail how to install ODBC drivers on your Windows NT server.

Creating the Access Database

Now you will construct a Microsoft Access database. The database will contain important information about the registrants and the costs they incur. You can build the database either by using Microsoft Access directly or by using the Data Manager included with Visual Basic. For this exercise, you will create the database by using the Data Manager. If you prefer to create the database in Access, you can do so and then return to the exercise at the "Defining the Datasource" section. In any case, you will create a database with the structure shown in Table 7-1.

Table 7-1. The Registrations Table

Field Name	Data Type
Name	Text
Company	Text
Address	Text
City	Text
State	Text
Zip	Text
Email	Text
CardType	Text
CardNumber	Text
CardExpDate	Text
Ticket	Text
Shirt	Text
Hat	Text
Mug	Text
Total	Text

Step 1

Start Visual Basic 4.0. Open the Data Manager by selecting Add-Ins/Data Manager from the Visual Basic menu bar. The Data Manager will start, and you will see a form with File and Help menus.

Step 2

Create a new database by selecting New Database from the File menu. After the New Database dialog box appears, navigate to the folder \bookdata\project2, type in the filename eventreg.mdb, and click on the OK (or Save) button.

Step 3

Add a new table to the database by clicking on the New button. The Add Table dialog box should appear. Name the new table Registrations.

Step 4

Add the fields from Table 7-1 to the database one at a time by filling in the Field Name text box with the appropriate name. For each field, select Text from the Data Type combo box and set the field size to 250. Click on the right arrow button to add each field. The fields will appear in the list box in the center of the dialog box. Figure 7-3 shows the completed Registrations table in the Add Table dialog box.

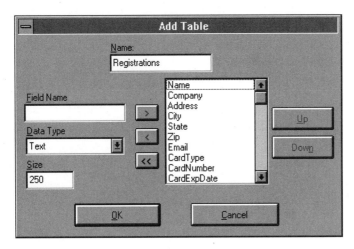

Figure 7-3.
The Add Table dialog box showing the completed Registrations table.

Step 5

Click on the OK button in the Add Table dialog box. The Registrations table should appear in the Data Manager. Figure 7-4 shows the event registration database with the Registrations table added. Minimize the Data Manager so that you can access the database directly anytime during the exercise. When you are working with ODBC drivers, direct access via the Data Manager can be helpful for troubleshooting.

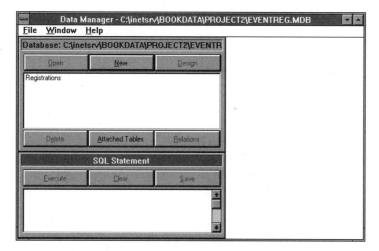

Figure 7-4.
The event registration database with the Registrations table added.

Defining the Datasource

At this point in the exercise, you should have built the database by using either the Data Manager or Microsoft Access. Regardless of which method you used, your database should have the structure shown in Table 7-1 (page 243). If your database is ready, you can go on to create the ODBC datasource used in the exercise. Make sure that the database is complete and that the appropriate ODBC drivers have been installed.

Step 1
From the Control Panel or an ODBC group, start the ODBC Administrator. When the ODBC Administrator starts, you will see the Data Sources dialog box.

Step 2
Install the new datasource by clicking on the System DSN button in the Data Sources dialog box. The System Data Sources dialog box should appear. In the System Data Sources dialog box, click on the Add button. The Add Data Source dialog box will then appear.

Step 3
In the Add Data Source dialog box, select the Microsoft Access ODBC driver and click on the OK button. The ODBC Microsoft Access Setup dialog box should appear. This dialog box is used to set up the datasource.

Step 4

Give your datasource a name by typing *eventreg* into the Data Source Name text box. This is the name you will use to identify the database whenever you utilize an ODBC driver. This name can be anything you want and is not directly related to the name of the database you created previously.

Step 5

Enter a brief description for your datasource in the Description text box. This can be any text you want and has no effect on the application.

Step 6

Establish your datasource as the database you created previously by clicking on the Select button. Now you will see a dialog box that lets you select the file for this datasource. Navigate to the \bookdata\project2 folder, select the eventreg.mdb database you created previously, and click the OK button. Figure 7-5 shows a sample of the ODBC Microsoft Access Setup dialog box after the eventreg.mdb database has been set up. When you are done, click the OK button. Your new datasource should now be visible in the System Data Sources dialog box.

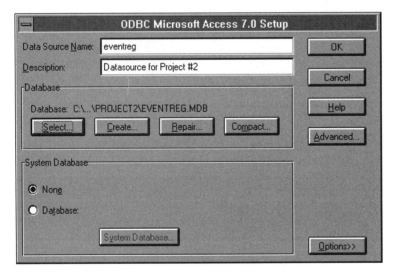

Figure 7-5.
The ODBC Microsoft Access Setup dialog box after the eventreg.mdb database has been set up.

Step 7

Click on the Close buttons in the System Data Sources dialog box and in the Data Sources dialog box to exit the ODBC Administrator. Your datasource is now ready to be accessed from the web!

Creating the HTML Page

In this section, you will build the HTML page that contains the data input form for event registration. This HTML page will utilize VBScript to perform some simple data validation and generate some interesting interactive content. You will use both intrinsic and ActiveX controls to create the page, and you will investigate interactions with both types of controls. The page you will create was shown earlier, in Figure 7-1 (page 240).

The HTML tags you will use to create your web page are described here, but many other tags exist. Many HTML tags also have attributes that are not discussed here. For a description of the fundamental HTML tags, along with their attributes, see Appendix A.

The Head Section

The web page begins with a simple head section. The head section contains the title for your web page and the script section. You will build the head section first and insert the script section later. Because HTML is nothing more than ASCII text, you will construct the page by using Notepad. Any text editor, including Microsoft Word, will work, but all files must be saved as ASCII text and typically have the extension *htm*.

While you are creating this file, you should be aware of one special consideration: some text editors, such as the one included with Windows NT 3.51, support the Unicode format. Unicode is a text format that uses 2 bytes per character. Unicode was designed to provide support for languages with more than 256 characters. When you are using a text editor that supports Unicode, be sure to save the text in ASCII format and not in Unicode format. ASCII format uses only 1 byte per character and is the format that browsers will expect.

Step 1

Begin your HTML page by opening a new document in Notepad or in a similar text editor. Add the following code to begin the head section:

```
<HTML>
<HEAD>
```

Step 2

Add a title to your page by using the <TITLE></TITLE> tags. The text that appears between the <TITLE></TITLE> tags will be displayed by the browser in the title bar of the browser and not actually on the page. Place the following code in your page to add the title and close up the head section:

```
<TITLE>Event Registration</TITLE>

</HEAD>
```

The Body Section

The body section contains all of the page's formatted text information and the controls that make up the user input form. You use HTML tags to create all the content, both static and interactive, that is displayed in the browser.

Step 1

You define the body section using the <BODY></BODY> tags. The <BODY></BODY> tags have several attributes that allow you to customize the look and feel of the page. You will use the BACKGROUND attribute to add a background image to the page. A background image, backgnd2.gif, is available on the companion CD, in the project2 folder. Any image can be used as a background. If the image is not large enough to cover the background area, the Internet Explorer will automatically tile the image to cover the area. Start the body section by adding the following code after the head section:

```
<BODY BACKGROUND="backgnd2.gif">
```

Step 2

This web page will use two different forms to contain controls. The first form, frmEvent, will be used to access an ActiveX Label control that displays advertisements to the user while he or she is registering for an event. The second form, frmRegister, will be used to contain the information that will be sent to your datasource. Add the first form to your HTML page by using the following code:

```
<FORM NAME="frmEvent">
```

Step 3

You format the Event form in a table by using the <TABLE></TABLE> tags. HTML tables allow sophisticated formatting of the content of a web page. You can space text, images, and controls with precision and create web pages that would otherwise not be possible. Add the following code to start the table:

```
<TABLE WIDTH=550 CELLPADDING=5 BORDER=0>
```

Step 4

In the table, you specify table rows by using the <TR></TR> tags, and table cells by using the <TD></TD> or <TH></TH> tags. You can place text, images, or controls in cells. In the first cell of the table, you will place an ActiveX Label control that will be used as a marker for the page. This label will appear at the far left side of the page and will display the page name, Event Registration. Add the label to the page by using the following code:

```
<TR>
    <TD ROWSPAN=14>
    <OBJECT
    CLASSID="clsid:99B42120-6EC7-11CF-A6C7-00AA00A47DD2"
    ID="lblFree"
    HEIGHT=300
    WIDTH=90
    >
    <PARAM NAME="Angle" VALUE="90">
    <PARAM NAME="ForeColor" VALUE="#FF0000">
    <PARAM NAME="Caption" VALUE="Event Registration">
    <PARAM NAME="FontName" VALUE="Arial Black">
    <PARAM NAME="FontSize" VALUE="22">
    <PARAM NAME="Visible" VALUE="True">
    </OBJECT>
    </TD>
```

Notice that the <OBJECT></OBJECT> tags are used to load the ActiveX Label control. The <PARAM> tag is used to change several of the properties for the label. Note that the Angle property value was changed to 90 so that the text runs vertically from bottom to top on the page. This gives an appealing look to the page.

Step 5

While the user is entering information into the form, you can display some advertising messages. You will use another Label control to display the various messages, which will be changed by a Timer control periodically. Add the following code to your page to place the Label control into the table:

```
<TD ALIGN="CENTER" COLSPAN=10>
<OBJECT
CLASSID="clsid:99B42120-6EC7-11CF-A6C7-00AA00A47DD2"
ID="lblBanner"
HEIGHT=40
WIDTH=400
>
```

(continued)

continued

```
<PARAM NAME="ForeColor" VALUE="#0000FF">
<PARAM NAME="Caption" VALUE="Register Here!">
<PARAM NAME="FontName" VALUE="Arial">
<PARAM NAME="FontSize" VALUE="20">
<PARAM NAME="FontBold" VALUE="True">
<PARAM NAME="Visible" VALUE="True">
</OBJECT>
</TD>
</TR>
```

Step 6

Now that you have a form to contain the labels, you will build a second form within the first one to contain the information entered by the user. Once again, the <FORM></FORM> tags are used. This time you make use of the ACTION attribute, which directs the information from the form to the back-end process. The ACTION attribute contains the URL of the process that is to receive the information. In this case, you are using OLEISAPI as the back-end process. Add the following code to place the second form inside the first form:

```
<TR>
<TD COLSPAN=6>
<FORM NAME="frmRegister" METHOD="POST" ACTION=
"/Scripts/oleisapi.dll/eventreg.Person.Register">
```

Take special note of how the ACTION attribute is implemented. The ACTION attribute invokes oleisapi.dll through the /Scripts folder. /Scripts is an alias set up in IIS as a pointer to the path c:\inetsrv\scripts. This alias is valuable because it hides the true path to your files. Hackers who want to damage a site could otherwise gain valuable information about the site's folder structure by examining the HTML code through the browser. Folder aliases help hide that information. Also, the /Scripts folder must be designated as an *Execute* folder (or directory) in IIS. Execute folders can contain executable content instead of just read-only content.

Consider the parts of the ACTION attribute. /Scripts defines the location of the oleisap.dll, eventreg is the name of the in-process ActiveX component, Person is the name of a public class in eventreg.dll, and Register is the name of a method in the Person class. You will create the in-process ActiveX component, eventreg.dll, later in this chapter, in the section titled "Creating the In-Process ActiveX Component." For more information on the oleisapi.dll or IIS, see Chapter 5.

Step 7

The input form is also formatted as a table to maintain a consistent interface for the user. Each control is labeled with text and formatted. The first controls are Radio controls, implemented with the <INPUT> tag. These controls are used to determine whether the registrant wants first-, second-, or third-class tickets. Add these Radio controls to your page with the following code:

```
<TABLE WIDTH=400 BORDER=0>
    <B><FONT SIZE=2>
    <TR>
        <TD COLSPAN=1>
        Tickets
        </TD>
        <TD NOWRAP COLSPAN=1>
        <INPUT TYPE="RADIO" VALUE="First"
        NAME="optTicket" CHECKED OnClick="Tickets(50)">
        First-Class $50
        <P><P>
        </TD>
        <TD NOWRAP COLSPAN=1>
        <P><P>
        <INPUT TYPE="RADIO" VALUE="Second"
        NAME="optTicket" OnClick="Tickets(20)">
        Second-Class $20
        </TD>
        <TD NOWRAP COLSPAN=1>
        <P><P>
        <INPUT TYPE="RADIO" VALUE="Third"
        NAME="optTicket" OnClick="Tickets(10)">
        Third-Class $10
        </TD>
    </TR>
```

Note that each of the Radio controls has the same NAME attribute but a different VALUE attribute. Because they have the same name, the controls behave as mutually exclusive options. Therefore, only one Radio control can be selected at a time. The value assigned to the selected item will be passed to the back-end process when the form is submitted.

Step 8

Offering options that are not mutually exclusive is the job of the Checkbox control. In this step, you will implement a set of three checkboxes that allow the user to purchase additional items. In this example, you offer a hat, a mug, and a shirt. If the user selects one or more of these, you will add the cost to the final bill. Add the Checkbox controls to your page with the following code:

```
<TR>
    <TD COLSPAN=1>
    </TD>
    <TD NOWRAP COLSPAN=1>
    <INPUT TYPE="CHECKBOX" NAME="chkHat"
    VALUE="Yes" OnClick="Calculate">
    Hat $10
    </TD>
    <TD NOWRAP COLSPAN=1>
    <INPUT TYPE="CHECKBOX" NAME="chkMug"
    VALUE="Yes" OnClick="Calculate">
    Mug $5
    </TD>
    <TD NOWRAP COLSPAN=1>
    <INPUT TYPE="CHECKBOX" NAME="chkShirt"
    VALUE="Yes" OnClick="Calculate">
    Shirt $20
    </TD>
</TR>
```

Step 9

The user enters data into the form by using Text controls. These controls are also implemented with the <INPUT> tag. For each piece of information, you provide a text box with some text next to it as a label. Add the Text controls with the following code:

```
<TR>
    <TD COLSPAN=1>
    Name
    </TD>
    <TD COLSPAN=3>
    <INPUT TYPE="TEXT" NAME="txtName" SIZE=72>
    </TD>
</TR>
<TR>
    <TD COLSPAN=1>
    Company
    </TD>
```

```
    <TD COLSPAN=3>
    <INPUT TYPE="TEXT" NAME="txtCompany" SIZE=72>
    </TD>
</TR>
<TR>
    <TD COLSPAN=1>
    Address
    </TD>
    <TD COLSPAN=3>
    <INPUT TYPE="TEXT" NAME="txtAddress" SIZE=72>
    </TD>
</TR>
<TR>
    <TD COLSPAN=1>
    City
    </TD>
    <TD COLSPAN=1>
    <INPUT TYPE="TEXT" NAME="txtCity" SIZE=20>
    </TD>
    <TD COLSPAN=1 ALIGN="RIGHT">
    State
    <INPUT TYPE="TEXT" NAME="txtState" SIZE=2
    MAXLENGTH=2>
    </TD>
    <TD COLSPAN=1 ALIGN="RIGHT">
    Zip
    <INPUT TYPE="TEXT" NAME="txtZip" SIZE=9
    MAXLENGTH=9>
    </TD>
</TR>
<TR>
    <TD COLSPAN=1>
    Email
    </TD>
    <TD COLSPAN=11>
    <INPUT TYPE="TEXT" NAME="txtEmail" SIZE=47>
    </TD>
</TR>
<TR>
    <TD COLSPAN=1>
    </TD>
    <TD NOWRAP COLSPAN=1>
    <INPUT TYPE="RADIO" VALUE="Visa"
    NAME="optCardType" CHECKED>
```

(continued)

continued

```
            VISA
            <P><P>
            </TD>
            <TD NOWRAP COLSPAN=1>
            <P><P>
            <INPUT TYPE="RADIO" VALUE="MC" NAME="optCardType">
            MasterCard
            </TD>
            <TD COLSPAN=1>
            </TD>
        </TR>
        <TR>
            <TD COLSPAN=1>
            Card #
            </TD>
            <TD COLSPAN=1>
            <INPUT TYPE="TEXT" NAME="txtCardNumber" SIZE=20>
            </TD>
            <TD COLSPAN=1>
            Exp Date
            <INPUT TYPE="TEXT" NAME="txtCardExpDate" SIZE=4>
            </TD>
            <TD COLSPAN=1 ALIGN="CENTER">
            TOTAL
            </TD>
        </TR>
```

Step 10

Another Label control gives the user a way to keep track of his or her total
expenditures. This Label control is updated every time the user selects a different ticket or product. The program also provides a Reset button that clears
all of the text entry fields and a Submit button that packages all of the data and
sends it to the back-end process. Add these controls with the following code:

```
    <TR>
        <TD COLSPAN=3>
        </TD>
        <TD ALIGN="CENTER">
        <OBJECT
        CLASSID="clsid:99B42120-6EC7-11CF-A6C7-00AA00A47DD2"
        ID="lblTotal"
        HEIGHT=20
        WIDTH=100
        >
```

```
<PARAM NAME="ForeColor" VALUE="#000000">
<PARAM NAME="Caption" VALUE="$50.00">
<PARAM NAME="BackStyle" VALUE="0">
<PARAM NAME="FontName" VALUE="Arial">
<PARAM NAME="FontSize" VALUE="20">
<PARAM NAME="FontBold" VALUE="True">
<PARAM NAME="Visible" VALUE="True">
</OBJECT>
<INPUT TYPE="HIDDEN" NAME="txtTotal" VALUE="50">
</TD>
</TR>
<TR>
<TD COLSPAN=3 ALIGN="CENTER">
<INPUT TYPE="SUBMIT" VALUE="Register Now!">
<INPUT TYPE="RESET">
</TD>
</TR>
</FONT></B>
</TABLE>
</FORM>
</TD>
</TR>
</TABLE>
```

Step 11

The last part of the HTML code inserts a Timer control into the form. The
Timer control is used to periodically change the advertising messages displayed
to the user. As is true of any other control, this control is inserted with the
<OBJECT></OBJECT> tags. Notice that you set the delay to 5000. This means
that a Timer event will fire every 5 seconds. Use the following code to add the
Timer control and complete the body section of your web page:

```
<OBJECT
CLASSID="clsid:59CCB4A0-727D-11CF-AC36-00AA00A47DD2"
ID="tmrEvent"
>
<PARAM NAME="Interval" VALUE="5000">
<PARAM NAME="Enable" VALUE="True">
</OBJECT>

</FORM>
</BODY>
</HTML>
```

The Script Section

In the script section of the HTML code, VBScript code is used to total the cost for registering and to perform some simple client-side validation before the data gets passed to the server. VBScript code is also used to add some dynamic behavior to the web page, by changing the caption of one of the Label controls. The script section is organized into separate modules containing subroutines that work together. The script section is inserted between the <HEAD> </HEAD> tags of the HTML code.

Step 1

Begin the first script module by defining and initializing the value of a variable to hold the total cost for the registration. You initially set the first-class ticket as the default value by setting the CHECKED attribute of the <INPUT> tag, so make the default value of the initial ticket cost $50. Add the following code to set up the initial cost:

```
<SCRIPT LANGUAGE="VBScript">
<!--
    Option Explicit
    Dim curTotal
    Dim curTicket
    curTicket=50
```

Notice that the beginning comment tag, <!--, is used. Its purpose is to hide the script code from browsers that do not understand scripting code. A closing comment tag, -->, will be used at the end of this script module.

Step 2

Every time the user selects a different option for the event, the program calculates the total cost. In this way, the user can see the running total for the options that are currently selected. A simple routine is called to set the total whenever options change. Add the following code to calculate the total cost:

```
Sub Calculate
    Dim MyForm
    Set MyForm=Document.frmRegister
    curTotal=curTicket
    If MyForm.chkHat.Checked Then
        curTotal=curTotal+10
    End If
    If MyForm.chkMug.Checked Then
        curTotal=curTotal+5
```

```
      End If
      If MyForm.chkShirt.Checked Then
          curTotal=curTotal+20
      End If
      MyForm.lblTotal.Caption="$" & curTotal & ".00"
      MyForm.txtTotal.Value=curTotal
  End Sub
```

Step 3

To track the type of ticket selected and the cost incurred, you built a set of three mutually exclusive Radio controls. Radio controls are normally ideal for control arrays, but VBScript does not support them, so instead of using control arrays, this program calls a routine from the OnClick event of each Radio control. The program passes an index into the routine, indicating which control was selected. Add the following code to calculate the ticket price when a new Radio control is selected:

```
Sub Tickets(curValue)
    curTicket=curValue
    Calculate
End Sub
```

Step 4

Complete this script module by adding the closing comment and script tags:

```
-->
</SCRIPT>
```

Step 5

Begin a new script module in which to hold the validation code for the form. The validation will be simple and will consist of ensuring that certain fields actually have some data in them. The program uses the OnBlur event, which correlates to Visual Basic's LostFocus event, to check whether a text box contains a value. Add the following code module to perform the validation for this form:

```
<SCRIPT LANGUAGE="VBScript">
<!--
    Option Explicit
    Sub txtName_OnBlur
        Dim MyForm
        Set MyForm=Document.frmRegister
        If MyForm.txtName.Value="" Then
```

(continued)

257

continued

```
            MsgBox "Please enter Name",16,"Register"
        End If
    End Sub

    Sub txtAddress_OnBlur
        Dim MyForm
        Set MyForm=Document.frmRegister
        If MyForm.txtAddress.Value="" Then
            MsgBox "Please enter Address",16,"Register"
        End If
    End Sub

    Sub txtCity_OnBlur
        Dim MyForm
        Set MyForm=Document.frmRegister
        If MyForm.txtCity.Value="" Then
            MsgBox "Please enter City",16,"Register"
        End If
    End Sub

    Sub txtState_OnBlur
        Dim MyForm
        Set MyForm=Document.frmRegister
        If MyForm.txtState.Value=" " Then
            MsgBox "Please enter State",16,"Register"
        End If
    End Sub

    Sub txtZip_OnBlur
        Dim MyForm
        Set MyForm=Document.frmRegister
        If MyForm.txtZip.Value="" Then
            MsgBox "Please enter Zip Code",16,"Register"
        End If
    End Sub

    Sub txtEmail_OnBlur
        Dim MyForm
        Set MyForm=Document.frmRegister
        If MyForm.txtEmail.Value="" Then
            MsgBox "Please enter Email Address",16,"Register"
        End If
    End Sub
```

```
Sub txtCardNumber_OnBlur
    Dim MyForm
    Set MyForm=Document.frmRegister
    If MyForm.txtCardNumber.Value="" Then
        MsgBox "Please enter Card Number",16,"Register"
    End If
End Sub

Sub txtCardExpDate_OnBlur
    Dim MyForm
    Set MyForm=Document.frmRegister
    If MyForm.txtCardExpDate.Value="" Then
        MsgBox "Please enter Card Expiration Date",16,"Register"
    End If
End Sub
-->
</SCRIPT>
```

Note that the reference to the form is obtained by using Document.*formname*. This is an important concept. All forms must be accessed with the Document object.

Step 6

Finally, you will add some VBScript code to periodically change the text in the label caption, as a form of advertising. This example uses the Timer control's Timer event to change the caption. The code will display a random message every 5 seconds. Add the following code to change the message:

```
<SCRIPT LANGUAGE="VBScript">
<!--
    Option Explicit
    Sub tmrEvent_Timer
        Dim intIndex
        Dim strBanner
        Dim MyForm
        Set MyForm=Document.frmEvent
        Randomize Timer
        intIndex=Int(3*Rnd)+1
        Select Case intIndex
            Case 1
                strBanner="Order a Shirt!"
            Case 2
                strBanner="Order a Hat!"
```

(continued)

259

continued

```
        Case 3
            strBanner="Order a Mug!"
        End Select
        MyForm.lblBanner.Caption=strBanner
    End Sub
-->
</SCRIPT>
```

That completes the HTML code. Listing 7-1 shows the completed HTML code, along with comments.

```
<HTML>
<HEAD>
<TITLE>Event Registration</TITLE>

<!--
This is the code for the event registration page.
The page contains the following elements:

Type of ticket
Option to purchase additional items
Personal information
Credit card information
Total cost
Submit and Reset buttons

Once the user completes the registration
form, he or she can submit the information
to a database where it can be further
processed.
-->

<SCRIPT LANGUAGE="VBScript">
<!--
    Option Explicit
    Dim curTotal
    Dim curTicket
    curTicket=50

    Sub Calculate
```

Listing 7-1.
The complete code for the HTML page.

```
'Author: New Technology Solutions, Inc.
'Purpose: Calculate total cost
'5/23/96 Original

    Dim MyForm
    Set MyForm=Document.frmRegister
    curTotal=curTicket
    If MyForm.chkHat.Checked Then
        curTotal=curTotal+10
    End If
    If MyForm.chkMug.Checked Then
        curTotal=curTotal+5
    End If
    If MyForm.chkShirt.Checked Then
        curTotal=curTotal+20
    End If
    MyForm.lblTotal.Caption="$" & curTotal & ".00"
    MyForm.txtTotal.Value=curTotal
End Sub

Sub Tickets(curValue)
    curTicket=curValue
    Calculate
End Sub
-->
</SCRIPT>

<SCRIPT LANGUAGE="VBScript">
<!--
    Option Explicit

    'Author: New Technology Solutions, Inc.
    'Purpose: The procedures in this module
    'make sure data has been entered
    '5/18/96 Original

Sub txtName_OnBlur
    Dim MyForm
    Set MyForm=Document.frmRegister
    If MyForm.txtName.Value="" Then
        MsgBox "Please enter Name",16,"Register"
    End If
End Sub
```

(continued)

Listing 7-1 *continued*

```
Sub txtAddress_OnBlur
    Dim MyForm
    Set MyForm=Document.frmRegister
    If MyForm.txtAddress.Value="" Then
        MsgBox "Please enter Address",16,"Register"
    End If
End Sub

Sub txtCity_OnBlur
    Dim MyForm
    Set MyForm=Document.frmRegister
    If MyForm.txtCity.Value="" Then
        MsgBox "Please enter City",16,"Register"
    End If
End Sub

Sub txtState_OnBlur
    Dim MyForm
    Set MyForm=Document.frmRegister
    If MyForm.txtState.Value="" Then
        MsgBox "Please enter State",16,"Register"
    End If
End Sub

Sub txtZip_OnBlur
    Dim MyForm
    Set MyForm=Document.frmRegister
    If MyForm.txtZip.Value="" Then
        MsgBox "Please enter Zip Code",16,"Register"
    End If
End Sub

Sub txtEmail_OnBlur
    Dim MyForm
    Set MyForm=Document.frmRegister
    If MyForm.txtEmail.Value="" Then
        MsgBox "Please enter Email Address",16,"Register"
    End If
End Sub

Sub txtCardNumber_OnBlur
    Dim MyForm
    Set MyForm=Document.frmRegister
```

```
            If MyForm.txtCardNumber.Value="" Then
                MsgBox "Please enter Card Number",16,"Register"
            End If
        End Sub

        Sub txtCardExpDate_OnBlur
            Dim MyForm
            Set MyForm=Document.frmRegister
            If MyForm.txtCardExpDate.Value="" Then
                MsgBox "Please enter Card Expiration Date",16,"Register"
            End If
        End Sub
    -->
    </SCRIPT>

    <SCRIPT LANGUAGE="VBScript">
    <!--
        Option Explicit
        Sub tmrEvent_Timer

        'Author: New Technology Solutions, Inc.
        'Purpose: Change label periodically
        '5/21/96 Original

            Dim intIndex
            Dim strBanner
            Dim MyForm
            Set MyForm=Document.frmEvent
            Randomize Timer
            intIndex=Int(3*Rnd)+1
            Select Case intIndex
                Case 1
                    strBanner="Order a Shirt!"
                Case 2
                    strBanner="Order a Hat!"
                Case 3
                    strBanner="Order a Mug!"
            End Select
            MyForm.lblBanner.Caption=strBanner
        End Sub
    -->
    </SCRIPT>
```

(continued)

Listing 7-1 *continued*

```
</HEAD>
<BODY BACKGROUND="backgnd2.gif">
<FORM NAME="frmEvent">

<TABLE WIDTH=550 CELLPADDING=5 BORDER=0>
    <TR>
        <TD ROWSPAN=14>

        <!--
        This is a vertical page label
        -->

        <OBJECT
        CLASSID="clsid:99B42120-6EC7-11CF-A6C7-00AA00A47DD2"
        ID="lblFree"
        HEIGHT=300
        WIDTH=90
        >
        <PARAM NAME="Angle" VALUE="90">
        <PARAM NAME="ForeColor" VALUE="#FF0000">
        <PARAM NAME="Caption" VALUE="Event Registration">
        <PARAM NAME="FontName" VALUE="Arial Black">
        <PARAM NAME="FontSize" VALUE="22">
        <PARAM NAME="Visible" VALUE="True">
        </OBJECT>
        </TD>
        <TD ALIGN="CENTER" COLSPAN=10>

        <!--
        This label handles the advertising messages
        -->

        <OBJECT
        CLASSID="clsid:99B42120-6EC7-11CF-A6C7-00AA00A47DD2"
        ID="lblBanner"
        HEIGHT=40
        WIDTH=400
        >
        <PARAM NAME="ForeColor" VALUE="#0000FF">
        <PARAM NAME="Caption" VALUE="Register Here!">
        <PARAM NAME="FontName" VALUE="Arial">
        <PARAM NAME="FontSize" VALUE="20">
```

```
        <PARAM NAME="FontBold" VALUE="True">
        <PARAM NAME="Visible" VALUE="True">
        </OBJECT>
        </TD>
</TR>
<TR>

        <!--
        This is the actual registration form.
        Notice that a table inside a table is used
        for attractive formatting on the screen.
        -->

        <TD COLSPAN=6>
        <FORM NAME="frmRegister" METHOD="POST" ACTION=
        "/Scripts/oleisapi.dll/eventreg.Person.Register">

        <TABLE WIDTH=400 BORDER=0>
            <B><FONT SIZE=2>
            <TR>
                <TD COLSPAN=1>
                Tickets
                </TD>
                <TD NOWRAP COLSPAN=1>
                <INPUT TYPE="RADIO" VALUE="First"
                NAME="optTicket" CHECKED OnClick="Tickets(50)">
                First-Class $50
                <P><P>
                </TD>
                <TD NOWRAP COLSPAN=1>
                <P><P>
                <INPUT TYPE="RADIO" VALUE="Second"
                NAME="optTicket" OnClick= "Tickets(20)">
                Second-Class $20
                </TD>
                <TD NOWRAP COLSPAN=1>
                <P><P>
                <INPUT TYPE="RADIO" VALUE="Third"
                NAME="optTicket" OnClick= "Tickets(10)">
                Third-Class $10
                </TD>
            </TR>
```

(continued)

Listing 7-1 *continued*

```
    <TR>
        <TD COLSPAN=1>
        </TD>
        <TD NOWRAP COLSPAN=1>
        <INPUT TYPE="CHECKBOX" NAME="chkHat"
        VALUE="Yes" OnClick="Calculate">
        Hat $10
        </TD>
        <TD NOWRAP COLSPAN=1>
        <INPUT TYPE="CHECKBOX" NAME="chkMug"
        VALUE="Yes" OnClick="Calculate">
        Mug $5
        </TD>
        <TD NOWRAP COLSPAN=1>
        <INPUT TYPE="CHECKBOX" NAME="chkShirt"
        VALUE="Yes" OnClick="Calculate">
        Shirt $20
        </TD>
    </TR>
    <TR>
        <TD COLSPAN=1>
        Name
        </TD>
        <TD COLSPAN=3>
        <INPUT TYPE="TEXT" NAME="txtName" SIZE=72>
        </TD>
    </TR>
    <TR>
        <TD COLSPAN=1>
        Company
        </TD>
        <TD COLSPAN=3>
        <INPUT TYPE="TEXT" NAME="txtCompany" SIZE=72>
        </TD>
    </TR>
    <TR>
        <TD COLSPAN=1>
        Address
        </TD>
        <TD COLSPAN=3>
        <INPUT TYPE="TEXT" NAME="txtAddress" SIZE=72>
        </TD>
    </TR>
```

```
<TR>
    <TD COLSPAN=1>
    City
    </TD>
    <TD COLSPAN=1>
    <INPUT TYPE="TEXT" NAME="txtCity" SIZE=20>
    </TD>
    <TD COLSPAN=1 ALIGN="RIGHT">
    State
    <INPUT TYPE="TEXT" NAME="txtState" SIZE=2
    MAXLENGTH=2>
    </TD>
    <TD COLSPAN=1 ALIGN="RIGHT">
    Zip
    <INPUT TYPE="TEXT" NAME="txtZip" SIZE=9
    MAXLENGTH=9>
    </TD>
</TR>
<TR>
    <TD COLSPAN=1>
    Email
    </TD>
    <TD COLSPAN=11>
    <INPUT TYPE="TEXT" NAME="txtEmail" SIZE=47>
    </TD>
</TR>
<TR>
    <TD COLSPAN=1>
    </TD>
    <TD NOWRAP COLSPAN=1>
    <INPUT TYPE="RADIO" VALUE="Visa"
    NAME="optCardType" CHECKED>
    VISA
    <P><P>
    </TD>
    <TD NOWRAP COLSPAN=1>
    <P><P>
    <INPUT TYPE="RADIO" VALUE="MC" NAME="optCardType">
    MasterCard
    </TD>
    <TD COLSPAN=1>
    </TD>
```

(continued)

Listing 7-1 *continued*

```
    </TR>
    <TR>
        <TD COLSPAN=1>
        Card #
        </TD>
        <TD COLSPAN=1>
        <INPUT TYPE="TEXT" NAME="txtCardNumber" SIZE=20>
        </TD>
        <TD COLSPAN=1>
        Exp Date
        <INPUT TYPE="TEXT" NAME="txtCardExpDate" SIZE=4>
        </TD>
        <TD COLSPAN=1 ALIGN="CENTER">
        TOTAL
        </TD>
    </TR>
    <TR>
        <TD COLSPAN=3>
        </TD>
        <TD ALIGN="CENTER">
        <OBJECT
        CLASSID=
        "clsid:99B42120-6EC7-11CF-A6C7-00AA00A47DD2"
        ID="lblTotal"
        HEIGHT=20
        WIDTH=100
        >
        <PARAM NAME="ForeColor" VALUE="#000000">
        <PARAM NAME="Caption" VALUE="$50.00">
        <PARAM NAME="BackStyle" VALUE="0">
        <PARAM NAME="FontName" VALUE="Arial">
        <PARAM NAME="FontSize" VALUE="20">
        <PARAM NAME="FontBold" VALUE="True">
        <PARAM NAME="Visible" VALUE="True">
        </OBJECT>
        <INPUT TYPE="HIDDEN" NAME="txtTotal" VALUE="50">
        </TD>
    </TR>
    <TR>
        <TD COLSPAN=3 ALIGN="CENTER">
```

```
                    <INPUT TYPE="SUBMIT" VALUE="Register Now!">
                    <INPUT TYPE="RESET">
                    </TD>
              </TR>
              </FONT></B>
         </TABLE>
         </FORM>
         </TD>
     </TR>
</TABLE>

<!--
This is the Timer control
-->

<OBJECT
CLASSID="clsid:59CCB4A0-727D-11CF-AC36-00AA00A47DD2"
ID="tmrEvent"
>
<PARAM NAME="Interval" VALUE="5000">
<PARAM NAME="Enable" VALUE="True">
</OBJECT>

</FORM>
</BODY>
</HTML>
```

Creating the In-Process ActiveX Component

Now that the web page is complete, you can concentrate on the back-end functionality of the event registration program. This functionality takes over when the user "submits" the form. Submitting the form passes all of the data from the VALUE attributes to the process indicated by the ACTION attribute. In this case, the program is passing the data to an in-process ActiveX component, formerly called an OLE server, that works with oleisapi.dll. You will use Visual Basic 4.0 to create this component. Figure 7-6 (page 270) shows a flowchart of how the event registration information is processed. As you work through the rest of this project, this flowchart will become clearer.

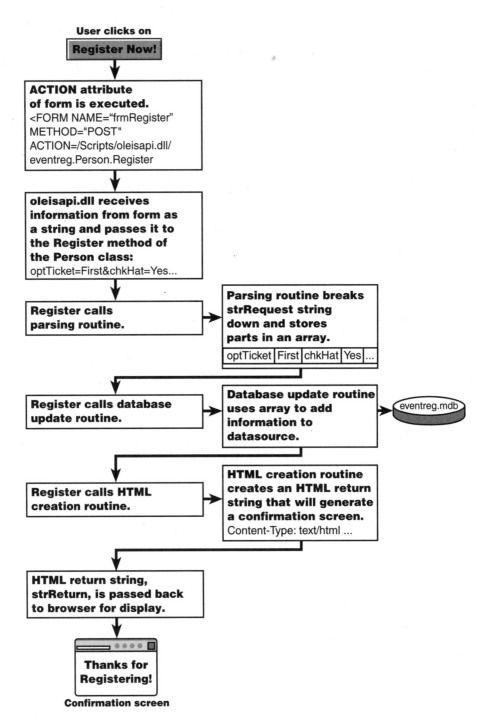

Figure 7-6.
A flowchart showing how event registration information is processed.

The Person Class

The heart of your in-process ActiveX component is the Person class. This class module contains a method called Register, which is called by oleisapi.dll. The Register method takes two string arguments, strRequest and strReturn. The strRequest argument contains the data passed by the ACTION attribute of the form, and the strReturn argument contains the return HTML code to be displayed by the browser.

Step 1

Start a new Visual Basic project. Remove the default form by selecting Remove File from the File menu. Since this component will be running on the server, any forms created in Visual Basic will be displayed only on the server, not on the client computer. For this project, creating a user interface in Visual Basic is not necessary.

Step 2

Add a new class module to your project by selecting Class Module from the Insert menu. When the class module is visible, press F4 to display its properties sheet. Change the properties of the class module as follows:

Instancing	2 - Creatable, MultiUse
Name	Person
Public	True

Setting the Public property to True allows OLEISAPI to access the functions in this module. Changing the Instancing property to Creatable, MultiUse allows an object from this class to be created, if one is not already running. The Name property is the name used in the ACTION attribute of your calling form. Figure 7-7 (page 272) shows the properties sheet for the Person class.

Figure 7-7.
The properties sheet for the Person class.

Step 3

When the form is submitted, OLEISAPI creates an object from the Person class and then calls the Register method. The Register method receives the information from the form and takes action to make entries in the database. After all the actions have been taken, the program dynamically creates an HTML page and returns it to the browser. To start the Register method, type the following into the code window for the Person class:

```
Option Explicit

Public Sub Register(strRequest As String, strReturn As String)
```

The Register method accepts two string arguments, and both are passed *by reference.* By reference is the default argument-passing convention in Visual Basic. When you pass an argument by reference, you pass the address of the string argument, as opposed to a copy of the actual data. This is important in our program because OLEISAPI expects your routine to return HTML code by changing the text located at the address specified by strReturn.

Step 4

The Register routine is responsible for calling additional functionality contained in your class module. The Register method will call the routine to parse the incoming string, call the routine to update the information in the database, call the routine to create the return HTML page, and call an error handler if a runtime error occurs. You will create these routines in later steps. We begin the Register method by enabling the error-handling routine and declaring a dynamic array that will hold the parsed incoming string:

```
On Error GoTo RegisterErr

    ReDim arrArgVal(0) As String
```

The first thing your program will need to do is parse the incoming string. Parsing is handled by a routine called sParseRequest. The sParseRequest routine takes the incoming string (which has a format of Field=Value), breaks it up into parts, and stores the parts in an array called arrArgVal( ). Add the following code to call the parsing routine:

```
    Call sParseRequest(strRequest, arrArgVal())
```

Next the parsed information in the array will be added to the datasource. This is handled in a routine called sUpdateData. Add the following code to call the database update routine:

```
    Call sUpdateData(arrArgVal())
```

Next a routine is called to create the HTML code that will be returned to the browser. This routine, fCreateHTML, creates an HTML confirmation screen that is returned as a string. The string is assigned to strReturn. Remember that strReturn is passed by reference, which means that when it is modified, this change is reflected wherever it is referenced. Therefore, assigning the created HTML string to strReturn is all that is required to have the confirmation screen returned and eventually displayed in the browser. Add the following code to call the routine for creating the HTML string and assigning it to strReturn:

```
    strReturn = fCreateHTML(arrArgVal())
```

All code should have an error trap to handle runtime errors. Later you will build a central error-handling routine that can generate HTML pages to display errors . Add the following code (next page) to call the error-handling routine:

```
RegisterExit:
    Exit Sub

RegisterErr:
    strReturn = fCreateHTMLError(Err.Number, Err.Description)
    Resume RegisterExit
End Sub
```

Step 5

Now you will create the routines that the Register method calls. The first thing the program must do is parse the incoming data. The data is sent from the client in the argument strRequest, which is a string that contains all of the input data from the submitted form. The data has the following format:

field1=value1&field2=value2…&fieldn=valuen

Spaces in the values are replaced with plus signs, and nonalphanumeric characters are replaced with hexadecimal representations of the data. For example, if you pass a phone number as *(800) 555 1212*, it will appear in your request string as

```
%28800%29+555+1212
```

As you can see, the percent sign indicates that a hexadecimal value follows. The spaces are replaced by plus signs. This format is consistent for all data that is passed and allows you to build an algorithm to decode it. This step shows you how this is accomplished.

Now you will create a parsing routine that will break the string down and populate an array with the fields and values. This array, arrArgVal( ), is an array of strings. The parsing routine creates an array that alternates between fields and values. This way, you can access all of the data in the array by using For…Next loops. Add the following code to the Person class to start the parsing routine:

```
Private Sub sParseRequest(strRequest As String, _
    arrArgVal() As String)

On Error GoTo ParseRequestErr

    Dim intIndex As Integer
    Dim intPosition As Integer
    Dim intStart As Integer
    Dim strParse As String
    Dim strTemp As String
```

```
Dim intTest As Integer

intIndex = 0
intStart = 1
```

To capture all of the data sent to the back-end server, your code must loop through all of the characters in the request string. You can identify each field by looking for the equals sign. Add the following code to your routine to search for equals signs and find the field entries:

```
Do While InStr(intStart, strRequest, "=", 1) > 0

        intIndex = intIndex + 1
        ReDim Preserve arrArgVal(intIndex + 1)

        intPosition = InStr(intStart, strRequest, "=", 1)
        arrArgVal(intIndex) = Trim$(Mid$(strRequest, intStart, _
                intPosition - intStart))

        intIndex = intIndex + 1
        intStart = intPosition + 1
        intPosition = InStr(intStart, strRequest, "&", 1)
```

Once you have identified the field, you can find the associated value by searching for the ampersand symbol (&). This symbol separates field and value pairs. Once a field and a value are known, they can easily be stored in an array. Add the following code to finish the parsing process:

```
    If intPosition > 0 Then
        arrArgVal(intIndex) = Trim$(Mid$(strRequest, _
            intStart, intPosition - intStart))
        intStart = intPosition + 1
    Else
        arrArgVal(intIndex) = Trim$(Right$(strRequest, _
            Len(strRequest) - intStart + 1))
        intStart = Len(strRequest)
    End If
Loop
```

When the entries have been parsed, they might still contain hexadecimal characters that are used to represent nonalphanumeric symbols. These hexadecimal values are always preceded by percent signs. They can be converted back to ASCII format with the Val function. Add the code at the top of page 276 to convert the hexadecimal characters back to ASCII format and change plus signs back to spaces.

```
        For intIndex = 1 To UBound(arrArgVal)
        strTemp = ""
        intPosition = 1
        Do
            Select Case Mid$(arrArgVal(intIndex), intPosition, 1)
                Case "+"
                    strTemp = strTemp & " "
                    intPosition = intPosition + 1
                Case "%"
                    strTemp = strTemp & Chr$(Val("&H" & _
                        Mid$(arrArgVal(intIndex), intPosition + 1, 2)))
                    intPosition = intPosition + 3
                Case Else
                    intTest = Asc(Mid$(arrArgVal(intIndex), _
                        intPosition, 1))
                    If Not (intTest < 32 Or (intTest > 126 And _
                        intTest < 145) Or (intTest > 146 And _
                        intTest < 160)) Then
                        strTemp = strTemp & _
                        Mid$(arrArgVal(intIndex), intPosition, 1)
                    End If
                    intPosition = intPosition + 1
            End Select
        Loop While intPosition <= Len(arrArgVal(intIndex))
        arrArgVal(intIndex) = strTemp
    Next
```

To complete the sParseRequest routine, add the following code to perform error handling:

```
ParseRequestExit:
    Exit Sub

ParseRequestErr:
    ReDim arrArgValue(4)
    arrArgValue(1) = "Error"
    arrArgValue(2) = Err.Description
    arrArgValue(3) = "Number"
    arrArgValue(4) = Format$(Err.Number)
    Resume ParseRequestExit

End Sub
```

Step 6

After the fields and values have been parsed and stored in an array, your application must update the database. The database is updated with Remote Data Object (RDO) technology. RDO is a feature of Visual Basic 4.0, Enterprise Edition, that is specifically designed to interact with ODBC datasources. RDO itself is nothing more than a component that wraps the ODBC API. This API provides direct access to ODBC functionality. RDO itself adds little overhead to the ODBC functionality, so the update performance is excellent.

Before you use RDO, you must make sure that you have set a reference to it. Select References from the Tools menu, and set a reference to the Remote Data Object. Figure 7-8 shows the References dialog box with the Microsoft Remote Data Object 1.0 selected.

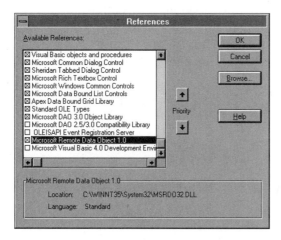

Figure 7-8.
The References dialog box with RDO selected.

Now you can add the following code to your project, to begin the database update routine:

```
Private Sub sUpdateData(arrArgVal() As String)
    On Error GoTo UpdateDataErr

        Dim strSQL As String
        Dim i As Integer
        Dim dbRegistrations As RDO.rdoConnection
```

You open a connection to the datasource with the OpenConnection method of the rdoConnection object. This method opens the datasource for use and takes as an argument the name of the datasource to be opened. In this case, you will open the datasource you created earlier in this project by adding the following code:

```
Set dbRegistrations = rdoEngine.rdoEnvironments(0). _
OpenConnection("eventreg")
```

To add the data to the database, you must create a SQL INSERT statement. The INSERT statement will add the fields and values you specify. In this case, you will use the field names as they were passed in from the browser. The HTML code you built previously uses the field names from the datasource as the NAME attributes for the form. The only catch is that the names in the form are prefixed with a three-letter designation. For example, the ticket information is referenced as optTicket in the HTML code, and the field name in the database is Ticket. Therefore, you must strip the first three letters of each field name prior to building the SQL INSERT string. The SQL INSERT string takes the following form:

INSERT INTO *table* (*field1, field2, ...fieldn*) VALUES (*'value1', 'value2',... 'valuen'*)

Add the following code to build the SQL INSERT string from the parsed input data:

```
strSQL = "INSERT INTO Registrations ("

For i = 1 To UBound(arrArgVal) - 1 Step 2
    strSQL = strSQL & Trim$(Right$(arrArgVal(i), _
        Len(arrArgVal(i)) - 3)) & ","
Next
strSQL = Left$(strSQL, Len(strSQL) - 1) & ") "
strSQL = strSQL & "VALUES ("
For i = 2 To UBound(arrArgVal) Step 2
    strSQL = strSQL & "'" & Trim$(arrArgVal(i)) & "',"
Next
strSQL = Left$(strSQL, Len(strSQL) - 1) & ") "
```

Executing the SQL statement is simply a matter of using the Execute method, which takes action immediately. Add the following code to execute the SQL INSERT statement:

```
dbRegistrations.Execute strSQL
```

Like all routines, this subroutine needs proper closing and error handling. To complete the database update routine, add the following code to close the database connection and handle errors:

```
UpdateDataExit:
    dbRegistrations.Close
    Set dbRegistrations = Nothing
    Exit Sub

UpdateDataErr:
    Resume UpdateDataExit

End Sub
```

Step 7

Once the database has been updated, the program must supply a return HTML page for the browser to display. The HTML page is formatted as a single string that is returned through the strReturn argument. OLEISAPI expects the return HTML page to be located at the memory location addressed by strReturn. Add the following code to start the formatting of the return HTML page:

```
Private Function fCreateHTML(arrArgVal() As String) As String

On Error GoTo CreateHTMLErr

    Dim strHTML As String
```

The key to the proper formatting of the return string is to supply the correct header. The header portion of the return string identifies the kind of information that the browser will be receiving. (Browsers can handle more types of data than just HTML code—they can accept sound and video clips, for example.) The header must be followed by a blank line. Add the following code to set up the correct header:

```
    strHTML = "Content-Type: text/html" & vbCrLf & vbCrLf
```

The rest of the code just completes the return string by using HTML tags. Add the following code to finish the return string and include error-handling for this routine:

```
    strHTML = strHTML & "<HTML><HEAD><TITLE>Registered!"
    strHTML = strHTML & "</TITLE></HEAD><BODY "
    strHTML = strHTML & "BGCOLOR=#FFFFFF><CENTER>"
    strHTML = strHTML & "<H2>Thanks for Registering!</H2>"
```

(continued)

continued

```
        strHTML = strHTML & "</CENTER></BODY></HTML>"
        fCreateHTML = strHTML

CreateHTMLExit:
    Exit Function

CreateHTMLErr:
    fCreateHTML = fCreateHTMLError(Err.Number, Err.Description)
    Resume CreateHTMLExit

End Function
```

Step 8

The ActiveX component must handle any runtime errors that occur. The main error-handling routine will create a return HTML page for any error that occurs. This means that all errors will be reported back to the browser in HTML code. Add the following code to your project, to provide runtime error handling:

```
Private Function fCreateHTMLError(lngNumber As Long, _
    strDescription As String) As String

    Dim strHTML As String

    strHTML = strHTML = "Content-Type: text/html" & vbCrLf _
        & vbCrLf
    strHTML = strHTML & _
        "<HTML><HEAD><TITLE>Error Report</TITLE></HEAD><BODY>"
    strHTML = strHTML & _
        "<H2><CENTER>OLEISAPI ERROR!</CENTER></H2><P>"
    strHTML = strHTML & _
        "<TABLE><TR><TH>NUMBER</TH><TD>" & Format$(lngNumber) _
        & "</TD></TR>"
    strHTML = strHTML & "<TR><TH>DESCRIPTION</TH><TD>" & _
        strDescription & "</TD></TR>"
    strHTML = strHTML & "</TABLE></BODY></HTML>"
    fCreateHTMLError = strHTML

End Function
```

You have now finished creating the Person class. This class module contains all of the functionality necessary to access the database and return HTML pages. Listing 7-2 shows the complete code for the Person class.

```
Option Explicit

Public Sub Register(strRequest As String, strReturn As String)

'Author: New Technology Solutions, Inc.
'Purpose: Receive calls from OLEISAPI
'5/1/96 Original

On Error GoTo RegisterErr

    ReDim arrArgVal(0) As String

    'Parse the incoming string
    Call sParseRequest(strRequest, arrArgVal())

    'Update the database
    Call sUpdateData(arrArgVal())

    'Return the HTML page to the browser
    strReturn = fCreateHTML(arrArgVal())

RegisterExit:
    Exit Sub

RegisterErr:
    strReturn = fCreateHTMLError(Err.Number, Err.Description)
    Resume RegisterExit
End Sub

Private Sub sParseRequest(strRequest As String, _
    arrArgVal() As String)

'Author: New Technology Solutions, Inc.
'Purpose: Parse request string into entries in array
'5/1/96 Original

On Error GoTo ParseRequestErr

    'Incoming string is in the format
    'Field1=Value1&Field2=Value2

    Dim intIndex As Integer
    Dim intPosition As Integer
```

Listing 7-2. *(continued)*

The complete code for the Person class.

Listing 7-2 *continued*

```
Dim intStart As Integer
Dim strParse As String
Dim strTemp As String
Dim intTest As Integer

intIndex = 0
intStart = 1

Do While InStr(intStart, strRequest, "=", 1) > 0

    intIndex = intIndex + 1
    ReDim Preserve arrArgVal(intIndex + 1)

    'Search for equals sign to get field name
    intPosition = InStr(intStart, strRequest, "=", 1)
    arrArgVal(intIndex) = Trim$(Mid$(strRequest, intStart, _
        intPosition - intStart))

    intIndex = intIndex + 1
    intStart = intPosition + 1
    intPosition = InStr(intStart, strRequest, "&", 1)

    'Search for ampersand to get value
    If intPosition > 0 Then
        arrArgVal(intIndex) = Trim$(Mid$(strRequest, _
            intStart, intPosition - intStart))
        intStart = intPosition + 1
    Else
        arrArgVal(intIndex) = Trim$(Right$(strRequest, _
            Len(strRequest) - intStart + 1))
        intStart = Len(strRequest)
    End If
Loop

For intIndex = 1 To UBound(arrArgVal)

'This loop cleans up each entry, changing
'plus signs back to spaces and restoring
'ASCII characters represented by hexadecimal
'notation preceded by percent signs

strTemp = ""
intPosition = 1
Do
```

```
        Select Case Mid$(arrArgVal(intIndex), intPosition, 1)
            Case "+"
                strTemp = strTemp & " "
                intPosition = intPosition + 1
            Case "%"
                strTemp = strTemp & Chr$(Val("&H" & _
                    Mid$(arrArgVal(intIndex), intPosition + 1, 2)))
                intPosition = intPosition + 3
            Case Else

                'Remove any ASCII characters not supported
                'by Windows
                intTest = Asc(Mid$(arrArgVal(intIndex), _
                    intPosition, 1))
                If Not (intTest < 32 Or (intTest > 126 And _
                    intTest < 145) Or (intTest > 146 And _
                    intTest < 160)) Then
                    strTemp = strTemp & _
                    Mid$(arrArgVal(intIndex), intPosition, 1)
                End If
                intPosition = intPosition + 1
        End Select
    Loop While intPosition <= Len(arrArgVal(intIndex))
    arrArgVal(intIndex) = strTemp
Next

ParseRequestExit:
    Exit Sub

ParseRequestErr:
    ReDim arrArgValue(4)
    arrArgValue(1) = "Error"
    arrArgValue(2) = Err.Description
    arrArgValue(3) = "Number"
    arrArgValue(4) = Format$(Err.Number)
    Resume ParseRequestExit

End Sub

Private Sub sUpdateData(arrArgVal() As String)

    'Author: New Technology Solutions, Inc.
    'Purpose: Update database with registration info
    '5/23/96 Original

    On Error GoTo UpdateDataErr
```

(continued)

Listing 7-2 *continued*

```
        Dim strSQL As String
        Dim i As Integer
        Dim dbRegistrations As RDO.rdoConnection

        'Open a connection to the datasource by using
        'Remote Data Objects
        Set dbRegistrations = rdoEngine.rdoEnvironments(0). _
        OpenConnection("eventreg")

        'Build SQL INSERT string
        strSQL = "INSERT INTO Registrations ("

        For i = 1 To UBound(arrArgVal) - 1 Step 2
            strSQL = strSQL & Trim$(Right$(arrArgVal(i), _
                Len(arrArgVal(i)) - 3)) & ","
        Next
        strSQL = Left$(strSQL, Len(strSQL) - 1) & ") "
        strSQL = strSQL & "VALUES ("
        For i = 2 To UBound(arrArgVal) Step 2
            strSQL = strSQL & "'" & Trim$(arrArgVal(i)) & "',"
        Next
        strSQL = Left$(strSQL, Len(strSQL) - 1) & ") "

        'Execute SQL statement
        dbRegistrations.Execute strSQL

UpdateDataExit:
    'Close connection
    dbRegistrations.Close
    Set dbRegistrations = Nothing
    Exit Sub

UpdateDataErr:
    Resume UpdateDataExit

End Sub

Private Function fCreateHTML(arrArgVal() As String) As String

'Author: New Technology Solutions, Inc.
'Purpose: Generate a sample return HTML page
'5/1/96 Original

On Error GoTo CreateHTMLErr
```

```
        Dim strHTML As String

        strHTML = "Content-Type: text/html" & vbCrLf & vbCrLf
        strHTML = strHTML & "<HTML><HEAD><TITLE>Registered!"
        strHTML = strHTML & "</TITLE></HEAD><BODY "
        strHTML = strHTML & "BGCOLOR=#FFFFFF><CENTER>"
        strHTML = strHTML & "<H2>Thanks for Registering!</H2>"
        strHTML = strHTML & "</CENTER></BODY></HTML>"
        fCreateHTML = strHTML

CreateHTMLExit:
        Exit Function

CreateHTMLErr:
        fCreateHTML = fCreateHTMLError(Err.Number, Err.Description)
        Resume CreateHTMLExit

End Function

Private Function fCreateHTMLError(lngNumber As Long, _
        strDescription As String) As String

'Author: New Technology Solutions, Inc.
'Purpose: Create an HTML page describing an error
'5/1/96 Original

        Dim strHTML As String

        strHTML = strHTML = "Content-Type: text/html" & vbCrLf _
                & vbCrLf
        strHTML = strHTML & _
                "<HTML><HEAD><TITLE>Error Report</TITLE></HEAD><BODY>"
        strHTML = strHTML & _
                "<H2><CENTER>OLEISAPI ERROR!</CENTER></H2><P>"
        strHTML = strHTML & _
                "<TABLE><TR><TH>NUMBER</TH><TD>" & Format$(lngNumber) _
                & "</TD></TR>"
        strHTML = strHTML & "<TR><TH>DESCRIPTION</TH><TD>" & _
                strDescription & "</TD></TR>"
        strHTML = strHTML & "</TABLE></BODY></HTML>"
        fCreateHTMLError = strHTML

End Function
```

The Main Module

Once the Person class has been completed, all of the functionality for your ActiveX component is finished. However, you must perform some simple house-keeping tasks to complete the entire component. First of all, every Visual Basic project must start from a form, or from a subroutine named Main. Your project does not have any forms, so you must provide a Sub Main subroutine to start the ActiveX component. A code module is the only component of Visual Basic that can contain the Sub Main procedure from which you start the application.

Step 1

Add a module to your application by selecting Module from the Insert menu.

Step 2

Add the Main procedure to the module by adding the following code:

```
Public Sub Main()
End Sub
```

It is not necessary to place any code in this new procedure. The Main procedure is simply a requirement of Visual Basic for creating the ActiveX component.

At this point, save your project in the \bookdata\project2 subfolder.

Finalizing the ActiveX Component

All of the code for your ActiveX component is now complete. All you have left to do is to build a final compiled component. The final component will be an in-process ActiveX component that will be called by oleisapi.dll when the user submits a form.

Step 1

First you must establish your project as an in-process ActiveX component. Access the project's options by selecting Options from the Tools menu and clicking on the Project tab. In the Project tab, set the following properties:

Project Name	Eventreg
StartMode	OLE Server
Description	OLEISAPI Event Registration Component

Figure 7-9 shows the settings made in the Project tab of the Options dialog box.

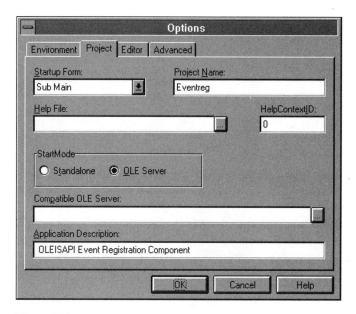

Figure 7-9.
The Project tab of the Options dialog box.

The StartMode property tells Visual Basic that this project is an ActiveX component. This will make the functionality of the application available to oleisapi.dll. This is a crucial part of the final development.

Step 2

Create a compiled in-process ActiveX component by selecting Make OLE DLL FILE from the File menu. Name your ActiveX component *eventreg.dll,* and save it in the \scripts\project2 folder you previously set up.

Step 3

For oleisapi.dll to locate eventreg.dll, eventreg.dll must be registered in the server's system Registry. If you created eventreg.dll on the Windows NT server itself, eventreg.dll will automatically be entered into the system Registry. If you created the eventreg.dll on a client computer, you will need to copy the component to the Windows NT server and register it manually. If the component is not properly registered, it will not work.

To register eventreg.dll on the server, you will need a copy of the regsvr32.exe registration utility. The registration utility is typically found in the clisvr folder of any Visual Basic 4.0 32-bit installation. The registration utility can be executed from MS-DOS or from the Windows Run command with the following syntax:

drive:\path\regsvr32.exe drive:\path\mycomponent.dll

For eventreg.dll, the line required for registration might look like this:

```
c:\vb4\clisvr\regsvr32.exe c:\inetsrv\scripts\project2\eventreg.dll
```

If the registration is successful, you will see a message box indicating that eventreg.dll is properly registered. Figure 7-10 shows a sample of the message box.

Figure 7-10.
A message box confirming successful registration of eventreg.dll.

Running the Project

Before you run the project, make sure that all of the files you created are stored in the proper folders. The eventreg.mdb database should be in the \bookdata\project2 folder, eventreg.dll should be in the \scripts\project2 folder, and eventreg.htm and backgnd2.gif should be in the \wwwroot\project2 folder. Make sure that eventreg.dll is properly registered and that the ACTION attribute of the frmRegister form in eventreg.htm is properly defined. Additionally, oleisapi.dll must be in the scripts folder. For more information on setting up the oleisapi.dll, see "Setting Up OLEISAPI," in Chapter 5 (page 156). Once everything is properly configured, you should be able to open the web page in the Internet Explorer and view the event registration form.

Wait a few moments after the page loads. You should see the text change in the ActiveX label at the top of the page. This indicates that the Timer control and associated VBScript code are working correctly. If the code is correct, a new random message will appear every 5 seconds.

Test the client-side validation routine by leaving a text field blank. As you tab to a new field, the VBScript code will detect the blank text box and stop you. You should see an appropriate message prompting you to enter some text.

Figure 7-11 shows the event registration form and a message box prompting the user to enter text.

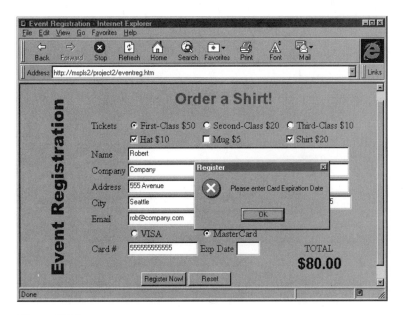

Figure 7-11.
The event registration form and a message box prompting the user to enter text.

After checking the validation procedure, fill out the form and submit it to the back end by clicking on the Register Now! button. You should receive an appropriate confirmation message from the server. Figure 7-12 (page 290) shows the confirmation screen.

You can check to see whether your data is in the database by opening the database in the Data Manager or in Microsoft Access. Figure 7-13 (page 290) shows a sample record in the eventreg.mdb database as viewed with the Data Manager in Visual Basic.

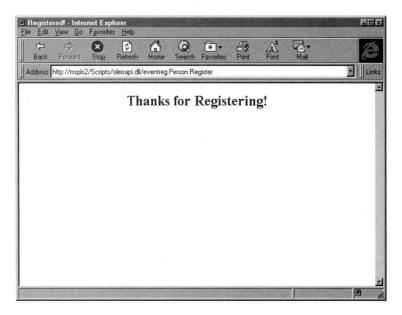

Figure 7-12.
The confirmation screen.

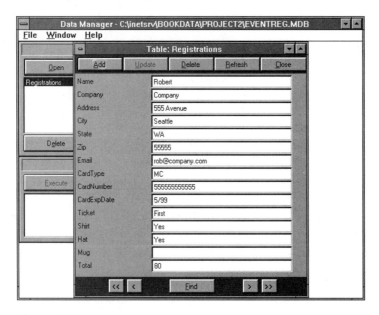

Figure 7-13.
A sample record as viewed with the Data Manager.

Project #3: An Online Bookstore

The project presented in this chapter creates an online bookstore that allows users to conduct a search of its inventory of book titles and make a purchase. This project uses the Internet Database Connector (IDC) to create a search engine that allows users to search for a book by subject, title, or author. Selections are returned to the user in a tabular format, and the user is also offered the option to order books online. Books that have special prices associated with them are marked with a unique image designating them as "special" purchases.

Because this project is intended to be a complete online solution, you will need to be familiar with Microsoft Windows NT Server, Microsoft Windows NT networks in general, and Microsoft Windows 95. We assume that you will be constructing the necessary files directly on the Windows NT server. However, it is possible to construct them on a computer with Windows 95 and then transfer them to a Windows NT server for final configuration and testing.

Requirements

Construction of the online bookstore project requires the following components:

- Windows NT Server version 3.51 or 4.0 with the Microsoft Internet Information Server (IIS) installed
- Windows 95 with the Microsoft Internet Explorer 3.0 installed
- Microsoft Access 7.0 ODBC drivers (available on the companion CD)
- Microsoft Access (optional)

- Microsoft PowerPoint Animation Player (available on the companion CD)
- Microsoft Calendar control (available on the companion CD)
- Microsoft Timer control (available on the companion CD)

Design Objective

The design objective of this project is to create an online bookstore. The system will provide a mechanism for searching the available book title database with various criteria. The system will call attention to books in the inventory that are designated as "special" and will allow users to order books online. The browsing will be done via an HTML web page that uses IDC in IIS. A primary goal is to make the web site highly interactive and dynamic. Figure 8-1 shows the home page for the online bookstore.

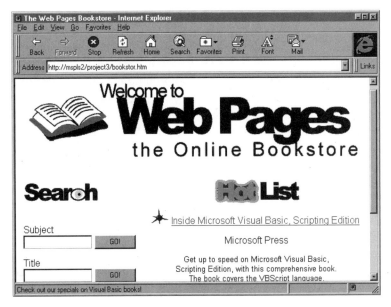

Figure 8-1.
The home page for the online bookstore.

When the user enters a subject, he or she will be able to view information on all books that correspond to that subject. The user will also be able to find additional books written by the author of a favorite title. If the user's request returns more than 20 selections, the system will warn the user and provide helpful instructions on how to perform better queries.

When the user has identified a book to purchase, the system will allow him or her to enter important information, such as name, address, and credit card number, to complete the transaction. Prior to committing the transaction, the system will validate data on the client side to ensure that data is present in each required field. When the form has been correctly filled out, it will be submitted to a back-end database.

On the back end, the data for the book inventory will be stored in an Access database. The same database will be used to store the customer order information. This data can be accessed later to process the orders. Any changes to the database, such as the inventory of books or the specials offered, will be reflected immediately on the web site.

Prerequisites

Before beginning this exercise, you will need to create a folder structure to hold your work. If you have worked on any of the other projects presented in this book, some of this structure might already be in place. (Note that for a standard installation of IIS, you should already have a folder named inetsrv and two subfolders named wwwroot and scripts.) From the Windows NT server's File Manager, create the following folders:

drive\inetsrv\bookdata\project3	For the bookstore database
drive\inetsrv\scripts\project3	For the idc and htx files
drive\inetsrv\wwwroot\project3	For the HTML file and associated graphics

Figure 8-2 (page 294) shows an example of the Project 3 folder structure.

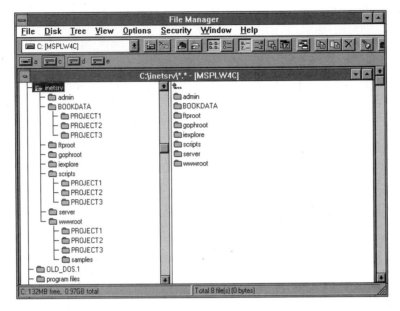

Figure 8-2.
An example of the Project 3 folder structure.

Creating the Datasource

To complete this project, you must create an ODBC datasource. Before you can create the datasource, you must have the ODBC drivers for Microsoft Access properly installed. If you need to install ODBC drivers, see the newsletter project in Chapter 6, which explains in detail how to install ODBC drivers on your server.

Creating the Access Database

Although you could certainly create the database for this exercise manually, the number of entries required for a complete online store makes manual database construction unreasonable for this project. Instead, copy the bookstor.mdb database from the project3 folder on the companion CD and store it in the bookdata\project3 folder you created earlier. The database used with this project is a modified version of the biblio.mdb database that ships with Microsoft Visual Basic.

This project uses several structured query language (SQL) queries to implement the search engine for the bookstore. These SQL queries perform multiple table joins and are dependent on the relationships in the database. For this reason, you must have a firm understanding of several tables for this project. The structures of the database tables, which are already implemented in bookstor.mdb, are shown in Tables 8-1 through 8-4.

Table 8-1. **The Customers Table**

Field Name	Data Type
Name	Text
Company	Text
Address	Text
City	Text
State	Text
Zip	Text
Email	Text
CardType	Text
CardNumber	Text
ExpDate	Text
Title	Text

Table 8-2. **The Authors Table**

Field Name	Data Type
Au_ID	Long
Author	Text
Year Born	Integer

Table 8-3. **The Title Author Table**

Field Name	Data Type
ISBN	Text
Au_ID	Long

Table 8-4. **The Titles Table**

Field Name	Data Type
Title	Text
Year Published	Integer
ISBN	Text
PubID	Long
Description	Text
Notes	Text
Subject	Text
Comments	Memo
Special	Boolean
Price	Currency

Defining the Datasource

Like all databases that are accessed with IDC, the bookstore database must be an ODBC datasource defined in the ODBC Administrator. Additionally, the datasource must be a system DSN. Create the system DSN by following the steps below.

Step 1

From the Control Panel or an ODBC group, start the ODBC Administrator. When the ODBC Administrator starts, you will see the Data Sources dialog box.

Step 2

Install the new datasource by clicking on the System DSN button in the Data Sources dialog box. The System Data Sources dialog box should appear. In the System Data Sources dialog box, click on the Add button. The Add Data Source dialog box will then appear.

Step 3

In the Add Data Source dialog box, select the Microsoft Access ODBC driver and click on the OK button. The ODBC Microsoft Access Setup dialog box should appear. This dialog box is used to set up the datasource.

Step 4

Give your datasource a name by typing *bookstore* into the Data Source Name text box. This is the name you will use to identify the database whenever you utilize an ODBC driver. This name can be anything you want and is not directly related to the name of the database you copied from the companion CD.

Step 5

Enter a brief description for your datasource in the Description text box. This can be any text you want and has no effect on the application.

Step 6

Establish your datasource as the database you copied previously by clicking on the Select button. Now you will see a dialog box that lets you select the file for this datasource. Navigate to the \bookdata\project3 folder in which you copied the database and select bookstor.mdb. Figure 8-3 shows a sample of the ODBC Microsoft Access Setup dialog box after the bookstor.mdb database has been set up. When you are done, click on the OK button. Your new datasource should now be visible in the System Data Sources dialog box.

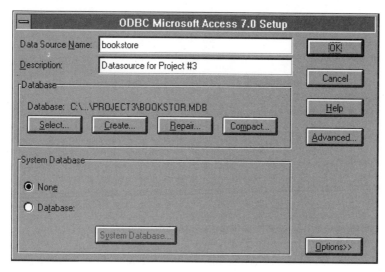

Figure 8-3.
The ODBC Microsoft Access Setup dialog box after the bookstor.mdb database has been set up.

Step 7

Click on the Close buttons in the System Data Sources dialog box and the Data Sources dialog box to exit the ODBC Administrator. Your datasource is now ready to be accessed from the web!

Creating the Home Page

In this project you will create several pages for the web site. The pages include a home page that introduces the bookstore, a query results page that lets the user examine book titles, and an order page that lets the user purchase a book. Each of these pages is enhanced with graphics and ActiveX controls to make the user's experience dynamic.

The home page introduces the bookstore and calls attention to selected titles. The code for this page uses several techniques to make the page interesting. Timer controls are utilized throughout the page to implement dynamic help systems and changing text displays. The goal of this home page is to grab the attention of the customer.

Step 1

Begin the home page by starting a new document in a text editor such as Notepad. This document will be saved in the \wwwroot\project3 folder you set up earlier for this project. The name of this page will be bookstor.htm. Add the following code to build the head section:

```
<HTML>
<HEAD>
<TITLE>The Web Pages Bookstore</TITLE>

</HEAD>
```

Remember that the script section will be placed inside the head section. You will add a script section later in the project.

Step 2

In the <BODY> tag of the home page, the OnLoad attribute is used to specify a Microsoft Visual Basic, Scripting Edition, routine that will run when this page is first loaded. The variables and ActiveX controls used on this page are initialized in this routine. Later in the exercise, you will construct this Page_Initialize routine. For now, simply add the reference and some graphics to the page by adding the following code:

```
<BODY BGCOLOR="WHITE" OnLoad="Page_Initialize">
<CENTER>
<BASEFONT FACE="ARIAL">
<IMG SRC="banner.gif" ALT="Web Pages Bookstore"
WIDTH=575 HEIGHT=130>

<P>
<BR>
```

Step 3

This web page uses a table to arrange the information in a pleasant display. You will divide the web page into two sections: a search section and a "hot list" section. The search section will allow searches by subject, title, or author. The hot list section will showcase books that deserve special attention. Begin the table, and add the graphics for each of these areas by adding the following code:

```
<TABLE WIDTH=600>
    <TR>
        <TD>
        <IMG SRC="search.gif" ALT="Search"
        WIDTH=132 HEIGHT=34>
        </TD>
        <TD ALIGN="CENTER">
        <IMG SRC="hotlist.gif" ALT="Hot List"
        WIDTH=153 HEIGHT=48>
        </TD>
    </TR>
```

Step 4

In the code for the search section, you will define three different text boxes that can accept input for searches. Each of these text boxes can submit data to IDC. The boxes represent the three different types of searches supported by the site: search by subject, by title, or by author. Each box calls a different idc file to run its query. You will create the idc files later in this project. For now, simply add the text boxes by adding the following code:

```
<TR>
    <TD>
    <FORM ACTION="/scripts/project3/subject.idc"
    METHOD="POST" NAME="frmSubject">
    Subject<BR>
    <INPUT TYPE="TEXT" NAME="txtSubject">
    <INPUT TYPE="SUBMIT" VALUE="GO!">
    </FORM>
    <P>

    <FORM ACTION="/scripts/project3/title.idc"
    METHOD="POST" NAME="frmTitle">
    Title<BR>
    <INPUT TYPE="TEXT" NAME="txtTitle">
    <INPUT TYPE="SUBMIT" VALUE="GO!">
    </FORM>
    <P>
```

(continued)

299

continued

```
<FORM ACTION="/scripts/project3/author.idc"
METHOD="POST" NAME="frmAuthor">
Author<BR>
<INPUT TYPE="TEXT" NAME="txtAuthor">
<INPUT TYPE="SUBMIT" VALUE="GO!">
</FORM>
</TD>
```

Step 5

The hot list section highlights a book for immediate purchase. You will implement the hot list by displaying some text about a particular book and offering a jump to let the user purchase the book. Use the following code to implement the hot list:

```
        <TD ALIGN="CENTER">
        <IMG SRC="spike_re.gif" ALT="Picture">
        <FONT FACE="ARIAL" SIZE=3>
        <A HREF="/scripts/project3/title.idc?txtTitle=
Inside+Microsoft+Visual+Basic, +Scripting+Edition">
        Inside Microsoft Visual Basic, Scripting Edition</A>
        <P>Microsoft Press<P>
        </FONT>
        <FONT FACE="ARIAL" SIZE=2>
        Get up to speed on Microsoft Visual Basic,<BR>
        Scripting Edition, with this comprehensive book.<BR>
        The book covers the VBScript language,<BR>
        ActiveX controls, and the Microsoft Internet<BR>
        Information Server.<BR>
        A must-have for any Visual Basic for<BR>
        Applications developer!!<BR>
        Click for more information!
        </FONT>
        </TD>
    </TR>
</TABLE>
</CENTER>
```

Step 6

This project uses three Timer controls to achieve some dynamic effects in the web page. The three timers are contained in a form called frmHelp. The first timer, tmrHelp, fires if there has been no user activity for 30 seconds and asks the user whether he or she needs help. The purpose of this timer is to offer some help with using the search engine if the user is idle for a relatively long period of time.

If the user asks for help after the first timer fires, a second timer, tmrDemo, is started. The second timer runs a demonstration program that places sample text in the text boxes for the various search engine selections. The demonstration also shows how to use wildcards in the input text boxes.

A third timer, tmrStatus, is used to generate commercial messages that appear on the status line of the browser. The messages are strings of text that appear one letter at a time, as if they were typed in by a teletype machine. This is an easy technique for adding some movement to your web page.

The three timers are placed in the web page with the <OBJECT> </OBJECT> tags. The timers have only two significant properties: Interval and Enabled. These properties allow you to set the number of milliseconds between timer events and to turn the timers on and off. Add these Timer controls to the web page with the following code:

```
<FORM NAME="frmHelp">

    <OBJECT
    CLASSID="clsid:59CCB4A0-727D-11CF-AC36-00AA00A47DD2"
    ID="tmrHelp"
    WIDTH=39
    HEIGHT=10
    >
    <PARAM NAME="Interval" VALUE="30000">
    <PARAM NAME="Enabled" VALUE="True">
    </OBJECT>

    <OBJECT
    CLASSID="clsid:59CCB4A0-727D-11CF-AC36-00AA00A47DD2"
    ID="tmrDemo"
    WIDTH=39
    HEIGHT=10
    >
    <PARAM NAME="Interval" VALUE="1000">
    <PARAM NAME="Enabled" VALUE="False">
    </OBJECT>

    <OBJECT
    CLASSID="clsid:59CCB4A0-727D-11CF-AC36-00AA00A47DD2"
    ID="tmrStatus"
```

(continued)

continued

```
      WIDTH=39
      HEIGHT=10
      >
      <PARAM NAME="Interval" VALUE="200">
      <PARAM NAME="Enabled" VALUE="False">
      </OBJECT>
</FORM>
```

Step 7

The body section of the home page is completed with a marquee. The <MARQUEE></MARQUEE> tags are special tags that display moving text. The <MARQUEE></MARQUEE> tags have several attributes that allow you to customize the moving text. For a description of the attributes available with these tags, see Appendix A.

Add the following code to insert a marquee on your home page and to complete the body section:

```
<FONT FACE="ARIAL" SIZE=4 COLOR="BLUE">
<MARQUEE>Check out our great Internet books!</MARQUEE>
</FONT>
</BODY>
</HTML>
```

Step 8

To complete the code that creates the dynamic behavior of the home page, you will add some VBScript code that will execute when the timers fire. Remember, the script section itself resides in the head section. All the VBScript code you write for this page will be placed inside one set of <SCRIPT></SCRIPT> tags.

You can use the OnLoad attribute of the <BODY></BODY> tags to specify a routine that will be executed when the page is first loaded. In a previous step, you created the <BODY></BODY> tags and specified the OnLoad attribute as OnLoad="Page_Initialize". When an OnLoad event occurs, the VBScript Page_Initialize routine gets called. You can use this routine to initialize variables and properties of ActiveX controls prior to displaying the web page. This functionality is similar to that of the Form_Load event found in Visual Basic.

In the home page code, you will specify several script-level variables that can be accessed by any routine. These variables are used to track the number of iterations of the various timer events. You can use these variables to create some animation effects. The variables are defined outside of all of the procedures but are located within the <SCRIPT></SCRIPT> tags. You will use the Page_Initialize routine to initialize these variables as well as to set properties for the page's ActiveX controls. Add the following code to initialize your web page:

```
<SCRIPT LANGUAGE="VBScript">
<!--
    Dim intLoop
    Dim intTextLoop
    Dim TempMsg1, TempMsg2, TempMsg3

    Sub Page_Initialize
        Dim MyForm
        Set MyForm=Document.frmHelp
        MyForm.tmrStatus.Enabled=True
        intLoop=0
        intTextLoop=0
    End Sub
```

In this routine, you have enabled the tmrStatus timer and initialized the counting integers to 0. The tmrStatus timer is used to type the commercial messages into the status bar of the browser. This routine turns it on when the page loads, which starts the animation immediately.

Step 9

The home page contains a form that lets the user search the Bookstore database by subject, title, or author. The form accepts wildcards to allow broader searches, but some users might not be familiar with the use of wildcards. If the user does not interact with the web page for 30 seconds, the page will display a prompt to see whether he or she needs help. The Timer control tmrHelp waits 30 seconds and then displays a message box. If the user answers "Yes," requesting help, another timer, tmrDemo, is turned on to start the help demonstration. You will code the help demonstration in the next step.

The code for tmrHelp is set to disable the timer after it fires once. You turn off the timer so that it does not cause the message box to display more than one time. If the user refuses help the first time, the page will not prompt him or her again. Add the following code to display the help message box after 30 seconds of inactivity:

```
Sub tmrHelp_Timer

        Dim intAnswer
        Dim MyForm
        Set MyForm=Document.frmHelp
```

(continued)

continued

```
       MyForm.tmrhelp.Enabled=False

       TempMsg1="You have been idle for a while. Do you "
       TempMsg2="need some help?"
       intAnswer=MsgBox(TempMsg1 & TempMsg2, 36, "Web Pages")
       If intAnswer=7 Then
           Exit Sub
       Else
           MyForm.tmrDemo.Enabled=True
       End if
   End Sub
```

Step 10

If the user answers "Yes" to the help message, the tmrDemo timer is enabled. This timer animates a help demonstration that displays a series of messages and also displays sample query requests in the subject, title, and author text boxes. The animation is driven by the timer and the script-level variable intLoop, which tracks the number of times the Timer event has occurred. Each time the timer fires, a new step in the animation program is run. Add the following code to place the help demonstration into the web page:

```
   Sub tmrDemo_Timer

       intLoop=intLoop+1

       Dim MyForm
       Set MyForm=Document.frmHelp

       Select Case intLoop
           Case 1
               MyForm.tmrDemo.Enabled=False
               TempMsg1="You can type directly into the Subject, "
               TempMsg2="Author, or Title boxes."
               Msgbox TempMsg1 & TempMsg2, 0, "Web Pages"
               MyForm.tmrDemo.Enabled=True
           Case 2
               Document.frmSubject.txtSubject.Value="Computers"
               Document.frmTitle.txtTitle.Value=""
               Document.frmAuthor.txtAuthor.Value=""
```

```
    Case 3
        Document.frmSubject.txtSubject.Value=""
        Document.frmTitle.txtTitle.Value= _
        "Inside Microsoft Visual Basic, Scripting Edition"
        Document.frmAuthor.txtAuthor.Value=""
    Case 4
        Document.frmSubject.txtSubject.Value=""
        Document.frmTitle.txtTitle.Value=""
        Document.frmAuthor.txtAuthor.Value="Hillier"
    Case 5
        MyForm.tmrDemo.Enabled=False
        TempMsg1="The following wildcards are allowed: "
        TempMsg2="% - Any String, _ - Any Character, [ ] - "
        TempMsg3="Any Range, [^] - Not Any Range"
        MsgBox TempMsg1 & TempMsg2 & TempMsg3, 0, "Web Pages"
        MyForm.tmrDemo.Enabled=True
    Case 6
        Document.frmSubject.txtSubject.Value="Comp%"
        Document.frmTitle.txtTitle.Value=""
        Document.frmAuthor.txtAuthor.Value=""
    Case 7
        Document.frmSubject.txtSubject.Value=""
        Document.frmTitle.txtTitle.Value="%Microsoft%"
        Document.frmAuthor.txtAuthor.Value=""
    Case 8
        Document.frmSubject.txtSubject.Value=""
        Document.frmTitle.txtTitle.Value=""
        Document.frmAuthor.txtAuthor.Value="Hill%"
    Case Else
        MyForm.tmrDemo.Enabled=False
        Document.frmSubject.txtSubject.Value=""
        Document.frmTitle.txtTitle.Value=""
        Document.frmAuthor.txtAuthor.Value=""
    End Select
End Sub
```

Step 11

Your web page provides additional animation by displaying commercial messages in the status bar of the browser. Your code writes text to the status bar with the Window object. The Window object is an object that can be accessed from VBScript directly. The StatusText property allows you to write directly to the status bar.

The commercial messages are animated with a Timer control. A new letter from a message string is displayed in the status bar each time the timer fires. In this way, the messages appear in the status bar as if they were typed in by a teletype machine. Add the commercial messages to your project with the following code:

```
Sub tmrStatus_Timer

    Dim MyForm
    Set MyForm=Document.frmHelp
    Dim Msg1
    Dim Msg2

    Msg1="Check out our specials on Visual Basic books!"
    TempMsg1="For quality training, call New Technology "
    TempMsg2="Solutions, Inc., at 203-239-6874!"
    Msg2=TempMsg1 & TempMsg2
    intTextLoop=intTextLoop + 1
    If intTextLoop > 0 And intTextLoop < Len(Msg1)+1 Then
        Window.Status=Left(Msg1,intTextLoop)
    End If
    If intTextLoop > Len(Msg1) + 25  And _
    intTextLoop < Len(Msg1) + Len(Msg2) + 26 Then
        Window.Status=Left(Msg2,intTextLoop-Len(Msg1)-25)
    End If
    If intTextLoop > Len(Msg1) + Len(Msg2) + 50 Then
        intTextLoop=0
    End If
End Sub
-->
</SCRIPT>
```

The home page code is now complete. Save this file as bookstor.htm in the \wwwroot\project3 folder. To view the completed home page, you will need to copy the necessary graphics. From the companion CD, copy *.gif and *.ppz from the project3\wwwroot\project3 folder into the \wwwroot\project3 folder on the Windows NT server. These are all the graphics you need for Project 3. Figure 8-4 shows the lower portion of the finished home page, which includes the marquee text and the status bar teletype text. Listing 8-1 shows the complete code, along with comments, for the home page.

Figure 8-4.
The lower portion of the Web Pages Bookstore home page.

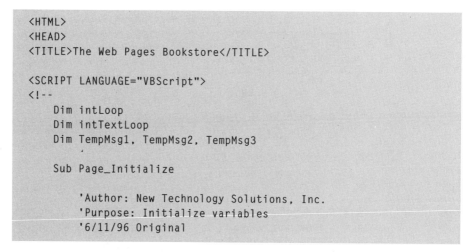

Listing 8-1.
The home page HTML code in the bookstor.htm file.

(continued)

Listing 8-1 *continued*

```
        Dim MyForm
        Set MyForm=Document.frmHelp
        MyForm.tmrStatus.Enabled=True
        intLoop=0
        intTextLoop=0
End Sub

Sub tmrHelp_Timer

        'Author: New Technology Solutions, Inc.
        'Purpose: Offer help to the user
        'if he or she is idle for 30 seconds
        '6/11/96 Original

        Dim intAnswer
        Dim MyForm
        Set MyForm=Document.frmHelp

        'Turn off the timer.  The help message
        'box should appear only once.
        MyForm.tmrhelp.Enabled=False

        TempMsg1="You have been idle for a while. Do you "
        TempMsg2="need some help?"
        intAnswer=MsgBox(TempMsg1 & TempMsg2, 36, "Web Pages")
        If intAnswer=7 Then 'No selected
            Exit Sub
        Else 'Yes selected

            'Turn on the demo timer to
            'show animation
            MyForm.tmrDemo.Enabled=True
        End if
End Sub

Sub tmrDemo_Timer

        'Author: New Technology Solutions, Inc.
        'Purpose: Run a search demo for the user
        'who needs help
        '6/11/96 Original

        intLoop=intLoop+1
```

```
Dim MyForm
Set MyForm=Document.frmHelp

'This code animates the search text
'boxes, showing sample entries
'while the user watches

Select Case intLoop
    Case 1
        MyForm.tmrDemo.Enabled=False
        TempMsg1="You can type directly into the Subject, "
        TempMsg2="Author, or Title boxes."
        Msgbox TempMsg1 & TempMsg2, 0, "Web Pages"
        MyForm.tmrDemo.Enabled=True
    Case 2
        Document.frmSubject.txtSubject.Value="Computers"
        Document.frmTitle.txtTitle.Value=""
        Document.frmAuthor.txtAuthor.Value=""
    Case 3
        Document.frmSubject.txtSubject.Value=""
        Document.frmTitle.txtTitle.Value= _
        "Inside Microsoft Visual Basic, Scripting Edition"
        Document.frmAuthor.txtAuthor.Value=""
    Case 4
        Document.frmSubject.txtSubject.Value=""
        Document.frmTitle.txtTitle.Value=""
        Document.frmAuthor.txtAuthor.Value="Hillier"
    Case 5
        MyForm.tmrDemo.Enabled=False
        TempMsg1="The following wildcards are allowed: "
        TempMsg2="% - Any String, _ - Any Character, [ ] - "
        TempMsg3="Any Range, [^] - Not Any Range"
        MsgBox TempMsg1 & TempMsg2 & TempMsg3, 0, "Web Pages"
        MyForm.tmrDemo.Enabled=True
    Case 6
        Document.frmSubject.txtSubject.Value="Comp%"
        Document.frmTitle.txtTitle.Value=""
        Document.frmAuthor.txtAuthor.Value=""
    Case 7
        Document.frmSubject.txtSubject.Value=""
        Document.frmTitle.txtTitle.Value="%Microsoft%"
        Document.frmAuthor.txtAuthor.Value=""
```

(continued)

Listing 8-1 *continued*

```
                Case 8
                    Document.frmSubject.txtSubject.Value=""
                    Document.frmTitle.txtTitle.Value=""
                    Document.frmAuthor.txtAuthor.Value="Hill%"
                Case Else
                    MyForm.tmrDemo.Enabled=False
                    Document.frmSubject.txtSubject.Value=""
                    Document.frmTitle.txtTitle.Value=""
                    Document.frmAuthor.txtAuthor.Value=""
        End Select
End Sub

Sub tmrStatus_Timer

        'Author: New Technology Solutions, Inc.
        'Purpose: Run commercials on the status
        'bar while this page is visible
        '6/13/96 Original

        Dim MyForm
        Set MyForm=Document.frmHelp
        Dim Msg1
        Dim Msg2

        Msg1="Check out our specials on Visual Basic books!"
        TempMsg1="For quality training, call New Technology "
        TempMsg2="Solutions, Inc., at 203-239-6874!"
        Msg2=TempMsg1 & TempMsg2

        'This code displays messages in the status bar.
        'A new letter is added once every 200 milliseconds,
        'imitating the action of a teletype machine.
        intTextLoop=intTextLoop + 1
        If intTextLoop > 0 And intTextLoop < Len(Msg1)+1 Then
            Window.Status=Left(Msg1,intTextLoop)
        End If
        If intTextLoop > Len(Msg1) + 25  And _
        intTextLoop < Len(Msg1) + Len(Msg2) + 26 Then
            Window.Status=Left(Msg2,intTextLoop-Len(Msg1)-25)
        End If
        If intTextLoop > Len(Msg1) + Len(Msg2) + 50 Then
            intTextLoop=0
        End If
End Sub
```

```
-->
</SCRIPT>

</HEAD>

<!--
Note the OnLoad attribute, which specifies the procedure
to be run when the page is first loaded
-->

<BODY BGCOLOR="WHITE" OnLoad="Page_Initialize">
<CENTER>
<BASEFONT FACE="ARIAL">
<IMG SRC="banner.gif" ALT="Web Pages Bookstore"
WIDTH=575 HEIGHT=130>

<P>
<BR>
<TABLE WIDTH=600>
    <TR>

        <TD>
        <IMG SRC="search.gif" ALT="Search"
        WIDTH=132 HEIGHT=34>
        </TD>
        <TD ALIGN="CENTER">
        <IMG SRC="hotlist.gif" ALT="Hot List"
        WIDTH=153 HEIGHT=48>
        </TD>
    </TR>
    <TR>

        <!--
        In this row, three forms are defined for performing
        the three different queries.  Each query calls the
        Internet Database Connector.
        -->

        <TD>
        <FORM ACTION="/scripts/project3/subject.idc"
        METHOD="POST" NAME="frmSubject">
        Subject<BR>
        <INPUT TYPE="TEXT" NAME="txtSubject">
        <INPUT TYPE="SUBMIT" VALUE="GO!">
        </FORM>
        <P>
```

(continued)

Listing 8-1 *continued*

```
        <FORM ACTION="/scripts/project3/title.idc"
        METHOD="POST" NAME="frmTitle">
        Title<BR>
        <INPUT TYPE="TEXT" NAME="txtTitle">
        <INPUT TYPE="SUBMIT" VALUE="GO!">
        </FORM>
        <P>

        <FORM ACTION="/scripts/project3/author.idc"
        METHOD="POST" NAME="frmAuthor">
        Author<BR>
        <INPUT TYPE="TEXT" NAME="txtAuthor">
        <INPUT TYPE="SUBMIT" VALUE="GO!">
        </FORM>
        </TD>

        <TD ALIGN="CENTER">
        <IMG SRC="spike_re.gif" ALT="Picture">
        <FONT FACE="ARIAL" SIZE=3>
        <A HREF="/scripts/project3/title.idc?txtTitle=
Inside+Microsoft+Visual+Basic,+Scripting+Edition">
        Inside Microsoft Visual Basic, Scripting Edition</A>
        <P>Microsoft Press<P>
        </FONT>
        <FONT FACE="ARIAL" SIZE=2>
        Get up to speed on Microsoft Visual Basic,<BR>
        Scripting Edition, with this comprehensive book.<BR>
        The book covers the VBScript language,<BR>
        ActiveX controls, and the Microsoft Internet<BR>
        Information Server.<BR>
        A must-have for any Visual Basic for<BR>
        Applications developer!!<BR>
        Click for more information!
        </FONT>
        </TD>
    </TR>
</TABLE>
</CENTER>

<FORM NAME="frmHelp">

    <!--
    This timer control will ask the user if he or she
    needs help when he or she has been idle for 30
```

```
seconds.  It is programmed in VBScript to ask
only one time, so as not to be annoying!
-->

<OBJECT
CLASSID="clsid:59CCB4A0-727D-11CF-AC36-00AA00A47DD2"
ID="tmrHelp"
WIDTH=39
HEIGHT=10
>
<PARAM NAME="Interval" VALUE="30000">
<PARAM NAME="Enabled" VALUE="True">
</OBJECT>

<!--
This timer is used to animate the help demonstration
when the user asks for help
-->

<OBJECT
CLASSID="clsid:59CCB4A0-727D-11CF-AC36-00AA00A47DD2"
ID="tmrDemo"
WIDTH=39
HEIGHT=10
>
<PARAM NAME="Interval" VALUE="1000">
<PARAM NAME="Enabled" VALUE="False">
</OBJECT>

<!--
This timer is used to send messages about products and
services to the user through the status bar
-->

<OBJECT
CLASSID="clsid:59CCB4A0-727D-11CF-AC36-00AA00A47DD2"
ID="tmrStatus"
WIDTH=39
HEIGHT=10
>
<PARAM NAME="Interval" VALUE="200">
<PARAM NAME="Enabled" VALUE="False">
</OBJECT>
</FORM>
```

(continued)

313

Listing 8-1 *continued*

```
<FONT FACE="ARIAL" SIZE=4 COLOR="BLUE">
<MARQUEE>Check out our great Internet books!</MARQUEE>
</FONT>
</BODY>
</HTML>
```

Building the Search Engine

The search engine for your web site is based on the IDC facilities of IIS. Constructing the search engine is a matter of writing an idc file for each of the queries you want to be able to execute. On this site, users can search by subject, title, or author. Therefore, you will need an idc file for each of these queries.

Step 1

Open a new document in your text editor. This document will allow the user to conduct a search by subject. Add the following code to specify the datasource, template, maximum number of return records, and SQL query for the subject search:

```
DataSource:Bookstore
Template:c:\inetsrv\scripts\project3\selected.htx
MaxRecords:21
SQLStatement:
+SELECT Titles.Title,Titles.Description,
+Titles.Price,Authors.Author,Titles.Special
+FROM Titles,Authors,[Title Author]
+WHERE Titles.Subject LIKE '%txtSubject%'
+AND Titles.ISBN=[Title Author].ISBN
+AND [Title Author].Au_ID=Authors.Au_ID
```

Note the MaxRecords line. This lines sets the maximum number of records that can be returned from a query. In this situation, it is 21 records. Save this file as subject.idc in the \scripts\project3 folder that you set up at the beginning of this project.

Step 2

Open a new document in your text editor. This document will allow the user to conduct a search by title. Add the following code to specify the datasource, template, maximum number of return records, and SQL query for the title search:

```
DataSource:Bookstore
Template:c:\inetsrv\scripts\project3\selected.htx
```

```
MaxRecords:21
SQLStatement:
+SELECT Titles.Title,Titles.Description
+,Authors.Author,Titles.Price,Titles.Special
+FROM Titles,[Title Author],Authors
+WHERE Titles.Title LIKE '%txtTitle%'
+AND Titles.ISBN=[Title Author].ISBN
+AND [Title Author].Au_ID=Authors.Au_ID
```

Save this file as title.idc in the \scripts\project3 folder that you set up at the beginning of this project.

Step 3

Open a new document in your text editor. This document will allow the user to conduct a search by author. Add the following code to specify the datasource, template, maximum number of return records, and SQL query for the author search:

```
DataSource:Bookstore
Template:c:\inetsrv\scripts\project3\selected.htx
MaxRecords:21
SQLStatement:
+SELECT Titles.Title,Titles.Description
+,Authors.Author,Titles.Price,Titles.Special
+FROM Titles,[Title Author],Authors
+WHERE Authors.Author LIKE '%txtAuthor%'
+AND Authors.Au_ID=[Title Author].Au_ID
+AND [Title Author].ISBN=Titles.ISBN
```

Save this file as author.idc in the \scripts\project3 folder that you set up at the beginning of this project.

Creating the Selected Titles Page

After IDC has executed the query, it returns the results as a web page. The book information is formatted into a table in which the title, description, author, and price are displayed. If any of the books listed in the table has a special price, an image designating the book as a "special" is displayed next to the entry in the table.

While the user is browsing the list of books, he or she can order a book at any time by clicking on the Order Info button associated with that book. You will build the order form later in the project. A More button for each entry is also available for users who want to see more titles by the same author.

Step 1

Start a new document in your text editor. This document will be saved as selected.htx in the \scripts\project3 folder. The head section is a simple section with a title.

```
<HTML>
<HEAD>
<TITLE>Selected Titles</TITLE>
</HEAD>
```

Step 2

The Selected Titles page is announced with an image banner. You add the image with the <IMG> tag. You will also specify a font for the entire page with the <BASEFONT> tag. Although the <BASEFONT> tag allows you to specify one font for the whole page, the font can be modified with subsequent <FONT> tags. One of the ways in which you can use the <FONT> tag to modify the base font is by using the SIZE attribute. For example, to increase the font size by 1 relative to the current <BASEFONT> setting, you specify <FONT SIZE=+1>. Similarly, you can use the minus sign to decrease the font size. For more information on <FONT> tags, consult Appendix A of this book. Add the following code to display the image and set the base font:

```
<BODY BGCOLOR="WHITE">
<BASEFONT FACE="ARIAL" SIZE=4>
<CENTER>

<IMG SRC="/project3/selected.gif" ALT="Selected Titles"
WIDTH=390 HEIGHT=100>
```

Step 3

All the information for the selected books is placed in a table. The strategy for the table setup is to define the column headings and then populate the rows through a loop. Add the following code to define the column headings:

```
<TABLE BORDER CELLPADDING=5>
<TR>
    <TH>
    Title
    </TH>
    <TH>
    Description
    </TH>
    <TH>
```

```
Author
</TH>
<TH>
Price
</TH>
</TR>
```

Step 4

Once the column headings have been defined, your code will use the
<%begindetail%> and <%enddetail%> tags to cause IDC to loop through ev-
ery record in the result set and populate subsequent rows of the table.

For each of the displayed selections, your web page will include an Order
Info button for ordering a book and a More button that will display more titles
by the same author. The functions of these buttons are carried out by additional
queries sent to IDC. You will build an additional order idc file later in this
project. For now, add the following code to populate the table with the returned
records and set up the Order Info and More buttons:

```
<%begindetail%>
    <TR>
        <TD>
        <%If Special EQ "1"%>
            <IMG SRC="/project3/special.gif"
            HEIGHT=25 WIDTH=75><BR>
        <%EndIf%>

        <FONT SIZE=-2>
        <B><%Title%></B><BR>

        <FORM METHOD="POST"
        ACTION="/scripts/project3/order.idc">
        <INPUT TYPE="HIDDEN" VALUE="<%Title%>"
        NAME="txtTitle">
        <INPUT TYPE="SUBMIT" VALUE="Order Info...">
        </FORM>

        </FONT>
        </TD>

        <TD>
        <FONT SIZE=-2>
        <%Description%>
        </FONT>
        </TD>
```

(continued)

continued

```
<TD>
<FONT SIZE=-2>
<%Author%><BR>

<FORM METHOD="POST"
ACTION="/scripts/project3/author.idc">
<INPUT TYPE="HIDDEN" VALUE="%<%Author%>%"
NAME="txtAuthor">
<INPUT TYPE="SUBMIT" VALUE="More...">
</FORM>

</FONT>
</TD>

<TD>
<FONT SIZE=-2>
<%Price%>
</FONT>
</TD>
</TR>
```

Take note of how the code displays the "special" image in this page for any book that is a special purchase. This code also shows how the VALUE settings for a query can be placed inside hidden fields for subsequent use in a query. For example, in the preceding code fragment, the Title field is placed in a hidden field so that the order query can be run with the title as a search criterion. The advantage is that the user doesn't have to enter the title to perform the order query. You can place the Title field in a hidden field, using code such as this:

```
<INPUT TYPE="HIDDEN" VALUE="<%Title%>"
```

Step 5

In the idc files you created previously, you specified that the maximum number of returned records was 21. If 21 records are returned, your code will display a warning and some help to prompt the user to narrow the search. The code determines which record the page is on by examining the built-in CurrentRecord variable. You can use this variable with the <%If%>, <%Else%>, and <%EndIf%> tags to set up decision structures. In this case, you will display the warning if CurrentRecord is 20. CurrentRecord indicates the number of times the <%begindetail%> section has been processed. Therefore, if CurrentRecord equals 20, it is processing record 21. Add the following code to display a warning and some help if more than 20 selections are returned:

```
<%If CurrentRecord EQ 20%>
    <TR>
        <TD COLSPAN=4>
        <IMG SRC="/project3/toomany.gif"
        ALT="Too Many Selections"
        WIDTH=315 HEIGHT=90><P>
        </TD>
    </TR>
    <TR>
        <TD COLSPAN=4>
        You have specified criteria that return information
        on more than 20 books. You should be more specific
        to narrow your search.
        <P>
        Here is an example of narrowing your selection:
        <P>
        <I>Title</I> = <FONT COLOR="GREEN">%V%</FONT>
        returns information on all books with the letter "V"
        in their titles.
        <P>
        Change this to:<BR>
        <I>Title</I> = <FONT COLOR="GREEN">%Visual Basic%</FONT>
        to return information on books with the words "Visual
        Basic" in their titles.
        <P>
        </TD>
    </TR>
    <%EndIf%>
<%enddetail%>

</TABLE>
</CENTER>
</BODY>
</HTML>
```

You have now completed the HTML code that displays the selected records in a table. Save this file as selected.htx in the \scripts\project3 folder. Figure 8-5 shows a sample of the Selected Titles page, and Listing 8-2 shows the complete code for selected.htx.

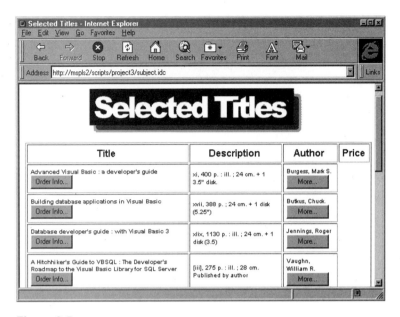

Figure 8-5.
The Selected Titles page.

```
<HTML>
<HEAD>
<TITLE>Selected Titles</TITLE>
</HEAD>

<BODY BGCOLOR="WHITE">
<BASEFONT FACE="ARIAL" SIZE=4>
<CENTER>

<IMG SRC="/project3/selected.gif" ALT="Selected Titles"
WIDTH=390 HEIGHT=100>

<TABLE BORDER CELLPADDING=5>
<TR>
    <TH>
    Title
    </TH>
    <TH>
    Description
    </TH>
```

Listing 8-2.
The Selected Titles page code in the selected.htx file.

```
        <TH>
        Author
        </TH>
        <TH>
        Price
        </TH>
</TR>

<%begindetail%>

        <TR>
            <TD>
            <%If Special EQ "1"%>
                <IMG SRC="/project3/special.gif"
                HEIGHT=25 WIDTH=75><BR>
            <%EndIf%>

            <FONT SIZE=-2>
            <B><%Title%></B><BR>

            <FORM METHOD="POST"
            ACTION="/scripts/project3/order.idc">
            <INPUT TYPE="HIDDEN" VALUE="<%Title%>"
            NAME="txtTitle">
            <INPUT TYPE="SUBMIT" VALUE="Order Info...">
            </FORM>

            </FONT>
            </TD>

            <TD>
            <FONT SIZE=-2>
            <%Description%>
            </FONT>
            </TD>

            <TD>
            <FONT SIZE=-2>
            <%Author%><BR>

            <FORM METHOD="POST"
            ACTION="/scripts/project3/author.idc">
            <INPUT TYPE="HIDDEN" VALUE="%<%Author%>%"
            NAME="txtAuthor">
            <INPUT TYPE="SUBMIT" VALUE="More...">
            </FORM>
```

(continued)

Listing 8-2 *continued*

```
        </FONT>
        </TD>

        <TD>
        <FONT SIZE=-2>
        <%Price%>
        </FONT>
        </TD>
    </TR>

    <%If CurrentRecord EQ 20%>
        <TR>
            <TD COLSPAN=4>
            <IMG SRC="/project3/toomany.gif"
            ALT="Too Many Selections"
            WIDTH=315 HEIGHT=90><P>
            </TD>
        </TR>
        <TR>
            <TD COLSPAN=4>
            You have specified criteria that return information
            on more than 20 books. You should be more specific
            to narrow your search.
            <P>
            Here is an example of narrowing your selection:
            <P>
            <I>Title</I> = <FONT COLOR="GREEN">%V%</FONT>
            returns information on all books with the letter "V"
            in their titles.
            <P>
            Change this to:<BR>
            <I>Title</I> =
            <FONT COLOR="GREEN">%Visual Basic%</FONT>
            to return information on books with the words "Visual
            Basic" in their titles.
            <P>
            </TD>
        </TR>
    <%EndIf%>
<%enddetail%>

</TABLE>
</CENTER>
</BODY>
</HTML>
```

The Book Order Query

If a user is interested in ordering a book, he or she can click on the Order Info button. IDC is used again to query the database and return the title, description, and any comments on the selected book. The results are then displayed in an HTML extension file.

Add this functionality by starting a new document in a text editor. The file will be saved as order.idc in the \scripts\project3 folder. Add the following code to set up the book order query:

```
Datasource:Bookstore
Template:c:\inetsrv\scripts\project3\order.htx
SQLStatement:
+SELECT Title,Description,Comments,Special,Subject
+FROM Titles
+WHERE Title LIKE '%txtTitle%'
```

Creating the Book Order Page

The Book Order page allows the user to see the title, description, and any comments on the selected book and gives him or her a chance to order the book. In the code for this page, you will build an HTML form that will be used to submit information to IDC to make a purchase. You will use an ActiveX Calendar control in this page and will write some VBScript code to perform client-side data validation. If you do not have the ActiveX Calendar control installed, you can install it from this book's companion CD.

Step 1

Start a new document in your text editor. This file will be saved as order.htx in the same \scripts\project3 folder with your other htx files. Add the following code to build the head section for the Book Order page:

```
<HTML>
<HEAD>
<TITLE>Book Order</TITLE>
<BASEFONT FACE="ARIAL" SIZE=3>

</HEAD>
```

You will add a script section later.

Step 2

The book title, description, and any comments are displayed prominently on the page for the user. If the book is a special purchase, you will again display a special image. Add the following code to display the title, description, and any comments for the selected book:

```
<BODY BGCOLOR="WHITE" OnLoad="Page_Initialize">
<CENTER>

<IMG SRC="/project3/order.gif" ALT="Book Order"
WIDTH=360 HEIGHT=96><P>

<%begindetail%>

<%If Special EQ "1"%>
    <IMG SRC="/project3/special.gif" ALT="Special"
    HEIGHT=25 WIDTH=75>
    <IMG SRC="/project3/special.gif" ALT="Special"
    HEIGHT=25 WIDTH=75>
    <IMG SRC="/project3/special.gif" ALT="Special"
    HEIGHT=25 WIDTH=75>
<%EndIf%>

<P>
<%Title%>
<P>
<%Description%>
<P>
<FONT SIZE=-1>
<%Comments%>
<P>
<HR>
<P>
```

Step 3

The order form is constructed of intrinsic controls and ActiveX controls. Data such as name and address is contained in simple text boxes. The expiration date of the credit card is entered with an ActiveX Calendar control. Later in this exercise, you will write some code that uses the Click event of the calendar to store the data in the form. Add the following code to build the order form in the web page:

```
<FORM ACTION="/scripts/project3/purchase.idc"
METHOD="POST" NAME="frmPurchase">

<TABLE BGCOLOR="GRAY">
    <TR>
        <TD COLSPAN=6>
        <FONT FACE="ARIAL" SIZE=4>
        <MARQUEE>
        Place your order here!
        </MARQUEE>
        </FONT>
    </TR>
    <TR>
        <TH ALIGN="LEFT">
        Name
        </TH>
        <TD COLSPAN=5>
        <INPUT TYPE="TEXT" NAME="txtName" SIZE=70>
        </TD>
    </TR>
    <TR>
        <TH ALIGN="LEFT">
        Company
        </TH>
        <TD COLSPAN=5>
        <INPUT TYPE="TEXT" NAME="txtCompany" SIZE=70>
        </TD>
    </TR>
    <TR>
        <TH ALIGN="LEFT">
        Address
        </TH>
        <TD COLSPAN=5>
        <INPUT TYPE="TEXT" NAME="txtAddress" SIZE=70>
        </TD>
    </TR>
    <TR>
        <TH ALIGN="LEFT">
        City
        </TH>
        <TD>
        <INPUT TYPE="TEXT" NAME="txtCity" SIZE=20>
        </TD>
```

(continued)

continued

```
        <TH ALIGN="LEFT">
        State
        </TH>
        <TD>
        <INPUT TYPE="TEXT" NAME="txtState" SIZE=2 MAXLENGTH=2>
        </TD>
        <TH ALIGN="LEFT">
        Zip
        </TH>
        <TD>
        <INPUT TYPE="TEXT" NAME="txtZip" SIZE=5 MAXLENGTH=5>
        </TD>
    </TR>
    <TR>
        <TH COLSPAN=2 ALIGN="LEFT">
        Credit Card
        </TH>
        <TD COLSPAN=2>
        <INPUT TYPE="RADIO" NAME="optCardType"
        VALUE="VISA" CHECKED>VISA
        </TD>
        <TD COLSPAN=2>
        <INPUT TYPE="RADIO" NAME="optCardType"
        VALUE="MC">MC
        </TD>
    </TR>
    <TR>
        <TH ALIGN="LEFT">
        Card #
        </TH>
        <TD COLSPAN=5>
        <INPUT TYPE="TEXT" NAME="txtCardNumber" SIZE=70>
        </TD>
    </TR>
    <TR>
        <TH ALIGN="LEFT">
        Email
        </TH>
        <TD COLSPAN=5>
        <INPUT TYPE="TEXT" NAME="txtEmail" SIZE=70>
        </TD>
    </TR>
    <TR>
        <TH ALIGN="LEFT">
        Exp Date
        </TH>
```

```
            <TD COLSPAN=5>
            <OBJECT
            CLASSID="clsid:8E27C92B-1264-101C-8A2F-040224009C02"
            ID="calPurchase"
            WIDTH=372
            HEIGHT=200
            >
            <PARAM NAME="BackColor" VALUE="12632256">
            </OBJECT><BR>
            <INPUT TYPE="TEXT" NAME="txtExpDate" VALUE="">
        </TR>
        <TR>
            <TD>
            <INPUT TYPE="HIDDEN" VALUE="<%Title%>" NAME="txtTitle">
            </TD>
            <TD>
            <INPUT TYPE="BUTTON" VALUE="Order!"NAME="btnOrder">
            </TD>
            <TD>
            <INPUT TYPE="RESET">
            </TD>
        </TR>
    </TABLE>
</FORM>

<%enddetail%>


</CENTER>
</BODY>
</HTML>
```

Step 4

The body section is finished. Now you need to add some VBScript code to allow the user to complete the transaction. In this step, you will initialize the Calendar control with the current date. This is done with the Page_Initialize routine that is called from the OnLoad attribute of the <BODY></BODY> tags. Add the following VBScript code to initialize the Calendar control when the page is loaded:

```
<SCRIPT LANGUAGE="VBScript">
<!--
    Sub Page_Initialize

        Dim MyForm
        Set MyForm=Document.frmPurchase
        MyForm.calPurchase.Year=Year(Now)
```

(continued)

continued

```
        MyForm.calPurchase.Month=Month(Now)
        MyForm.calPurchase.Day=Day(Now)
        MyForm.txtExpDate.Value=MyForm.calPurchase.Value
    End Sub
```

Step 5

Whenever the user clicks on the Calendar control to change the date, the new date will appear in a text box control. This way, the user can either enter the credit card expiration date directly into the text box or use the ActiveX Calendar control to enter the expiration date. Add the following code to update the text box when the calendar is clicked:

```
Sub calPurchase_Click

    Dim MyForm
    Set MyForm=Document.frmPurchase
    MyForm.txtExpDate.Value=MyForm.calPurchase.Value
End Sub
```

Step 6

When the user has finished filling out the form, your code will validate the data. The validation for this page is done when the Order! button is clicked. If any of the fields is empty, you will display a message box prompting the user to enter data. If all the fields contain data, the form is submitted with the Submit method. Add the following routine to perform the data validation and call the Submit method:

```
Sub btnOrder_OnClick

    Dim blnValid
    Dim MyForm
    Set MyForm=Document.frmPurchase

    blnValid=True
    If MyForm.txtName.Value="" Then blnValid=False
    If MyForm.txtCompany.Value="" Then blnValid=False
    If MyForm.txtAddress.Value="" Then blnValid=False
    If MyForm.txtCity.Value="" Then blnValid=False
    If MyForm.txtState.Value="" Then blnValid=False
```

```
        If MyForm.txtZip.Value="" Then blnValid=False
        If MyForm.txtCardNumber.Value="" Then blnValid=False
        If MyForm.txtEMail.Value="" Then blnValid=False
        If blnValid=False Then
            MsgBox "All of the required fields must contain data" _
            ,16,"Book Order"
        Else
            MyForm.Submit
            End If
    End Sub
-->
</SCRIPT>
```

You have now completed the Book Order page. Save the page as order.htx in the \scripts\project3 folder with your other htx files from this project. Figures 8-6 and 8-7 show a sample of the Book Order page. Listing 8-3 shows the complete code, along with comments, for order.htx.

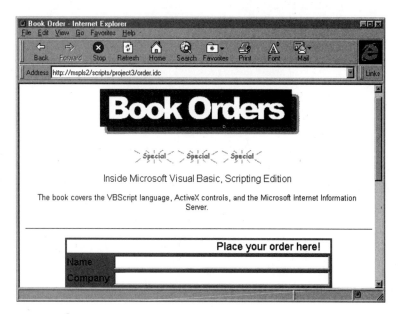

Figure 8-6.
The Book Order page.

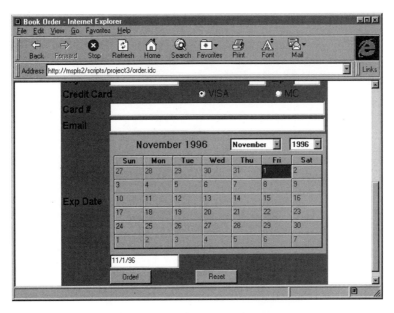

Figure 8-7.
The ActiveX Calendar control on the Book Order page.

```
<HTML>
<HEAD>
<TITLE>Book Order</TITLE>
<BASEFONT FACE="ARIAL" SIZE=3>

<SCRIPT LANGUAGE="VBScript">
<!--
    Sub Page_Initialize

        'Author: New Technology Solutions, Inc.
        'Purpose: Initialize page
        '6/12/96 Original

        Dim MyForm
        Set MyForm=Document.frmPurchase
        MyForm.calPurchase.Year=Year(Now)
        MyForm.calPurchase.Month=Month(Now)
        MyForm.calPurchase.Day=Day(Now)
        MyForm.txtExpDate.Value=MyForm.calPurchase.Value
    End Sub
```

Listing 8-3.
The Book Order page code in the order.htx file.

```
    Sub calPurchase_Click

        'Author: New Technology Solutions, Inc.
        'Purpose: Store the expiration date
        '6/13/96 Original

        Dim MyForm
        Set MyForm=Document.frmPurchase
        MyForm.txtExpDate.Value=MyForm.calPurchase.Value
    End Sub

    Sub btnOrder_OnClick

        'Author: New Technology Solutions, Inc.
        'Purpose: Validate form data
        'before form is submitted
        '6/12/96 Original

        Dim blnValid
        Dim MyForm
        Set MyForm=Document.frmPurchase

        blnValid=True
        If MyForm.txtName.Value="" Then blnValid=False
        If MyForm.txtCompany.Value="" Then blnValid=False
        If MyForm.txtAddress.Value="" Then blnValid=False
        If MyForm.txtCity.Value="" Then blnValid=False
        If MyForm.txtState.Value="" Then blnValid=False
        If MyForm.txtZip.Value="" Then blnValid=False
        If MyForm.txtCardNumber.Value="" Then blnValid=False
        If MyForm.txtEMail.Value="" Then blnValid=False
        If blnValid=False Then
            MsgBox "All of the required fields must contain data" _
            ,16,"Book Order"
        Else
            MyForm.Submit
        End If
    End Sub
-->
</SCRIPT>

</HEAD>
<BODY BGCOLOR="WHITE" OnLoad="Page_Initialize">
<CENTER>
```

(continued)

Listing 8-3 *continued*

```
<IMG SRC="/project3/order.gif" ALT="Book Order"
WIDTH=360 HEIGHT=96><P>

<!--
Display the selected book title
and the description
-->

<%begindetail%>

<%If Special EQ "1"%>
    <IMG SRC="/project3/special.gif" ALT="Special"
    HEIGHT=25 WIDTH=75>
    <IMG SRC="/project3/special.gif" ALT="Special"
    HEIGHT=25 WIDTH=75>
    <IMG SRC="/project3/special.gif" ALT="Special"
    HEIGHT=25 WIDTH=75>
<%EndIf%>

<P>
<%Title%>
<P>
<%Description%>
<P>
<FONT SIZE=-1>
<%Comments%>
<P>
<HR>
<P>

<!--
This form allows the user
to purchase the book. The data
is sent to a database for
later processing.
-->

<FORM ACTION="/scripts/project3/purchase.idc"
METHOD="POST" NAME="frmPurchase">

<TABLE BGCOLOR="GRAY">
    <TR>
        <TD COLSPAN=6>
        <FONT FACE="ARIAL" SIZE=4>
        <MARQUEE>
```

```
        Place your order here!
        </MARQUEE>
        </FONT>
</TR>
<TR>
        <TH ALIGN="LEFT">
        Name
        </TH>
        <TD COLSPAN=5>
        <INPUT TYPE="TEXT" NAME="txtName" SIZE=70>
        </TD>
</TR>
<TR>
        <TH ALIGN="LEFT">
        Company
        </TH>
        <TD COLSPAN=5>
        <INPUT TYPE="TEXT" NAME="txtCompany" SIZE=70>
        </TD>
</TR>
<TR>
        <TH ALIGN="LEFT">
        Address
        </TH>
        <TD COLSPAN=5>
        <INPUT TYPE="TEXT" NAME="txtAddress" SIZE=70>
        </TD>
</TR>
<TR>
        <TH ALIGN="LEFT">
        City
        </TH>
        <TD>
        <INPUT TYPE="TEXT" NAME="txtCity" SIZE=20>
        </TD>
        <TH ALIGN="LEFT">
        State
        </TH>
        <TD>
        <INPUT TYPE="TEXT" NAME="txtState" SIZE=2 MAXLENGTH=2>
        </TD>
        <TH ALIGN="LEFT">
        Zip
        </TH>
```

(continued)

Listing 8-3 *continued*

```
        <TD>
        <INPUT TYPE="TEXT" NAME="txtZip" SIZE=5 MAXLENGTH=5>
        </TD>
    </TR>
    <TR>
        <TH COLSPAN=2 ALIGN="LEFT">
        Credit Card
        </TH>
        <TD COLSPAN=2>
        <INPUT TYPE="RADIO" NAME="optCardType"
        VALUE="VISA" CHECKED>VISA
        </TD>
        <TD COLSPAN=2>
        <INPUT TYPE="RADIO" NAME="optCardType"
        VALUE="MC">MC
        </TD>
    </TR>
    <TR>
        <TH ALIGN="LEFT">
        Card #
        </TH>
        <TD COLSPAN=5>
        <INPUT TYPE="TEXT" NAME="txtCardNumber" SIZE=70>
        </TD>
    </TR>
    <TR>
        <TH ALIGN="LEFT">
        Email
        </TH>
        <TD COLSPAN=5>
        <INPUT TYPE="TEXT" NAME="txtEmail" SIZE=70>
        </TD>
    </TR>
    <TR>
        <TH ALIGN="LEFT">
        Exp Date
        </TH>
        <TD COLSPAN=5>
        <OBJECT
        CLASSID="clsid:8E27C92B-1264-101C-8A2F-040224009C02"
        ID="calPurchase"
        WIDTH=372
        HEIGHT=200
        >
```

```
        <PARAM NAME="BackColor" VALUE="12632256">
        </OBJECT><BR>
        <INPUT TYPE="TEXT" NAME="txtExpDate" VALUE="">
    </TR>
    <TR>
        <TD>
        <INPUT TYPE="HIDDEN" VALUE="<%Title%>" NAME="txtTitle">
        </TD>
        <TD>
        <INPUT TYPE="BUTTON" VALUE="Order!" NAME="btnOrder">
        </TD>
        <TD>
        <INPUT TYPE="RESET">
        </TD>
    </TR>
</TABLE>
</FORM>

<%enddetail%>

</CENTER>
</BODY>
</HTML>
```

The Purchase Query

When the user has filled out the form and submitted the purchase order, IDC must execute an INSERT query to save the record in the bookstor.mdb database. The data is stored in the Customers table, from which you can access the data and fill the order. When the order has been received, a confirmation screen is displayed to the user.

The only step in this section creates the idc file for the INSERT query. The file will be saved as purchase.idc. Open a new document in your text editor, add the following code, and save the file in the \scripts\project3 folder with the rest of your idc files:

```
DataSource:Bookstore
Template:c:\inetsrv\scripts\project3\purchase.htx
SQLStatement:
+INSERT INTO Customers
+(Name,Company,Address,City,State,Zip,CardType,
+CardNumber,ExpDate,Email,Title)
```

```
+VALUES
+('%txtName%','%txtCompany%','%txtAddress%',
+'%txtCity%','%txtState%','%txtZip%',
+'%optCardType%','%txtCardNumber%',
+'%txtExpDate%','%txtEmail%','%txtTitle%')
```

Creating the Confirmation Page

The confirmation page is displayed by IDC after the purchase data has been saved. In the confirmation page, you will thank the user for his or her purchase and then display commercial information on the subject matter of the purchase. For example, if the user has purchased *Inside Microsoft Visual Basic, Scripting Edition,* he or she will be directed to the New Technology Solutions, Inc., web site for more information.

Step 1

Start a new document in your text editor. This document will be the confirmation page. The document will be saved as purchase.htx in the \scripts\project3 folder with the rest of your htx files. Create the head section of the page by adding the following code:

```
<HTML>
<HEAD>
<TITLE>Thank You</TITLE>
</HEAD>
```

Step 2

The body section begins with an image that displays a message thanking the user. Add the image to the body section with the following code:

```
<BODY BGCOLOR="WHITE">
<CENTER>

<IMG SRC="/project3/thanks.gif" ALT="Thank you for your purchase"
WIDTH=450 HEIGHT=100><P>
<BR>
```

Step 3

If the user has purchased a book with the keyword *database* in the title, you will direct him or her to other books about database programming. Note how the page accesses the purchased book's title by referencing the form input variable. You can reference form input variables in an htx file by prefixing them with idc. Add the following code to display the titles of additional database books:

```
<%If idc.txtTitle CONTAINS "database"%>
    <FONT FACE="ARIAL" SIZE=3>
    Check out these other hot titles on
    database development!<P>
    <A HREF="/scripts/project3/title.idc?txtTitle=
Applying+SQL+in+Business">
    Applying SQL in Business
    </A><P>
    <A HREF="/scripts/project3/title.idc?txtTitle=
Paradox+made+easy">
    Paradox made easy
    </A><P>
    <A HREF="/scripts/project3/title.idc?txtTitle=
Oracle7;+the+complete+reference">
    Oracle7; the complete reference
    </A><P>
    </FONT>
<%EndIf%>
```

Step 4

If the title of the purchased book contains the keyword *visual,* the page directs the user to the Microsoft web site, in which he or she can learn more about visual tools. A link is built directly into the page with the anchor tag only if the title of the book contains the word *visual.* Add the following code to display the Microsoft link:

```
<%If idc.txtTitle CONTAINS "visual"%>
    <FONT FACE="ARIAL" SIZE=3>
    For more information on visual tools, <BR>
    check out the <A HREF="http://www.microsoft.com">
    Microsoft</A> web site!
    </FONT><P>
<%EndIf%>
```

Step 5

If the title of the purchased book contains the keyword *programming,* the user is treated to a Microsoft PowerPoint animation. This PowerPoint show is displayed with the PowerPoint Animation Player, which is an ActiveX control. The control is available on the companion CD and will display any PowerPoint slide show in a web page. Consult Project #1, in Chapter 6, for more information about the PowerPoint Animation Player and how to install it. Add the code at the top of page 338 to display the slide show.

```
<%If idc.txtTitle CONTAINS "programming"%>

    <OBJECT
    CLASSID="clsid:EFBD14F0-6BFB-11CF-9177-00805F8813FF"
    WIDTH=320
    HEIGHT=240
    >
    <PARAM NAME="File" VALUE="/project3/bootcamp.ppz">
    <EMBED
    WIDTH=320 HEIGHT=240 SRC="/project3/bootcamp.ppz"
    >
    </EMBED>
    <NOEMBED>This page contains a Microsoft PowerPoint
    animation that your browser was unable to view.
    </NOEMBED>
    </OBJECT><P>
<%EndIf%>
```

Step 6

Finally, if the title contains the keyword *script,* the user is directed to the New Technology Solutions, Inc., web site. This link is installed in the same way as the previous link to the Microsoft web site. Add the following code to place this link in the web page:

```
<%If idc.txtTitle CONTAINS "script"%>
    <FONT FACE="ARIAL" SIZE=3>
    For more information on VBScript,<BR>
    check out the <A HREF="http://www.vb-bootcamp.com">
    New Technology Solutions, Inc.,</A> web site!
    </FONT><P>
<%EndIf%>

</CENTER>
</BODY>
</HTML>
```

Your project is now complete! Save the file you created as purchase.htx in the \scripts\project3 folder with your other htx files. Figure 8-8 shows a sample confirmation page. Listing 8-4 shows the complete code, along with comments, for purchase.htx.

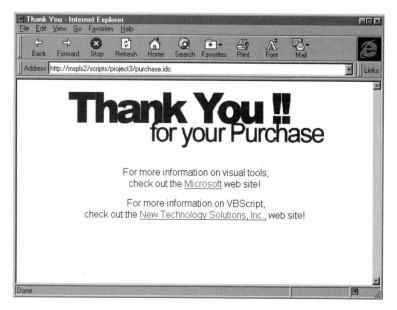

Figure 8-8.
A sample confirmation page.

```
<HTML>
<HEAD>
<TITLE>Thank You</TITLE>
</HEAD>

<BODY BGCOLOR="WHITE">
<CENTER>

<IMG SRC="/project3/thanks.gif" ALT="Thank you for your purchase"
WIDTH=450 HEIGHT=100><P>
<BR>

    <%If idc.txtTitle CONTAINS "database"%>
        <FONT FACE="ARIAL" SIZE=3>
        Check out these other hot titles on
        database development!<P>
        <A HREF="/scripts/project3/title.idc?txtTitle=
Applying+SQL+in+Business">
        Applying SQL in Business
        </A><P>
```

Listing 8-4.   *(continued)*
Confirmation page code in the purchase.htx file.

Listing 8-4 *continued*

```
        <A HREF="/scripts/project3/title.idc?txtTitle=
Paradox+made+easy">
        Paradox made easy
        </A><P>
        <A HREF="/scripts/project3/title.idc?txtTitle=
Oracle7;+the+complete+reference">
        Oracle7; the complete reference
        </A><P>
        </FONT>
    <%EndIf%>


    <%If idc.txtTitle CONTAINS "visual"%>
        <FONT FACE="ARIAL" SIZE=3>
        For more information on visual tools,<BR>
        check out the <A HREF="http://www.microsoft.com">
        Microsoft</A> web site!
        </FONT><P>
    <%EndIf%>


    <%If idc.txtTitle CONTAINS "programming"%>

        <!--
        This is a PowerPoint viewer control used
        to embed a PowerPoint presentation in the
        web page
        -->

        <OBJECT
        CLASSID="clsid:EFBD14F0-6BFB-11CF-9177-00805F8813FF"
        WIDTH=320
        HEIGHT=240
        >
        <PARAM NAME="File" VALUE="/project3/bootcamp.ppz">
        <EMBED
        WIDTH=320 HEIGHT=240 SRC="/project3/bootcamp.ppz"
        >
        </EMBED>
        <NOEMBED>This page contains a Microsoft PowerPoint
        animation that your browser was unable to view.
        </NOEMBED>
        </OBJECT><P>
    <%EndIf%>
```

```
      <%If idc.txtTitle CONTAINS "script"%>
          <FONT FACE="ARIAL" SIZE=3>
          For more information on VBScript,<BR>
          check out the <A HREF="http://www.vb-bootcamp.com">
          New Technology Solutions, Inc.,</A> web site!
          </FONT><P>
      <%EndIf%>

</CENTER>
</BODY>
</HTML>
```

Running the Project

Run the project by opening bookstor.htm from the Internet Explorer. When you see the home page, wait 30 seconds to see whether the help message box appears. When the message box appears, click on Yes and watch the animated help demonstration to make sure that it runs correctly. Figure 8-9 shows the home page with the help message box displayed.

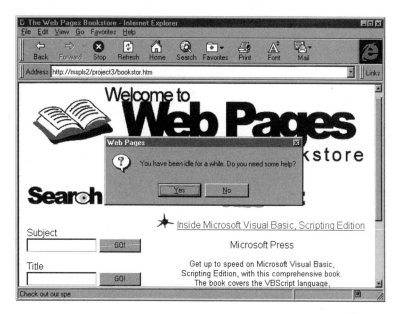

Figure 8-9.
The help message box displayed on the bookstore home page.

After you have tested the help demonstration, type the search string %programming% into the title search text box and click on the GO! button. Check to make sure that IDC returns a table full of book selections on subjects containing the keyword *programming*. Since there are many books about programming, more than 20 matching titles may be found. Figure 8-10 shows the message that is displayed at the bottom of the returned table if more than 20 matching titles are found.

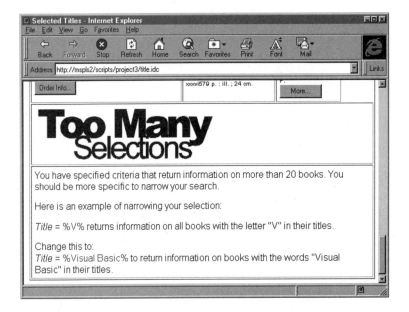

Figure 8-10.
The message displayed when more than 20 matching titles are found.

Select a book and click on the Order Info button. The Book Order page should appear.

In the Book Order page, verify the behavior of the ActiveX Calendar control by clicking on various dates and checking to see whether they appear in the text box. After you have tested the Calendar control, check the form validation routine by clicking the Order! button when the form has blank fields. The validation message box should appear. Figure 8-11 shows the message box that is displayed if one or more of the fields in the order form does not contain data.

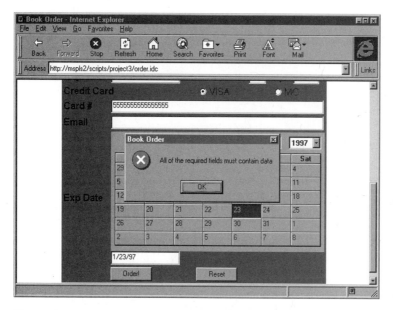

Figure 8-11.
A data validation message box displayed in the order form.

Finally, fill out the form and submit the order by clicking the Order! button. Depending on which book you have ordered, different confirmation screens appear. Figure 8-12 (page 344) shows the confirmation screen that appears if the ordered book has the terms *database, visual,* and *programming* in the title. The confirmation screen includes links to other database-related books, a link to Microsoft's web site, and a PowerPoint animation.

If everything is working correctly, book orders will be stored in the Customers table of the bookstore database. Figure 8-13 (page 344) shows some of the fields for a book order in the bookstor.mdb database, as viewed in Microsoft Access for Windows 95.

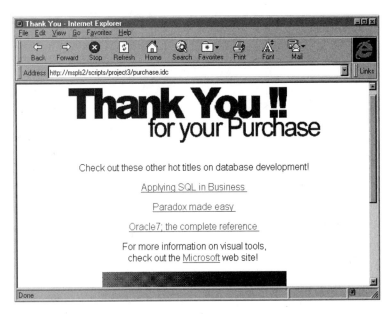

Figure 8-12.

The confirmation screen for a purchased book containing the terms database, visual, *and* programming *in the title.*

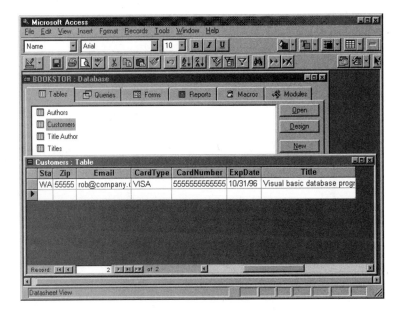

Figure 8-13.

A book order in the bookstore database.

C H A P T E R   N I N E

Project #4:
An Interactive Order Form
Built with ActiveX Control Pad

Although no integrated debugging environment (IDE) is currently available for Microsoft Visual Basic, Scripting Edition, Microsoft has created several tools to assist VBScript developers. In previous chapters, we have discussed the ActiveX Control Lister, which is used to place ActiveX controls in a web page, and content development tools such as Microsoft FrontPage. In Chapter 4, you first saw a development tool called Microsoft ActiveX Control Pad, which allows you to integrate HTML code, ActiveX controls, HTML layouts, and VBScript or JavaScript code to create interactive web pages. In this project, we will discuss ActiveX Control Pad in detail and use it to construct an interactive order form for purchasing computer products online. This project is designed to simply show you how to use ActiveX Control Pad, so it isn't necessary to construct the files directly on the server. Before you begin the project, you'll take a look at the various features of ActiveX Control Pad and some examples of their use.

Requirements

You will need the following components to complete the examples and the project in this chapter:

- Windows 95 with the Microsoft Internet Explorer 3.0 installed
- ActiveX Control Pad (available on the companion CD)
- Microsoft Timer Control (Available on the companion CD)

Prerequisites

Before you begin the examples and the project in this chapter, you might want to create a folder to save the related files. Note that any necessary graphics, as well as the completed examples and projects, are available on the companion CD, in the project4 folder.

ActiveX Control Pad Features

ActiveX Control Pad supports several features that can help you develop interactive web pages, but ActiveX Control Pad cannot be considered a true IDE because it lacks such features as debugging support. ActiveX Control Pad is really just a development utility, but it is still a step forward in ActiveX web page development. The following features are supported by ActiveX Control Pad:

- The HTML Source Editor, which allows you to create and edit HTML code

- The ActiveX Control Editor, which allows you to insert ActiveX controls in a web page and set their properties

- The Script Wizard, which helps you create VBScript code

- The HTML Layout control, an ActiveX control that is installed with ActiveX Control Pad and renders HTML layouts

- The HTML Layout Editor, a two-dimensional WYSIWYG editor that allows you to create HTML layouts with multiple ActiveX controls

- Several new ActiveX controls for use in web pages

In the next few sections, you'll practice with several examples that demonstrate these major features of ActiveX Control Pad.

The HTML Source Editor

The HTML Source Editor provides an environment for creating and editing HTML code. The HTML Source Editor is functionally equivalent to any other ASCII editor and can be used even if the other ActiveX Control Pad features, such as the ActiveX Control Editor or the Script Wizard, are not used. The HTML Source Editor is a Multiple Document Interface (MDI) editor, which means that you can use it to work on several HTML documents at the same time. Figure 9-1 shows the HTML Source Editor in ActiveX Control Pad.

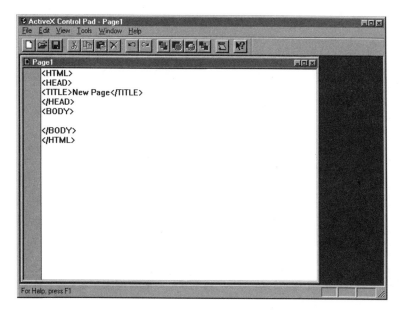

Figure 9-1.
The HTML Source Editor.

The ActiveX Control Editor

The ActiveX Control Editor allows you to insert ActiveX controls into a web page and set their properties. Only one control can be inserted at a time. You access the ActiveX Control Editor by selecting Insert ActiveX Control from the Edit menu. The Insert ActiveX Control dialog box is then displayed. A list box shows all of the ActiveX controls that have entries in the Registry. If you scroll the list box to the right, the class ID for each control is shown. Selecting a control in the list and then clicking the OK button begins the insertion process.

Figure 9-2 (page 348) shows the Insert ActiveX Control dialog box.

The ActiveX control will be inserted into the HTML code at the location specified by the text editor's cursor. When the OK button has been clicked, two new windows appear: the Edit ActiveX Control window and the Properties window. Figure 9-3 (page 348) shows these windows after the Microsoft Forms 2.0 Label control has been selected.

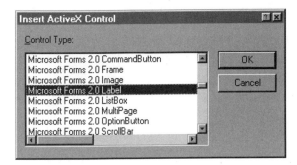

Figure 9-2.
The Insert ActiveX Control dialog box.

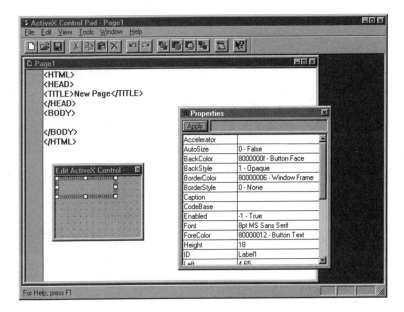

Figure 9-3.
The Edit ActiveX Control window and the Properties window.

The Edit ActiveX Control window allows you to resize the control and specify its appearance in the completed web page. Many of the controls that come with ActiveX Control Pad also support in-place editing of the Caption property. Simply click on the caption in the Edit ActiveX Control window and type the new entry.

To set other properties for the current control, you use the Properties window. The ActiveX Control Pad Properties window is similar to the Properties window found in Microsoft Visual Basic. In this window, you can edit any of the design-time properties supported by the ActiveX control. As in Visual

Basic, runtime properties are not available in the Properties window. However, you can access them in your VBScript code.

You complete the insertion of the ActiveX control by closing the Edit ActiveX Control window. When this window is closed, the Properties window is automatically closed and the <OBJECT></OBJECT> tags and other necessary code are added to the HTML Source Editor at the current cursor location. The design-time properties you set in the Properties window are added to the page with <PARAM> tags.

When the controls have been added to the HTML document, you can edit them either by typing directly in the HTML code or by selecting Edit ActiveX Control from the Edit menu. The Edit ActiveX Control command will be available only when your cursor is somewhere in the code for the control. Selecting Edit ActiveX Control causes the Edit ActiveX Control and Properties windows to open. You can make your changes to the control and then close the window to update your HTML code.

When a new control is added, the HTML Source Editor flags the control by displaying a control icon in the left margin next to it. You can also edit an ActiveX control by simply clicking on its control icon. Similar icons are displayed in the left margin for other objects in the HTML code—for example, a script icon for a scripting module, and an HTML Layout icon for an HTML layout. Figure 9-4 shows the HTML Source Editor after the Label control has been inserted. Note the control icon for the Label control in the left margin of the figure.

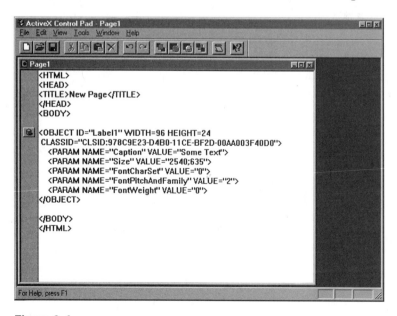

Figure 9-4.
The HTML Source Editor after the Label control has been inserted.

Example #1: Using the ActiveX Control Editor

In this example, you will use the ActiveX Control Editor to create a simple web page containing a pie chart, and then you will view it in the Internet Explorer. After you have created the HTML page, you will edit it and create a bar chart.

Step 1

Create a new folder named example1 in a convenient location on your computer.

Step 2

Launch ActiveX Control Pad. A new HTML Source Editor window containing the following code will appear:

```
<HTML>
<HEAD>
<TITLE>New Page</TITLE>
</HEAD>
<BODY>

</BODY>
</HTML>
```

Step 3

Add a form to the web page by adding the following code between the <BODY></BODY> tags:

```
<FORM NAME="frmTest">

</FORM>
```

Step 4

Place your cursor between the <FORM></FORM> tags and insert a new ActiveX control by selecting Insert ActiveX Control from the Edit menu. When the Insert ActiveX Control dialog box appears, select the Chart object and click OK. The Edit ActiveX Control window and the Properties window should now be visible.

Step 5

In the Properties window, change the Chart properties as follows:

ChartType	1 - Special Pie Chart
Height	144
ID	chtTest
Width	186

Figure 9-5 shows the Edit ActiveX Control and Properties windows after the Chart properties have been set.

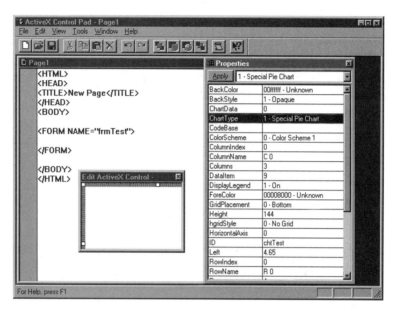

Figure 9-5.
The Edit ActiveX Control and Properties windows for the pie chart.

Step 6

Close the Edit ActiveX Control window to insert the Chart control code into your HTML document. The following code should appear between the <FORM></FORM> tags in your HTML code:

```
<OBJECT ID="chtTest" WIDTH=248 HEIGHT=192
    CLASSID="CLSID:FC25B780-75BE-11CF-8B01-444553540000">
    <PARAM NAME="_ExtentX" VALUE="6562">
    <PARAM NAME="_ExtentY" VALUE="5080">
    <PARAM NAME="Rows" VALUE="4">
    <PARAM NAME="Columns" VALUE="3">
    <PARAM NAME="ChartType" VALUE="1">
    <PARAM NAME="Data[0][0]" VALUE="9">
    <PARAM NAME="Data[0][1]" VALUE="10">
    <PARAM NAME="Data[0][2]" VALUE="11">
    <PARAM NAME="Data[1][0]" VALUE="7">
    <PARAM NAME="Data[1][1]" VALUE="11">
    <PARAM NAME="Data[1][2]" VALUE="12">
    <PARAM NAME="Data[2][0]" VALUE="6">
    <PARAM NAME="Data[2][1]" VALUE="12">
```

(continued)

continued

```
    <PARAM NAME="Data[2][2]" VALUE="13">
    <PARAM NAME="Data[3][0]" VALUE="11">
    <PARAM NAME="Data[3][1]" VALUE="13">
    <PARAM NAME="Data[3][2]" VALUE="14">
    <PARAM NAME="HorizontalAxis" VALUE="0">
    <PARAM NAME="VerticalAxis" VALUE="0">
    <PARAM NAME="hgridStyle" VALUE="0">
    <PARAM NAME="vgridStyle" VALUE="0">
    <PARAM NAME="ColorScheme" VALUE="0">
    <PARAM NAME="BackStyle" VALUE="1">
    <PARAM NAME="Scale" VALUE="100">
    <PARAM NAME="DisplayLegend" VALUE="0">
    <PARAM NAME="BackColor" VALUE="16777215">
    <PARAM NAME="ForeColor" VALUE="32768">
</OBJECT>
```

Step 7

Save the HTML document page as pie.htm in the example1 folder you created earlier. You will use it later, in Example #2. Open pie.htm in the Internet Explorer. You should see a web page that shows a pie chart. Figure 9-6 shows the pie chart in the Internet Explorer.

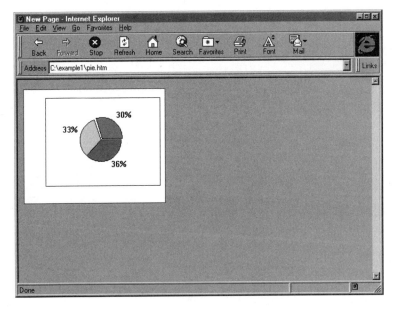

Figure 9-6.
A web page containing a Chart control inserted with ActiveX Control Pad.

Step 8

Switch back to ActiveX Control Pad, and, in the HTML Source Editor, locate the control icon next to the <OBJECT> tag for the Chart control. Click once on the control icon to open the editing windows. In the Properties window, change the ChartType property to 14 - Simple Bar Chart. You should see the pie chart change immediately to a bar chart in the Edit ActiveX Control window. Close the Edit ActiveX Control window. From the File menu, select Save As, and save the HTML document as bar.htm in the example1 folder. Open bar.htm in the Internet Explorer to view the bar chart. Figure 9-7 shows the bar chart in the Internet Explorer.

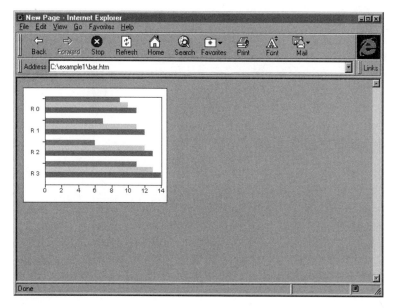

Figure 9-7.
A web page containing a Chart control edited with ActiveX Control Pad.

The Script Wizard

The Script Wizard is a tool that allows you to map actions to events and add scripting code. You invoke the Script Wizard by selecting Script Wizard from the Tools menu.

The Script Wizard supports two views: the list view and the code view. You can switch between views by clicking on the View radio buttons. Each view in the Script Wizard has three panes: an event pane, an action pane, and a script pane. The event pane shows objects and events. It allows you to select an event to which you will apply a script. The action pane shows actions, properties, variables, procedures, and objects. It allows you to select the action, property, variable, or procedure that you want to map to an event. The script pane, in list view, displays the results of event/action mapping. It also gives you the option of modifying and reordering the actions. In code view, the script pane displays the resulting script and allows you to edit it. Figure 9-8 shows a sample of the Script Wizard in list view and Figure 9-9 shows a sample in code view.

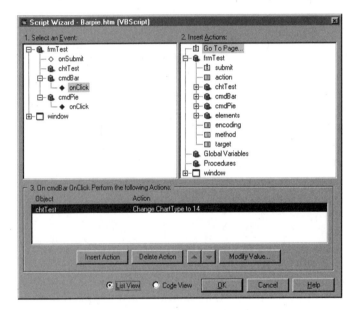

Figure 9-8.
A sample of the Script Wizard in list view.

Example #2: Using the Script Wizard

In this example, you will use the Script Wizard to modify the code you wrote in Example #1. You will add some button controls to the page to allow the user to manually change the chart style. You will use the Script Wizard to map the OnClick events of the buttons to the ChartType property of the chart.

Step 1
Create a folder named example2 in a convenient location on your computer.

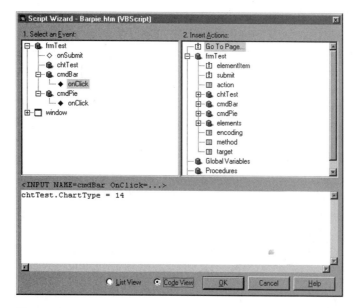

Figure 9-9.
A sample of the Script Wizard in code view.

Step 2

Open the bar.htm file you created in Example #1 in ActiveX Control Pad. Select Save As from the File menu, and save the file as barpie.htm in the example2 folder you just created. Add two intrinsic buttons to frmTest by placing the following code in the HTML Source Editor just before the </FORM> tag:

```
<P><INPUT TYPE=BUTTON VALUE="Bar Chart" NAME="cmdBar">
<P><INPUT TYPE=BUTTON VALUE="Pie Chart" NAME="cmdPie">
```

Step 3

Start the Script Wizard by selecting Script Wizard from the Tools menu. The Script Wizard should appear. Make sure the wizard is in list view.

Step 4

In the event pane, double-click on the frmTest object to find the cmdBar button object. Double-click on the cmdBar object to reveal the OnClick event. Single-click on the OnClick event to select it.

Step 5

In the action pane, double-click on the frmTest object to find the chtTest object. Double-click on the chtTest object to reveal the ChartType property.

Step 6

Double-click on the ChartType property. A ChartType property dialog box is displayed. Figure 9-10 shows the ChartType property dialog box.

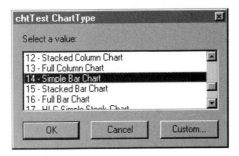

Figure 9-10.
The ChartType property dialog box.

In the dialog box, select 14 - Simple Bar Chart and click OK. The script pane of the Script Wizard displays the results as shown in Figure 9-11.

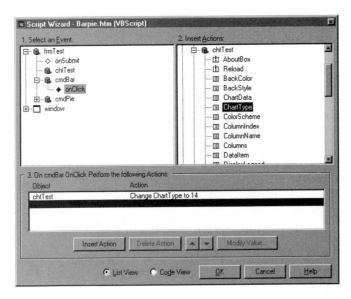

Figure 9-11.
The Script Wizard in list view after a cmdBar OnClick action has been added.

Step 7

Switch to code view by selecting the appropriate radio button in the Script Wizard. In code view, you can see the equivalent VBScript code for the actions you specified. Figure 9-12 shows the Script Wizard in code view.

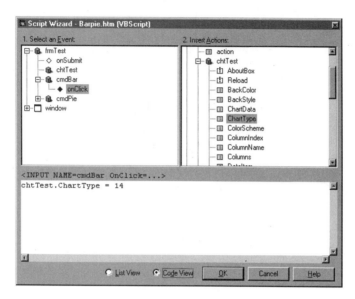

Figure 9-12.
The Script Wizard in code view after a cmdBar OnClick action has been added.

Click the OK button to insert this code into your HTML document. The Script Wizard modifies the code for the cmdBar <INPUT> tag in the following way:

```
<INPUT LANGUAGE="VBSEcript" TYPE=BUTTON VALUE="Bar Chart"
ONCLICK="chtTest.ChartType = 14" NAME="cmdBar">
```

Step 8

Repeat steps 3 through 7, replacing references to the cmdBar button with references to the cmdPie button. In step 6, select 1 - Special Pie Chart in the ChartType property dialog box.

Step 9

Save the page, and open it in the Internet Explorer. You should be able to change the chart type by clicking each of the buttons on the page. Figure 9-13 (page 358) shows how the page looks in the Internet Explorer.

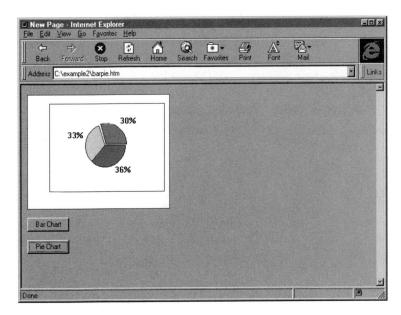

Figure 9-13.
Barpie.htm after button controls and VBScript code generated with the Script Wizard have been added.

The HTML Layout Control and the HTML Layout Editor

HTML is a *stream-based* language. In other words, the HTML information for a web page is loaded serially as the page is parsed by the browser. When the browser finds <OBJECT> tags, it loads the objects and places them in positions according to their locations in the HTML code. Exact positioning of objects in a page is not possible, however. HTML does not support the positioning properties, such as Left and Top, that are so familiar to Visual Basic developers. Instead, you make "suggestions" to the browser regarding control placement. A table, for example, can suggest relative object placement, but you cannot be certain of the exact pixel location of any object.

In an effort to overcome this limitation, Microsoft has been working with the World Wide Web Consortium to promote the adoption of a standard for HTML known as *style sheets*. Style sheets allow you to apply styles to HTML pages. Style sheets can allow you to apply styles to text, as in Microsoft Word, and they allow you to specify the placement of objects.

The Internet Explorer 3.0 does support text-based style sheets, but the implementation of style sheets to control object placement is unsupported. Many of the style sheet specifications are still being defined. However, ActiveX Control Pad contains an ActiveX control that provides the functionality of an object-based style sheet. This control is called the HTML Layout control. The HTML Layout control is an ActiveX control that references HTML layouts and renders them at runtime. An HTML layout is a container for multiple controls that have precise sizes and arrangements. HTML layouts are similar to forms in Visual Basic, but the HTML layout does not act like a form in code—you cannot use it to reference controls in VBScript code. HTML layouts are saved as standard text files with an alx extension. They contain information about the properties and placement of controls, as well as any VBScript code necessary for the controls. Inside the HTML layout file, the control information is surrounded by <DIV></DIV> tags, which group related elements. The basic syntax for the control information in the HTML layout or alx file is as follows:

```
<DIV BACKGROUND="#rrggbb" ID="division_name"
STYLE="LAYOUT:FIXED;WIDTH:integerpt;HEIGHT:integerpt;">

    <OBJECT ID="control_name"

    CLASSID="CLSID:class_ID" STYLE="TOP:integerpt;LEFT:integerpt;
    WIDTH:integerpt;HEIGHT:integerpt;DISPLAY:display;
    TABINDEX:integerpt;ZINDEX:integerpt;">

        <PARAM ...>
        . . .
    </OBJECT>

    multiple object tags defining the controls used in the layout

</DIV>
```

HTML layouts are created with the HTML Layout Editor. The HTML Layout Editor provides the WYSIWYG placement functionality of an object-based style sheet during the interim while these sheets are being defined. Figure 9-14 (page 360) shows the HTML Layout Editor, along with a toolbox containing controls.

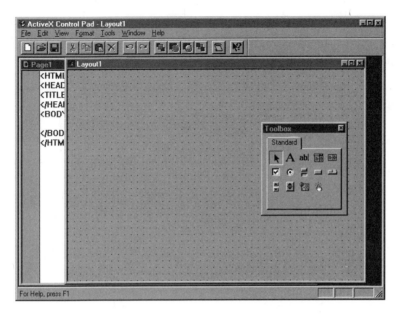

Figure 9-14.
The HTML Layout Editor and the control toolbox.

Once you have created an HTML layout, you must reference it with the HTML Layout control in order to use it in a web page. You insert the HTML Layout control into a web page by using the <OBJECT></OBJECT> tags, just as you do with any other control. The HTML Layout control then references an HTML layout file, or alx file, by specifying its name and location. The syntax for inserting the HTML Layout control is as follows:

<OBJECT

CLASSID="CLSID:812AE312-8B8E-11CF-93C8-00AA00C08FDF"

ID="*name*" STYLE="LEFT:*integer*;TOP:*integer*">

<PARAM NAME="ALXPATH" REF VALUE="*file_location*">

</OBJECT>

In Example #3, you will create a simple web page animation with the HTML Layout Editor and various ActiveX controls. The goal is to create a web page in which the animation is not limited to a certain region but takes place across the entire page. This is possible only if you have control over the layout of the entire page.

If you have used Visual Basic 4.0, you might have done the butterfly example that is described in the product documentation. That simple animation example uses a Timer control to alternate the appearance of two different images. In Example #3B, you will use the same strategy with the HTML Layout Editor.

Example #3A: Using the HTML Layout Control

The HTML file you will create for this application is intended only to hold the HTML Layout control. The HTML Layout will span the entire web page; all of the content and all of the ActiveX controls will be placed within it. This development approach is very similar to that used for creating a form in Visual Basic.

Step 1

Create a folder named example3 in a convenient location on your computer.

Step 2

Start a new HTML file in ActiveX Control Pad. The default title for the web page is New Page. Change the title from New Page to Simple Animation. Then add the BGCOLOR attribute to the <BODY> tag and set it to WHITE. Your HTML code in the HTML Source Editor should look like this:

```
<HTML>
<HEAD>
<TITLE>Simple Animation</TITLE>
</HEAD>
<BODY BGCOLOR="WHITE">

</BODY>
</HTML>
```

Step 3

Now you need to add a form to the web page to hold the HTML Layout control. Add the form by placing the following code in the body section of the page:

```
<FORM NAME="frmAnimate">

</FORM>
```

Step 4

Now you will add the HTML Layout control to the HTML document. Make sure that your cursor is positioned between the <FORM></FORM> tags in the HTML Source Editor. From the Edit menu, select Insert HTML Layout. You will be presented with a dialog box that allows you to specify the name for a new HTML layout. In the File Name input box, type animate.alx and select the example3 folder you created earlier. Figure 9-15 shows the new HTML Layout dialog box.

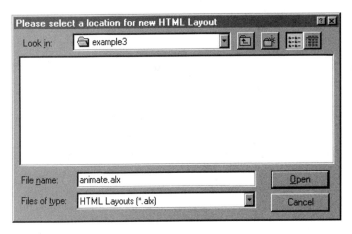

Figure 9-15.
The new HTML Layout dialog box.

Click the Open button. A message box will be displayed, indicating that the file does not exist and asking whether you want to create it. Click the Yes button. The HTML Layout control will be inserted between the <FORM></FORM> tags, and an HTML Layout icon will be displayed in the left margin. By default, the absolute path is included with the animate.alx reference in the VALUE attribute of the ALXPATH property. (For example, the VALUE attribute may be file:C:\example3\animate.alx.) Remove the path information so that the HTML Layout control will look for animate.alx in the current folder. Figure 9-16 shows the resulting code in the HTML Source Editor.

Step 5

Your HTML page is now complete. From ActiveX Control Pad, select Save from the File menu. Save the file as animate.htm in the example3 folder, where you also saved animate.alx.

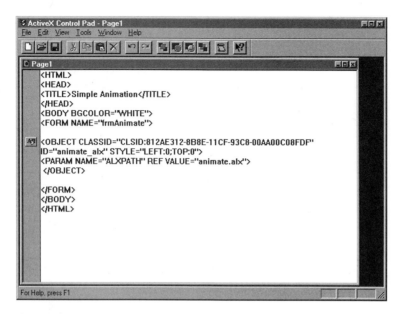

Figure 9-16.
The HTML Source Editor after the HTML Layout control has been inserted and the animate.alx path has been removed.

Example #3B: Using the HTML Layout Editor

The HTML Layout control reads the information for each object from the HTML layout file or alx file. This file is a simple text file, but you can create the file graphically by using the HTML Layout Editor.

Step 1

Access the HTML Layout Editor by clicking the HTML Layout icon next to the <OBJECT> tag in the HTML Source Editor. The HTML Layout Editor and the toolbox should appear. The toolbox has various controls that you can add to your HTML layout and is very similar to the toolbox in Visual Basic.

In the HTML Layout Editor, change the background color by clicking anywhere on the HTML Layout window with the right mouse button and selecting Properties. In the Properties window, you can change the background color by selecting BackColor and clicking the ... button that appears. This brings up a Color dialog box, from which you can select a background color. Select a white background, and click the OK button. Also set the Height and Width properties in the Properties window as follows:

Height	266
Width	460

363

Figure 9-17 shows the HTML Layout Editor, along with the Properties window and the toolbox, after the background color, height, and width properties have been set.

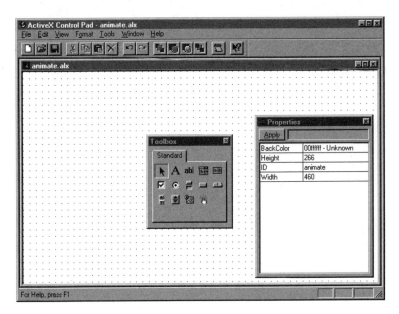

Figure 9-17.
The HTML Layout Editor after the background color, height, and width properties have been set.

Step 2

Add a Label control to the HTML layout by clicking on the Label control in the toolbox and dragging a rectangle onto the HTML Layout Editor window. Access the properties of the label by right-clicking on the Label control and selecting Properties. Set the Label control properties as follows:

BackStyle	0 - Transparent
Caption	My First Animated Web Page
Font	Arial, Bold, 28
Height	42
Left	17
TextAlign	2 - Center
Top	8
Width	420

Step 3

To display the butterfly, you will first need to copy the butterfly images to the example3 folder. Copy bfly1.gif and bfly2.gif from the project4 folder on the companion CD to your example3 folder. You will add two ISImage controls to the HTML layout to hold the images of the butterfly. Select the ISImage control from the toolbox, and drag out a rectangle to add the first Image control to the HTML layout. Repeat the process to add the second Image control. Set the Image1 control properties as follows:

Height	60
ID	Image1
Left	10
PicturePath	bfly1.gif
Top	200
Visible	-1 - True
Width	60

Set the Image2 control properties as follows:

Height	60
ID	Image2
Left	10
PicturePath	bfly2.gif
Top	200
Visible	0 - False
Width	60

Step 4

You will need to add a Timer control to your web page, but the default toolbox does not offer this option. However, you can add a Timer control to the toolbox by clicking on any control in the toolbox with the right mouse button and selecting Additional Controls. You'll see a dialog box listing all of the registered controls on your computer. Select the Timer object (Figure 9-18, on page 366, shows the Additional Controls dialog box) and click OK. The Timer control should now be in the toolbox.

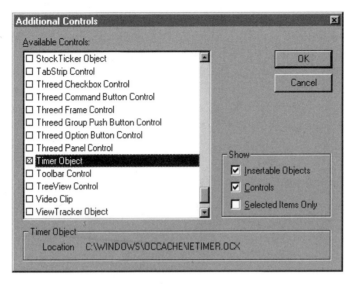

Figure 9-18.
The Additional Controls dialog box.

Step 5

Add a Timer control to the HTML layout by selecting it from the toolbox and clicking on the layout. Set the Timer control properties as follows:

ID	Timer1
Interval	500

The layout portion of the page is now complete. You just need to make a final adjustment to the Zorder of the Label control. Right-click on the Label control, and select Bring To Front. This will make the butterfly appear to fly behind the label. Save the layout by selecting Save from the File menu. Figure 9-19 shows the layout after the controls have been placed.

Step 6

Creating the animation is a matter of creating a Timer event handler that will modify the Visible, Left, and Top properties of the Image controls. Although the Script Wizard is available to generate code, its functionality is not rich enough to support the kind of VBScript code you need to write. Instead, you will write the code directly in a text editor such as Notepad.

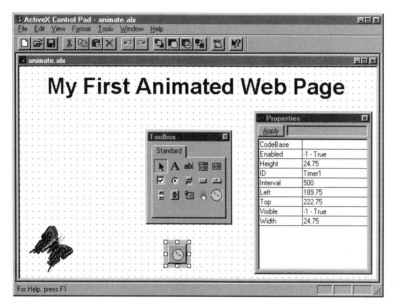

Figure 9-19.
The completed layout page for Example #3.

Click on the HTML Layout Editor window with the right mouse button, and select View Source Code from the menu. You'll see a message box indicating that the current layout will be saved and closed. You will then be asked whether you want to continue. Click the Yes button, and the source code for the animate.alx file will appear in the Notepad text editor. Your code should be similar to this:

```
<DIV BACKGROUND="#ffffff" ID="animate"
STYLE="LAYOUT:FIXED;WIDTH:460pt;HEIGHT:266pt;">
    <OBJECT ID="Image1"
    CLASSID="CLSID:D4A97620-8E8F-11CF-93CD-00AA00C08FDF"
    STYLE="TOP:200pt;LEFT:10pt;WIDTH:60pt;HEIGHT:60pt;ZINDEX:0;">
        <PARAM NAME="PicturePath" VALUE="bfly1.gif">
        <PARAM NAME="BorderStyle" VALUE="0">
        <PARAM NAME="SizeMode" VALUE="3">
        <PARAM NAME="Size" VALUE="2117;2117">
        <PARAM NAME="PictureAlignment" VALUE="0">
        <PARAM NAME="VariousPropertyBits" VALUE="19">
    </OBJECT>
```

(continued)

367

continued

```
<OBJECT ID="Image2"
CLASSID="CLSID:D4A97620-8E8F-11CF-93CD-00AA00C08FDF"
STYLE="TOP:200pt;LEFT:10pt;WIDTH:60pt;HEIGHT:60pt;DISPLAY:NONE;
ZINDEX:1;">
    <PARAM NAME="PicturePath" VALUE="bfly2.gif">
    <PARAM NAME="BorderStyle" VALUE="0">
    <PARAM NAME="SizeMode" VALUE="3">
    <PARAM NAME="Size" VALUE="2117;2117">
    <PARAM NAME="PictureAlignment" VALUE="0">
    <PARAM NAME="VariousPropertyBits" VALUE="19">
</OBJECT>
<OBJECT ID="Timer1"
CLASSID="CLSID:59CCB4A0-727D-11CF-AC36-00AA00A47DD2"
STYLE="TOP:223pt;LEFT:190pt;WIDTH:25pt;HEIGHT:25pt;ZINDEX:2;">
    <PARAM NAME="_ExtentX" VALUE="873">
    <PARAM NAME="_ExtentY" VALUE="873">
    <PARAM NAME="Interval" VALUE="500">
</OBJECT>
<OBJECT ID="Label1"
CLASSID="CLSID:978C9E23-D4B0-11CE-BF2D-00AA003F40D0"
STYLE="TOP:8pt;LEFT:17pt;WIDTH:420pt;HEIGHT:42pt;ZINDEX:3;">
    <PARAM NAME="BackColor" VALUE="16777215">
    <PARAM NAME="VariousPropertyBits" VALUE="8388627">
    <PARAM NAME="Caption" VALUE="My First Animated Web Page">
    <PARAM NAME="Size" VALUE="14817;1482">
    <PARAM NAME="FontName" VALUE="Arial">
    <PARAM NAME="FontEffects" VALUE="1073741825">
    <PARAM NAME="FontHeight" VALUE="560">
    <PARAM NAME="FontCharSet" VALUE="0">
    <PARAM NAME="FontPitchAndFamily" VALUE="2">
    <PARAM NAME="ParagraphAlign" VALUE="3">
    <PARAM NAME="FontWeight" VALUE="700">
</OBJECT>
</DIV>
```

Step 7

Next you will add a VBScript section to the animate.alx file that will handle Timer events. Add the following code before the <DIV> tag to begin the VBScript Timer1 subroutine:

```
<SCRIPT LANGUAGE="VBScript">
    Sub Timer1_Timer

    End Sub
</SCRIPT>
```

Step 8

Inside the Timer1 subroutine, you will alternate the Visible properties of the butterfly images and move them to simulate animation. Add the following code to the Timer1 subroutine:

```
If Image1.Visible Then
    Image2.Left=Image1.Left+10
    Image2.Top=Image1.Top-10
    If Image2.Top<0 Then
        Image2.Top=230
        Image2.Left=10
    End If
Else
    Image1.Left=Image2.Left+10
    Image1.Top=Image2.Top-10
    If Image1.Top<0 Then
        Image1.Top=230
        Image1.Left=10
    End If
End If
Image1.Visible=Not(Image1.Visible)
Image2.Visible=Not(Image2.Visible)
```

This completes the necessary VBScript code. Save animate.alx, and close Notepad.

Running the Application

Make sure that animate.htm has been saved, and then open animate.htm in the Internet Explorer. The butterfly should move from the lower left to the upper right, across the web page, and then start again. The butterfly should cross behind the label at the top of the page. Figure 9-20 (page 370) shows the animation example in the Internet Explorer.

An Interactive Order Form

In this project, you will use ActiveX Control Pad to create an interactive order form that allows the user to purchase computer products online. The form will utilize Image controls in an HTML layout to add animation to the product purchase procedure. The page will keep a running total of the purchases and allow the user to submit the order to a back-end process. Although the form you create here can easily be used with any of the ISAPI processes covered in this book, this exercise will focus on the client side of the application; processing of the data is left to you.

Figure 9-20.
The completed animation example.

The bytecomp.htm File

The HTML file for this web page consists of some simple text and graphics and an HTML Layout control. In this page, you will limit the active region of the HTML Layout control instead of using the entire page. The interactive action of the web page involves only the product selection portion, not the informational text and other images, such as the web page banner.

Step 1

Create a folder named bytecomp in a convenient location on your computer. This web page uses several images that can be found on the companion CD, in the project4\bytecomp folder. Copy all the gif files from this folder on the companion CD into the bytecomp folder that you just created.

Step 2

Start a new HTML file in ActiveX Control Pad. Change the title of the page in the default HTML to the company name ByteComp, Inc., and add the BGCOLOR="WHITE" attribute to the <BODY> tag. Your HTML code should look like what you see at the top of page 371:

```
<HTML>
<HEAD>
<TITLE>ByteComp, Inc.</TITLE>
</HEAD>
<BODY BGCOLOR="WHITE">

</BODY>
</HTML>
```

Step 3

Add the following code to the body section of your web page to place one of the image files as a banner at the top:

```
<CENTER>
<IMG SRC="banner.gif" ALT="ByteComp Order Form"
HEIGHT=100 WIDTH=500><P>
```

Step 4

The HTML Layout control will be contained within a form. Add the form to your page by adding the following code after the banner in the body section:

```
<FORM NAME="frmBytes">

</FORM>
</CENTER>
```

Step 5

Place your cursor between the <FORM></FORM> tags. Add an HTML Layout control to your page by selecting Insert HTML Layout from the Edit menu. In the new HTML Layout dialog box, navigate to your bytecomp folder, name the file bytecomp.alx, and click the Open button. A message box should be displayed, indicating that the file does not exist and asking whether you want to create it. Click the Yes button. This action creates the HTML layout file, bytecomp.alx, in your bytecomp folder and returns you to the HTML Source Editor. The HTML Layout control is inserted between the <FORM></FORM> tags. Delete the absolute path from the ALXPATH property. This action will cause the HTML Layout control to search the current folder for the alx file (instead of searching a specific folder), which will make your web page more portable. Note that you can use any valid URL to specify the location of the alx file. Your HTML file is now complete, and you can save it as bytecomp.htm in your bytecomp folder. Figure 9-21 (page 372) shows the code for bytecomp.htm in the HTML Source Editor.

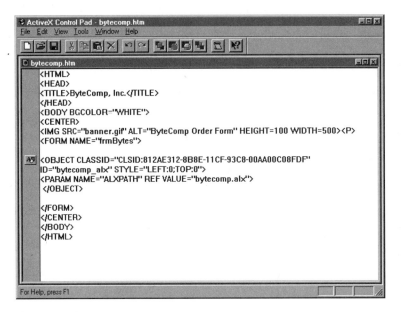

Figure 9-21.
The bytecomp.htm file in the HTML Source Editor.

The bytecomp.alx File

You will use the HTML Layout Editor to construct the bytecomp.alx file. In the HTML Layout Editor, you will design an interactive ordering region that allows the user to click a button to select the product he or she wants to purchase. Clicking a product's button will move the product's icon and add the cost of the product to the total for the purchase. You will also use the HTML Layout Editor to construct an order form that will be submitted when the user has finished making his or her selections.

Step 1

Access the HTML Layout Editor by clicking the HTML Layout icon next to the <OBJECT> tag in the bytecomp.htm file. When the HTML Layout Editor is visible, immediately right-click anywhere in the HTML Layout Editor window, and select Properties. Set the properties as follows:

BackColor	white
Height	270
Width	450

Step 2

Locate the ToggleButton control in the toolbox. Draw a toggle button in the HTML Layout Editor window, and set its properties as follows:

Caption	(*Empty*)
Height	17
Left	112
Top	16
Width	17

Step 3

Copy the toggle button and add seven more buttons by pasting the copy onto the HTML layout. The user will click on these toggle buttons in the browser to select the products to be purchased. Line the toggle buttons up by selecting all of them and setting the Left properties to 112. Space them vertically by setting their Top properties, naming each toggle button as you align it. The ID and Top properties for all eight toggle buttons are shown here:

ID	Top
btnFloppy	16
btnHardDrv	45
btnCDROM	74
btnMonitor	103
btnKeyboard	132
btnMouse	161
btnModem	191
btnJoystick	220

Step 4

Locate the ISImage control on the toolbox. Place eight Image controls on the HTML layout for the images of the products that the user can purchase. Each of these Image controls will hold one of the images from the companion CD, all of which should now be in your bytecomp folder. Set the following properties for all eight Image controls:

Height	30
Left	154
Width	40

Set the ID, PicturePath, and Top properties for the individual Image controls as shown here:

ID	PicturePath	Top
imgFloppy	floppy.gif	16
imgHardDrv	harddrv.gif	42
imgCDROM	cdrom.gif	62
imgMonitor	monitor.gif	96
imgKeyboard	keyboard.gif	125
imgMouse	mouse.gif	152
imgModem	modem.gif	184
imgJoystick	joystick.gif	210

Your layout should look like the one shown in Figure 9-22. Be sure to save your layout at this point by selecting Save from the File menu in the HTML Layout Editor. You should save your layout frequently during this project, to avoid losing data.

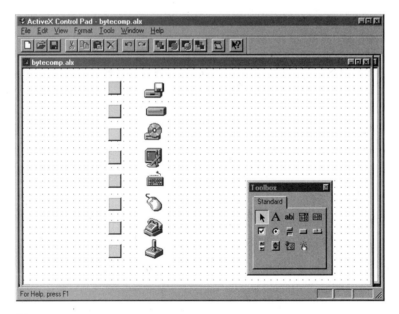

Figure 9-22.
Buttons and images in the HTML Layout Editor.

Step 5

Locate the Label control in the toolbox. Add a label for each of the images that represents a product. These labels will be used to identify each product to the user. Set the following properties for all eight labels:

BackStyle	0 - Transparent
Font	Arial, Bold, 10
Height	17
Left	5
Width	100

Set the Caption, ID, and Top properties for the individual labels as shown here:

Caption	ID	Top
Floppy Drive ($200)	lblFloppy	16
Hard Drive ($400)	lblHardDrv	45
CD-ROM Drive ($400)	lblCDROM	74
Monitor ($250)	lblMonitor	103
Keyboard ($125)	lblKeyboard	132
Mouse ($60)	lblMouse	161
28.8 Modem ($150)	lblModem	191
Joystick ($35)	lblJoystick	220

Step 6

Now you will build the order form that will collect the customer's shipping and billing information. The order form will be similar to the order forms you built previously with HTML, but in this case you will have complete control over the appearance of the form. This is a significant difference from the HTML order forms you built earlier, which used <TABLE></TABLE> tags to "suggest" a layout to the browser.

Locate the TextBox control in the toolbox. Add seven text boxes to the HTML layout for use in the order form. Set the Font and Height properties for all seven text boxes as follows:

Font	Arial, Bold, 9
Height	17

Set the ID, Left, Top, and Width properties for each individual text box as shown here:

ID	Left	Top	Width
txtName	225	34	146
txtCompany	225	70	146
txtAddress	225	106	146
txtCity	225	144	52
txtState	293	144	24
txtZip	324	144	47
txtCardNumber	225	189	146

Step 7

Locate the Label control in the toolbox. Use the Label control to label each of the text boxes you created for the order form. For all seven labels, set the BackStyle and Height properties as follows:

BackStyle	0 - Transparent
Height	9

Set the Caption, ID, Left, Top, and Width properties for each individual label as shown here:

Caption	ID	Left	Top	Width
Name	lblName	225	23	32
Company	lblCompany	225	59	47
Address	lblAddress	225	95	88
City	lblCity	225	133	45
State	lblState	293	133	23
Zip	lblZip	324	133	36
Credit Card Number	lblCardNumber	225	178	88

Step 8

Add another Label control to the layout to show the total purchase cost. Set this Label control's properties as follows:

BackStyle	0 - Transparent
Caption	$0.00
Font	Comic Sans MS, Bold, 24
Height	38

ID	lblTotal
Left	227
Top	214
Width	142

Step 9

When a customer picks a product, your web page will move the image of the product from the left side of the page to the right side of the page. The animation will be driven by a Timer control. In this step, you will add a Timer control to your layout.

If the Timer control is not in the toolbox, you can add it by right-clicking on any control in the toolbox and selecting Additional Controls. The Additional Controls dialog box will appear, and you can select the Timer object. Click the OK button to place the Timer control in the toolbox.

Add a Timer control to the HTML layout by selecting it from the toolbox and clicking on the layout. The exact position of the timer is not critical, since timers are not visible at runtime. Set the Timer control properties as follows:

Enabled	0 - False
ID	tmrBytes
Interval	50
Left	8
Top	240

Step 10

Save the entire layout by selecting Save from the File menu. The layout is now complete. (In the next section, you will add some VBScript code to the byte.alx file to bring the web page to life.) Figure 9-23 (page 378) shows the completed HTML layout.

Step 11

Open the source file for the HTML layout by clicking in the HTML Layout Editor window with the right mouse button and selecting View Source Code. A message box will be displayed, indicating that the current layout will be saved and closed and asking whether you want to continue. Click the Yes button to display the source code in the Notepad text editor. Note that the alx file is largely a collection of <OBJECT></OBJECT> tags that position the various controls in the HTML layout. Note also that the STYLE attribute in the <OBJECT> tag is used to specify the position of the control in the HTML layout.

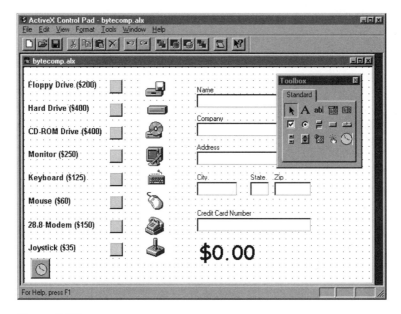

Figure 9-23.
The completed order form layout.

Here is the code for the floppy drive ToggleButton control:

```
<OBJECT ID="btnFloppy"
CLASSID="CLSID:8BD21D60-EC42-11CE-9E0D-00AA006002F3"
STYLE="TOP:16pt;LEFT:112pt;WIDTH:17pt;HEIGHT:17pt;TABINDEX:0;ZINDEX:0;">
    <PARAM NAME="BackColor" VALUE="2147483663">
    <PARAM NAME="ForeColor" VALUE="2147483666">
    <PARAM NAME="DisplayStyle" VALUE="6">
    <PARAM NAME="Size" VALUE="600;600">
    <PARAM NAME="FontCharSet" VALUE="0">
    <PARAM NAME="FontPitchAndFamily" VALUE="2">
    <PARAM NAME="ParagraphAlign" VALUE="3">
    <PARAM NAME="FontWeight" VALUE="0">
</OBJECT>
```

When you have finished viewing bytecomp.alx in Notepad, close it. Save bytecomp.htm, and close ActiveX Control Pad.

Adding the VBScript Code

In this section, you will place VBScript code in the bytecomp.alx file to make the web page interactive. Although the Script Wizard is available in ActiveX

Control Pad, you will find it easier to use a text editor to add the code for this project. The VBScript code you add will animate the icons for the selected products by moving them across the page when the products are selected. You will also use VBScript code to track the total cost for the purchase.

Step 1
Open bytecomp.alx in Notepad.

Step 2
The beginning of the script section defines several variables for use with the web page. One variable is defined for the total cost, and several variables are defined to mark the starting position for each image before it is animated. None of these variables is defined within a procedure, and therefore they all are global to the entire web page. Add the following code at the top of the bytecomp.alx file to define the variables:

```
<SCRIPT LANGUAGE="VBScript">

    Dim intTotal
    intTotal=0

    Dim dblFloppy
    Dim dblHardDrv
    Dim dblCDROM
    Dim dblMonitor
    Dim dblKeyboard
    Dim dblMouse
    Dim dblModem
    Dim dblJoystick

    dblFloppy=154
    dblHardDrv=154
    dblCDROM=154
    dblMonitor=154
    dblKeyboard=154
    dblMouse=154
    dblModem=154
    dblJoystick=154
```

Step 3
When a button is clicked, the total cost of the purchase is computed. The timer on the web page is also started—if it is not already running—so that the product's image can be moved to the right-hand side of the form. Add the code beginning on page 380 to handle the Click events for each button:

```
Sub btnFloppy_Click
    tmrBytes.Enabled=True
    If btnFloppy.Value=True Then
        intTotal=intTotal+200
    Else
        intTotal=intTotal-200
    End If
    lblTotal.Caption="$" & intTotal & ".00"
End Sub

Sub btnHardDrv_Click
    tmrBytes.Enabled=True
    If btnHardDrv.Value=True Then
        intTotal=intTotal+400
    Else
        intTotal=intTotal-400
    End If
    lblTotal.Caption="$" & intTotal & ".00"
End Sub

Sub btnCDROM_Click
    tmrBytes.Enabled=True
    If btnCDROM.Value=True Then
        intTotal=intTotal+400
    Else
        intTotal=intTotal-400
    End If
    lblTotal.Caption="$" & intTotal & ".00"
End Sub

Sub btnMonitor_Click
    tmrBytes.Enabled=True
    If btnMonitor.Value=True Then
        intTotal=intTotal+250
    Else
        intTotal=intTotal-250
    End If
    lblTotal.Caption="$" & intTotal & ".00"
End Sub

Sub btnKeyboard_Click
    tmrBytes.Enabled=True
    If btnKeyboard.Value=True Then
        intTotal=intTotal+125
    Else
        intTotal=intTotal-125
    End If
    lblTotal.Caption="$" & intTotal & ".00"
End Sub
```

```
Sub btnMouse_Click
    tmrBytes.Enabled=True
    If btnMouse.Value=True Then
        intTotal=intTotal+60
    Else
        intTotal=intTotal-60
    End If
    lblTotal.Caption="$" & intTotal & ".00"
End Sub

Sub btnModem_Click
    tmrBytes.Enabled=True
    If btnModem.Value=True Then
        intTotal=intTotal+150
    Else
        intTotal=intTotal-150
    End If
    lblTotal.Caption="$" & intTotal & ".00"
End Sub

Sub btnJoystick_Click
    tmrBytes.Enabled=True
    If btnJoystick.Value=True Then
        intTotal=intTotal+35
    Else
        intTotal=intTotal-35
    End If
    lblTotal.Caption="$" & intTotal & ".00"
End Sub
```

Step 4

When an item is selected, its icon is moved from the middle of the form to the right side. This movement is animated with a Timer control. The Timer control checks the location of each product image on the page and moves it as necessary. Add the following code to animate the product images:

```
Sub tmrBytes_Timer
    Call Animate(btnFloppy,imgFloppy,dblFloppy)
    Call Animate(btnHardDrv,imgHardDrv,dblHardDrv)
    Call Animate(btnCDROM,imgCDROM,dblCDROM)
    Call Animate(btnMonitor,imgMonitor,dblMonitor)
    Call Animate(btnKeyboard,imgKeyboard,dblKeyboard)
    Call Animate(btnMouse,imgMouse,dblMouse)
    Call Animate(btnModem,imgModem,dblModem)
    Call Animate(btnJoystick,imgJoystick,dblJoystick)
End Sub
```

(continued)

continued

```
Sub Animate(MyButton,MyImage,MyStart)
    MyImage.ZOrder 1
    If MyButton.Value=True and MyImage.Left<MyStart+240 Then
        MyImage.Left=MyImage.Left+20
    End If
    If MyButton.Value=False and MyImage.Left>MyStart+20 Then
        MyImage.Left=MyImage.Left-20
    End If
End Sub
```

Step 5

When a user wants more information about a product, he or she can simply click the right mouse button on the product image. The MouseDown event for each image triggers the appearance of a message box that offers additional product information. Add the following code to provide this information:

```
Sub imgFloppy_MouseDown(Button,Shift,X,Y)
    If Button=2 Then
        MsgBox "1.44MB Drive and Ten Disks",64,"ByteComp"
    End If
End Sub

Sub imgHardDrv_MouseDown(Button,Shift,X,Y)
    If Button=2 Then
        MsgBox "1GB Internal IDE Drive",64,"ByteComp"
    End If
End Sub

Sub imgCDROM_MouseDown(Button,Shift,X,Y)
    If Button=2 Then
        MsgBox "4X IDE CD-ROM Drive",64,"ByteComp"
    End If
End Sub

Sub imgMonitor_MouseDown(Button,Shift,X,Y)
    If Button=2 Then
        MsgBox "14-Inch VGA Monitor",64,"ByteComp"
    End If
End Sub

Sub imgKeyboard_MouseDown(Button,Shift,X,Y)
    If Button=2 Then
        MsgBox "128-Key Ergonomic Keyboard",64,"ByteComp"
    End If
```

```
    End Sub

    Sub imgMouse_MouseDown(Button,Shift,X,Y)
        If Button=2 Then
            MsgBox "Two-Button Serial Mouse",64,"ByteComp"
        End If
    End Sub

    Sub imgModem_MouseDown(Button,Shift,X,Y)
        If Button=2 Then
            MsgBox "28.8 Internal Modem",64,"ByteComp"
        End If
    End Sub

    Sub imgJoystick_MouseDown(Button,Shift,X,Y)
        If Button=2 Then
            MsgBox "Aviation-Style Joystick",64,"ByteComp"
        End If
    End Sub
```

Step 6

The order form in your project should perform some simple data validation.
You will use the KeyPress event to trap keystrokes sent to txtCardNumber and
reject any keystrokes but numbers and hyphens. Add the following code to
provide some simple validation:

```
    Sub txtCardNumber_KeyPress(KeyASCII)
        txtCardNumber.Locked=True
        If KeyASCII=8 Then txtCardNumber.Locked=False
        If KeyASCII=45 Then txtCardNumber.Locked=False
        If KeyASCII>47 and KeyASCII<58 Then
            txtCardNumber.Locked=False
        End If
    End Sub
</SCRIPT>
```

Running the Project

Your project is now complete. Save bytecomp.alx and open bytecomp.htm in
the Internet Explorer. Test the animation by selecting products and watching
their icons move. Make sure that the total is updated as products are selected.
Also test the right mouse button support, and check the data validation routine
for the credit card number. Figure 9-24 (page 384) shows the completed order
form in action, as well as products selected for purchase, the total cost, and the
message box that is displayed if you right-click on the modem image. Listing
9-1 (page 384) shows the complete, commented VBScript code for the project.

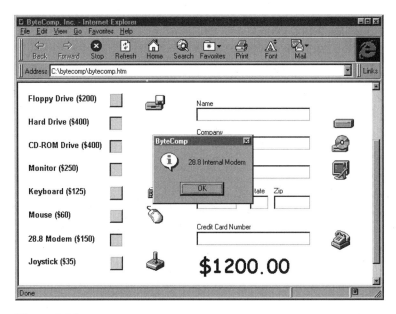

Figure 9-24.
The completed order form in action.

```
<SCRIPT LANGUAGE="VBScript">
'Variable for total purchase price
    Dim intTotal
    intTotal=0

    'Variables for storing the starting Left coordinates
    'for each product image
    Dim dblFloppy
    Dim dblHardDrv
    Dim dblCDROM
    Dim dblMonitor
    Dim dblKeyboard
    Dim dblMouse
    Dim dblModem
    Dim dblJoystick

    dblFloppy=154
    dblHardDrv=154
    dblCDROM=154
    dblMonitor=154
    dblKeyboard=154
```

Listing 9-1.
The VBScript code for the interactive order form example.

```
dblMouse=154
dblModem=154
dblJoystick=154

'The Click events for the
'buttons are used to update
'the total purchase price

Sub btnFloppy_Click
    tmrBytes.Enabled=True
    If btnFloppy.Value=True Then
        intTotal=intTotal+200
    Else
        intTotal=intTotal-200
    End If
    lblTotal.Caption="$" & intTotal & ".00"
End Sub

Sub btnHardDrv_Click
    tmrBytes.Enabled=True
    If btnHardDrv.Value=True Then
        intTotal=intTotal+400
    Else
        intTotal=intTotal-400
    End If
    lblTotal.Caption="$" & intTotal & ".00"
End Sub

Sub btnCDROM_Click
    tmrBytes.Enabled=True
    If btnCDROM.Value=True Then
        intTotal=intTotal+400
    Else
        intTotal=intTotal-400
    End If
    lblTotal.Caption="$" & intTotal & ".00"
End Sub

Sub btnMonitor_Click
    tmrBytes.Enabled=True
    If btnMonitor.Value=True Then
        intTotal=intTotal+250
    Else
        intTotal=intTotal-250
    End If
    lblTotal.Caption="$" & intTotal & ".00"
End Sub
```

(continued)

Listing 9-1 *continued*

```
Sub btnKeyboard_Click
    tmrBytes.Enabled=True
    If btnKeyboard.Value=True Then
        intTotal=intTotal+125
    Else
        intTotal=intTotal-125
    End If
    lblTotal.Caption="$" & intTotal & ".00"
End Sub

Sub btnMouse_Click
    tmrBytes.Enabled=True
    If btnMouse.Value=True Then
        intTotal=intTotal+60
    Else
        intTotal=intTotal-60
    End If
    lblTotal.Caption="$" & intTotal & ".00"
End Sub

Sub btnModem_Click
    tmrBytes.Enabled=True
    If btnModem.Value=True Then
        intTotal=intTotal+150
    Else
        intTotal=intTotal-150
    End If
    lblTotal.Caption="$" & intTotal & ".00"
End Sub

Sub btnJoystick_Click
    tmrBytes.Enabled=True
    If btnJoystick.Value=True Then
        intTotal=intTotal+35
    Else
        intTotal=intTotal-35
    End If
    lblTotal.Caption="$" & intTotal & ".00"
End Sub

Sub tmrBytes_Timer

    'Author: New Technology Solutions, Inc.
    'Purpose: Call Animate routine for each image
    '6/22/96 Original
```

```
        Call Animate(btnFloppy,imgFloppy,dblFloppy)
        Call Animate(btnHardDrv,imgHardDrv,dblHardDrv)
        Call Animate(btnCDROM,imgCDROM,dblCDROM)
        Call Animate(btnMonitor,imgMonitor,dblMonitor)
        Call Animate(btnKeyboard,imgKeyboard,dblKeyboard)
        Call Animate(btnMouse,imgMouse,dblMouse)
        Call Animate(btnModem,imgModem,dblModem)
        Call Animate(btnJoystick,imgJoystick,dblJoystick)
End Sub

Sub Animate(MyButton,MyImage,MyStart)

    'Author: New Technology Solutions, Inc.
    'Purpose: Animate an image control
    '6/22/96 Original

    MyImage.ZOrder 1
    If MyButton.Value=True and MyImage.Left<MyStart+240 Then
        MyImage.Left=MyImage.Left+20
    End If
    If MyButton.Value=False and MyImage.Left>=MyStart+20 Then
        MyImage.Left=MyImage.Left-20
    End If
End Sub


'MouseDown events are used to supply
'additional product information when
'the right mouse button is clicked

Sub imgFloppy_MouseDown(Button,Shift,X,Y)
    If Button=2 Then
        MsgBox "1.44MB Drive and Ten Disks",64,"ByteComp"
    End If
End Sub

Sub imgHardDrv_MouseDown(Button,Shift,X,Y)
    If Button=2 Then
        MsgBox "1GB Internal IDE Drive",64,"ByteComp"
    End If
End Sub

Sub imgCDROM_MouseDown(Button,Shift,X,Y)
    If Button=2 Then
        MsgBox "4X IDE CD-ROM Drive",64,"ByteComp"
    End If
End Sub
```

(continued)

Listing 9-1 *continued*

```
    Sub imgMonitor_MouseDown(Button,Shift,X,Y)
        If Button=2 Then
            MsgBox "14-Inch VGA Monitor",64,"ByteComp"
        End If
    End Sub

    Sub imgKeyboard_MouseDown(Button,Shift,X,Y)
        If Button=2 Then
            MsgBox "128-Key Ergonomic Keyboard",64,"ByteComp"
        End If
    End Sub

    Sub imgMouse_MouseDown(Button,Shift,X,Y)
        If Button=2 Then
            MsgBox "Two-Button Serial Mouse",64,"ByteComp"
        End If
    End Sub

    Sub imgModem_MouseDown(Button,Shift,X,Y)
        If Button=2 Then
            MsgBox "28.8 Internal Modem",64,"ByteComp"
        End If
    End Sub

    Sub imgJoystick_MouseDown(Button,Shift,X,Y)
        If Button=2 Then
            MsgBox "Aviation-Style Joystick",64,"ByteComp"
        End If
    End Sub

    Sub txtCardNumber_KeyPress(KeyASCII)

        'Author: New Technology Solutions, Inc.
        'Purpose: Validate credit card entry
        '6/22/96 Original

        txtCardNumber.Locked=True
        If KeyASCII=8 Then txtCardNumber.Locked=False
        If KeyASCII=45 Then txtCardNumber.Locked=False
        If KeyASCII>47 and KeyASCII<58 Then
            txtCardNumber.Locked=False
        End If
    End Sub
</SCRIPT>
```

C H A P T E R   T E N

Emerging Internet Technologies

Internet technologies are constantly changing. The biggest challenge I faced when writing this book about Internet application development was the fact that the technology is like shifting sand. Major advancements were occurring, literally as I wrote. Inevitably, some of the technology that will be available when this book is published did not exist when the text was created. These are certainly exciting times for developers.

In an effort to include as much information as possible, I have devoted this chapter to the advances in Internet development that occurred late in the writing of the book. In fact, some of the technologies discussed in this section exist at the time of this writing only as announcements from Microsoft. At any rate, the following sections will give you a sight-seeing tour of the leading edge of Internet development.

Windows NT 4.0

In August of 1996, Microsoft released Windows NT Server 4.0 and Windows NT Workstation 4.0. This release of Windows NT Server supports Internet development directly by including the Microsoft Internet Information Server (IIS) as an integral part of the system. The popular Microsoft Windows 95 interface has also been integrated into Windows NT Server.

The IIS release that ships with Windows NT Server 4.0 is version 2.0. This version of IIS is reportedly 40 percent faster than version 1.0, which shipped as a separate product that could be installed in Windows NT Server 3.51. Windows NT Server 4.0 includes the following new features:

- ■ **Support for remote server administration via a web browser**
  With a remote server administration utility, administrators can perform management tasks, such as creating and deleting accounts, by using any HTML 2.0–compatible web browser.

- **Support for Distributed Component Object Model (DCOM) applications**   DCOM is an extension to COM that allows components to communicate across a network. For example, DCOM supports the connection and communication of components residing on different computers.

- **A new version of Domain Name System (DNS)**   DNS allows computers on an intranet to use domain names to communicate. DNS maintains the correlation between intuitive domain-name addresses and numerical IP addresses. This revamped service includes a graphical administration utility and is integrated with the Windows Internet Naming Service (WINS), which allows administrators to dynamically update domain-name addresses and IP addresses.

- **Point-to-Point Tunneling Protocol (PPTP)**   PPTP is a technology that allows users to securely connect to corporate networks across the Internet. This protocol can create virtual networks between any designated computers on the Internet.

Improvements were also made in Windows NT Workstation. These enhancements include built-in Internet access through the Internet Explorer, the Windows 95 interface, and expanded user and multimedia support.

Normandy

Microsoft has developed a family of servers for Internet service providers. These servers, code-named *Normandy*, are built on Windows NT Server and IIS. The Normandy servers are designed to support users on high-traffic web sites. An early release of Normandy is expected in the fourth quarter of 1996. Here are some of the features:

A mail server that supports the Simple Mail Transfer Protocol (SMTP) and the Post Office Protocol (POP3) for sending and receiving Internet mail.

A news server that supports the Network News Transfer Protocol (NNTP) for tracking news.

A chat server that allows Internet service providers to set up chat rooms for users.

A merchant server that allows Internet service providers to create and maintain online stores.

A personalization server allowing Internet service providers to retain information about users and adapt it, to personalize content.

An information-retrieval server allowing easy search of web sites.

A content-replication server that allows larger sites to manage multiple gigabytes of data. (This server can update the data with the site online and is able to update only the data that has changed.)

A membership server that securely stores profile information about the users of the service.

Microsoft SQL Server 6.5

Microsoft SQL Server 6.5 is the latest upgrade to the powerful Microsoft BackOffice database. The product has many enhancements for administrators and developers alike. Some of these features are listed here:

Distributed Transaction Coordinator (DTC) manages transactions across multiple SQL Server systems.

A heterogeneous data replication component allows data to be exchanged with databases other than SQL Server.

Web Assistant automatically formats SQL Server data into HTML code.

DBA Assistant automates such tasks as data backup, consistency checking, and statistical updating.

Microsoft dbWeb

Microsoft dbWeb is an Internet Server API (ISAPI) application that forms an interface between IIS and an ODBC datasource. It allows you to quickly make information in ODBC databases accessible from a web page. With Microsoft dbWeb, you can easily set up database queries. This utility also provides insert, delete, and update capabilities. The advantage of dbWeb is that it allows web page developers to publish database information without writing any code. No HTML or ISAPI knowledge is required. All the HTML code required to publish an ODBC datasource is generated by dbWeb.

Microsoft dbWeb consists of an administrator application for creating web content and a service for publishing the content. The administrator application allows you to easily specify the data fields that can be searched and the fields that will be published. You can even specify different sets of data for the same datasource. Each set of data is managed as one of a number of *schemas* associated with the datasource (see page 394).

The dbWeb Service controls the processing between ODBC and IIS. The service processes the data requests and generates the return HTML page for the browser. Users can search the data with a simple query screen that is also generated by the service.

Installing dbWeb

Microsoft dbWeb is a Windows NT application. To use dbWeb, you must install it on a Windows NT server that has the following components installed:

- Windows NT Server version 3.51 with Service Pack 4, or Windows NT Server 4.0 or later.

- The Microsoft Internet Information Server version 1.0 or later.

- ODBC 2.5 or later. Microsoft dbWeb allows you to install the ODBC Desktop Driver Pack 3.0 after dbWeb has been installed.

Installing dbWeb is a simple matter of running its setup utility. The Microsoft dbWeb utility is free and available from Microsoft's web site, (http://www.microsoft.com/intdev/). If you have downloaded dbWeb from the Microsoft web site, your setup file will be a self-extracting compressed file with an exe extension. Simply run the exe file to install the application. If you accept all the default settings, dbWeb installs the following folders on your server:

drive\dbWeb	The root directory
drive\dbWeb\Admin	The dbWeb Administrator
drive\dbWeb\odbc32	ODBC files
drive\dbWeb\Server	The dbWeb Service
drive\inetsrv\scripts\dbWeb	The dbWeb DLL file, dbwebc.dll
drive\inetsrv\wwwroot\dbWeb	Sample dbWeb files

When the installation is complete, dbWeb places an icon for the ODBC 3.0 setup file in the Microsoft dbWeb group. To install the ODBC Desktop Driver Pack 3.0 on your server, double-click on the ODBC Setup icon in the Microsoft dbWeb group. The use of dbWeb requires these drivers, so you should run the setup routine if you do not have the ODBC Desktop Driver Pack 3.0 installed. You will then see several popular ODBC drivers listed in the ODBC Administrator. You can use these to set up ODBC datasources.

The dbWeb Administrator

The dbWeb Administrator allows you to easily specify the data to be published on your web site. It is the primary development interface for dbWeb. You start the administrator by double-clicking on the dbWeb Administrator icon in the Microsoft dbWeb group. Figure 10-1 shows the dbWeb Administrator interface.

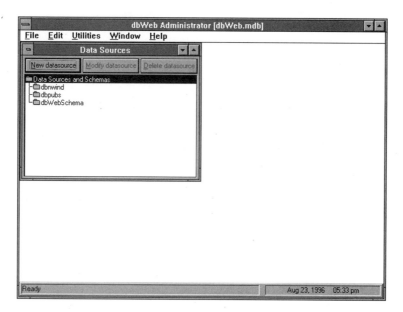

Figure 10-1.
The dbWeb Administrator.

The dbWeb Administrator manages ODBC datasources in the Data Sources window. If the Data Sources window is not already open, you can open it by selecting Open from the File menu. You'll see a dialog box that allows you to select a Microsoft Access database. The database you are selecting here is not the database to be published but rather the database that dbWeb will use to track ODBC datasources. The default database is dbweb.mdb, but you can create others. Select dbweb.mdb, located in the dbWeb/Admin folder, and click on the OK button to open it.

After you have opened dbweb.mdb, you will see in the Data Sources window several example ODBC datasources that can be published. You can easily add your own datasource to be published, by selecting Data Sources And Schemas in the Data Sources window and then clicking on the New Datasource button. Clicking on this button causes the Data Source dialog box to appear. Figure 10-2 (page 394) shows the Data Source dialog box.

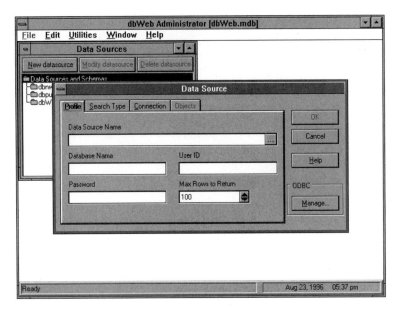

Figure 10-2.
The Data Source dialog box.

Inside the Data Source dialog box, you can select a new datasource by clicking on the ellipsis button that appears next to the Data Source Name box. Clicking on this button displays a list of all of the datasources available on your server. Simply select the datasource you want to publish and click on the OK button. The Data Source dialog box allows you to add information and make additional settings. Once you are finished with the Data Source dialog box, click on the OK button, and your new ODBC datasource will appear in the Data Sources window. If you want to set up a new ODBC datasource on your server, refer to Chapter 6 for detailed instructions on how to set up an ODBC datasource, using the ODBC Administrator.

You publish the database by using definitions (or schemas) that you build in dbWeb. Datasources can have multiple schemas that define the fields that are published and the fields that can be searched. You can create a new schema by using the Schema Wizard, or you can create one manually. Adding a new schema to your datasource is extremely easy if you use the Schema Wizard. The Schema Wizard walks you through the process of creating a schema for your datasource by asking which fields you want to publish and which fields should be used in the searches. When you finish with the wizard, your new schema will appear in the Data Sources window.

You begin the schema-creation process by selecting a datasource in the Data Sources window and clicking on the New Schema button. A dialog box is displayed that allows you to select either the Schema Wizard or an option for creating a schema manually. Figure 10-3 shows a sample of the first dialog box of the Schema Wizard. Figure 10-4 shows the New Schema window used for creating a schema manually.

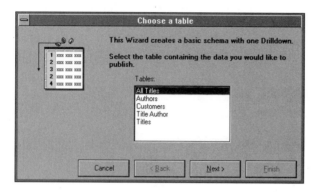

Figure 10-3.
A sample of the first dialog box of the Schema Wizard.

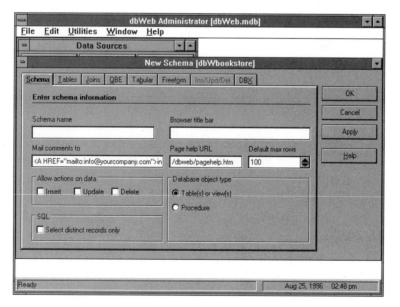

Figure 10-4.
The New Schema window for creating a schema manually.

The dbWeb Service

Information in a database can be published by the dbWeb Service, which processes the data requests and formats the return HTML page. The service is installed automatically when you install dbWeb; however, it is not automatically started by the setup routine. In fact, it is installed as a manual service that you must start yourself. To start the service, launch the Services administrator by double-clicking on the Services icon located in the Control Panel. In the Services dialog box, start the dbWeb Service by selecting dbWeb Service from the service list and clicking on the Start button. Figure 10-5 shows the Services dialog box.

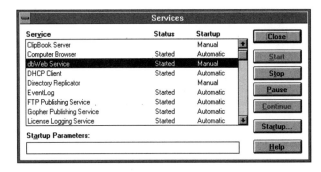

Figure 10-5.
The Services dialog box.

If you want the service to start automatically when you start your server, change the service from manual to automatic. You can do this by double-clicking on dbWeb Service from the service list. The Service dialog box appears. This box has an option with which you can change the startup type from manual to automatic. Figure 10-6 shows the Service dialog box.

Viewing the data in the Internet Explorer is simple once the service is running. All you have to do is call the appropriate URL and specify the schema to publish. Here is an example of the URL format, which uses the getqbe method:

http://*www_address*/scripts/dbweb/dbwebc.dll/*schema*?getqbe

www_address and *schema* are different for each host name and schema published. You can either type this address directly into the browser or simply access it from a link in an existing web page. Regardless of how it is accessed, the dbWeb Service builds a web page that is based on the schema. Figure 10-7 shows a simple query page published by dbWeb.

From the query page, users can access your database by specifying search criteria. The dbWeb Service provides an interface that allows users to search for exact matches or partial strings. When the user has built a query, he or she simply clicks on the Submit Query button to execute it. The result is displayed in tabular format. Figure 10-8 (page 398) shows a sample of the returned results.

Figure 10-6.
The Service dialog box.

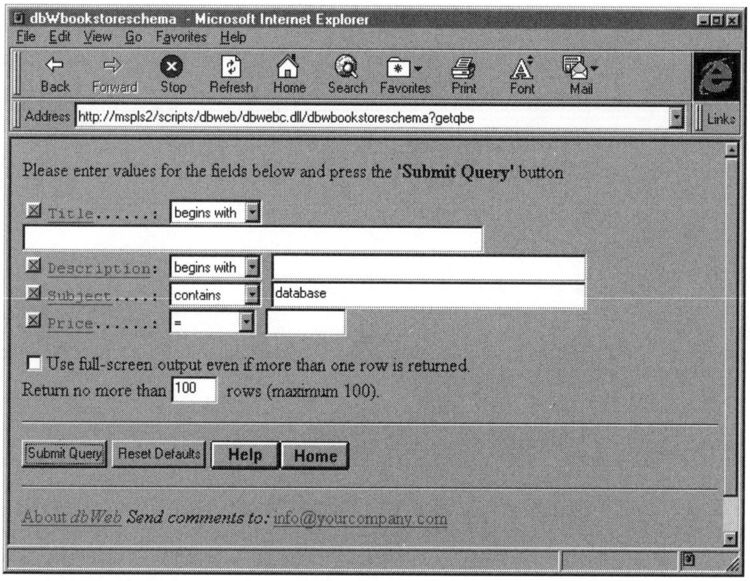

Figure 10-7.
A dbWeb query page.

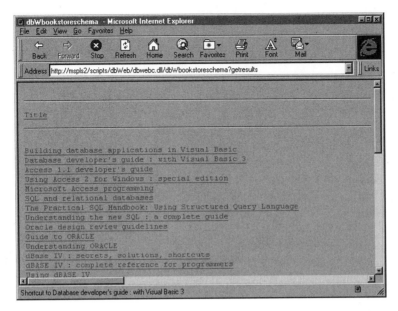

Figure 10-8.
The data returned from a dbWeb query.

Into the Future

This chapter has introduced some of the technologies that are beginning to bloom as this book nears completion. I have no doubt that the number and variety of Internet development tools will continue to grow exponentially. New design environments for ActiveX development, as well as new content tools, can be expected to appear frequently.

To bring yourself up to date on the dynamic, fast-moving topics that were discussed in this book or that are too new to have been discussed here, point your web browser to the following URL:

http://www.microsoft.com/mspress/updates/243/

On this web page, I will be discussing new developments that are related to this book.

Future editions of this book will cover new advances in Microsoft Visual Basic, Scripting Edition, and anything else new that I can get my hands on. Until then, I'll continue to have great fun developing for the Internet.

An HTML Primer

Although it is not my intention to teach HTML programming in this book, many Visual Basic programmers do not have a lot of experience with HTML. In this appendix, I provide brief descriptions of the fundamental HTML tags supported by the Microsoft Internet Explorer 3.0 as a starting point for those of you who want to learn the language. HTML is changing constantly, so you should consider this appendix as a foundation for future learning.

An Introduction to HTML Documents

You define an HTML document by placing the <HTML> tag at the beginning of the document and the </HTML> tag at the end of the document.

Occasionally a document will also have a header that appears before the first <HTML> tag to describe the type of information in the document. For example, documents that send return strings back to the browser from OLEISAPI will often have headers. For HTML, the header is

```
Content-Type: text/html
```

The header must be followed by a blank line.

The <!DOCTYPE> tag is the first tag in your HTML document. It specifies the version of HTML used in the document. <!DOCTYPE> is a required tag for HTML 3.2–compliant documents and has the following format:

```
<!DOCTYPE HTML PUBLIC "-//W3C//DTD HTML 3.2//EN">
```

An HTML document has two sections: the head and the body. Although Microsoft Visual Basic, Scripting Edition code can appear anywhere in the document, in this book we place VBScript code in a third section, called the script section, which we place inside the head section. The following empty HTML structure shows how these sections are placed in relation to each other:

```
<HTML>
<HEAD>
<SCRIPT>
</SCRIPT>
</HEAD>
<BODY>
</BODY>
</HTML>
```

The Head Section

The head section is where the title of the web page is placed and typically where the base and style tags are placed. The title of the page appears in the title bar of the browser. The base and style tags are described later, under the heading "The HTML Tags." Here is an example of the title tag used in the head section:

```
<HTML>
<HEAD>
<TITLE>My Document</TITLE>
</HEAD>
```

The Script Section

In this book, the script section is where we place VBScript code. Although the script section appears within the head section, this book identifies it as a separate section because of its importance. The script section should contain comment tags (<!-- and -->) so that scripting code will not be displayed by older browsers that do not support scripting. The script section is defined by the tags <SCRIPT></SCRIPT>, which have the following syntax:

```
<SCRIPT LANGUAGE="language" [EVENT="event"] [FOR="object"]>
<!--
    scripting code
-->
</SCRIPT>
```

The attributes are as follows:

LANGUAGE specifies the scripting language used for the scripting code in the section. For the Internet Explorer 3.0, the possible languages are JavaScript and VBScript.

EVENT specifies the event associated with this script section. You can use as many script sections as you want.

FOR specifies the object associated with the event. You can attach code to events in several different ways.

Here is an example that shows the use of the <SCRIPT></SCRIPT> tags and their attributes:

```
<HTML>
<HEAD>
<SCRIPT LANGUAGE="VBScript">
<!--
    Sub btnOne_OnClick
        MsgBox "You clicked button One"
    End Sub
-->
</SCRIPT>
<SCRIPT LANGUAGE="VBScript" EVENT="OnClick" FOR="btnTwo">
<!--
    MsgBox "You clicked button Two"
-->
</SCRIPT>
</HEAD>
<BODY>
<FORM NAME="frmOne">
<INPUT TYPE="BUTTON" NAME="btnOne" VALUE="One">
<INPUT TYPE="BUTTON" NAME="btnTwo" VALUE="Two">
</FORM>
</BODY>
</HTML>
```

For more information on Microsoft Visual Basic, Scripting Edition, consult Chapters 2–4, as well as the companion CD.

The Body Section

The body section will perhaps be the one that is most unfamiliar to Visual Basic programmers who are new to HTML. The body section contains the bulk of the formatted information that appears on a web page. This section is defined by the <BODY></BODY> tags, which have the following syntax:

<BODY [BACKGROUND="*url*"] [BGCOLOR="#*rrggbb*"]
[BGPROPERTIES="FIXED"] [LEFTMARGIN="*integer*"]
[LINK="#*rrggbb*"] [OnLoad="*subroutine*"] [TEXT="#*rrggbb*"]
[TOPMARGIN="*integer*"] [OnUnload="*subroutine*"] [VLINK="#*rrggbb*"]>

</BODY>

The attributes are as follows:

BACKGROUND specifies a URL of an image to be used as the background graphic.

BGCOLOR is the background color (in hexadecimal RGB format or as a recognized color name).

BGPROPERTIES, when set to FIXED, specifies that the background image should not scroll.

LEFTMARGIN is an integer that specifies the left margin for the page.

LINK specifies the color (in hexadecimal RGB format or as a recognized color name) for all the links in the document.

OnLoad specifies the event handler that gets called when the page is first loaded.

TEXT specifies the color (in hexadecimal RGB format or as a recognized color name) for all text in the document.

TOPMARGIN is an integer that specifies the top margin for the page.

OnUnload specifies the event handler that gets called when the current page is unloaded.

VLINK specifies the color (in hexadecimal RGB format or as a recognized color name) for all links that have been visited during the current session.

Note that the Internet Explorer recognizes the following color names, in addition to hexadecimal RGB values: Aqua, Black, Blue, Fuchsia, Gray, Green, Lime, Maroon, Navy, Olive, Purple, Red, Silver, Teal, White, and Yellow.

Here is a short example that shows the use of the <BODY></BODY> tags and some of their attributes:

```
<HTML>
<HEAD>
<SCRIPT LANGUAGE="VBScript">
<!--
    Sub TestMessage
        MsgBox "OnLoad fired"
    End Sub
-->
</SCRIPT>
</HEAD>
```

```
<BODY BACKGROUND="/images/truck.gif" BGCOLOR="#FFFFFF"
BGPROPERTIES="FIXED" LEFTMARGIN="60" LINK="#FF6600"
OnLoad="TestMessage" TEXT="Fuchsia" TOPMARGIN="60" VLINK="#330099">
This is some text.
</BODY>
</HTML>
```

The HTML Tags

The body section can contain a number of other tags that are used to format information in a web page. The next several pages describe the most useful tags and their attributes.

The Anchor Tag

The anchor tag defines anchors and links in a document. It can be used to define a destination or a jump to another web page. It can also be used to invoke a back-end process, such as the Internet Database Connector (IDC). The anchor tag is defined by the <A></A> tags, which have the following syntax:

<A [HREF="*link*"] [NAME="*name*"] [TARGET="*target_window*"]
[TITLE="*title*"]>

</A>

The attributes are as follows:

HREF specifies the destination URL link.

NAME specifies the anchor name.

TARGET specifies a frame window. Target also allows several target windows to be specified. *_blank* specifies loading the link into a new untitled window. *_parent* specifies loading the link into the parent of the document that the link is in. *_self* specifies loading the link into the same frame window that the link is in. *_top* specifies loading the link into the full window.

TITLE specifies the title that appears when the link is selected.

Here are some examples that show the use of the anchor tag to create links and anchors:

```
<A HREF="http://www.vb-bootcamp.com">Here is a link</A>
```

```
<A NAME="Anchor1">Here is an anchor named Anchor1 on the Linktest.htm
page</A>
```

(continued)

continued

```
<A HREF="#Anchor1">Here is a link to Anchor1 somewhere else on the
Linktest.htm page</A>
<A HREF="http://www.company.com/Linktest.htm#Anchor1">Here is a link
to Anchor1 on a different HTML page</A>

<A HREF="http://www.company.com"><IMG SRC="truck.gif"></A>
Here is an example of an image that is a link

<A HREF="frametest.htm" TARGET="contents">Here is a link to display
frametest.htm in the frame named contents.</A>
```

The Base Tag

The base tag is used to specify a base URL from which all other relative URLs in the document are referenced. The base tag is placed in the head section rather than in the body section. The base tag is defined by the <BASE> tag, which has the following syntax:

> <BASE [HREF="*url*"] [TARGET="*target_window*"]>

The attributes are as follows:

HREF specifies the root URL for the current page.

TARGET specifies a target window. Target also allows several target windows to be specified. *_blank* specifies loading the link into a new untitled window. *_parent* specifies loading the link into the parent of the document that the link is in. *_self* specifies loading the link into the same frame window that the link is in. *_top* specifies loading the link into the full window.

Here is an example that shows the use of the base tag:

```
<HTML>
<HEAD>
<TITLE>Base Example</TITLE>
<BASE HREF="http://www.vb-bootcamp.com" TARGET="contents">
</HEAD>
```

The BaseFont Tag

The BaseFont tag defines a base font for the entire HTML document. These settings can be overridden by settings in the font tag. The BaseFont tag is defined by the <BASEFONT></BASEFONT> tags, which have the following syntax:

> <BASEFONT [COLOR="*#rrggbb*"] [NAME="*name*"] [SIZE="*integer*"]>

The attributes are as follows:

COLOR specifies the base font color (in hexadecimal RGB format or as a recognized color name).

NAME specifies the name of the base font.

SIZE is an integer that specifies the size of the base font, which can be 1 through 7. The smallest size is 1, the largest is 7, and the default is 3.

Here is an example:

```
<BASEFONT COLOR="#FF0000" NAME="Arial" SIZE="4">
```

The BGSound Tag

The BGSound tag allows you to play sounds in your web page. You can use the tag's attributes to control the source and the number of times the sound is played. Accepted sound formats are AU, WAV, and MIDI. The BGSound tag is defined by the <BGSOUND> tag, which has the following syntax:

<BGSOUND SRC="*url*" [LOOP="*integer*"]>

The attributes are as follows:

SRC specifies the URL at which the sound to be played is located.

LOOP is an integer that specifies the number of times the sound is played. This attribute can be set to a finite integer value or to the keyword INFINITE.

Here is an example:

```
<BGSOUND SRC="/sounds/music.wav" LOOP="INFINITE">
```

The Break Tag

The break tag generates a line break in text. It has the following syntax:

<BR [CLEAR="*clear*"]>

The sole attribute is as follows:

CLEAR specifies where the text that follows will continue around an object. CLEAR can be one of the following: LEFT, RIGHT, or ALL. LEFT indicates that the text that follows will continue at the next clear left margin. RIGHT indicates that the text that follows will continue at the next clear right margin. ALL indicates that the text that follows will continue at the next clear left *and* right margins.

Here is an example:

```
<BR CLEAR="RIGHT">
```

The Comment Tag

The comment tag is used to place comments in HTML code. Comment tags should be used within the <SCRIPT></SCRIPT> tags so that scripting code will not be displayed by older browsers that do not support scripting. Comments can be defined either by the <COMMENT></COMMENT> tags or by the <!-- and --> tags. They have the following syntax:

        <COMMENT>
        </COMMENT>

or

        <!--
        -->

Here are some short examples that show the use of the comment tags:

```
<COMMENT>
Text within these tags will not be displayed by the browser
</COMMENT>

<!--
Text within these tags will not be displayed by the browser
-->

<SCRIPT LANGUAGE="VBScript">
<!--
    scripting code
-->
</SCRIPT>
```

The Div Tag

The div tag allows you to group elements within your HTML code into sections so that the grouped elements can be given a style. The div tag is defined by the <DIV></DIV> tags, which have the following syntax:

        <DIV [ALIGN="*align*"] [CLASS="*class*"]>

        </DIV>

The attributes are as follows:

ALIGN specifies the default horizontal alignment of the div section. ALIGN can be one of the following: LEFT, CENTER, or RIGHT.

CLASS specifies the type of section—chapter, abstract, or appendix, for example.

Here is an example that shows the use of the div tag:

```
<DIV ALIGN="CENTER" CLASS="Main Text">
    Text and objects within this section
</DIV>
```

The Font Tag

The font tag is used to specify the font, the font color, and the font size for a block of text. The font tag is defined by the <FONT></FONT> tags, which have the following syntax:

<FONT [COLOR="#*rrggbb*"] [FACE="*font1*[, *font2*[, *font3*[, ...]]]"] [SIZE="*integer*"]>

</FONT>

The attributes are as follows:

COLOR specifies the font color (in hexadecimal RGB format or as a recognized color name).

FACE specifies the font and allows a font list to be specified in case your first font choice is not available on the system. If none of the fonts specified in the list is on the system, the default font will be used. Typically, the default font is set in the user's browser.

SIZE is an integer that specifies the size of the font, which can be 1 through 7. The smallest size is 1 and the largest is 7. Plus and minus symbols can be used to increase or decrease the size of the font relative to the BASEFONT size setting.

Here is an example that shows the use of the font tag:

```
<FONT COLOR="Blue" FACE="Lithos, Arial" SIZE="+2">
Some text
</FONT>
```

The Form Tag

The form tag is used to generate an HTML form. Forms act as containers for user input. Any controls used within the <FORM></FORM> tags can be referenced in VBScript code. The form tag is defined by the <FORM></FORM> tags, which have the following syntax:

```
<FORM [ACTION="url"] [METHOD="GET or POST"]
[NAME="form_name"] [OnSubmit="subroutine"]
[TARGET="target_window"]>

</FORM>
```

The attributes are as follows:

ACTION specifies the URL of the back-end process that will receive the form's data.

METHOD specifies the method of data exchange between the client and the server. Valid values are GET and POST. You use POST when you are accessing back-end processes, such as the Internet Database Connector (IDC) or an ActiveX component, through OLEISAPI. GET is used to append arguments to the end of a URL. See Chapter 5 and the Microsoft Internet Information Server documentation for more information on back-end processing.

NAME specifies the name of the form. This is the name you reference in VBScript.

OnSubmit specifies the event handler that gets called when the form is submitted.

TARGET specifies a target window. Target also allows several target windows to be specified. _blank_ specifies loading the link into a new untitled window. _parent_ specifies loading the link into the parent of the document that the link is in. _self_ specifies loading the link into the same frame window that the link is in. _top_ specifies loading the link into the full window.

Here is an example that shows the use of the form tag and its attributes :

```
<HTML>
<HEAD>
<SCRIPT LANGUAGE="VBScript">
<!--
    Sub TestMessage
        MsgBox "OnSubmit fired"
    End Sub
```

```
-->
</SCRIPT>
</HEAD>
<BODY>
<FORM ACTION="/Scripts/test.idc" METHOD="POST" NAME="frmTest"
OnSubmit="TestMessage">
<INPUT TYPE="TEXT"><BR>
<INPUT TYPE="SUBMIT">
</FORM>
</BODY>
</HTML>
```

For information on the <INPUT> tag, see the discussion of the <INPUT> tag (pages 414–416).

The Frame Tag

The frame tag allows you to specify the attributes of a frame—for example, a name for the frame, whether the frame is scrollable, what HTML file to display in the frame, and other attributes. You typically use multiple frame definitions in conjunction with the frameset tag (see the next entry). When you use the frame tag and the frameset tag, you can divide the browser window into different frames or panes. (If you are interested in creating floating frames, see the entry on the iframe tag.) A frame is defined with the <FRAME> tag and has the following syntax:

<FRAME [FRAMEBORDER="1 *or* 0"] [MARGINHEIGHT="*integer*"]
[MARGINWIDTH="*integer*"] [NAME="*frame_name*"] [NORESIZE]
[SCROLLING="YES *or* NO"] [SRC="*html_file*"]>

The attributes are as follows:

FRAMEBORDER specifies whether a three-dimensional border will be displayed around a frame. 1 displays a 3-D border, and 0 displays a flat border. (By default, FRAMEBORDER is 1.)

MARGINHEIGHT is an integer that specifies the top and bottom margins inside the frame, in pixels.

MARGINWIDTH is an integer that specifies the left and right margins inside the frame, in pixels.

NAME specifies the name of the frame window.

NORESIZE, when specified, prevents the user from resizing the frame.

SCROLLING specifies whether the frame is scrollable (YES is a scrolling frame, and NO is a nonscrolling frame).

SRC specifies the HTML file to be displayed in the frame.

Here is an example that shows the use of the frame tag:

```
<FRAME FRAMEBORDER="0" MARGINHEIGHT="100" NAME="content" NORESIZE
SCROLLING="NO" SRC="content.htm">
```

The Frameset Tag

The frameset tag specifies a container for frames, framesets, and noframes. The frameset tag is defined by the <FRAMESET></FRAMESET> tags, which have the following syntax:

<FRAMESET [COLS="*col1, col2, col3, …*"] [FRAMEBORDER="1 *or* 0"]
[FRAMESPACING="*integer*"] [ROWS="*row1, row2, row3, …*"]>

</FRAMESET>

The attributes are as follows:

COLS specifies the dimensions of the frame columns. The column dimensions can be specified by percentage (%), pixels, or a relative size (*). For example, COLS="25%, 100, *" specifies three frame columns, where the width of the first column is 25 percent of the width of the browser window, the width of the second column is 100 pixels, and the width of the third column is the remaining portion of the browser window.

FRAMEBORDER specifies whether a three-dimensional border will be displayed around a frameset. 1 displays a 3-D border, and 0 displays a flat border. (By default, FRAMEBORDER is 1.)

FRAMESPACING is an integer that specifies the size of the space between frames, in pixels.

ROWS specifies the dimensions of the frame rows. The row dimensions can be specified by percentage (%), pixels, or a relative size (*). For example, ROWS="25%, 100, *" specifies three frame rows, where the height of the first row is 25 percent of the height of the browser window, the height of the second row is 100 pixels, and the height of the third row is the remaining portion of the browser window.

Inner framesets inherit the FRAMEBORDER and FRAMESPACING attributes; therefore, you only need to set these values once, in the outer frameset.

Here is an example that creates a page with three frames: a 100-pixel-high heading frame, which spans the entire browser window, and two frames below the heading frame. The lower left frame is 20 percent of the width of the browser window, and the lower right frame is the remaining portion.

```
<FRAMESET ROWS="100,*">
<FRAME NAME="heading" NORESIZE SCROLLING="NO" SRC="heading.htm">
<FRAMESET COLS="20%,*">
<FRAME NAME="contents" SRC="contents.htm">
<FRAME NAME="results" SRC="results.htm">
</FRAMESET>
</FRAMESET>
```

The Horizontal Rule Tag

The horizontal rule tag places a horizontal line across the page. The horizontal rule tag is defined by the <HR> tag, which has the following syntax:

<HR [ALIGN="*align*"] [COLOR= "#*rrggbb*"] [NOSHADE]
[SIZE="*integer*"] [WIDTH="*integer*"]>

The attributes are as follows:

ALIGN specifies the alignment of the line. ALIGN can be one of the following: LEFT, RIGHT, or CENTER.

COLOR is the color of the line (in hexadecimal RGB format or as a recognized color name).

NOSHADE, when specified, displays a solid line with no shadow.

SIZE is the thickness of the line, in pixels.

WIDTH is the length of the line, either in pixels or as a percentage of the page width.

Here is an example:

```
<HR ALIGN="RIGHT" COLOR="Blue" SIZE="10" WIDTH="40%">
```

The Iframe Tag

The iframe tag specifies a floating frame. A floating frame is a frame that can be placed anywhere on a web page. The iframe tag is defined by the <IFRAME></IFRAME> tags, which have the following syntax:

<IFRAME [ALIGN="*align*"] [FRAMEBORDER="1 *or* 0"]
[HEIGHT="*integer*" WIDTH="*integer*"] [MARGINHEIGHT="*integer*"]
[MARGINWIDTH="*integer*"] [NAME="*name*"] [SCROLLING="YES *or*
NO"] [SRC="*html_file*"]> </IFRAME>

411

The attributes are as follows:

ALIGN specifies the alignment of the floating frame or the surrounding text. ALIGN can be one of the following: LEFT, RIGHT, TOP, CENTER, MIDDLE, or BOTTOM. LEFT and RIGHT specify the alignment of the frame. The rest specify the alignment of the surrounding text.

FRAMEBORDER specifies whether a three-dimensional border will be displayed around the floating frame. 1 displays a 3-D border, and 0 displays no border. (By default, FRAMEBORDER is 1.)

HEIGHT is an integer that specifies the height of the floating frame, in pixels. HEIGHT can also be specified as a percentage. If HEIGHT is specified, WIDTH must also be specified.

MARGINHEIGHT is an integer that specifies the top margin inside the floating frame, in pixels.

MARGINWIDTH is an integer that specifies the left margin inside the floating frame, in pixels.

NAME specifies the floating frame's name.

SCROLLING specifies whether the floating frame is scrollable. (YES is a scrolling frame, and NO is a nonscrolling frame.)

SRC specifies the HTML file to be displayed in the floating frame.

WIDTH is an integer that specifies the width of the floating frame, in pixels. WIDTH can also be specified as a percentage. If WIDTH is specified, HEIGHT must also be specified.

Here is an example that shows the use of the iframe tag:

```
<IFRAME ALIGN="RIGHT" HEIGHT="200" WIDTH="80%" MARGINWIDTH="40"
MARGINHEIGHT="40" NAME="DATA" SCROLLING="NO" SRC="HOME.HTM"></IFRAME>
```

The Image Tag

The image tag is used to place images in the page. It can be used in conjunction with an anchor tag to create simple image links and image maps. An image link is an image that, when you click on it, displays the specified link. An image map is an image that has specified clickable areas that display different links, according to where you click on the image. The image tag is defined by the <IMG> tag, which has the following syntax:

<IMG [ALIGN="*align*"] [ALT="*text*"] [BORDER="*integer*"]
[CONTROLS] [DYNSRC="*url*"] [HEIGHT="*integer*"]
[HSPACE="*integer*"] [ISMAP] [LOOP="*integer*"] [SRC="*url*"]
[START="*start_event*"] [USEMAP="*map_name*"] [VSPACE="*integer*"]
[WIDTH="*integer*"]>

The attributes are as follows:

ALIGN specifies the alignment of the image or the surrounding text.
ALIGN can be one of the following: LEFT, RIGHT, TOP, CEN-
TER, MIDDLE, or BOTTOM. LEFT and RIGHT specify the
alignment of the image. The rest specify the alignment of the
surrounding text.

ALT specifies the text that will display while the image is loading and is
the text that displays when the cursor is moved over the image.

BORDER is an integer that specifies the thickness of the border around
the graphic. If the image is a link, the border is the appropriate
link color; otherwise, the border is invisible.

CONTROLS, when specified, displays a set of video controls if a video
clip is present.

DYNSRC specifies a URL to a video clip or VRML file. DYNSRC stands
for Dynamic Source.

HEIGHT is an integer that specifies the height of the image, which
allows the browser to correctly format the page even before the
image is downloaded. If the actual dimensions of the image differ
from the height specified, the image is stretched accordingly.

HSPACE is an integer that specifies the left and right margins for the
image. It is similar to BORDER, but the margins are not colored if
the image is a link.

ISMAP specifies that the image is a server-side image map. When the
user clicks on the image, the *x-* and *y*-coordinates of the click are
sent as arguments to the URL specified in the anchor tag. The
arguments are formatted as *URL?x,y.*

LOOP is an integer that specifies the number of times a video clip will
play. LOOP can also be set to the keyword INFINITE.

SRC specifies the URL for the image to be displayed.

START specifies when the DYNSRC file should start to play; *start_event* can be FILEOPEN or MOUSEOVER.

USEMAP specifies that the image is a client-side image map; *map_name* is the file containing the coordinate information.

VSPACE is an integer that specifies the top and bottom margins for the image. It is similar to BORDER, but the margins are not colored if the image is a link.

WIDTH is an integer that specifies the width of the image, which allows the browser to format the page correctly even before the image is downloaded. If the actual dimensions of the image differ from the width specified, the image is stretched accordingly.

Here is an example that shows the use of the image tag and some of its attributes with the anchor tag:

```
<A HREF="/scripts/test.idc?Name=Scot">
<IMG ALT="Test Button" BORDER="0"
SRC="http://www.vb-bootcamp.com/button.gif">
</A>
```

The Input Tag

The input tag is used to add intrinsic controls to a web page. Intrinsic controls are controls that are part of the browser and do not have to be downloaded from the server. Intrinsic controls can be referenced in VBScript code. The input tag is defined by the <INPUT > tag, which has the following syntax:

<INPUT [TYPE="*control*"] [ALIGN="*align*"] [CHECKED]
[MAXLENGTH="*integer*"] [NAME="*name*"] [SIZE="*integer*"]
[SRC="*url*"] [VALUE="*value*"] [*Events*]>

The attributes are as follows:

TYPE specifies the type of control. TYPE can be one of the following: BUTTON, CHECKBOX, HIDDEN, IMAGE, PASSWORD, RADIO, RESET, SUBMIT, TEXT, or TEXTAREA. The IMAGE type allows you to use a clickable image instead of the SUBMIT button to submit information.

ALIGN, when included with the IMAGE type, specifies the alignment of the surrounding text. ALIGN can be one of the following: TOP, MIDDLE, or BOTTOM.

CHECKED, when included with the CHECKBOX or RADIO type, specifies that the check box or radio control is to be selected by default.

MAXLENGTH is an integer that specifies the maximum number of characters allowed in the PASSWORD, TEXT, and TEXTAREA controls.

NAME specifies the name of the form input variable associated with the control. Form input variables are passed to back-end processes when the form is submitted.

SIZE is an integer that specifies the width, in characters, for the PASS-WORD and TEXT controls. For the TEXTAREA control, the width and height can be specified with the following format: "*width,height*".

SRC, when included with the IMAGE type, specifies the URL at which the image to be displayed is located.

VALUE specifies the default value of the form input variable for the PASSWORD, TEXT, and TEXTAREA controls. For the CHECKBOX and RADIO controls, VALUE is the form input variable value of the control when submitted. For the RESET and SUBMIT controls, VALUE is the caption on the button.

Events are events that fire when the control's value is submitted. Each control supports different events.

See Chapter 3 for more information on intrinsic controls. Here is an example that shows the use of the input tag:

```
<FORM ACTION="/scripts/test.idc" METHOD="POST" NAME="frmTest">
<INPUT TYPE="BUTTON" NAME="btnOne" VALUE="Push Me"><BR>
<INPUT TYPE="CHECKBOX" CHECKED NAME="chkOne" VALUE="CHECK"><BR>
<INPUT TYPE="HIDDEN" NAME="txtHid" VALUE="Hidden Value"><BR>
<INPUT TYPE="IMAGE" SRC="truck.gif"><BR>
```

(continued)

415

continued

```
<INPUT TYPE="PASSWORD" MAXLENGTH="8" NAME="txtPas" SIZE="10"
VALUE="Change Me"><BR>
<INPUT TYPE="RADIO" NAME="OPTIONS" VALUE="One">One<BR>
<INPUT TYPE="RADIO" NAME="OPTIONS" VALUE="Two">Two<BR>
<INPUT TYPE="RADIO" NAME="OPTIONS" VALUE="Three">Three<BR>
<INPUT TYPE="RESET" VALUE="Reset Me"><BR>
<INPUT TYPE="SUBMIT" VALUE="Submit Form"><BR>
<INPUT TYPE="TEXT" MAXLENGTH="30" NAME="txtText" SIZE="50"
VALUE="Default Text"><BR>
<INPUT TYPE="TEXTAREA" NAME="txtTextA" SIZE="50,5" VALUE="Default
Text"><BR>
</FORM>
```

The List Tags

The tags described here are used to generate lists on a web page.

The List Item Tag

The list item tag defines an individual item in a list. Multiple list item tags are typically used with the directory, menu, ordered, and unordered list tags. The list item tag is defined by the <LI> tag, which has the following syntax:

<LI [TYPE="*type*"] [VALUE="*integer*"]>

The attributes are as follows:

TYPE specifies the style of the ordered list. (By default, TYPE is 1.) TYPE can be one of the following: *A* for uppercase letters, *a* for lowercase letters, *I* for uppercase Roman numerals, *i* for lowercase Roman numerals, or *1* for Arabic numbers.

VALUE is an integer that specifies the order value for the current list item.

The Directory, Menu, and Unordered List Tags

The directory, menu, and unordered list tags each define a bulleted list. They are defined, respectively, by the <DIR></DIR>, <MENU></MENU>, and <UL></UL> tags. Here are three examples that show the use of these list tags:

```
<DIR>
<LI>Item 1
<LI>Item 2
```

```
<LI>Item 3
</DIR>

<MENU>
<LI>Item 1
<LI>Item 2
<LI>Item 3
</MENU>

<UL>
<LI>Item 1
<LI>Item 2
</UL>
```

The Ordered List Tag

The ordered list tag defines a numbered list. The ordered list is defined by the <OL></OL> tags, which have the following syntax:

<OL [START="*integer*"] [TYPE="*type*"]

<LI>*Item1*

<LI>*Item2*

…

</OL>

The attributes are as follows:

START is an integer that specifies a starting ordering value. (By default, START is 1.)

TYPE specifies the style of the ordered list. (By default, TYPE is 1.) TYPE can be one of the following: *A* for uppercase letters, *a* for lowercase letters, *I* for uppercase Roman numerals, *i* for lowercase Roman numerals, or *1* for Arabic numbers.

Here is an example that shows the use of the ordered list tag:

```
<OL START="5" TYPE="i">
<LI>Item v
<LI TYPE="1" VALUE="8">Item 8
<LI>Item 9
</OL>
```

The Select List Tag

The select list tag is used to implement an intrinsic list box. The select list tag is defined by the <SELECT></SELECT> tags, and the individual items are designated with <OPTION > tag:

```
<SELECT [MULTIPLE] [NAME="name"] [SIZE="integer"]>
<OPTION VALUE="value1">Item1
<OPTION VALUE="value2">Item2
<OPTION VALUE="value3" [SELECTED]>Item3
...
</SELECT>
```

The attributes of the select list tags are as follows:

MULTIPLE allows multiple selections.

NAME is the name of the form input variable associated with the control.

SIZE is the height of the control in characters.

The attributes of the option tag are as follows:

SELECTED specifies that the item is to be selected by default.

VALUE specifies the value of the control when submitted.

Here is an example of the select list and option tags:

```
<SELECT NAME="Trucks">
<OPTION VALUE="1">Ford
<OPTION VALUE="2" SELECTED>Chevy
<OPTION VALUE="3">Dodge
</SELECT>
```

The Marquee Tag

The marquee tag creates scrolling text. The marquee tag is defined by the <MARQUEE></MARQUEE> tags, which have the following syntax:

```
<MARQUEE [ALIGN="align"] [BEHAVIOR="behavior"]
[BGCOLOR="#rrggbb"] [DIRECTION="direction"] [HEIGHT="integer"]
[HSPACE="integer"] [LOOP="integer"] [SCROLLAMOUNT="integer"]
[SCROLLDELAY="integer"] [VSPACE="integer"] [WIDTH="integer"]>

</MARQUEE>
```

The attributes are as follows:

ALIGN specifies how the marquee will align with the surrounding text. ALIGN can be one of the following: TOP, MIDDLE, or BOTTOM.

BEHAVIOR specifies the nature of the text animation. BEHAVIOR can be one of the following: SCROLL, SLIDE, or ALTERNATE.

BGCOLOR specifies the background color (in hexadecimal RGB format or as a recognized color name) for the marquee.

DIRECTION specifies the direction in which the text will move, which is left by default. DIRECTION can be one of the following: LEFT or RIGHT.

HEIGHT is an integer that specifies the height of the marquee, in pixels. It can also be specified as a percentage (%).

HSPACE is an integer that specifies the left and right margins, in pixels, between the marquee's outer edge and the browser window.

LOOP is an integer that specifies the number of times that the marquee will scroll. LOOP can also be set to the keyword INFINITE.

SCROLLAMOUNT is an integer that specifies the distance, in pixels, that the text is moved for each scroll movement.

SCROLLDELAY is an integer that specifies the number of milliseconds between each scroll movement.

VSPACE is an integer that specifies the top and bottom margins, in pixels, between the marquee's outer edge and the browser window.

WIDTH is an integer that specifies the width of the marquee, in pixels. It can also be specified as a percentage (%).

Here is an example that shows the use of the marquee tag:

```
<MARQUEE BGCOLOR="White" BEHAVIOR="SCROLL" DIRECTION="RIGHT"
HSPACE="60" SCROLLAMOUNT="10" SCROLLDELAY="100" VSPACE="40"
WIDTH="60%">This is scrolling text.
</MARQUEE>
```

The Noframes Tag

The noframes tag allows you to display a message to users whose browsers do not support frames. The message will not be displayed by a browser that does support frames. The noframes tag is used within the </FRAMESET> <FRAMESET> tags. The noframes tag is defined by the <NOFRAMES> </NOFRAMES> tags. Here is an example of their use:

```
<FRAMESET>
    <NOFRAMES>
    This page contains frames, which are not supported by your
    browser.
    </NOFRAMES>
</FRAMESET>
```

The Object Tag

The object tag allows objects (for example, ActiveX controls, applets, or images) to be inserted into an HTML document. The object tag is defined by the <OBJECT></OBJECT> tags, which have the following syntax:

<OBJECT [ALIGN="*align*"] [BORDER="*integer*"] [CLASSID="*url*"] [CODEBASE="*url*"] [CODETYPE="*codetype*"] [DATA="*url*"] [DECLARE] [HEIGHT="*integer*"] [HSPACE="*integer*"] [ID="*id*"] [NAME="*url*"] [SHAPES] [STANDBY="*message*"] [TYPE="*type*"] [USEMAP="*url*"] [VSPACE="*integer*"] [WIDTH="*integer*"]>

</OBJECT>

The attributes are as follows:

ALIGN specifies where to place the object. ALIGN can be one of the following: LEFT, CENTER, RIGHT, TEXTTOP, MIDDLE, TEXTMIDDLE, BASELINE, or TEXTBOTTOM.

BORDER is an integer that specifies the width of the border that is displayed around the visible area of the object when the object is part of a hyperlink.

CLASSID specifies either a URL used to locate the object or a class identifier for the object. For ActiveX controls, CLASSID is used to specify the class identifier. The class identifier is a unique alpha-numeric code assigned to each ActiveX control and is stored in the system Registry of the client computer.

CODEBASE specifies a URL used to locate the object. For ActiveX controls, CODEBASE specifies the location of the control.

CODETYPE specifies the Internet Media Type of the code specified by the CLASSID attribute. Since this information can be accessed before the code is retrieved, it is possible to skip over unsupported media types.

DATA specifies a URL that references the object's data (for example, a gif file for an image object).

DECLARE, when specified, indicates that the object is not to be instantiated, only declared.

HEIGHT is an integer that specifies the height of a box enclosing the visible area of the object. Use HEIGHT instead of accessing the Height property.

HSPACE is an integer that specifies the space to the left and right of the visible area of the object.

ID specifies the name of the object as it is referenced in code. The ID attribute is just like the Name property of an OCX control.

NAME provides a way to determine whether an object within a form block should be involved in the Submit process. If the object has its NAME attribute specified, its VALUE property will be included in any Submit action for a form.

SHAPES, when specified, indicates that the object element contains shape-defined links on the visible area of the object.

STANDBY specifies a text string that can be displayed in the browser while the object and data are being loaded.

TYPE specifies the Internet Media Type of the data specified by the DATA attribute. Since this information can be accessed before the data is retrieved, it is possible to skip over unsupported media types.

USEMAP specifies a URL for a client-side image map in a format proposed by Spyglass, Inc.

VSPACE is an integer that specifies the space above and below the visible area of the object.

WIDTH is an integer that specifies the width of a box enclosing the visible area of the object. Use WIDTH instead of accessing the Width property.

For more information and updates on the object tag, review the information at the World Wide Web consortium website, http://www.w3.org/pub/WWW/. See the next entry for an example that uses the object and param tags.

The Param Tag

The param tag sets the property values for an object and is used within the <OBJECT></OBJECT> tags. The param tag is defined by the <PARAM> tag, which has the following syntax:

<PARAM [NAME="*name*"] [TYPE="*type*"]
[VALUE="*value*"] [VALUETYPE="*valuetype*"]>

The attributes are as follows:

NAME specifies the property name.

TYPE specifies the Internet Media Type.

VALUE specifies the value for the named property.

VALUETYPE specifies how the value is to be interpreted. VALUETYPE can be one of the following: DATA, REF, or OBJECT. DATA indicates that the value is to be passed directly to the object as a string. OBJECT indicates that the value is a URL of an OBJECT element in the same document. REF indicates that the value is a URL.

Here is an example that uses the object and param tags for an ActiveX control:

```
<OBJECT
    CLASSID="CLSID:99B42120-6EC7-11CF-A6C7-00AA00A47DD2"
    CODEBASE=
    "http://www.company.com/controls/ielabel.ocx#version=4,70,0,1112"
    ALIGN="LEFT"
    ID="IeLabel1"
    TYPE="application/x-oleobject"
    VSPACE="0"
    HEIGHT="60"
    WIDTH="100"
    >
    <PARAM NAME="Caption" VALUE="Label Text">
    <PARAM NAME="Angle" VALUE="0">
    <PARAM NAME="Alignment" VALUE="4">
    <PARAM NAME="ForeColor" VALUE="#000000">
    <PARAM NAME="BackColor" VALUE="#C0C0C0">
    <PARAM NAME="FontName" VALUE="Arial">
    <PARAM NAME="FontSize" VALUE="12">
</OBJECT>
```

The Paragraph Tag

The paragraph tag generates a paragraph break in text. It has the following syntax:

<P [ALIGN="*align*"]>

The sole attribute is as follows:

ALIGN sets the alignment of the paragraph that follows it, which is left-aligned by default. ALIGN can be one of the following: LEFT, CENTER, or RIGHT.

Here is an example:

```
This text will be aligned left
<P ALIGN="RIGHT">
This text will be aligned right
```

The Style Tag

The style tag allows you to define style sheets and is typically placed in the head section. A style sheet is a collection of rules that can be easily applied and updated to format HTML pages. Style sheets are similar to styles used in Microsoft Word. For more information on style sheets, review the information at the World Wide Web Consortium web site, http://www.w3.org/pub/WWW/. Here is an example that uses style sheets, which are defined within the <STYLE></STYLE> tags:

```
<HTML>
<HEAD>
<TITLE>Style Example</TITLE>
<STYLE>
<!--
BODY {
    background: white;
    color: gray
}
H1 {
    color: green;
    font-weight: bold;
    font-size: 20pt;
    font-family: arial;
}
-->
</STYLE>
</HEAD>
```

(continued)

continued

```
<BODY>
The background is white and the text is gray.<BR>
<H1>Here is some text with the H1 style applied.
The text is green, bold, 20pt, Arial font.</H1><BR>
Here is some more gray text.<BR>
</BODY>
</HTML>
```

The Table Tag

The table tag is used to format information into a table. This is one of the most flexible formats in HTML. Use this tag frequently to add variety to your web pages. The table tag is defined by the <TABLE></TABLE> tags. The table rows are designated with the <TR></TR> tags, and individual cells are designated with the <TD></TD> or <TH></TH> tags. The table heading tags, <TH></TH>, are the same as the table cell tags, <TD></TD>, but they cause the cell data to be in boldface when it is displayed. The <CAPTION></CAPTION> tags specify the caption for the table. The <TABLE></TABLE> tags have the following syntax:

<TABLE [ALIGN="*align*"] [BACKGROUND="*url*"]
[BGCOLOR="*#rrggbb*"] [BORDER="*integer*"
[BORDERCOLOR="*#rrggbb*"] [BORDERCOLORDARK="*#rrggbb*"]
[BORDERCOLORLIGHT="*#rrggbb*"]] [CELLPADDING="*integer*"]
[CELLSPACING="*integer*"] [COLS="*integer*"] [FRAME="*frame*"]
[RULES="*rules*"] [WIDTH="*integer*"]>

</TABLE>

The attributes are as follows:

ALIGN specifies the alignment of the table, which is left-aligned by default. ALIGN can be one of the following: LEFT, CENTER, or RIGHT.

BACKGROUND specifies a URL of an image to be used as a background graphic.

BGCOLOR specifies the background color (in hexadecimal RGB format or as a recognized color name).

BORDER is an integer that specifies the size of the table border, in pixels. If BORDER is not specified, the border is 0.

BORDERCOLOR specifies the border color (in hexadecimal RGB format or as a recognized color name) and must be used with BORDER.

BORDERCOLORDARK specifies the shadow color (in hexadecimal RGB format or as a recognized color name) of a 3-D border and must be used with BORDER.

BORDERCOLORLIGHT specifies the highlight color (in hexadecimal RGB format or as a recognized color name) of a 3-D border and must be used with BORDER.

CELLPADDING is an integer that specifies the horizontal and vertical space, in pixels, between the data in a cell and the cell border.

CELLSPACING is an integer that specifies the horizontal and vertical space, in pixels, between cells.

COLS is an integer that specifies the number of columns in the table. If specified, it helps to speed up processing of the table.

FRAME specifies which outer borders are displayed. FRAME can be one of the following: VOID, ABOVE, BELOW, HSIDES, LHS, RHS, VSIDES, BOX, or BORDER.

RULES specifies which inner borders are displayed. RULES can be one of the following: NONE, GROUPS, ROWS, COLS, or ALL.

WIDTH is an integer that specifies the width of the table, in pixels. The width can also be specified as a percentage (%).

The caption is defined with the <CAPTION> tag, which has the following syntax:

<CAPTION [ALIGN="*align*"] [VALIGN="*valign*"]>

</CAPTION>

The attributes are as follows:

ALIGN specifies the alignment of the caption, which is center-aligned by default. ALIGN can be one of the following: LEFT, CENTER, or RIGHT.

VALIGN specifies the vertical alignment of the caption, which is bottom-aligned by default. VALIGN can be one of the following: TOP, MIDDLE, BOTTOM, or BASELINE.

The table rows are defined with the <TR></TR> tags, which have the following syntax:

```
<TR [ALIGN="align"] [BACKGROUND="url"] [BGCOLOR="#rrggbb"]
[BORDERCOLOR="#rrggbb"] [BORDERCOLORDARK="#rrggbb"]
[BORDERCOLORLIGHT="#rrggbb"] [VALIGN="valign"]>
```

```
</TR>
```

The attributes are as follows:

ALIGN specifies the alignment of the row, which is left-aligned by default. ALIGN can be one of the following: LEFT, CENTER, or RIGHT.

BACKGROUND specifies a URL of an image to be used as a background graphic for the table row.

BGCOLOR specifies the background color (in hexadecimal RGB format or as a recognized color name) of the row.

BORDERCOLOR specifies the border color (in hexadecimal RGB format or as a recognized color name) for the row. It will work only if a value other than 0 is specified for the BORDER attribute of the <TABLE></TABLE> tags.

BORDERCOLORDARK specifies the shadow color (in hexadecimal RGB format or as a recognized color name) of a 3-D border for the row. It will work only if a value other than 0 is specified for the BORDER attribute of the <TABLE></TABLE> tags.

BORDERCOLORLIGHT specifies the highlight color (in hexadecimal RGB format or as a recognized color name) of a 3-D border for the row. It will work only if a value other than 0 is specified for the BORDER attribute of the <TABLE></TABLE> tags.

VALIGN specifies the vertical alignment of the text in a row, which is middle-aligned by default. VALIGN can be one of the following: TOP, MIDDLE, BOTTOM, or BASELINE.

The table cells are defined with the <TD></TD> and <TH></TH> tags, which have the following syntax:

```
<TD or TH [ALIGN="align"] [BACKGROUND="url"]
[BGCOLOR="#rrggbb"] [BORDERCOLOR="#rrggbb"]
[BORDERCOLORDARK="#rrggbb"][BORDERCOLORLIGHT="#rrggbb"]
[COLSPAN="integer"] [NOWRAP] [ROWSPAN="integer"]
[VALIGN="valign"]>
```

```
</TD or /TH>
```

The attributes are as follows:

ALIGN specifies the horizontal alignment of the text in a cell, which is center-aligned by default. ALIGN can be one of the following: LEFT, CENTER, or RIGHT.

BACKGROUND specifies a URL of an image to be used as a background graphic for the cell.

BGCOLOR specifies the background color (in hexadecimal RGB format or as a recognized color name) for the cell.

BORDERCOLOR specifies the border color (in hexadecimal RGB format or as a recognized color name) for the cell. It will work only if a value other than 0 is specified for the BORDER attribute of the <TABLE></TABLE> tags.

BORDERCOLORDARK specifies the shadow color (in hexadecimal RGB format or as a recognized color name) of a 3-D border for the cell. It will work only if a value other than 0 is specified for the BORDER attribute of the <TABLE></TABLE> tags.

BORDERCOLORLIGHT specifies the highlight color (in hexadecimal RGB format or as a recognized color name) of a 3-D border for the cell. It will work only if a value other than 0 is specified for the BORDER attribute of the <TABLE></TABLE> tags.

COLSPAN is an integer that specifies the number of table columns the cell should span.

NOWRAP, when specified, indicates that text should not wrap in a cell.

ROWSPAN is an integer that specifies the number of table rows this cell spans.

VALIGN specifies the vertical alignment of the text in a cell, which is middle-aligned by default. VALIGN can be one of the following: TOP, MIDDLE, BOTTOM, or BASELINE.

Here is an example that shows the table tags and some of their attributes:

```
<TABLE ALIGN="RIGHT" BACKGROUND="truck.gif" BORDER="3"
BORDERCOLOR="Blue" BORDERCOLORDARK="Green" WIDTH="80%">
    <CAPTION ALIGN="RIGHT" VALIGN="TOP">
    Caption to appear flush right on top of the table
    </CAPTION>
```

(continued)

427

continued

```
<TR>
    <TH COLSPAN="3">
    Column Heading
    </TH>
</TR>
<TR ALIGN="RIGHT" BGCOLOR="#FFFFFF">
    <TH>
    Column One
    </TH>
    <TH>
    Column Two
    </TH>
    <TH>
    Column Three
    </TH>
</TR>
<TR>
    <TD>
    Data for Column One
    </TD>
    <TD>
    Data for Column Two
    </TD>
    <TD ALIGN="RIGHT">
    Data for Column Three
    </TD>
</TR>
</TABLE>
```

The TextArea Tag

The TextArea tag is used to implement the intrinsic TextArea control, which is a multiline text box. The TextArea tag is defined by the <TEXTAREA> </TEXTAREA> tags, which have the following syntax:

<TEXTAREA [COLS="*integer*"] [NAME="*name*"] [ROWS="*integer*"]>

</TEXTAREA>

The attributes are as follows:

COLS is an integer that specifies the width of the text area, in characters.

NAME specifies the name of the form input variable associated with the control. Form input variables are passed to a back-end process when the form is submitted.

ROWS is an integer that specifies the height of the text area, in lines of text.

Here is an example of the use of the TextArea tag:

```
<TEXTAREA COLS="40" NAME="txtData" ROWS="5">
This is text that appears in the TextArea control
</TEXTAREA>
```

The Text Formatting Tags

The following table lists the common text formatting tags. These tags are used to change the style and size of text. All of these tags are used with the *<TAG>text to format</TAG>* syntax.

Tag	Usage
<ADDRESS></ADDRESS>	Used to format a company address on the web page.
<B></B>	Used to make text bold.
<BLOCKQUOTE></BLOCKQUOTE>	Indents left and right margins. Most often used for quotations.
<CENTER></CENTER>	Used to center text and images horizontally on the page.
<CODE></CODE>	Used to make a small font. Most often used for code samples.
<EM></EM>	Used to emphasize text, most often by displaying text in italic.
<H1></H1> <H2></H2> <H3></H3> <H4></H4> <H5></H5> <H6></H6>	Used to format the size of text on the page; H1 is the largest size, and H6 is the smallest.
<I></I>	Used to italicize text.
<STRIKE></STRIKE>	Used to create strikethrough text.
<STRONG></STRONG>	Used to emphasize text, most often by displaying text in bold.
<U></U>	Used to underline text.

Colors in HTML Documents

Like the <BODY> tag, many other HTML tags have attributes that add color to a page. In the Internet Explorer, these colors can be specified in RGB format, with a # sign in front of the hexadecimal number. The format is "#rrggbb"; an example of green is "#00FF00". The colors can also be specified with named arguments. The Internet Explorer recognizes the following color names: Aqua, Black, Blue, Fuchsia, Gray, Green, Lime, Maroon, Navy, Olive, Purple, Red, Silver, Teal, White, and Yellow.

Coding Standards

When you are learning any new language, it helps to have some standard rules to follow. The standards presented here are a combination of the generally accepted standards for Microsoft Visual Basic for Applications programs and the standards I have developed through my experience with Microsoft Visual Basic, Scripting Edition. Although you can freely modify these standards to fit your needs, you might want to consider using them as a starting point when you begin to develop your own interactive web applications.

HTML Standards

I recommend that you place your HTML code into three separate sections: the head, the script, and the body sections. This empty HTML code structure shows the relationship between these main sections:

```
<HTML>
<HEAD>
<SCRIPT>
<!--
-->
</SCRIPT>
</HEAD>
<BODY>
</BODY>
</HTML>
```

The Head Section

The head section contains the root URL (specified by the <BASE> tag), the <TITLE></TITLE> tags, and the script section. Here's an example:

```
<HEAD>
<BASE HREF="http://www.vb-bootcamp.com">
<TITLE>Coding Standards</TITLE>
```

(continued)

continued

```
<SCRIPT LANGUAGE="VBScript">
<!--
-->
</SCRIPT>
</HEAD>
```

The Script Section

In the examples shown in this book, I place all of the VBScript code into the script section within the head section. Although VBScript code can appear anywhere in an HTML document, placing it in this area provides a consistent look and feel to your code, making it easier to debug and maintain. You can use as many sets of <SCRIPT></SCRIPT> tags as you need; however, I strongly recommend that you place all of the script sections together at the top of the page, just inside the head section. The <SCRIPT></SCRIPT> tags separate code into code modules and can affect the scope of variables declared within them. The script section should contain comment marks to hide the code from old browsers that do not support scripting. Here's an example showing a simple script section:

```
<HEAD>
<SCRIPT LANGUAGE="VBScript">
<!--
    Sub subroutine name
        VBScript code
    End Sub
-->
</SCRIPT>
<SCRIPT LANGUAGE="VBScript" EVENT="OnClick" FOR="btnOne">
<!--
    VBScript code for the btnOne OnClick event
-->
</SCRIPT>
</HEAD>
```

The Body Section

All of the code for the formatted text and forms that will appear on the actual HTML page is placed in the body section. The controls in the forms can be referenced by VBScript code in the script section. Here's a brief example showing a body section:

```
<BODY>
<FORM NAME="frmTest">
<INPUT TYPE="BUTTON" NAME="btnOne" VALUE="Push Me!">
</FORM>
</BODY>
```

VBScript Standards

The following coding standards are derived from the existing Visual Basic for Applications coding standards. If you are familiar with Visual Basic for Applications, you will have no trouble adopting these standards.

Object Naming

Every object in your VBScript code should have a name that indicates the class of the object and its function in the program. The common approach is to use a three-letter, lowercase prefix followed by a meaningful name. For example, a text box that has an address in it might be named *txtAddress*. The following table presents some suggested prefixes for the most common intrinsic and ActiveX controls:

Object Class	Suggested Prefix
Intrinsic Text, TextArea, and Password controls	txt
Intrinsic Button, Submit, and Reset controls	btn or cmd
Intrinsic Select control	lst
Intrinsic Radio Button control	opt
Intrinsic CheckBox control	chk
ActiveX Label control	lbl
ActiveX Timer control	tmr
ActiveX Graph control	gph
ActiveX TextBox control	txt
ActiveX ListBox control	lst
ActiveX ComboBox control	cbo
ActiveX Spin control	spn
ActiveX Button control	btn or cmd
ActiveX CheckBox control	chk
ActiveX Option Button control	opt

433

Variable Naming

Every variable in VBScript code should have a meaningful name that specifies the scope of the variable, the data type of the variable, and the function of the variable. As with objects, prefixes are used to indicate the most important information. Although VBScript supports only the variant data type, you should use the appropriate prefix to indicate the type of variant in use (for example, a script-level counter might be named *sintCount*). The following table presents the standard VBScript variable prefixes:

Data Type	Prefix
Boolean	bln
Byte	byt
Date/Time	dtm
Double	dbl
Error	err
Integer	int
Long	lng
Object	obj
Single	sng
String	str

The scope of a variable is also indicated with a prefix, as shown in the following table:

Scope	Declaration Area	Prefix
Procedure-level: available only to the procedure in which it is defined	Inside functions and subroutines	None
Script-level: available to the entire script code	Outside functions and subroutines	s

Comments

Both HTML and VBScript code should be well commented. As a rule, an HTML document should have inline comments where appropriate. VBScript code should be commented inline but should also have a header comment for each function or subroutine. A function header for a VBScript routine should contain at least the author, purpose, and revision history information.

The following code shows how VBScript and HTML code can be commented:

```
<HEAD>
<SCRIPT LANGUAGE="VBScript">
<!--
    Sub OperationPad(intIndex)

        'Author: New Technology Solutions, Inc.
        'Purpose: Handle addition, subtraction, multiplication, and
        'division
        '5/1/96 Original

        Call DoPending()
        'VBScript Comment: Reset all flags
        intKeyStrokes = 0
        blnDecimal = 0
        Call UpdateDisplay(dblStorage)    'Update calculator display
    End Sub
-->
</SCRIPT>
</HEAD>
<BODY>
<FORM NAME="frmCalculator">    <!-- Form containing the calculator -->
<!--
This is the seven button
-->
<INPUT TYPE="BUTTON" NAME="btnSeven" VALUE="7" OnClick="Call NumPad(7)">
</FORM>
</BODY>
```

Case Sensitivity

Although both VBScript and HTML are case insensitive, in this book I show HTML code, HTML attributes, and HTML keywords in uppercase to distinguish them from VBScript, which is shown in mixed case. Here's an example that demonstrates this usage:

```
<SCRIPT LANGUAGE="VBScript">
<!--
    Sub btnOne_Click
        MsgBox "Hello"
    End Sub
-->
</SCRIPT>
<FORM>
<INPUT TYPE="BUTTON" VALUE="Push Me" NAME="btnOne">
</FORM>
```

The <!DOCTYPE> Tag

Although the <!DOCTYPE> tag is not used in the examples in this book, you should be aware of it. It is the first tag in your HTML document and specifies the version of HTML used in the document. <!DOCTYPE> is a required tag for HTML 3.2–compliant documents and has the following format:

```
<!DOCTYPE HTML PUBLIC "-//W3C//DTD HTML 3.2//EN">
```

Features of Microsoft Visual Basic for Applications That Are Not Supported in Microsoft Visual Basic, Scripting Edition

Microsoft Visual Basic, Scripting Edition, is a subset of Microsoft Visual Basic for Applications (VBA). Therefore, many of the features and keywords used in VBA can also be used in VBScript. Some features and keywords that can be used in VBA are not supported in VBScript, however. This table lists those features and keywords.

Category	Omitted Feature/Keyword
Array handling	Array function Option Base Private, Public Declaring arrays with lower bound <>0
Collection	Add, Count, Item, Remove Using ! character to access collections
Conditional compilation	#Const #If...Then...#Else
Constants/Literals	Const All intrinsic constants Type-declaration characters
Control flow	DoEvents For Each...Next GoSub...Return, GoTo

(continued)

continued

Category	Omitted Feature/Keyword
Control flow *(continued)*	On Error GoTo On…GoSub, On…GoTo Line Numbers, Line Labels With…End With
Conversion	CCur, CVar, CVDate Format Str, Val
Data types	All intrinsic data types except Variant Type…End Type
Date/Time	Date statement, Time statement Timer
DDE	LinkExecute LinkPoke LinkRequest LinkSend
Debugging	Debug.Print End, Stop
Declaration	Declare (for declaring DLLs) Property Get, Property Let, Property Set Public, Private, Static ParamArray, Optional New
Error handling	Erl, Error On Error…Resume Resume, Resume Next
File Input/Output	All
Financial functions	All
Object manipulation	CreateObject GetObject TypeOf
Objects	Clipboard Collection
Operators	Like
Options	Deftype Option Base Option Compare Option Private Module

Category	Omitted Feature/Keyword
Strings	Fixed-length strings
	LSet, RSet
	Mid statement
	StrConv
Using objects	TypeName
	Using! to access collections

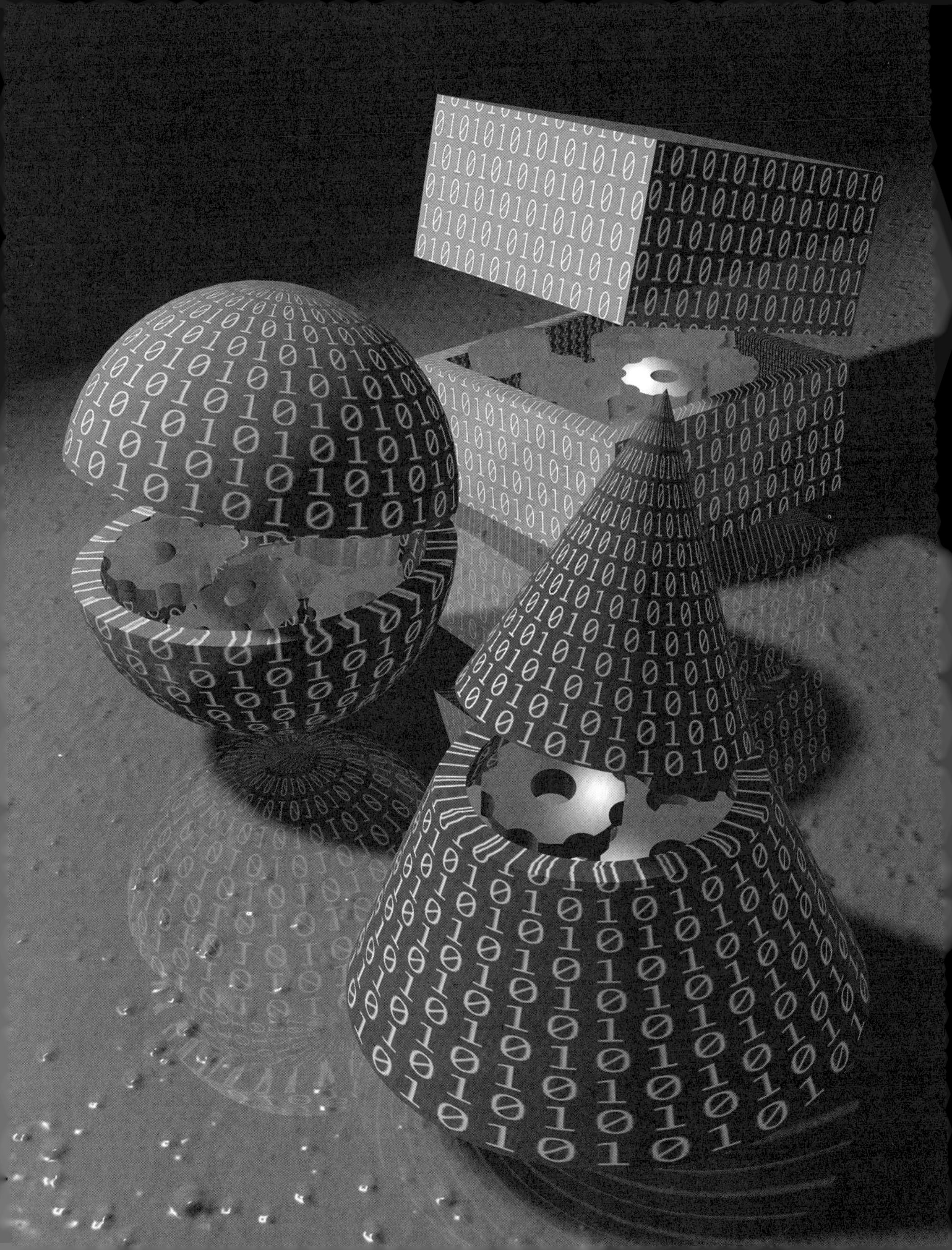

Interactive Web Sites

The web sites listed here are good resources for up-to-the-minute information on many of the subjects covered in this book. All the links to these sites are available on the companion CD, on a web page in the folder named websites.

Sites for Use with This Book

Inside Microsoft Visual Basic, Scripting Edition
http://www.microsoft.com/mspress/updates/243/
This site has information on new developments related to this book.

New Technology Solutions, Inc.
http://www.vb-bootcamp.com/
This site has examples from the book, as well as software articles for ActiveX developers.

Microsoft
http://www.microsoft.com/
This site is Microsoft's home page, which contains recent announcements and links to Microsoft technologies.

Microsoft Visual Basic, Scripting Edition
http://www.microsoft.com/vbscript/
This site has documentation, samples, and a download area for VBScript.

Microsoft Internet Explorer
http://www.microsoft.com/ie/
This site has information and a download area for the Internet Explorer.

Microsoft Site Builder Workshop
http://www.microsoft.com/intdev/

This site has links to many helpful Microsoft web site resources.

Microsoft ActiveX Resource Area
http://www.microsoft.com/activex/

This site has information on Microsoft ActiveX resources.

Microsoft ActiveX Software Development Kit
http://www.microsoft.com/intdev/sdk/

This site has information and a download area for the ActiveX SDK.

Microsoft ActiveX Control Pad
http://www.microsoft.com/workshop/author/cpad/

This site has information, a tutorial, and a download area for the ActiveX Control Pad.

Microsoft HTML Reference
http://www.microsoft.com/workshop/author/newhtml/

This site has an Internet Explorer author's guide and an HTML reference.

Microsoft Internet Information Server
http://www.microsoft.com/InfoServ/

This site has information and a download area for IIS.

Microsoft PowerPoint Animation Player User Guide
http://internet/mspowerpoint/internet/player/userguide.htm

This site has a user guide for the Microsoft PowerPoint Animation Player.

Microsoft dbWeb
http://www.microsoft.com/intdev/dbweb/

This site has information, a tutorial, and a download area for the Microsoft dbWeb utility.

Resources for ActiveX Controls

CMP
http://www.activextra.com/
This site has general-use ActiveX controls.

CNET
http://www.cnet.com/activex/
This site has general-use ActiveX controls and information on registering controls.

CyberSource Corp.
http://www.software.net/components/activex.htm
This site has general-use ActiveX controls and reusable software components.

FarPoint Technologies
http://www.fpoint.com/
This site has general-use ActiveX controls.

Innovision
http://www.active-x.com/
This site has general-use ActiveX controls.

Media Architects
http://www.mediarch.com/
This site has multimedia ActiveX controls.

Micro Modeling Associates
http://www.micromodeling.com/
This site has ActiveX control demos and information on Microsoft Office and Microsoft BackOffice solutions.

Microsoft ActiveX Component Gallery
http://www.microsoft.com/activex/controls/
This site has demonstration and download areas for ActiveX controls.

Online Interactive
http://www.webtools.atoncesoftware.com/
This site has general-use ActiveX controls.

Part Bank
http://www.partbank.com/activex/
This site has general-use ActiveX controls.

Xtras
http://www.xtras.com/activex/
This site has general-use ActiveX controls.

Other Sites

Developers Workshop
http://www.developers.com/
This site has software development tools.

Fawcette Publications
http://www.windx.com/
This site has development tools and Visual Basic resources.

VeriSign, Inc.
http://www.verisign.com/
This site has digital authentication services.

Visual Basic Programmer's Journal
http://www.windx.com/
This is the developer exchange site for the *Visual Basic Programmer's Journal.*

Windows 95
http://www.windows95.com/
This is a non-Microsoft site that has shareware for Windows 95 users.

World Wide Web Consortium
http://www.w3.org/pub/WWW/
This site has information on current HTML specifications.

APPENDIX E

Glossary

ActiveX   A term describing the suite of products and technologies produced by Microsoft to support web development. ActiveX components are built on the Component Object Model (COM).

ActiveX control   A reusable software component that can be accessed from a variety of development environments, including web pages hosted by the Microsoft Internet Explorer.

address   An identifier for a computer or site on the Internet. For example, an IP address could be *123.45.6.78*, and an email address could be *fred@bedrock.com*.

Automation   A technology that allows a client application to create and control an object by using the exposed object's properties and methods.

bandwidth   The amount of data, measured in bits per second, that can be passed through a network.

browser   A client-side application used to view web documents.

client   An application or computer that communicates with and requests information from a server.

code signing   The process of embedding a digital signature inside software for the purpose of verifying its authenticity.

com   An Internet address extension indicating that the web site is a commercial site.

Common Gateway Interface (CGI)   The part of a web server that gathers input and calls other programs to process it. These programs are typically called *CGI programs* or *CGI scripts* and can be written in a variety of programming languages, such as PERL or C. CGI is an older standard (as compared, for example, to the newer ISAPI technology).

datasource   Typically, a database that has been defined with the ODBC Administrator and that is compliant with Open Database Connectivity (ODBC). These ODBC-compliant databases are given an alias name that becomes known as the datasource.

domain name   A unique alphanumeric name for an Internet site.

Domain Name System (DNS)   A system for translating alphanumeric domain-name addresses into Internet Protocol (IP) addresses.

dynamic-link library (DLL)   A file containing sets of reusable functions. These libraries can link into the memory space of an executable at runtime to provide additional functionality.

file transfer protocol (FTP)   A communications standard for transferring files between computers on the Internet. FTP is supported by the Microsoft Internet Information Server.

firewall   A security measure that protects information and prevents access to a computer or network system.

gateway   A computer that connects one network to another network operating on a different protocol.

Gopher   A file transfer system that allows users to search Gopher servers with menus. Gopher is supported by the Microsoft Internet Information Server.

Graphics Interchange Format (GIF)   A compressed graphics file format that is popular on the Internet.

home page   The first web page displayed when a web site is visited by a browser. Typically, the home page has links to other web pages within the web site.

host   A computer on a network that allows users to log on to it.

HTML attribute   A modifying parameter to an HTML tag, as in the BGCOLOR attribute of the BODY tag.

HTML tag   The principal formatting mechanism for web pages. HTML tags tell the browser what to do.

Hypertext Markup Language (HTML)   The coding standard for creating web pages. It is a subset of Standard Generalized Markup Language (SGML).

Hypertext Transfer Protocol (HTTP)   The communications standard that defines how web servers respond to requests.

in-process   A term that refers to components that are hosted inside the memory space of an application. ActiveX components run in-process with the Microsoft Internet Explorer.

Integrated Services Digital Network (ISDN)   A data transfer mechanism that can send data at a speed of up to 128 KB per second over a standard phone line.

Internet Database Connector (IDC)   An ISAPI DLL that allows access to data in an ODBC datasource from a web page.

Internet Protocol (IP)   The communications standard that handles the routing of packets across the Internet. IP works along with Transmission Control Protocol (TCP).

Internet Server Application Programming Interface (ISAPI)   The set of function calls that provides access to the functionality of the Microsoft Internet Information Server. Although ISAPI applications have many capabilities, several are used to publish databases. Some examples are the Internet Database Connector (IDC), OLEISAPI, and Microsoft dbWeb.

Internet service provider (ISP)   A third-party company that provides access to the Internet or rents server space for web sites. Examples of ISPs include the Microsoft Network, America OnLine, and CompuServe.

intranet   A local area network (LAN) that runs TCP/IP protocol and provides HTML publishing servers that can be accessed by a client using a browser. Typically, intranets are created by corporations for the purpose of publishing in-house data while taking advantage of platform-independent browsers.

intrinsic control   A user interface device supported inherently by HTML. Examples include the Button control and the Select control.

IP address   A four-part number used to uniquely identify each computer on the Internet. Each part can be a maximum of three integers, and parts are separated by a dot. The format of the address is *xxx.xxx.xxx.xxx*; an example is 123.45.6.78.

local area network (LAN)   A group of networked computers, usually confined to a single office or building.

Microsoft Internet Explorer   The Microsoft web browser.

Microsoft Internet Information Server (IIS)   A server designed for use with Windows NT Server. It provides WWW, FTP, and Gopher services.

mirror site   A site that offers copies of the same files that another site offers. Mirror sites are often used to provide additional sites from which users can download popular files.

Multipurpose Internet Mail Extensions (MIME)   A system of identifying Internet mail content to browsers and servers. MIME allows disparate types of information, as in multimedia, to be contained in email.

name resolution   The process of mapping domain names to their IP addresses.

Network News Transfer Protocol (NNTP)   A communications standard for distributing and retrieving news articles. The largest news distribution network is Usenet.

OLE   A technology that allows cross-process communication. Examples of OLE include linking, embedding, and drag and drop features. The term *OLE* previously referred to a wider range of technologies, many of which have been replaced by the term *ActiveX*.

OLEISAPI   An interface that allows web pages to access the functionality of software components on IIS. OLEISAPI is embodied in a single dynamic-link library called oleisapi.dll.

Open Database Connectivity (ODBC)   An open standard for communicating with datasources. Standardized communication results in "database independence," which allows a single front-end application to communicate with varying back-end datasources.

packet   A piece of electronic information sent over the Internet. Each packet contains the destination address, the sender's address, data, and error-handling information.

Post Office Protocol (POP3)   A protocol that specifies how a computer connects to a mail server and downloads email.

Remote Data Objects (RDO)   A set of objects that handle access to remote data, such as an ODBC datasource. These objects ship with Microsoft Visual Basic 4.0, Enterprise Edition.

script   A series of commands that can be executed.

scripting engine   An interpreter capable of executing the commands embedded in a script.

server   An application or computer that provides information or functional services to a client.

Simple Mail Transfer Protocol (SMTP)   A TCP/IP protocol that specifies how computers exchange email.

socket   A term denoting a communications link with the Internet. Several sockets can be open on a single computer at once.

Standard Generalized Markup Language (SGML)   A set of formatting tags that show the logical relationships between text segments.

Transmission Control Protocol/Internet Protocol (TCP/IP)   A communications standard for all computers on the Internet. On the sending end, TCP breaks the data to be sent into data segments. IP assembles segments into packets that contain data segments, as well as sender and destination addresses. IP then sends packets to the router for delivery. On the receiving end, IP receives the packets and breaks them down into data segments. TCP assembles the data segments into the original data set.

Uniform Resource Locator (URL)   An Internet address specifying a server to which users can connect with web browsers (for example, http://www.microsoft.com). It typically consists of a protocol, a host name, a folder structure, and a filename (for example, http://some_host.com/some_folder/some_web_page.htm).

web server   A server specifically designed for the Internet. Web servers typically provide data in the form of HTML pages using HTTP.

World Wide Web Consortium   An industry consortium that seeks to promote standards for the web.

INDEX

Numbers in italics refer to figures or tables.

SPECIAL CHARACTERS

<> (angle brackets), 11

A

<A> (anchor) tag
  HREF attribute, 15, 32, 143
  implementing menu structure with, 32
  overview, 403–4
ACTION attribute (<FORM> tag)
  biblio.idc example, 130–31
  CGI example, 122
  defined, 37, 408
  event registration example, 250
  IDC example, 124–25
  invoking IDC from, 124–25, 216
  invoking OLEISAPI from, 159
  newsletter subscription example, 210–11
Action property (Form object), *57*
ActiveX, defined, 445
ActiveX components
  creating, 157–60
  event registration example, 269–88
  generating with OLEISAPI Wizard, 184–90
  in-process vs. out-of-process, 156
  parsing example, 160–68
  registering on Windows NT server, 158, 287–88
ActiveX Control Editor, 347–53
ActiveX Control Lister, 87–88
ActiveX Control Pad
  ActiveX Control Editor, 347–53
  defined, 25
  HTML Layout control example, 90–91
  HTML Source Editor, 346–47

ActiveX Control Pad, *continued*
  interactive order form example, 369–88
  list of features, 346
  overview, 88–89, 345
  Script Wizard, 353–58
ActiveX controls
  on companion CD, 94–101
  defined, 7, 445
  inserting with ActiveX Control Lister, 87–88
  inserting with ActiveX Control Pad, 88–89, 347–53
  and Internet Explorer, 8
  Label control, 94–95, 248, 249–50
  list of attributes for <OBJECT> tag, 79–80
  Marquee control, 100–101
  menu support, 33–35
  New Item control, 97–98
  PowerPoint Animation Player, 205, 206–9
  standards for naming in VBScript, 433
  Stock Ticker control, 98–99
  Timer control, 95–97, 255, 259, 300–304, 306, 365–66, 368–69, 381–82
  and VBScript, 8
  Web site resources, 442–44
ActiveX Scripting standard, defined, 19
addresses, defined, 445
<ADDRESS> tag, 429
Alert method (Window object), *54*
aliases, use of, 250
ALIGN attribute
  <CAPTION> tag, 425
  <DIV> tag, 406
  <HR> tag, 411
  <IFRAME> tag, 412
  <IMG> tag, 413
  <INPUT> tag, 415
  <MARQUEE> tag, 419
  <OBJECT> tag, 79, 420
  <P> tag, 423
  <TABLE> tag, 424

ALIGN attribute, *continued*

    <TD> or <TH> tag, 427

    <TR> tag, 426

ALinkColor property (Document object), *55*

ALL_HTTP variable (htx files), *137*

ALT attribute (<IMG> tag), 413

alx files, 359, 371

Anchor object, 61

Anchors property (Document object), *56*

anchor tag, 15, 32, 143, 403–4. *See also* Link object

animate.alx file, 362, 367, 368

animate.htm file, 362, 369

animations

    adding PowerPoint animation to web pages,
        205, 206–9

    PowerPoint animation in online bookstore
        project, 337–38

    source code for butterfly, *367–68*

    Timer control in online bookstore project, 306

AppCodeName property (Navigator object), 62

Application property (Internet Explorer), *45*

AppName property (Navigator object), 62

AppVersion property (Navigator object), 62

AttachmentPathName property (MAPIMessages
    control), *227*

attributes, HTML, list of, 403–30

author.idc file, 315

AUTH_TYPE variable (htx files), *137*

Automation

    defined, 445

    overview, 41–44

    and Registry, 85

B

<B> (bold) tag, 429

BACKGROUND attribute

    <BODY> tag, 402

    <TABLE> tag, 424

    <TD> or <TH> tag, 427

    <TR> tag, 426

Back method (History object), 62

bandwidth, defined, 445

bar.htm file, 353

barpie.htm file, 355–58

<BASEFONT> tag, 316, 404–5

<BASE> tag, 404

<%begindetail%> tag (htx files), *137*, 317, 319

BEHAVIOR attribute (<MARQUEE> tag), 419

BGCOLOR attribute

    <BODY> tag, 402

    <MARQUEE> tag, 419

    <TABLE> tag, 424

    <TD> or <TH> tag, 427

    <TR> tag, 426

BGColor property (Document object), *56*

BGPROPERTIES attribute (<BODY> tag), 402

<BGSOUND> tag, 405

biblio.htm file, *130–31*

biblio.htx file, *135–36*

biblio.idc file, 130, 131–32, *132*

biblio.mdb file

    using for IDC record retrieval example, 129

    using for online bookstore project, 294–96

<BLOCKQUOTE> tag, 429

body section, HTML document

    defined, 14, 401

    list of tags, 403–30

    overview, 401–3

    standards for coding, 432–33

<BODY> tag

    code example, *402–3*

    list of attributes, 402

    overview, 14, 401–3

boldface, HTML document

    adding with <B> tag, 429

    adding with <STRONG> tag, 15

bookstor.htm file

    code listing, *307–14*

    creating, 298–306

    opening from Internet Explorer, 341–43

BORDER attribute
  <IMG> tag, 413
  <OBJECT> tag, 79, 420
  <TABLE> tag, 424
BORDERCOLOR attribute
  <TABLE> tag, 424
  <TD> or <TH> tag, 427
  <TR> tag, 426
BORDERCOLORDARK attribute
  <TABLE> tag, 425
  <TD> or <TH> tag, 427
  <TR> tag, 426
BORDERCOLORLIGHT attribute
  <TABLE> tag, 425
  <TD> or <TH> tag, 427
  <TR> tag, 426

 (line break) tag, 15, 405–6
browsers
  defined, 1, 445
  as desktop, 26
  VBScript compatibility, 25–26
Busy property (Internet Explorer), 45
butterfly animation example, 363–69
Button control, intrinsic, 69, 70–71
buy.idc file, 143
bytecomp.alx file, 372–83
bytecomp.htm file, 370–72

C

calculator example
  code listing, 113–20
  overview, 103–4
Calendar control (ActiveX), 323, 324, 327–28
<CAPTION> tag, 425
case, standards for using, 436
CELLPADDING attribute (<TABLE> tag), 425
CELLSPACING attribute (<TABLE> tag), 425
<CENTER> tag, 429
certificate authority, 92–93

CGI (Common Gateway Interface)
  for back-end processing, 121
  defined, 446
  vs. DLLs, 123
  vs. IDC, 124–25
  and Internet Information Server, 190–91
  vs. Internet Server API, 122–23
  vs. ISAPI, 6
  submitting form variables, 122
Chart control (ActiveX), 350–53
CheckBox control, intrinsic, 69, 71–72, 252
CHECKED attribute (<INPUT> tag), 415
CLASS attribute (<DIV> tag), 406
classes, JavaScript vs. VBScript support, 26–27, 30
CLASSID attribute (<OBJECT> tag), 79, 81, 84, 85, 420
class identifiers, 84–87
class modules
  ActiveX component requirement, 157–58
  creating, 271–85
CLEAR attribute (
 tag), 405
Clear method (Document object), 56
ClearTimeout method (Window object), 54
Click event vs. OnClick event, 69, 81
client applications, 8–9, 445
ClientToWindow method (Internet Explorer), 47
Close method (Document object), 56
Close method (Window object), 54
CODEBASE attribute (<OBJECT> tag), 79, 420
code modules
  adding Main subroutine, 286
  supported in VBScript, 35, 38–40
code signing, defined, 92–93, 445
<CODE> tag, 429
CODETYPE attribute (<OBJECT> tag), 79, 420
color
  in HTML documents, 402, 430
  properties of Document object, 55, 56
  for web page tables, 424–25, 426, 427

COLOR attribute
    <BASEFONT> tag, 405
    <FONT> tag, 407
    <HR> tag, 411
COLS attribute
    <FRAMESET> tag, 410
    <TABLE> tag, 425
    <TEXTAREA> tag, 428
COLSPAN attribute (<TD> or <TH> tag), 427
com extension, defined, 445
comments
    code examples, *435*
    in HTML documents, 406, 435
    in VBScript code, 435
<COMMENT> tag, 406
Common Gateway Interface. *See* CGI (Common Gateway Interface)
Compose method (MAPIMessages control), *227*
Confirm method (Window object), *54*
constants, intrinsic, 32
Container property (Internet Explorer), *45*
CONTENT_LENGTH variable (htx files), *137*
ContentType field (idc files), *133*
CONTENT_TYPE variable (htx files), *137*
control arrays
    defined, 30
    unsupported in VBScript, 30–31
    workaround for, 30–31
ControlBox control. *See* intrinsic Select control
Control Lister, 87–88
controls, ActiveX vs. intrinsic HTML, 68. *See also* ActiveX controls; intrinsic HTML controls
CONTROLS attribute (<IMG> tag), 413
Cookie property (Document object), *56*
CryptoAPI, 93
cryptography, 93
CurrentRecord variable (htx files), *137*

D

Data Access Objects (DAOs), 222
DATA attribute (<OBJECT> tag), 80, 421

databases. *See also* ODBC datasource
    biblio.mdb file, 129, 294–96
    event registration IDC example, 138–43
    eventreg.mdb file, 243, 246, 288
    members-only page IDC example, 151–55
    ODBC drivers for, 126
    product showcase IDC example, 143–51
    updating using RDO, 277–79
Data Manager, 198–200
datasource, defined, 446. *See also* ODBC datasource
Datasource field (idc files), *133*, 217
data types, in VBScript, 36
data validation
    testing in event registration project, 289
    testing in newsletter subscription project, 235–36
    VBScript code for, *212–16*
dbWeb. *See* Microsoft dbWeb
dbWeb Administrator, 393–95
dbWeb Service, 396–98
debugging VBScript code, 25, 31, 345
DECLARE attribute (<OBJECT> tag), 80, 421
DefaultParameters field (idc files), *133*
DefaultStatus property (Window object), *53*
desktop, unifying, 8, 26
detail tags, 136
<DIR> (directory list) tag, 416
DIRECTION attribute (<MARQUEE> tag), 419
Distributed Component Object Model (DCOM), 390
<DIV> tag
    adding VBScript routine, 368
    overview, 406–7
<DL> (definition list) tag, 15
DLL files, creating, 158
DLLs. *See* dynamic-link libraries (DLLs)
<!DOCTYPE> tag, 399, 436
Document object
    example of use, 64–66
    list of methods, *56–57*

Document object, *continued*
  list of properties, *55–56*
  overview, 54–57
  use in event registration project, 259
Document property (Internet Explorer), *45*
Document property (Window object), *53*
domain names, defined, 446
Domain Name System (DNS), 390, 446
downloading, security issues, 92–93
DownloadMail property (MAPISession control), *226*
dynamic-link libraries (DLLs)
  vs. CGI scripts, 123
  defined, 446
  for IIS, 6–7
  and Internet Services API, 123
DYNSRC attribute (<IMG> tag), 413

E

Elements array, 61
Elements property (Form object), *57*
<%else%> tag (htx files), *137*, 318
email.pl file, 122
<EM> (emphasis) tag, 15, 429
Encoding property (Form object), *57*
<%enddetail%> tag (htx files), *137*, 317
<%endif%> tag (htx files), *137*, 318
error-handling routines, 230, 280
EVENT attribute (<SCRIPT> tag), 400
event procedures
  Click event vs. OnClick event, 69, 81
  defined, 39
  in VBScript, 39–40
  Visual Basic for Applications vs. VBScript, 69
eventreg.dll file, 287–88
eventreg.htm file, 288
event registration project
  back-end processing, 269–88
  design objective, 240–41
  HTML code, *260–69*

event registration project, *continued*
  organizing files for, 241–42
  overview, 239, 240–41
  running application, 288–90
  system component requirements, 239–40
eventreg.mdb file, 243, 246, 288
events.htx file, *140–41*
events.idc file, *140*
Excel. *See* Microsoft Excel
Expires field (idc files), *133*

F

FACE attribute (<FONT> tag), 407
FGColor property (Document object), *56*
<%field_name%> tag (htx files), *137*
files
  operations not supported in VBScript, 31
  organizing for event registration project, 241–42
  organizing for newsletter project, 195–96
  organizing for online bookstore project, 293–94
file transfer protocol (FTP), 191, 446
firewall, defined, 446
floating frames, 411–12
folders
  organizing for event registration project, 241–42
  organizing for newsletter project, 195–96
  organizing for online bookstore project, 293–94
<FONT> tag, 15, 316, 407
FOR attribute (<SCRIPT> tag), 401
form input variables, *137*
Form object
  example of use, 66–68
  list of events, *58*
  list of methods, *58*
  list of properties, *57–58*
  overview, 57–58

forms, HTML
    for event registration project, 248–55
    overview, 37
    submitting, 37–38
    VBScript support for, 31, 37–38
    VBScript vs. Visual Basic, 37
Forms property (Document object), *56*
<FORM> tag
    ACTION attribute, 37, 122, 124–25, 130–31,
        159, 210–11, 216, 250
    adding HTML Layout control to, 371
    and Form object, 57–58
    NAME attribute, 37, 122
    overview, 31, 37, 408–9
    syntax, 37
Forward method (History object), 62
FRAME attribute (<TABLE> tag), 425
FRAMEBORDER attribute
    <FRAMESET> tag, 410
    <FRAME> tag, 409
    <IFRAME> tag, 412
frames
    defining with <FRAME> tag, 409–10
    floating, 411–12
    multiple, 410–11
    unsupported, 419–20
<FRAMESET> tag, 410–11
FRAMESPACING attribute (<FRAMESET>
    tag), 410
Frames property (Window object), *53*
<FRAME> tag, 409–10
FrontPage. *See* Microsoft FrontPage
FullName property (Internet Explorer), *45*
FullScreen property (Internet Explorer), *45*
functions, in VBScript, 39

G
GATEWAY_INTERFACE variable (htx files), *137*
gateways, defined, 446
Gauge control, 81–84
GET method, 37

GetProperty method (Internet Explorer), *47*
GoBack method (Internet Explorer), *47*
GoForward method (Internet Explorer), *47*
GoHome method (Internet Explorer), *47*
Go method (History object), 62
Gopher, 191, 446
GoSearch method (Internet Explorer), *47*
graphical user interface (GUI), 220–22
graphics, HTML document
    adding with <IMG> tag, 15, 412–14
    for online bookstore project, 306
Graphics Interchange Format (GIF), defined, 446

H
<H1> through <H6> (heading) tags, 15, 429
Hangman game, 90–91
Hangman HTML file, *91*
Hash property (Location object), *59*
header, HTML document, 399
headings, HTML document, 15, 429
head section, HTML document
    overview, 14, 400
    standards for coding, 431–32
<HEAD> tag, 14
HEIGHT attribute
    <IFRAME> tag, 412
    <IMG> tag, 413
    <MARQUEE> tag, 419
    <OBJECT> tag, 80, 421
Height property (Internet Explorer), *45*
"Hello, World" message, 16–17
Help files
    unsupported in VBScript, 31–32
    using hypertext instead, 32
Hidden control, intrinsic, *69, 72*
Hidden property (Form object), *57*
History object, 62
History property (Window object), *53*
home page. *See also* HTML documents
    defined, 446
    sample HTML code, *11–14*

host, defined, 447

HostName property (Location object), *59*

Host property (Location object), *58*

HREF attribute

  <A> tag, 143, 403

  <BASE> tag, 404

Href property (Location object), *58*

<HR> (horizontal rule) tag, 411

HSPACE attribute

  <IMG> tag, 413

  <MARQUEE> tag, 419

  <OBJECT> tag, 80, 421

htm files. *See also* HTML documents

  defined, 123, *124*

  generating with IDC Wizard, 181, 183

HTML. *See* HTML documents; Hypertext Markup
  Language (HTML)

HTML attribute, defined, 447

HTML documents. *See also* Document object

  adding controls with ActiveX Control Lister,
    87–88

  adding controls with ActiveX Control Pad,
    88–89, 347–53

  adding PowerPoint animation to, 205, 206–9

  biblio.mdb database example, 129–38

  body section, 401–3

  creating for event registration project, 247–69

  creating for newsletter subscription project,
    204–16

  editing code with HTML Source Editor, 346–47

  event registration IDC example, 138–43

  head section, 400

  including scripting languages, 19–27

  members-only page IDC example, 151–55

  and Microsoft dbWeb, 391, 396–98

  options for creating, 9

  overview, 399–403

  product showcase IDC example, 143–51

  sample code for simple page, *11–14*

  script section, 400–401

  sections of, 399–403, 431–33

  standards for coding, 431–33

HTML documents, *continued*

  use of case, 436

  where to put VBScript code, 400–401

HTML extension file. *See* htx files

HTML Layout control (ActiveX), 90–91, 359,
  360, 361–63

HTML Layout Editor

  butterfly animation example, 363–69

  constructing bytecomp.alx file, 372–78

  opening, 363

  overview, 359, *360*

HTML Layout files, 359, 371

HTML Source Editor, 346, *347, 361–63*

<HTML> tag, 399

HTML tags, defined, 447

HTTP_ACCEPT variable (htx files), *138*

httpodbc.dll file, 123, 131

htx files

  code, *135–36*

  generating with IDC Wizard, 181, 184

  list of HTTP variables available, *137–38*

  list of tags available, *137*

  list of variables available, *137*

  for newsletter subscription project, 218–19

  overview, 123, *124,* 135, 136

HWND property (Internet Explorer), *45*

Hypertext Markup Language (HTML)

  defined, 447

  extensions to, 16–17

  overview, 11–17

  VBScript as extender of, 5

Hypertext Transfer Protocol (HTTP),
  defined, 447

I

<I> (italic) tag, 429

ICP. *See* Internet Control Pack (ICP)

ID attribute (<OBJECT> tag), 80, 81, 421

IDC. *See* Internet Database Connector (IDC)

idc files

  biblio.idc example, 130, 131–32

idc files, *continued*

   generating with IDC Wizard, 181, 184

   list of ODBC options, *134*

   list of optional fields, *133*

   list of required fields, *133*

   for newsletter subscription project, 216, 217–18

   for online bookstore search engine, 314–15

   overview, 123, *124*

idcwiz.exe file, 181

<IFRAME> tag, 411–12

<%if%> tag (htx files), *137*, 318

IIS. *See* Internet Information Server (IIS)

<IMG> tag, 15, 412–14

immediate execution, defined, 40

INI files, 84–85

initialization files, 84–85

in-process, defined, 447. *See also* ActiveX components

input forms, 250–55

<INPUT> tag, 16, 39, 68, 251, 414–16

INSERT query, 335–36

integrated debugging environment (IDE), 25, 345

Integrated Services Digital Network (ISDN), 121, 447

interactive order form project

   and ActiveX Control Pad, 345, 346, 369–88

   bytecomp.alx file, 372–78

   bytecomp.htm file, 370–72

   creating order form for, 369–88

   file organization for, 346

   overview, 346, 369

   system component requirements, 345

interface, for publishing intranet newsletter, 220–22

internal networks. *See* intranets, defined

Internet, overview, 1–3

Internet Assistants. *See* Microsoft Office

Internet Control Pack (ICP), 9

Internet Database Connector (IDC)

   vs. CGI, 124–25

   defined, 123, 447

Internet Database Connector (IDC), *continued*

   event registration example, 138–44

   files for utilization, 123–24

   invoking, 216

   members-only page example, 151–55

   vs. OLEISAPI, 155–56

   overview, 6–7, 123–25

   product showcase example, 143–51

   record retrieval example, 129–38

   and search engine for bookstore project, 314–15

   using IDC Wizard with, 181–84

Internet Database Connector Wizard, 181–84

Internet Explorer. *See also* Window object

   and ActiveX controls, 8

   defined, 448

   graphical user interface (GUI), 1, *2*

   intrinsic HTML controls, 68–77

   JavaScript support, 22–24

   list of methods, *47–48*

   list of properties, *45–47*

   object model, 8, 43, *44*, 44–48

   as scripting host, 19

   scripting object model, 52–68

   using objects with, 48–51

Internet Information Server (IIS)

   architecture, 5–6

   and Common Gateway Interface (CGI), 190–91

   defined, 448

   and file transfer protocol (FTP), 191

   and Gopher, 191

   IDC Wizard, 181–84

   OLEISAPI Wizard, 181, 184–90

   overview, 121–22

   scripts directory, 156–57

   and Windows CGI, 190–91

Internet Protocol (IP), defined, 447

Internet Server API (ISAPI). *See also* Internet Database Connector (IDC); OLEISAPI

   defined, 6–7, 123, 447

   Microsoft dbWeb application, 391–98

Internet service providers
  defined, 447
  Microsoft servers for, 390–91
  vs. private servers, 121
intranet newsletter project
  design objective, 194–95
  file organization, 195–96
  overview, 193, 194–95
  running application, 235–37
  sending, 219–35
  system component requirements, 193–94
intranets, defined, 4, 448. *See also* HTML
    documents
intrinsic Button control, *69*, 70–71
intrinsic CheckBox control, *69*, 71–72
intrinsic constants, 32
intrinsic Hidden control, *69*, 72
intrinsic HTML controls
  defined, 448
  in forms, 68
  list of, *69–70*
  overview, 68–70
  standards for naming in VBScript, 433
intrinsic Password control, *70*, 72–73
intrinsic Radio control, *70*, 73–74
intrinsic Reset control, *70*, 74
intrinsic Select control, *70*, 75
intrinsic Submit control, *70*, 75–76
intrinsic TextArea control, *70*, 77
intrinsic Text control, *70*, 76–77
IP addresses, defined, 448
ISAPI. *See* Internet Server API (ISAPI)
isapiwiz.exe file, 181
ISDN, 121, 447
ISImage control (ActiveX)
  adding to HTML layout with HTML Layout
    Editor, 365
  adding by using HTML Layout Editor, 373–74
ISMAP attribute (<IMG> tag), 413
ISPs. *See* Internet service providers

italics, HTML document
  adding with <EM> tag, 15
  adding with <I> tag, 429

J
JavaScript
  "Hello, World" example, 21–22
  and Internet Explorer, 22–24
  language scalability, 27
  overview, 21
  syntax, 21, 26
  together with VBScript, 22–24
  use of objects, 26–27
  vs. VBScript, 21, 26–27
jumps, HTML document, 15

K
KeyPress event, 383

L
Label control (ActiveX)
  adding by using HTML Layout Editor, 364,
    375, 376–77
  adding by using HTML Source Editor, 347,
    348, 349
  in event registration example, 248, 249–50, 254
  overview, 94–95
LANGUAGE attribute (<SCRIPT> tag), 400
LastModified property (Document object), *56*
Layout control, HTML, 90–91
LEFTMARGIN attribute (<BODY> tag), 402
Left property (Internet Explorer), *45*
Length property (History object), 62
<LI> (list item) tag, 416
LINK attribute (<BODY> tag), 402
LinkColor property (Document object), *55*
Link object, 59–61
links, HTML document, 15
Links property (Document object), *56*
lists, HTML document, 15, 416–18
local area network (LAN), defined, 448

LocationName property (Internet Explorer), *45*

Location object, 58–59

Location property (Document object), *56*

Location property (Window object), *53*

LocationURL property (Internet Explorer), *46*

LOOP attribute

  <BGSOUND> tag, 405

  <IMG> tag, 413

  <MARQUEE> tag, 419

M

Mail API. *See* MAPI

mail server, connecting to, 226–27

Main subroutine, adding to event registration
    project, 286

MAPI

  adding controls, 220, 222

  connecting to mail server, 226

MAPIMessages control, 226, 227

MAPISession control, 226

MARGINHEIGHT attribute

  <FRAME> tag, 409

  <IFRAME> tag, 412

MARGINWIDTH attribute

  <FRAME> tag, 409

  <IFRAME> tag, 412

Marquee control (ActiveX), 100–101

<MARQUEE> tag, 302, 418–19

MaxFieldSize field (idc files), *133*

MAXLENGTH attribute (<INPUT> tag), 415

MaxRecords field (idc files), *133*

MaxRecords variable (htx files), *137*

MDI. *See* Multiple Document Interface (MDI)

members.htm file, *153*

members.htx file, *153–55*

members.idc file, *153*

MenuBar property (Internet Explorer), *46*

menus

  ActiveX controls for, 33–35

  HTML workaround, 32–35

  unsupported in VBScript, 32–35

<MENU> tag, 32, 416

METHOD attribute (<FORM> tag), 37, 122, 408

Method property (Form object), *57*

Microsoft Access

  creating database for event registration project,
    242–45

  creating database for intranet newsletter, 198

  creating database for online bookstore project,
    294–96

  event registration IDC example, 138–43

  installing ODBC drivers, 196–98

  members-only page IDC example, 151–55

  ODBC driver, 126, 127–28

  product showcase IDC example, 143–51

  record retrieval IDC example, 129–38

Microsoft Cryptographic Application Program-
    ming Interface, 93

Microsoft dbWeb

  dbWeb Administrator, 393–95

  dbWeb Service, 396–98

  installing, 392

  overview, 391–92

Microsoft Excel

  accessing through Automation, 8, 42

  object model, 43

Microsoft FrontPage, 9

Microsoft Internet Explorer. *See* Internet Explorer

Microsoft Internet Information Server.
    See Internet Information Server (IIS)

Microsoft Office, 9

  Internet Assistants, 9

Microsoft PowerPoint. *See* PowerPoint

Microsoft SQL Server, 126, 391

Microsoft Visual Basic. *See* Visual Basic

Microsoft Visual Basic, Scripting Edition.
    See VBScript

Microsoft Word, 9

mines.htm file, *171*

Minesweeper game

  code listings, *104–13, 171–81*

  Internet version utilizing OLEISAPI, 168–81

Minesweeper game, *continued*
   simple Internet version, 102–3
mirror site, defined, 448
mnuPopUp control, 33
modules, VBScript support for, 35, 38–40
MouseDown event, 382–83
MsgNoteText property (MAPIMessages control),
   227
MsgSubject property (MAPIMessages control), *227*
MULTIPLE attribute (<SELECT> tag), 418
Multiple Document Interface (MDI)
   applications unsupported in VBScript, 36
   and HTML Source Editor, 346–47
Multipurpose Internet Mail Extensions (MIME),
   defined, 448

N

NAME attribute
   <A> tag, 403
   <BASEFONT> tag, 405
   <FORM> tag, 37, 122, 408
   <FRAME> tag, 409
   <IFRAME> tag, 412
   <INPUT> tag, 415
   <OBJECT> tag, 80, 421
   <PARAM> tag, 81, 422
   <SELECT> tag, 418
   <TEXTAREA> tag, 428
Name property (Anchor object), 61
Name property (Internet Explorer), *46*
Name property (Window object), *53*
name resolution, defined, 448
naming
   objects in VBScript, 433
   variables in VBScript, 434
Navigate method (Internet Explorer), *47*
Navigate method (Window object), *54*
Navigator object, 62
Navigator property (Window object), *53*
Network News Transfer Protocol (NNTP), 390, 448

networks, private. *See* intranets, defined
New Item control (ActiveX), 97–98
newsletter subscription project, 193–237
<NOFRAMES> tag, 419–20
NORESIZE attribute (<FRAME> tag), 409
Normandy, 390–91
NOSHADE attribute (<HR> tag), 411
NOWRAP attribute (<TD> or <TH> tag), 427

O

object browser, 43, *44*
object models. *See also* scripting object model,
   Internet Explorer
   Internet Explorer, 8, 43, *44,* 44–48
   Microsoft Excel, 43
objects. *See also* system objects, VBScript
   support for
   class identifiers, 84–87
   naming in VBScript, 433
<OBJECT> tag
   code example, *422*
   limits, 90
   list of attributes, 79–80, 420–21
   overview, 420–21
   <PARAM> tag, 422
   tools for inserting ActiveX controls in, 87,
      88–89, 349, 360
OCX controls, 8. *See also* ActiveX controls
ODBC. *See* Open Database Connectivity (ODBC)
ODBC Administrator, 126, 197, 245, 296–97
ODBC datasource
   configuring, 126–29
   creating for event registration project, 242–47
   creating for newsletter subscription project,
      195, 196–203
   creating for online bookstore project, 294–97
   defining for event registration project, 245–47
   defining for newsletter subscription project,
      201–3
   defining for online bookstore project, 296–97

ODBC datasource, *continued*
  and Microsoft dbWeb, 391, 393–95
  referencing RDO, 223–24, 277
  setting up, 126–29
ODBC drivers
  and IDC, 123
  list of idc file options, 132, *134*
  for newsletter subscription project, 196–98
  setting up, 126–29
  SQL Server vs. other databases, 126
Office. *See* Microsoft Office
OLE, defined, 448
OLE controls. *See* ActiveX controls
OLE custom controls, 8
OLE Internet Server Application Programming
    Interface. *See* OLEISAPI
OLEISAPI
  defined, 7, 155, 449
  vs. IDC, 155–56
  invoking, 159–60
  Minesweeper game example, 168–81
  overview, 155–56
  parsing example, 160–68
  setting up, 156–57
oleisapi.dll file
  defined, 155, 156
  obtaining, 156
  placing, 156–57
OLEISAPI Wizard, 181, 184–90
<OL> (ordered list) tag, 15, 417
OnBlur event, 212, 257
OnClick attribute, 17
OnClick event vs. Click event, 69, 81
online bookstore project
  adding commercial message to web page, 305–6
  adding orders to database, 335–36
  book order queries, 323
  creating Book Order web page, 323–35
  creating Confirmation web page, 336–39
  creating datasource, 294–97
  creating home page, 298–304

creating search engine, 314–15
  creating Selected Titles web page, 315–22
  design objectives, 292–93
  organizing files for, 293–94
  overview, 291, 292–93
  running application, 341–43
  system component requirements, 291–92
  testing application, 341–43
OnLoad attribute (<BODY> tag), 298, 302, 402
OnLoad event (Window object), *54*
OnSubmit attribute (<FORM> tag), 408
OnSubmit event (Form object), *58*
OnUnload attribute (<BODY> tag), 402
OnUnload event (Window object), *54*
Open Database Connectivity (ODBC), 6, 449.
    See also ODBC datasource
Open method (Document object), *56*
Open method (Window object), *54*
option buttons. *See* intrinsic Radio control
Option Explicit statement, 36
<OPTION> tag, 418
order forms. *See* interactive order form project
order.htx file
  creating, 324–29
  online bookstore example, *330–35*
  product showcase example, *146–49*
order.idc file, *146*

P

<P> (paragraph) tag, 15, 423
packets, defined, 449
page view, defined, 26
<PARAM> tag, 81, 422
Parent property (Internet Explorer), *46*
Parent property (Window object), *53*
parsing
  event registration project example, 273–76
  OLEISAPI DLL example, 160–68
Password control, intrinsic, *70, 72–73*
Password field (idc files), *133*

Password property (MAPISession control), *226*

passwords, checking, 151–55

PATH_INFO variable (htx files), *138*

PathName property (Location object), *59*

Path property (Internet Explorer), *46*

PATH_TRANSLATED variable (htx files), *138*

Person class

    code listing, *281–85*

    creating, 271–80

    defined, 271

phone lines, 121

pie.htm file, 350–52

Point-to-Point Tunneling Protocol (PPTP), 390

Popup Menu control, 33

Port property (Location object), *59*

POST method, 37, 122

Post Office Protocol (POP3), 390, 449

PowerPoint, 9. *See also* PowerPoint
    Animation Player

PowerPoint Animation Player

    installing, 207–8

    online bookstore application, 337–38

    using with web pages, 205, 206–9

PowerPoint Animation Publisher

    creating compressed PowerPoint animations,
        208–9

    defined, 205

    installing, 207–8

ppanim.htm file, 209

ppanim.ppz file, 208, 209

prodshow.htm file, *144–45*

Prompt method (Window object), *54*

Protocol property (Location object), *58*

protocols, defined, 2

Public method, 158

Public property, 158

Publish application

    creating, 220–35

    running, 236–37

purchase.htx file

    creating, 336–38

purchase.htx file, *continued*

    online bookstore example, *339–41*

    product showcase example, *151*

purchase.idc file

    creating, 335–36

    product showcase example, *150*

PutProperty method (Internet Explorer), *47*

Q

queries, creating search engine for, 314–15

QUERY_STRING variable (htx files), *138*

Quit method (Internet Explorer), *47*

R

RAD. *See* Rapid Application Development (RAD)

Radio control, intrinsic, *70,* 73–74, 251

Rapid Application Development (RAD), 10

RecipDisplayName property (MAPIMessages
    control), *227*

References dialog box, 48, *49*

Referrer property (Document object), *56*

Refresh method (Internet Explorer), *48*

REGEDIT.EXE file, 86

register.htx file, *142*

register.idc file, *142*

registration utility, 158

Registry, Windows, 84, 85–87, 131, 158, 287–88

Registry Editor, 86

REMOTE_ADDR variable (htx files), *138*

Remote Data Objects (RDOs)

    defined, 449

    list of objects, *223*

    RDO model, *224*

    setting references to, 223, 277

    using to access ODBC source, 222, 223–24

REMOTE_HOST variable (htx files), *138*

REMOTE_USER variable (htx files), *138*

REQUEST_METHOD variable (htx files), *138*

RequiredParameters field (idc files), *133*

Reset control, intrinsic, *70,* 74

ROWS attribute
    <FRAMESET> tag, 410
    <TEXTAREA> tag, 429
ROWSPAN attribute (<TD> or <TH> tag), 427
RULES attribute (<TABLE> tag), 425
runtime errors, 280

S

schemas, defined, 394
Schema Wizard, 394–95
script, defined, 449
scripting engine
    defined, 19, 449
    vs. scripting host, 19, *20*
    VBScript, 20
scripting host, defined, 19
scripting languages. *See also* VBScript
    JavaScript, 21–24
    overview, 19–20, 21
    third-party vendors, 27
scripting object model, Internet Explorer
    Document object example, 64–66
    Form object example, 66–68
    object properties and methods, 52–62
    overview, 52
    Window object example, 62–64
SCRIPT_NAME variable (htx files), *138*
script section, HTML document
    as code module, 16, 19, 30, 35, 38, 39–40
    overview, 400–401
    standards for coding, 432
<SCRIPT> tag
    code examples, *301–2, 401*
    code modules within, 16, 19, 30, 35, 38, 39–40
    defining event procedures, 39–40
    importance of using, 432
    list of attributes, 400–401
    Option Explicit statement in, 36
  Script Wizard, 353–58

SCROLLAMOUNT attribute (<MARQUEE> tag), 419
SCROLLDELAY attribute (<MARQUEE> tag), 419
SCROLLING attribute
    <FRAME> tag, 409
    <IFRAME> tag, 412
search engine, creating, 314–15
Search property (Location object), *59*
security issues, 92–93
Select control, intrinsic, *70,* 75
SELECTED attribute (<OPTION> tag), 418
selected.htx file
    code listing, *320–22*
    creating, 315–20
<SELECT> tag, 68, 75, 417
Self property (Window object), *53*
Send method (MAPIMessages control), *227*
SERVER_NAME variable (htx files), *138*
SERVER_PORT variable (htx files), *138*
SERVER_PROTOCOL variable (htx files), *138*
servers, defined, 2, 449. *See also* web servers;
    Windows NT Server
SERVER_SOFTWARE variable (htx files), *138*
SessionID property (MAPIMessages control), *227*
SessionID property (MAPISession control), *226*
SetTimeout method (Window object), *54*
SHAPES attribute (<OBJECT> tag), 80, 421
signature block, 92–93
SignOff method (MAPISession control), *226*
SignOn method (MAPISession control), *226*
Simple Mail Transfer Protocol (SMTP), 390, 449
SIZE attribute
    <BASEFONT> tag, 405
    <FONT> tag, 407
    <HR> tag, 411
    <INPUT> tag, 415
    <SELECT> tag, 418
sockets, defined, 449
software tools, for web page development, 4–9
spell checker, accessing through Automation, 42

SQL_ACCESS_MODE option (idc files), *134*

SQL_LOGIN_TIMEOUT option (idc files), *134*

SQL_MAX_LENGTH option (idc files), *134*

SQL_MAX_ROWS option (idc files), *134*

SQL_NOSCAN option (idc files), *134*

SQL_OPT_TRACEFILE option (idc files), *134*

SQL_OPT_TRACE option (idc files), *134*

SQL_PACKET_SIZE option (idc files), *134*

SQL_QUERY_TIMEOUT option (idc files), *134*

SQL Server, 126, 391

SQL Statement field (idc files), *133,* 218

SQL_TRANSLATE_DLL option (idc files), *134*

SQL_TRANSLATE_OPTION option (idc files), *134*

SQL_TXN_ISOLATION option (idc files), *134*

SRC attribute
    <BGSOUND> tag, 405
    <FRAME> tag, 410
    <IFRAME> tag, 412
    <IMG> tag, 414
    <INPUT> tag, 415

Standard Generalized Markup Language
    (SGML), defined, 449

STANDBY attribute (<OBJECT> tag), 80, 421

START attribute
    <IMG> tag, 414
    <OL> tag, 417

StartMode property, 287

StatusBar property (Internet Explorer), *46*

Status property (Window object), *53*

StatusText property (Internet Explorer), *46,* 305

Stock Ticker control (ActiveX), 98–99

Stop method (Internet Explorer), *48*

<STRIKE> tag, 429

<STRONG> tag, 15, 429

STYLE attribute, 377

style sheets, proposed, 358–59

<STYLE> tag, 423–24

subject.idc file, 314

Submit control, intrinsic, *70,* 75–76

Submit method (Form object), *58*

submitting forms, 37–38, 122

subroutines, in VBScript, 39

subscrib.htm file, *213–16*

subscrib.htx file, 218–19

subscrib.idc file, 217–18

sweeper.cls file, *171–81*

syntax, JavaScript vs. VBScript, 21, 26

system datasource, setting up, 126–29

system objects, VBScript support for, 36

system Registry, 84, 85–87, 131, 158, 287–88

T

T-1 connections, 121

tables, HTML, creating for forms, 205–6, 248–49

<TABLE> tag
    <CAPTION> tag, 425
    code example, *427–28*
    overview, 424–28
    <TD> (table cell) tag, 426–27
    <TH> (table cell) tag, 426–27
    <TR> (table row) tag, 425–26

tags. *See also names of individual tags*
    defined, 11
    list of, 403–30

TARGET attribute
    <A> tag, 403
    <BASE> tag, 404
    <FORM> tag, 408

Target property (Form object), *57*

TCP/IP, 5, 450

<TD> (table cell) tag, 426–27

telephone lines, 121

Template field (idc files), *133,* 217

TextArea control, intrinsic, *70,* 77

<TEXTAREA> tag, 68, 428–29

TEXT attribute (<BODY> tag), 402

TextBox control (ActiveX), adding using
    HTML Layout Editor, 375–76

Text control, intrinsic, *70,* 76–77, 252–54

text files, for IDC implementation, 123–24

<TH> (table cell) tag, 426–27

Timer control (ActiveX), 95–97, 255, 259, 300–304, 306, 365–66, 368–69, 381–82

TITLE attribute (anchor tag), 403

title.idc file, 314–15

Title property (Document object), *56*

<TITLE> tag, 14

ToggleButton control, 373, 378

ToolBar property (Internet Explorer), *46*

TopLevelContainer property (Internet Explorer), *46*

TOPMARGIN attribute (<BODY> tag), 402

Top property (Internet Explorer), *45*

Top property (Window object), *53*

Transmission Control Protocol/Internet Protocol (TCP/IP), 5, 450

<TR> (table row) tag, 425–26

TYPE attribute
  <INPUT> tag, 414
  <LI> tag, 416
  <OBJECT> tag, 80, 421
  <OL> tag, 417
  <PARAM> tag, 422

Type property (Internet Explorer), *47*

U

<U> (underline) tag, 429

<UL> (unordered list) tag, 15, 416

Uniform Resource Locators (URLs), defined, 450. *See also* Location object

URLs. *See* Uniform Resource Locators (URLs), defined

UserAgent property (Navigator object), 62

usergrp.htm file, *139–40*

UserName field (idc files), *133*

UserName property (MAPISession control), *226*

V

VALIGN attribute
  <CAPTION> tag, 425
  <TD> or <TH> tag, 427

VALIGN attribute, *continued*
  <TR> tag, 426

VALUE attribute
  <INPUT> tag, 415
  <LI> tag, 416
  <OPTION> tag, 418
  <PARAM> tag, 81, 422

VALUETYPE attribute (<PARAM> tag), 81, 422

variables
  indicating scope in VBScript, 434
  naming in VBScript, 434
  procedure-level, 38–39
  script-level, 38–39
  in VBScript, 36, 38–39

variant data type, 434

VBScript
  adding code with Script Wizard, 353–58
  adding to newsletter subscription page, 212–16
  browser compatibility, 25–26
  code for interactive order form example, *384–88*
  coding standards, 433–34
  comments in, 435
  debugging code, 25, 31, 345
  defined, 4–5
  event procedures in, 39–40
  in event registration project, 256–69
  forms support, 37–38
  function headers, 435
  functions in, 39
  in HTML, 16
  Internet Explorer scripting object model, 52–68
  vs. JavaScript, 21, 26–27
  language scalability, 27
  list of features, *28–29*
  location in HTML documents, 400–401, 432
  modules support, 35, 38–40
  naming objects in, 433
  overview, 25–26
  scripting engine, 20

VBScript, *continued*
   subroutines in, 39
   syntax, 26
   use of case, 436
   use of objects, 26–27
   variables in, 38–39
   vs. Visual Basic for Applications, 437–39
   writing code for butterfly animation, 366–69
   writing code for interactive order form, 378–83
vbscript.dll file, 20
Visible property (Internet Explorer), *47*
Visual Basic
   class module requirement, 157–58
   creating class module, 271–85
   and the Internet, 9, 48, 49–51
   object browser, 43, *44*
Visual Basic for Applications (VBA)
   list of unsupported VBA features in, 437–39
   vs. VBScript, 30–36, 437–39
   VBScript as subset of, 5, 20, 25, 27–28
VLINK attribute (<BODY> tag), 402
VLinkColor property (Document object), *55*
VSPACE attribute
   <IMG> tag, 414
   <MARQUEE> tag, 419
   <OBJECT> tag, 80, 421

W

WebBots, defined, 9
web pages. *See* HTML documents
web servers. *See also* Internet Information
      Server (IIS)
   defined, 450
   and setting up a web presence, 5–7, 121–23
Web sites
   ActiveX control resources, 442–44
   related to this book, 441–42
WIDTH attribute
   <HR> tag, 411
   <IFRAME> tag, 412

WIDTH attribute, *continued*
   <IMG> tag, 414
   <MARQUEE> tag, 419
   <OBJECT> tag, 80, 421
   <TABLE> tag, 425
Width property (Internet Explorer), *45*
Window object
   examples of use, 62–64, 305
   list of events, *54*
   list of methods, *54*
   list of properties, *53*
   overview, 53–54
Windows API, unsupported in VBScript, 36
Windows CGI, and Internet Information Server,
      190–91
Windows Help files, unsupported in VBScript,
      31–32
Windows Internet Naming Service (WINS), 390
Windows NT Server
   organizing files for event registration project,
      241–42
   organizing files for newsletter project, 195–96
   organizing files for online bookstore project,
      293–94
   overview, 389–90
   as platform for web server, 5, 121–22
   system Registry, 158, 287–88
Windows NT Workstation, 389, 390
Wizards
   Internet Database Connector Wizard, 181–84
   OLEISAPI Wizard, 181, 184–90
   Schema Wizard, 394–95
   Script Wizard, 353–58
Word. *See* Microsoft Word
World Wide Web, 1. *See also* browsers; intranets,
      defined
World Wide Web Consortium, 25, 450
WriteLn method (Document object), *56*
Write method (Document object), *56*

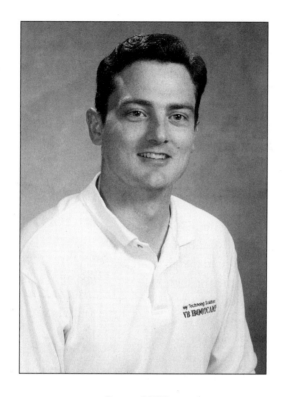

Scot Hillier

Scot Hillier, a graduate of Virginia Military Institute, is a former naval submarine officer. As a principal at New Technology Solutions, Inc., in North Haven, Connecticut, he has trained thousands of developers across the country since 1995. He is also the developer of the Visual Basic Add-In wizard AttilaVB/Pro (patent pending). Scot serves as regional director of the Microsoft Developer Days program in Hartford, Connecticut. His articles appear regularly in *Visual Basic Programmer's Journal.*

New Technology Solutions, Inc.

New Technology Solutions, in North Haven, Connecticut, provides training and tools to developers working with Microsoft Visual Basic. All of NewTech's training programs include our award-winning tools, 30 days of question-and-answer support, and access to our developers-only web site.

NewTech employees also write feature articles and columns for *Visual Basic Programmer's Journal* and are active in presenting technology topics at such conferences as VBITS and DCI's INTERNET WORLD. NewTech sponsors the Microsoft Developer Days event, in Boston and Hartford, as well as the Connecticut Visual Basic Special Interest Group, one of the largest VB user groups in the country. (You can browse http://www.microsoft.com/devdays/ for detailed information on Microsoft Developer Days.) Contact New Technology Solutions (or browse http://www.vb-bootcamp.com) to learn more about the following areas.

■ VB BOOTCAMP®

This is the flagship nationwide seminar for developers only. In just one or two days, you learn all the essentials of developing and deploying mission-critical business systems in Visual Basic.

■ INTRANET BOOTCAMP™

This course teaches you the key technologies and skills you need for deploying intranet technology using Microsoft Visual Basic, Scripting Edition (VBScript), as well as the Microsoft Internet Explorer and Microsoft Internet Information Server (IIS).

■ ON-SITE TRAINING

New Technology Solutions, Inc., offers on-site, hands-on technology training and tailors the training to your exact requirements. The company's clients include the FBI, Levi Strauss, Aetna, American Airlines, Chemical Bank, Prudential Insurance, and McDonald's. Call (203) 239-6874 to schedule training and arrange course content tailored to your needs.

VIDEO TRAINING

New Technology Solutions, Inc., offers the following training videos. All the tapes include source code, exercises, and a money-back guarantee. Call for pricing and availability.

- ❑ *VB BOOTCAMP/FUNDAMENTALS* (7 hours; for developers only)

- ❑ *VB BOOTCAMP/ADVANCED* (4 hours; covers advanced topics)

- ❑ *INTRANET/FUNDAMENTALS* (4 hours; covers VBScript and IIS)

- ❑ *INTRANET/ADVANCED* (4 hours; covers advanced intranets)

DISTANCE LEARNING PROGRAMS AND COMPUTER-BASED TRAINING

The company offers a variety of distance learning programs and CD-ROM–based training. Write for more information, or browse the New Technology Solutions web site:
http://www.vb-bootcamp.com

New Technology Solutions, Inc.

444-A Washington Avenue
North Haven, CT 06473
Phone: (203) 239-6874
Fax: (203) 239-7997
Email: info@vb-bootcamp.com
World Wide Web: http://www.vb-bootcamp.com

The manuscript for this book was prepared and submitted to Microsoft Press in electronic form. Text files were prepared with Microsoft Word 7.0 for Windows 95. Pages were composed by Microsoft Press with Adobe PageMaker 6.0 for Windows 95 (text in New Baskerville, and display type in Helvetica Bold). Composed pages were delivered to the printer as electronic prepress files.

Cover Graphic Designers
Greg Erickson
Robin Hjellen

Cover Illustrator
John Bleck

Interior Graphic Designer
Kim Eggleston

Interior Graphic Artists
Michael Victor
Lori Campbell

Compositors
E. Candace Gearhart
Susan Prettyman

Indexer
Julie Kawabata

Register Today!

Return this
Inside Microsoft® Visual Basic, Scripting Edition
registration card for
a Microsoft Press® catalog

U.S. and Canada addresses only. Fill in information below and mail postage-free. Please mail only the bottom half of this page.

1-57231-444-3A   *INSIDE MICROSOFT® VISUAL BASIC,*   *Owner Registration Card*
                      SCRIPTING EDITION

_____

NAME

_____

INSTITUTION OR COMPANY NAME

_____

ADDRESS

_____

_____

CITY   STATE   ZIP

Microsoft® Press
Quality Computer Books

For a free catalog of
Microsoft Press® products, call
1-800-MSPRESS

NO POSTAGE
NECESSARY
IF MAILED
IN THE
UNITED STATES

BUSINESS REPLY MAIL
FIRST-CLASS MAIL   PERMIT NO. 108   REDMOND, WA

POSTAGE WILL BE PAID BY ADDRESSEE

MICROSOFT PRESS REGISTRATION
INSIDE MICROSOFT® VISUAL BASIC,®
SCRIPTING EDITION
PO BOX 3019
BOTHELL WA 98041-9946